David Iredale and John Barrett

Discovering
Local History

Shire Publications

British Library Cataloguing in Publication Data: Iredale, David
Discovering local history. – (Discovering; no. 290)
1. Local history – Amateurs' manuals
2. Great Britain – History, Local – Research – Amateurs' manuals
I. Title II. Barrett, John, 1950-
941'.0072
ISBN 0 7478 0356 0

Front cover: *'A survey of the barony of Wooler, 1568' shows a typical medieval town with castle motte, broad high street, church and mill. (NRO.4188: reproduced with permission of the Northumberland Record Office.)*
Back cover: *Ludlow, Shropshire, was replanned soon after 1066 along a broad high street (centre) which served also as the market-place. The town prospered and was enlarged during the twelfth century with three parallel streets. An aerial view gives the historian a fine impression of the plan of the town. (Photograph by D. Iredale)*

ACKNOWLEDGEMENTS
The authors acknowledge with gratitude the contribution of Christine Clerk, who did the drawings on pages 14, 18, 21, 26, 29, 32, 39, 69, 70, 71, 74, 75, 78, 85, 86, 95, 100, 105, 107, 113, 116, 123, 127, 135, 136, 137, 179, 197, 198. The drawings on pages 150 and 215 are by G. Buchan. Photographs and other illustrations are acknowledged as follows: J. C. Adam, Forres, copied by A. Fraser, Forres, page 19; reproduced with permission of the Trustees of the British Library, page 41; London Borough of Hounslow, Chiswick Library Local Studies Collection, page 154; Moray Aerial Archaeology Group, page 27; Norfolk Record Ofice, page 165; Northumberland Record Office, front cover; G. Van Warmelo, page 94. The remaining photographs are by the authors, attributed as follows: John Barrett, pages 5, 15 (bottom), 60, 63, 72, 73 (both), 74, 78, 79, 81 (both), 82, 106, 108 (bottom), 120, 121, 122 (centre and bottom), 125, 128 (top), 130 (top right and bottom), 131 (both), 132, 138, 139, 163, 186 (bottom), 194, 196, 198 (top), 204, 205, 213 (bottom), 218, 219 (top); David Iredale, pages 15 (top), 21, 24, 51, 77, 80, 107, 108 (top), 109, 111, 112 (both), 114, 115, 122 (top), 126, 128 (bottom), 129 (both), 130 (top left), 133, 134, 148, 151, 153, 171, 172, 178 (top), 187, 199 (both), 200, 201, 202 (both), 203, 208, 209 (top three), 211, 212 (both), 213 (top), 215 (top), 216, 219 (bottom), 220, and back cover.

Published in 1999 by Shire Publications Ltd, Cromwell House, Church Street, Princes Risborough, Buckinghamshire HP27 9AA, UK. (Website: www.shirebooks.co.uk)
Copyright © 1999 by David Iredale and John Barrett. First published 1999. Number 290 in the Discovering series. ISBN 0 7478 0356 0.

Printed in Great Britain by CIT Printing Services Ltd, Press Buildings, Merlins Bridge, Haverfordwest, Pembrokeshire SA61 1XF.

Contents

Introduction

Local historians are usually ordinary people with a passion for the past and a love for their own town, village or native parish. They are, first and last, possessed by a sense of place. The particular landscape or community that is the focus for their passion is intimately known, every field or street, each church, school, farm, factory and prehistoric monument. The place has a definable boundary: administrative (a parish or borough), topographical (a valley or island), economic (a coalfield or landed estate) or social (a religious enclave or working-class suburb). There may be a distinctive type of countryside: forest, fen, arable landscape, a fell or dale, wold or heath; or an institution: monastery, college, cathedral, hospital, school, railway station, factory or mansion house.

Each community is just one unit in a broader social and economic region. Even the islanders of St Kilda way out in the Atlantic were part of the wider world as a detached portion of the ecclesiastical parish of Harris, governed by county officials based in Inverness, with ships bringing in Bibles, the estate factor and tourists, then carrying away feathers, oil, ling and tallow as rents in kind. Similar relationships exist for every community. The historian is sensitive to the position of the village within the parish, the parish within the county and the county within the country. The village may in some way have an influence on the outside world, but the wider world will certainly exert pressures on a small community. The historian is concerned with cause and effect, accepting that cultural and technological innovation have not always flowed from the Middle East to northern Europe, from continental Europe to Britain; or within Britain from south and east to north and west, from lowland zone to highland zone. Ireland was long a cultural powerhouse in the British Isles, evidenced in the physical landscape of tribal assembly enclosures, the spiritual landscapes of early Christianity, the linguistic and musical landscape of the Celtic west.

The past haunts the present. Ancestral genes pass through the generations, while material possessions and archives also survive remarkably. Historical events subtly shape the community psyche or, by revolutionary means, upset the noiseless tenor of parochial ways. Some historians glamorise or barbarise the past, populating the narrative with witches, wenches, hangings and heroines, while overlooking the basics of contraceptive practice, cost-of-living data and butt-purlin roof construction. A cosy view of the past is a particular ailment of the incomer-resident who, having deserted metropolitan Exton for rural Ambridge, imagines the rat-race is left far behind, forgetting quite that Ambridge, past as well as present, has the same race, if different rats. Learning from the past as a guide for the future is often said to be a great advantage of historical study. In 1934 Robert Douglas, medical officer of health for Moray and Nairn, privately published his *Annals of the Royal Burgh of Forres*, a reference book still in constant use. He set off on a balmy day during the first week in June to ascend a hill above the town and there to doze. In his dreams came St Laurence, patron saint of the parish, to survey the history of Forres, whose evolutionary stream swept forward to a future of full employment, healthy homes, extended life span and quicker processes of decomposition by means of cremation, all developments that might be expected to win the approval of a modern doctor and an admirer of current political reforms in Italy and Germany. St Laurence urged his townsfolk to adapt themselves to the laws of nature:

> As for those who disregard natural forces and become a menace to themselves and others, measures will be adopted by the community to rid the world of such undesirables. Forres in the past has had its quota of such inhabitants. They will not be tolerated in the future. Local government as we know it will disappear, the conduct of the inhabitants will be regulated by a code of laws moulded on natural laws and established by an international tribunal. The penalty of their infringement may be death.

The past haunts the present in Belfast.

The word *history* derives from Greek, meaning 'a learning or knowing through enquiry'. The historian's vision pans across the whole pageant of experience, drawing back to view a broad perspective, zooming in to take a sharp-focus close-up of a person, place or incident; freezing the frame to scrutinise a moment in time. The researcher asks why certain events occurred in certain ways; why at a certain place and time; why not otherwise; whether, how and why events are interconnected; how they relate to the world beyond the parish boundary. British and Irish history is usually, though erroneously, taken to concern only the two millennia since the Romans, for which written records supplement fieldwork and archaeology as sources of information. Traditionally, local history is seen as a sequence of events, discovering, chronicling and incidentally explaining the roots, growth, burgeoning, decay and regeneration of a community. Occasionally the narrative moves backwards, for example beginning with rural depopulation, then unravelling the strands of decline and fall. Usually the limit of date is determined by the researcher's own interests: the Second World War, the Romans, the Industrial Revolution, the Tudors and Stuarts. There may also be considerations of the accessibility or otherwise of sources for a particular period of history and chosen locality.

A history may be organised in various ways according to the researcher's particular interest and approach. Cultural historians think in terms of *Celts* (Britons, Picts and Gaels), *Romans, Anglo-Saxons, Vikings* (Danes and Norsemen) and *Normans*. Religious observance might be approached under two subdivisions: *Pagan belief* and *Christianity*, perhaps with a final chapter to consider the growth of, say, *Islam and New-age* belief, or indeed the decline of formal religious practice. The community might be considered under broad subject headings such as *Country-side, Houses, Economic activity* and *Maritime history*. Witchcraft is always a popular subject, chosen, for example, by the Victorian author W. H. Ainsworth. With true historical method Ainsworth carefully selected and defined a particular geographical area, the Forest of Pendle in Lancashire. He also selected a manage-able era, the generations between the Pilgrimage of Grace (1536) and the reign of James VI and I (1603-25). The son of a lawyer, Ainsworth researched his subject in legal papers from county courts of law and also studied the journal of Nicholas Assheton of Downham, a key figure in Pendle politics, which was just then being edited by F. R. Raines for publication by the Chetham Society (1848). Ainsworth walked his territory frequently, getting to know the lie of the land and learning to understand the character of its people. He climbed to the Armada beacon site on Pendle, visited the hamlets of Goldshaw and Sabden, studied the ruins of Whalley

Abbey and the houses of Downham and Roughlee, observed Lancashire folk customs and May-day festivities. When he came to write up his research he chose a format that would make the narrative as accessible as possible. Believing that community history should be read and enjoyed by a wide audience, he opted for a novel rather than an academic monograph. Nicholas Assheton became the principal character in a blockbuster of horror and sentiment, an example of 'faction' which, published in 1848 as *The Lancashire Witches*, is still readable (and read) today.

The historian cannot avoid studies of prehistory which rely on fieldwork and archaeology to uncover and interpret sites, finds and monuments. Territorial divisions, place-names, folklore, settlement sites and rituals may all owe their origins to prehistoric predecessors. Research in the archaeological literature reveals reports and theories of generations of excavators and investigators to produce information on each of the major eras of localised prehistory: the age of hunter-gatherers, from the emergence of humankind down to the more complex society of the Middle Stone Age (mesolithic); the New Stone Age (neolithic), roughly 5000 BC to 3200 BC; the Bronze Age, down to around 1200 BC; and Celtic societies, from 1200 BC onwards. There is still scope for educated speculation about the means by which people in the distant past contended with their environment. Prehistoric societies may be understood by study of the lives today of the indigenous peoples of New Guinea, Africa or South America. The historian obviously bears in mind the writings of anthropologists and archaeologists, who can sometimes feel resentful when the mere amateur trespasses into their territories. It is advisable to tread softly to avoid treading on sensitive academic toes. The historian who studies the human story from the time that ape-like creatures first stood upright to the present day should be careful to avoid the telescopic tendencies by which time becomes progressively compressed with receding distance: long centuries of prehistoric culture may sometimes be confined in a brief paragraph serving to preface a history beginning, in effect, with the Norman Conquest.

Comparing and studying several communities which need not be contiguous can illustrate useful themes such as patterns of poor relief, the decline of the English market town or evictions in County Mayo. By selecting places widely scattered across county or country, the historian compares and contrasts the shared or peculiar characteristics of the sample. M. Spufford selected the three Cambridgeshire villages of Chippenham, Orwell and Willingham for her work of social dissection, *Contrasting Communities* (Cambridge University Press, 1974).

It is always interesting to come upon differences rather than similarities, and upon exceptions to a general rule. A particular village might have had virtually no paupers in the war year 1813, when almost everywhere else long lists of paupers claiming relief are evidence of economic depression. A church may be physically isolated from the parochial population while in adjacent parishes the church stands as the focus of a community. Such divergences demand explanation and investigation. There is usually no mystery. A village with well-managed parochial charities and a benevolent landowner can overcome the economic impact of war and famine. Villagers evicted during agricultural reorganisation may be resettled with new businesses elsewhere, while their church, for legal reasons, cannot be so easily shifted. To draw a rounded and interesting picture usually requires knowledge of what happened in neighbouring places and of how communities further afield managed their affairs. The way of life in a given locality at the time of, say, St Patrick can in part be inferred from sources in the neighbourhood, such as a sherd of pottery, a monastic enclosure, a circular cropmark, a glass bead, an iron knife or a memorial inscription. More can be added if we allow the people to resemble other human beings, including ourselves, with similar urges, needs, fears, ambitions, prejudice, appetites and spirituality. More, too, becomes clear if we look to other and analogous cultures such as Roman Gaul, a civilisation contemporary with St Patrick, where written records, artefacts and buildings illustrate the influence of supernatural powers and human genius.

Speculation on sound evidence may be acceptable, particularly if people in history are permitted to behave in credible ways. All too often, wild and romantic interpretations enter the mind unbidden to explain ordinary things in absurd ways. A linear earthwork is quite wrongly and unnecessarily interpreted as the work of the gods or a runway for alien astronauts; the sandy hump of a Norman rabbit warren as the grave of King Arthur. There is generally no need to romanticise or fantasise, because interpreting the ordinary features in a locality is sufficiently enthralling. Our everyday experience, as well as historical sources, suggests that the concerns motivating people are basic and prosaic: securing a subsistence, satisfying appetites, exercising power, begetting a new generation. These basics may underlie the public expressions of courage, altruism, idealism and spirituality as well as lust, violence, greed, sloth and spite. History is not for the faint-hearted or for those who shrink from a mention of disease, death, drains, depravity and bodily functions. Historians relish the vigorous hard-edged soap opera that is everyday life in every past era and each particular place. Public spirit, belief in divine and supernatural forces, love of family and native place, all have considerable influence on behaviour, if records are to be trusted. Such factors begin to make sense of the voiceless bric-a-brac of tombs, pottery, beads, knives, cropmarks and other objects created by people in the past.

Interpretation of cultural change also requires us to expand horizons beyond regional boundaries. Archaeology may tell us when agriculture or metallurgy began in the particular place under scrutiny. The means by which such innovations were introduced are generally much less clear: whether by invaders who came to overwhelm and exterminate the natives, as happened in Tasmania and parts of the Americas; or by a smaller immigration and political takeover, as in the case of the Romans in Britain; or perhaps by commercial contacts, as with American influence on Japan in the nineteenth century and Japanese influence on Europe in the twentieth. Historians debate these matters. Opinions swing from one theory to another. Mass immigration and extermination dominated historical thinking in the nineteenth century when historians were more comfortable with the colonising ethos. More recently historians have favoured theories of change through subtler, gentler means, except of course where the evidence is otherwise, for example the attested mass movements of the Celtic world; episodes of extermination and ethnic cleansing during the modern era. The historian considering the evidence of cultural change will decide for himself how that change came about, by common-sense analysis of data and academic opinion. DNA research may eventually provide clues as to the racial origins of the various peoples who have inhabited the British Isles and reveal to what extent Britons and Picts were displaced by English and Scots during the first centuries AD. With evidence of DNA extracted from living populations and even, perhaps, recovered archaeologically, it may be possible to suggest how far change came through immigration, extermination or intermarriage, and how far through acculturation, in which people learned from abroad how to grow grain, smelt metal and worship the gods, importing for themselves not only ideas but hardware and new species of domestic crops and beasts.

Whatever the period, place, topic or format chosen there is an accepted plan of campaign to be followed that has served researchers well over the years. First, of course, the various sources of information have to be found: old people who remember the past, an article in a periodical from the library, an antiquarian book, a monument in the landscape, some distinctive hedgerow, an item of furniture, a tool or weapon in the museum or junk shop. Perhaps information is secreted away among the archives of a city lawyer or has been removed to America in an emigrant's baggage or even hidden beneath the ground, retrievable only through archaeological excavation. Information accumulates in no particular order, the sheer quantity a source of surprise and delight. The disparate items of information must be properly recorded in notebooks, on audio or video tape, in sketches and photographs. Photocopying books, maps and manuscripts saves a lot of time. Custodians of collections, archivists and librarians will advise on any copyright problems. Sometimes the original source of information is subsequently destroyed, for example a house or tomb standing in the way of roadworks, a manuscript accidentally incinerated. Then the historian's record, photocopies and sketches alone remain, sources for future generations and the result of the vital activity of preserving an aspect or image of the past. The collection of information is a marvellous and interesting pursuit in itself, and many people take their hobby no further, except perhaps to organise the gathered sources as logically as possible for future researchers to use.

The effectiveness of historical research depends in no small measure on the efficiency of the historian's filing system. History becomes an exercise in documentary control. Over the years the mass of research notes and paperwork swells. Small piles of paper on the study floor and huge stacks lying on the stairs become a source of exasperation. The piles of paper must be gathered into files, neatly disposed of into titled folders, binders, cabinets and labelled boxes. The historian requires also to develop information retrieval systems. The traditional method collates information from the notes in a card index of names, places and subjects. The modern historian exploits the potential of the personal computer. Notes are generally written in the library or archives on one side only of large (A4) loose-leaf sheets, widely spaced. Where feasible a separate sheet of paper is allocated to each source and site visit. Researchers quite often pursue paperless strategies, entering notes directly into a lap-top computer. Each source-note is headed with a running reference number and full description of the source. A field monument is conventionally identified by name, British national grid reference and a brief description:

SOURCE-NUMBER 273
SH632808
Penmon parish, Anglesey county, St Seiriol's well and cell, sixth century, baptistry roofed during the eighteenth century.

Requisite details for a published book or monograph comprise author, title, edition, place of publication, publisher, year of publication:

SOURCE-NUMBER 274
E. Allen, J. F. Clarke, N. McCord and D. J. Rowe *The North-east Engineers' Strike of 1871: The Nine Hours' League*, Newcastle upon Tyne, Frank Graham, 1971.

An article in a journal or periodical requires the author and title of the article with the name of the periodical, volume, number, date and inclusive page numbers:

SOURCE-NUMBER 275
D. Starkey 'The String untuned: a riot at Hoddesdon, 1534', *History Today*, Vol. XXIX (December 1979), pp. 795-9.

An archival source should be identified with the name of the holding institution, the collection, reference code and description of the document with date, page and folio number:

SOURCE-NUMBER 51
Essex Record Office, Chelmsford: D/DM M7, Mildmay of Moulsham muniments, new bylaws of Chelmsford with physical and monetary punishments for transgressors, signed by William Sidey, steward of the manor of Bishop's Hall, Latin heading, English text, 24th February 1563/4.

The sources do not necessarily speak for themselves in any clear manner, but have to be interpreted, a fascinating stage in research. This is real history. Each historian reads the sources himself, drawing his own conclusions about what is being said about the past. The advice of experts will always be welcome, for instance in translating a Latin charter or identifying features in an archaeological structure. The fresh eye of a visitor to the parish is sometimes required to make an observation or raise a question, even though the evidence has always stared the resident researcher in the face. The drystone wall bounding an eighteenth-century enclosure can be passed regularly for years until a newcomer notices a distinctive feature, a single slight hump at one point in the level of the wall. Such an aberration, though apparently natural, could tell of 'a feature under a feature' such as the earth and rubble of a denuded prehistoric burial cairn. The historian who actually lives in the community has the advantage of examining the landscape or townscape, year in year out, whatever the weather or season. He can await a light dusting of snow on a sunny February morning to photograph subtle relief features normally invisible. He keeps his eye on a farmer grubbing out the impenetrable gorse obscuring ancient structural foundations. Carvings on the stones of a tomb can be sought in a variety of lights, including – arguably best of all – candlelight or the rays of the sun rising or setting at the solstice. Of the landscape, the historian asks questions repeatedly until answers emerge, for the landscape always tells the truth.

The historian avoids reproducing snatches of documentary sources merely as 'bytes' of historical curiosity but seeks always to uncover underlying motives, meanings and significances. The accounts of the burgh of Elgin in Moray contain a precept to the treasurer to pay for:

Powder & Ball to shoot the Hylandmen ... coming down upon the account
of the late uproar at Trinity Fair 1708 ... £3:14:0.

Burgh archives reveal an allegation by the town council that a recruiting party from a highland regiment had attempted to impress certain of the townsfolk to enlist in the army, thereby sparking off a riot in which one was killed and a number of others wounded. The army, for its part, played up the danger of civil commotion and, by way of vindication, claimed that armed intervention had been required to protect a local MP, Brigadier-General Alexander Grant, from maltreatment by the mob. The background to this fracas was, of course, the first election (26th May 1708) of an MP for the constituency of Elgin, Cullen, Banff, Kintore and Inverurie to sit in the new all-Britain Parliament established by the Act of Union of 1707, a political innovation decidedly unpopular with the burgesses. The citizenry had therefore to be armed against any reprisal by the army or by the Grant clansmen seeking in their turn to avenge the insult offered by the royal burgh to their chief and the new British constitution.

The historian gives life and voice to yesterday's people. Frankness and detachment characterise the historian's dealings, especially when exposing people's failings and frailties or when disturbing their dust. Historians pile fact upon fact. Each documented building block is cemented with new research, theory and speculation. As further sites are excavated, as sealed archives become available, as other historians publish fresh interpretations, the historian revises, reconsiders, even rewrites, his work in progress.

The interpretation of sources may produce a view of the past approximating to what actually happened, though we cannot be sure we are correct. A comprehensive picture of the parish will usually be impossible. For some topics and eras evidence is slight. Inference or informed imagination alone can fill the gaps. On the other hand evidence may be so voluminous or so vastly contradictory that the historian selects and samples, rejecting much that another researcher sooner or later will recognise as the key to a conundrum. The whole truth of what happened in the past remains unknown, perhaps unknowable. Useful work is done as historians busily worry around the margins of immeasurable ignorance, more often than not merely redefining the problems rather than publishing the answers. At the same time the modern reader can never entirely cast aside the mental luggage of the present age or readily penetrate the consciousness of people in the past. The discipline of history is not subverted by this seditious scepticism. We may be satisfied, though, if our historical investigation at least gives others pause for thought. Historians admit that at best they make only trifling inroads upon the immeasurable realm of unknowableness that is the past.

Stepping into the past

From the start the researcher gets out and about in the community talking to people about their history; consulting the librarian, the archivist, the county archaeologist, landowners, farmers, the editor of the town newspaper, university academics, school teachers and council officials; extending knowledge; publicising interests and requirements. A first step into the past is joining or establishing a lively society involved in community history or heritage through which research and discoveries may be shared. The group is likely to discuss and publish articles on medieval, modern and industrial archaeology, regional history, vernacular architecture and family history. Existing societies will probably have annual publications containing the research of previous generations. Because past times appeal to a wide range of individuals the society will make available a pool of particular skills in languages, administration, illustration, computing, writing and indexing. In this cooperative way the history of Hatfield was researched by members of the Workers' Educational Association under the guidance of a professional tutor. A book was published and sold as twelve pamphlets (each priced at half a crown, 1961-4), with sales of the earlier financing the later pamphlets. A society may be simply a group of enthusiasts meeting in each other's homes. A more formally organised group will appoint a chairperson, secretary and treasurer and keep proper minutes and accounts. This kind of group may be able to secure funding to supplement subscription income, including grants from the county council, sponsorship from industry and lottery money to finance ambitious projects such as archaeological excavation and publication. Cooperation within a group maximises that most precious resource, time. Group members will devise simple strategies such as car pools and baby sitting to increase the time available to the group for, say, a detailed survey of houses in the village, a comprehensive review of place-names or a record of inscriptions in the churchyard. Since out-of-doors research, landscape studies and archival investigation may be possible only during daylight or office hours the time and assistance of retired or unemployed group members will be invaluable.

Even the largest group will from time to time need to 'get a man in' to advise on, direct or undertake a project. An expert thus employed will require to be paid at a professional rate. This may not be cheap, but it may be quicker and more satisfactory to ask a professional to come and date a farmhouse roof than for the group to argue and debate endlessly and to no purpose because no single member has the faintest idea about the history of carpentry. A group may advertise in the newspaper or supermarket for particular kinds of expert to assist in particular projects: a botanist for a hedgerow study, a doctor to assist in the analysis of a medical archive. A guest speaker, perhaps the archivist or archaeologist or a university lecturer, may be persuaded, as a public servant, to give a talk free of charge. Community organisations interested in such historically useful subjects as geology, photography, architecture, folklore, botany or climate can be drawn in to specific enterprises. The researcher may also wish to join the British Association for Local History, founded in 1982 'to promote the advancement of public education through the study of local history' in Britain and Ireland, whose current address is in *Whitaker's Almanack*.

Researching and writing history can be a rewarding personal activity or hobby, free of the constraints of society membership. Some of the best histories have been produced in this way, with publication aided by funds from universities or county councils, grant-making trusts and commercial firms who may be willing to pay for advertisements. Desk-top publishing has reduced publication costs though selling is

Local history seminars are useful to the historian.

LOCAL HISTORY SEMINARS

at

**Bishop Grosseteste College
LINCOLN**

in conjunction with
***The Department of Adult Education
University of Hull***

more of a challenge. By traditional but cautious methods D. E. Pullen privately published two of her successful London suburban histories, beginning with Sydenham (1974), using sales for Penge (Lodgemark Press, Chislehurst, 1978), then Forest Hill (1979). The fieldworkers G., M. and R. Ponting, G. R. Curtis and M. MacRae have privately published their own researches on Lewis and Harris, ensuring that the booklets are small, attractive and inexpensive enough to sell through tourist information centres.

Study courses offer a stimulating step into the past, though often requiring personal commitment, family support and a lot of travel, with evenings and weekends reserved for lectures and written exercises. Courses on historical research, languages, old handwriting and archaeology, even a simple GCSE history class, should provide an essential broad outline of national history and an introduction to the historian's way of thinking. Seminars in community history and related subjects are becoming increasingly popular, especially at weekends and holiday times, usually organised through university adult education centres. Typical is the Latin and palaeography summer school of Keele University, Staffordshire, where lectures on handwriting and the history and use of documents are introduced through a correspondence course and telephonic tutorials. Regional studies centres such as the University of Lancaster Centre for North-West Regional Studies and the University of Aberdeen Centre for Scottish Studies provide facilities where local historians study research techniques and regional sources in formal, usually evening, courses lasting up to three years, leading to certificates of competency in regional studies and/or fieldwork. Entry qualifications may be minimal (A-level at most) or waived entirely for mature students. A main powerhouse is Leicester University, which offers an intensive MA course (one year, full-time) in the department of English local history. This concentrates for two terms on lectures and fieldwork, covering the historical development of English society at regional and community level; topography with emphasis on the Midlands; popular culture of the labouring classes (folklore, art, witchcraft, literature, religion); documents and their uses; handwriting and record interpretation. The final term is devoted to the preparation of a dissertation on a chosen topic. It may be possible for the researcher to enrol for just a few modules of a degree course to acquire expertise in a relevant area. Lists of courses are usually available in public libraries, while additionally there may be databases of courses regionally and nationally. The annual *Directory of Vocational and Further Education* arranges colleges alphabetically, with their wide range of subjects also indexed alphabetically. For further information, including registers of full or part-time degree-level courses, the reference librarian holds the latest editions of standard reference books such as *British Qualifications* (published by Kogan Page) and the comprehensive guides to universities and degree courses compiled by the Careers Research and Advisory Centre (CRAC).

Words and music

Those aspects of the past that are general knowledge in the neighbourhood are worth thinking carefully about. Neighbours will have learned as children about famous battles fought nearby and will be aware, though goodness knows how, that a certain green lane was a Roman road and a field known as Mill Field the site of the manorial mill. These snippets require confirmation through research, but anecdotal evidence is a beginning, suggesting how much history is well known and a source of pride within the modern community. Residents who scowl at council officials and opinion pollsters tend to smile on historical enquirers whom they regard, at worst, merely as harmless eccentrics. This direct approach may be a means of accessing the folk beliefs, fairy tales, legends, traditional customs and popular games sometimes spurned as rustic, unruly, superstitious and irrelevant. A sensitive appreciation of popular culture, consciously preserved and transmitted by word of mouth down the generations, may even lead to significant manifestations of prehistory, perhaps inherited from pagan Celts or even from the Stone Age.

Legends are preserved for centuries, with a kernel of history within the onion-skin accretions of confusion and fancy. On the outskirts of Forres, Moray, there is a grey roadside boulder on which old men used to spit for luck. The stone is associated with a legend concerning the burning of three witches following their killing about 966 of King Dubh, ancestor of Shakespeare's Macduff. In fact this dark Witches' Stone, pointing to the midwinter sunset, has a reddish companion aligned on the midsummer sunset. There are reports of a third stone having been there until the 1930s. All belonged to a stone circle erected around 2500 BC. Spitting is a folk memory of a prehistoric ritual libation, originally probably of semen. The three medieval witches connect folk memory of a Celtic trinity of goddesses and Shakespeare's three weird sisters. A further level of association derives from the seventeenth-century obsession with witches. From the legend Forres emerges as a place of political and symbolic power, another Scone or Tara, a magical ground where kings were made and broken. The legend of King Dubh is linked with the fate of the seven kings of Pictland whose decapitated corpses are depicted on the ninth-century Sueno's Stone, also at Forres; with King Malcolm I, murdered by men of Moray; with King Duncan, killed near Forres by Macbeth; and with King Donald II, murdered at Forres in 900 and commemorated in an early fifteenth-century version of an older medieval oral tradition:

> Donald, Constantynis swne, Wes kyng in Scotland off powere,
> And held that state ellewyn yhere. In Murrawe syne he murthrysyd was
> In till that towne is cald Foras.
> Andrew Wyntoun *The Orygynale Cronykil of Scotland* (book VI, chapter X, lines 710-14).

The researcher does well to become acquainted with the music and dance of the region. Formal music may be inspired by topography and incident, for example Mendelssohn's *Hebrides* overture, a romantic impression of Fingal's Cave, Staffa, in 1829. Music of farmstead and workshop may be realised in distinctive instrumentation and performance such as the pipes of Northumberland, the bothy ballads of Aberdeenshire, the *piobaireachd* (pipe-music and laments) of Skye, the fiddlers of Shetland, the female walksters of Lewis, the brass bands of the Yorkshire coalfields. Doolin, County Clare, is notable in musicology as a repository and powerhouse of native tradition. The historian cannot be deaf to the music of Liverpool, which provided accompaniment for the social revolution of the 1960s. Music and words go hand in hand. The researcher hears and notes song in authentic performance at home, in the field or at the pub. A pioneer collector of popular song was Cecil Sharp (1859-1924), founder of the English Folk Dance and Song Society, who concentrated on rural song and dance in *Folk-Songs from Somerset* (Simpkin, Marshall & Company, 1904-19) and *The Sword Dances of Northern England Together with the Horn Dance of Abbots Bromley* (Novello & Company, 1911-13). Others who

Charles Grant of Aberlour, Banffshire, worked in the popular tradition of the hereditary fiddlers and pipers maintained by clan chiefs. His music book includes a lament for a laird dated 13th December 1850.

tramped the country in pursuit of folk song included Lucy Broadwood, Percy Grainger and Ralph Vaughan Williams. Subsequent researchers recognised the value of industrial folk song. Communities of pitmen, fishermen, weavers and whalers nurtured particular schools of musicianship and peculiar styles of ribald, radical or sentimental balladry. Music inspired dance such as the floral dance of Helston, the masculine clog dance of industrial Lancashire, the virile highland dance, reels and strathspeys. By preference, dance is recorded on film or videotape, though the imaginative observer will also develop strategies for describing graphically the various movements, steps and figures.

The researcher attends, observes, records and analyses adult folk customs and neighbourhood child lore, playground myths, chants, songs and games, discovering through interview the significance of each practice, pursuing early manifestations of ceremonies in archival sources, interpreting each custom in the light of historical background. Numerous tales and beliefs await collection and study in the context of historical monuments and natural features. One of the earliest observers of the customs of the common people was Henry Bourne, a curate in Newcastle upon Tyne, whose *Antiquitates Vulgares* ('Common Antiquities'; 1725) offered 'proper reflection' on each of the ceremonies, 'shewing which may be retain'd, and which ought to be laid aside'. The periodical *Folklore*, as well as *County Folk-lore Printed Extracts* and other publications of the Folklore Society (founded 1878), offers evidence based on oral and archival research. From 1936 onwards the volumes on *British Calendar Customs* concentrate on documentation from the period 1840-80, 'when many popular calendar customs were becoming evanescent and some that were very popular were discontinued', such as the Epping Hunt and Greenwich Fairs. Popular rites such as well-dressing, maypole-dancing, free-for-all football games, Hallowe'en guizing (guizing, 'going in disguise' and playing pranks at Hallowe'en, was a popular adult custom until the nineteenth century, revived as a children's custom in the twentieth) and mumming plays may be rooted in pagan Celtic or Anglo-Saxon cults. A memory of Celtic sacrificial ritual may endure in bowdlerised form in the curious hood game played each year on old Christmas day at Haxey, Lincolnshire, when twelve villagers dressed in flower-decked scarlet hats represent a preternatural creature of the earth known as the bogey, bodach or boggle-boo. The fool of the game, seated in a rope-swing over a fire, is the sacrificial victim. When the game ends in a free-for-all scrum to win possession of a length of leather-bound rope, modern participants unwittingly struggle for the garrotting noose of a Lindow man.

13

Not all folksy customs are of great antiquity. The morris (Moorish North African) dance of England, for instance, was introduced only following the crusades, though perhaps grafted on to older spring festival observances. Customs may prove romantic reinventions of genuine but moribund practices, with overt sexuality safely diffused and boisterous elements rigidly suppressed. Practices and customs that have in their short lifetimes become rooted in popular culture include the wearing of distinctive clan tartans created for George IV's Scottish visit; the Welsh *eisteddfodau* (gatherings) whose ritual *gorsedd* (meeting of bards and druids) was initiated by Edward Williams (Iolo Morganug) at London's Primrose Hill in 1792; St Patrick's Day parades; the guitar-strumming convivialities of the *ceilidh* (gathering for music and story); the stronger meat of the rock festival and rave; and the solstice festivals of Stonehenge and Glastonbury.

The Department of Irish Folklore, National University of Ireland, successor to the Irish Folklore Commission of 1935-71, collects, preserves and makes available reminiscences, legend, song, dance, music, belief and documents relating to such subjects as vernacular building, boat construction, domestic economy, religion, agriculture and transport. Research may be published in *Béaloideas* and *Scríbhinní Béaloidis*. Schoolchildren contributed thousands of pages of lore, particularly in projects of 1937-8 and 1980-1. The School of Scottish Studies, Edinburgh University, was established in 1951 as a research centre on folklore, topography, place-names and dialects. Farming, fishing, building, religion and domestic life and occupations are recorded visually in, for instance, the work of the anthropologist Werner Kissling (1896-1988) in the Hebrides and Dumfriesshire. Early fiddle music in manuscript, a tale archive, a linguistic survey, Lady Stewart-Murray's Gaelic traditional tales from clachan and croft and R. C. Maclagan's highland folklore are all referred to in the journals *Scottish Studies* and *Tocher*. Psalmody, ballads and stories are available on disc or cassette in the series *Scottish Tradition*.

Landscape studies

Studying the landscape, often known as fieldwork, offers a further step into the past, and a good foundation for this is two books by the pioneer academic W. G. Hoskins, *The Making of the English Landscape* (Hodder & Stoughton, 1955), now available in an illustrated edition (Hodder & Stoughton, 1988) updated by the landscape historian Christopher Taylor, and *Fieldwork in Local History* (Faber, 1967). The public library holds the main series of archaeological and architectural regional surveys as well as volumes on the 'making of the landscape' theme, including the series of Shell Guides to reading the landscape. Guides to typical sites for the fieldworker include the Exploring England's Heritage series (HMSO/English Heritage), P. Harbison's *Guide to the National Monuments in the Republic of Ireland* (Gill & Macmillan, 1970), the current edition of *Historic Monuments of Northern Ireland* (HMSO, Belfast), the Exploring Scotland's Heritage series (HMSO, Edinburgh), C. Houlder's *Wales: An Archaeological Guide; the Prehistoric, Roman and Early Medieval Field Monuments* (Faber, 1974) and the Guide to Ancient and Historic Wales series (HMSO/Cadw, Welsh Historic Monuments). The relevant volume of Nikolaus Pevsner's *Buildings of England* (volumes also for regions of Ireland, Scotland and Wales) is an affordable addition to the home bookshelf.

Fieldwork means getting out and about and looking at the landscape and townscape from a historical

Fieldwork means getting out and about.

The bicycle, important for rural mobility and women's liberation, is the local historian's preferred means of transport. Wayside features here span five millennia of local history. The signpost dates from the turnpike era. The early Christian cross is fashioned from a prehistoric standing stone that retains an aura of ancient mystery and magic in its popular Cornish name, Crows an Wra ('cross of the witch').

point of view. The landscape tells the truth. It may be read like a book. The text of the landscape is the cairn on the skyline, the milestone on the verge, the oratory by the lough. The language of the landscape is the activity of men and women, raising memorials to their passing presence. Fieldwork is concerned with what can be observed on the ground in town and country with the sensitive eye, without recourse to archaeology. The fieldworker is a walker and a cyclist, a gazer, enquirer and interpreter, slowly traversing fields, streets, river banks, coastlines and hills to appreciate the natural or man-made lie of the land. A bicycle carries the researcher and a full kit of research tools across the parish at the same convenient rate as the horse-drawn and pedestrian traffic of the past. The cyclist is not insulated by speed and comfort from terrain, track, weather, wildlife and conversation with the natives. Areas closed to the motorist welcome the cyclist,

An environmentally friendly mode of transport, this bicycle gives scale to the Norman doorway and Tudor window at the church of Thwaite St Mary, Norfolk.

who may ride along farm tracks and forestry roads, wheel along towpaths and bridleways and manoeuvre with no special difficulty across moors, streams and mountain passes, hence the encomium of praise by the artist and archaeologist Heywood Sumner:

> What bliss it was in childhood to read of the magical seven league boots, and to see their possessor ... striding across a landscape! A bicycle is our magic of seven leagues. It carries us where we will, and then, laid on the grass, it waits our further will. A few drops of oil and our own muscles are its sole demand, while in return it endows us with the magical power of the old fairy tale.
> H. Sumner *The Ancient Earthworks of Cranborne Chase* (1913), quoted in B. Cunliffe *Heywood Sumner's Wessex* (Roy Gasson Associates, Wimborne, 1985, page 76).

The fieldworker is not generally an archaeologist, a digger or a motorist. A landscape that flashes past the windows at sixty miles an hour cannot properly be appreciated. On occasion it may be necessary to travel far afield to visit comparator sites in adjacent parishes, distant counties or indeed anywhere in Europe, because throughout history people have been able to migrate widely, spreading culture and styles.

Fieldwork is best achieved when bearing in mind the adage 'The more you know, the more you will learn'. Fieldwork should be linked with other disciplines, so that what is seen in the landscape relates to information from the library, archives, neighbours and members of one or other of the community societies involved in research. Conversely, research in written sources helps in dating and understanding features observed, while the county archaeologist will direct energies into accessible channels to avoid pitfalls. The historian is so steeped in his subject that he usually knows intuitively when an archaeologically sensitive site is being opened and so may be proved right even when experts have dismissed the area as archaeologically barren. The researcher is in the front rank of curious onlookers when workmen begin to dig a trench for cables or water mains and will quickly recognise potsherds, bones and significant artefacts turned up by the shovels. The site foreman can always be asked if it is feasible to halt work while the planning department and archaeologist are contacted.

The *Sites and Monuments Record* (SMR) locates by place-name and Ordnance Survey (OS) national grid reference most archaeological sites, monuments and find-spots. The SMR is compiled and maintained locally, usually by the council archaeologist, typically in county planning offices in England, regional archaeological trusts in Wales and unitary authorities in Scotland. Planning officials also hold 'statutory lists of buildings of special architectural and historic interest' (listed buildings). These two registers are available for public consultation and are a usual starting point for historical studies.

The fieldworker considers natural features. A river, for example, has influenced people's lives, perhaps providing power for a corn mill, or maybe as the home of a pagan deity (Sabrina inhabiting the Severn). It is often a barrier between one community and another, a natural moat for a castle town, or alternatively a highway for goods, people and ideas. It is usually a legal (or poached!) source of fish for the traditional meatless Friday meal, certainly a cause for litigation over fishing rights. The fieldworker recognises that virtually every landscape in Britain and Ireland, even the rugged mountains of Snowdonia and the desolate flow country of Caithness, has been shaped by perhaps ten thousand years of human activity. The researcher questions how and why changes in landscape, vegetation or land use took place, whether rapidly or gradually, by slow evolution or according to some deliberate plan, and how changes affected people's lives and living standards. The historian peels back layer upon layer of history in a single landscape. Beneath the modern prairie-style fieldscape stretch the fields of eighteenth-century enclosure, and beneath those lie medieval common fields. Beneath the medieval furlongs are layers of prehistoric agriculture harking back to the Stone Age.

What is true of the landscape applies too to the built environment. The construction details, date and purpose of a bridge, castle, church or factory invite attention, leading to the crucial question of how a particular feature affected communities in the vicinity. The most visible man-made buildings in town and country date back only a century or so, though often incorporating older parts. The parish church may seem entirely Victorian, though careful observation might reveal sections of medieval walling, itself reusing Anglo-Saxon carved stone and Roman brick. The church may stand upon a prehistoric pagan cult site. Each landscape in each era had an appropriate set of standard features required by the civilised human community, including habitation and industrial sites, fields, temples, burial places, fortifications, tracks, boundary markers, walls, memorials and administrative centres. Most seem absent where localities are sealed under concrete, though even in London or Birmingham fieldwork may yield medieval pottery, monumental inscriptions, foundations of temples and early factories. In such instances it may help to survey sites and landscapes in adjacent still rural parishes and then infer from topography and historical analogy what should have existed before the developers moved in.

Fieldwork requires advance planning. Decisions must be made about where to go, what time of year is best, what equipment is required. A clear map is essential, preferably the Ordnance Survey Landranger (1:50,000, pink cover) and Pathfinder (1:25,000, green cover) series or the large-scale Ordnance Survey maps (1:10,560 and 1:2500) which are sufficiently detailed to show individual fields and buildings. All may be purchased in bookshops or borrowed from libraries. Photocopies of tithe, estate or enclosure plans and older out-of-copyright editions of the Ordnance Survey can be bought from libraries or archives for annotation on site. Sites and monuments are indicated by the OS in gothic lettering as 'Village', 'Settlement', 'Field System', 'Roman Fort (site of)', while battlefields have a crossed-swords symbol. Archaeological find-spots, though nothing may now be apparent on site, are indicated by a remark such as 'Human Bones and Pieces of Tartan found 1868'. Annotations reflect the state of knowledge at the time; thus a Pictish fort may be called a 'Danish Camp', while an eighteenth-century military road may be misidentified as a 'Roman Road'.

The fieldworker's basic tool kit might consist of a notebook and pencil for recording observations in the field, with watercolours and drawing pens for on-site sketches. Measurements of buildings, field systems and townscapes may be made simply by pacing out the distance. A size nine walking boot measures almost exactly one foot (305 mm). A 27 inch (689 mm) bicycle wheel travels approximately 7 feet (2.134 metres) in one revolution. A hand's breadth is about 8 inches (203 mm). The top joint of the thumb is 1 inch (25 mm). Sometimes it is advisable to employ such informal means, lest people should think you are a council official! For working alone or in confined spaces a pocket ultrasonic measuring device from a do-it-yourself shop is recommended. Accurate recording with metric measuring tapes, a steel ruler, a plumb line and a magnetic compass for establishing orientations is desirable. A camera and electronic flash are constant companions, with the scale shown by discreetly positioning a passer-by or a homely object such as a coin. Measuring rods graduated in metres or centimetres as appropriate give a professional look.

Building materials and architectural details should be recorded, showing the layout, orientation, dimensions (internal and external), ceiling height, roof pitch and structure, windows, chimneys and other relevant features. Wall structures, divided for convenience by a grid of vertical and horizontal tapes, can be recorded stone by stone by teams of fieldworkers and draughtsmen working from ladders and scaffolding. Detailed analysis of variations in texture, tooling, coursing, bonding, size and geology should reveal significant aspects of structural history. Phases of construction are indicated by blocked-up windows, redundant doorways, stones from earlier buildings, raised rooflines, repairs and fire damage. Filled-up beam

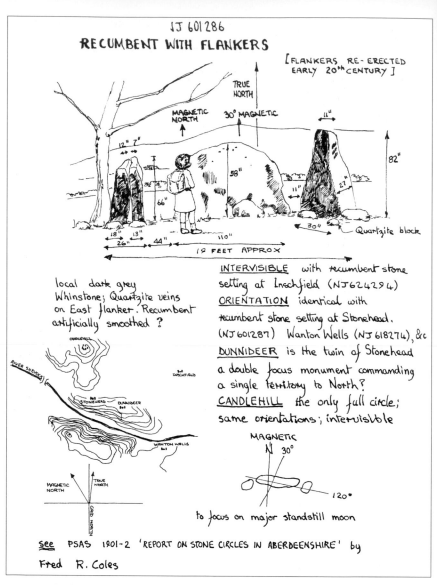

The fieldwork notebook of Christine Clerk, Elgin, 13th January 1991.

slots may be associated with the original scaffolding, internal furnishings, partitions or external timber outshots. The technology of computer-aided design (CAD) cannot be rivalled for hard-edged accuracy, offering a convenient means of storing architectural and cartographic data, easily retrievable on-screen or as a printout. CAD allows the generation of multilayered drawings in a variety of scales, projections and orientations. Instruction in the use of CAD and computer graphics is available through colleges of technology.

Field-walking involves systematically walking, with permission, across ploughland to plot and collect items turned up by the plough. In this group activity all members may participate as active walkers or sedentary planners, cataloguers or even caterers. The group might wish at an early stage to call in a landscape archaeologist. A team leader should undertake the essential background reading on national history, archaeology, sites, finds, monuments and technique. Field-walking requires no excavation, but a generalised awareness of archaeology will suggest how artefacts can be recognised, what may be collected from the site and what should be left, carefully marked, for retrieval by an expert at a later date. The ground for field-walking may be marked out in advance with pegs and tapes to plot find-spots precisely on a map. An extensive expedition might cross two hundred fields or more with walkers no closer than 60 feet (18 metres) but looking out to right and left as well as ahead for potsherds, flint tools, coins, nails, buttons, weapons, changes in soil colour and texture (a hearth may show traces of scattered charcoal, while dark soil with bits of bone may indicate a midden). Each item retrieved is carefully packed in cotton wool, and its location is noted, to permit detailed examination later. The law of treasure trove requires a searcher to notify valuable finds to the authorities and, as appropriate, to deposit them in the secure custody of a museum.

An example of an amateur field-walker was George Thomson, a farmer at Easter Gollachy, Banffshire. Thomson, who died in 1908, spent all his life following the plough. From the disturbed soil he collected hundreds of medieval and earlier implements, including several finds of national importance and a complete undisturbed cist burial of a Bronze Age chieftain. He recognised the value of his finds by maintaining close contact with other enthusiastic amateur historians and with experts in universities and national museums, who respected his careful methods. Thomson was eventually recognised as an expert himself, and people came for advice on artefacts and sites discovered on their own farms and in their kitchen gardens. Easter Gollachy farmhouse became a famous community museum. Thomson was a generous man, and from time to time he redrafted his will, increasing the

Field-walking on the dunes and pebble banks at Culbin, Moray, about 1911, for evidence of an agricultural landscape first tamed in the Bronze Age, finally destroyed by erosion and sand storms in the 1690s. The sandy landscape was later successfully afforested.

number of legatees on each occasion. When he died his antiquarian collections had to be sold so that the many bequests could be paid. Archives relating to the public auction reveal that whole cases of flint arrowheads were snapped up for a few pennies. A wonderful carved stone ball of late neolithic date was knocked down for fifteen shillings. Neolithic polished stone axeheads sold for between two and sixteen shillings depending on quality. A bronze axehead of about 2500 BC went for £1 2s 6d. Two skulls excavated from Bronze Age cist graves were sold together for 1s 3d. The ashes of a chief from a Bronze Age burial, described by the auctioneer as 'lot dust in box etc', raised just two shillings, the value of the box. Thomson's field notebooks in the custody of his descendants describe in words and pictures each object and the circumstances of its discovery, but where the items are now is not recorded either in the family papers or in the public records.

Archaeology

Buried sites may be located by careful probing with a metal rod, for instance to follow the line of a buried foundation or infilled ditch. Dowsing using a forked twig may (unaccountably) identify hidden features, such as water pipes. Bosing involves banging with a pickaxe at regular intervals across the ground to recognise alterations in sound above pits and walls. In addition, a variety of technical apparatus allows the historian to see beneath the soil. The popular metal detector needs to be used with skill and sensitivity if the information potentially available from any item is to be fully exploited. A find may be just one element in a more extensive site. Noting its exact position or context (perhaps in a pot or posthole or beneath a foundation) is important if the relationship between find and find-spot is to be understood and the significance of the site fully realised. There are, however, legal restrictions on the use of metal detectors, in the interests of landowners and archaeological study. Geophysical survey equipment would be brought by an expert called in to search for features below ground, especially solid remains such as walls or roads. Magnetic anomalies caused by a buried furnace, hearth or cremation pit may be detected by the proton magnetometer, the proton gradiometer and the differentiated flux-gate gradiometer. An expert will determine the age of a site and any objects by reference to a fixed timescale in the process known as chronometric or absolute dating. The expert will be aware of the advantages of dating prehistoric sites and burned artefacts by such modern techniques as thermoluminescence, potassium argon, uranium thorium, electron spin resonance, fission-track and archaeomagnetism. Technology takes much of the work of surveying and describing away from the amateur, who, however, remains crucial as facilitator, if not as operator, and in the vital role of explaining and interpreting the human significance of sites and finds.

Archaeology might be thought to follow naturally from a survey on the surface, but this rarely happens because excavation is highly specialised and expensive. Excavation under controlled conditions is essential when a site is scheduled for destruction, building construction, roadworks or mineral extraction. Archaeological importance is recognised through inclusion on the *Sites and Monuments Record*, the first register to consult whenever an interesting item is thrown up by a workman's shovel or exposed on a molehill. Building and demolition works should already have been notified for comment by the county archaeologist at the planning stage. The archaeologist cannot be on every site every day, so the historian keeps a lookout and brings any finds to the attention of a museum or archaeological field unit. Archaeological discoveries are usually made by the man or woman on the spot, the householder or the workman. In May 1996 a contractor digging a new cellar deep below ground in the centre of Elgin, Moray, discovered a medieval stone slab incised with a floreated cross. Recognising the object's significance, he called in historians and archivists, who suggested the stone may have originated in the parochial graveyard destroyed in 1826 for road improvements. Museum curators,

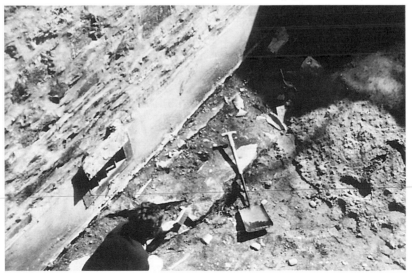

Archaeology does not necessarily follow a survey on the surface.

archaeologists and the treasure trove panel for Scotland then became involved, and an archaeological dig was mooted. The enthusiasm of the ordinary citizen, the total commitment to the home environment, is a powerful element in the process of lobbying to ensure a site is recognised, perhaps in spite of experts, then properly protected and, ultimately, excavated. The Department of the Environment publishes planning policy guidance for England and Wales, including *Archaeology and Planning* (known as PPG16, 1990) which details action appropriate in archaeologically sensitive areas. In the Republic of Ireland all unauthorised archaeological excavation was made illegal in 1994.

A researcher can liaise with the county archaeologist to help ensure that sites are appropriately protected and investigated. The historian who wishes to become involved may acquire the necessary skills by enrolling as a volunteer on an organised dig or by formal courses of instruction. The county archaeologist may find places on the team for amateurs and volunteers. The community history group, as facilitator, might raise funds through heritage grants, raffles, lectures, jumble sales

When the exercise yard of Forres prison was improved in 1992 fieldworkers identified the foundations and recorded the dimensions of some of the earliest medieval houses in the town, demolished in 1836.

and the national lottery to employ a professional freelance archaeological team to excavate and record. The work may be publicised nationally by the Council for British Archaeology's progress lists, such as *Discovery and Excavation in Scotland*. During the excavation the archaeologist arranges for the conservation and preservation of artefacts and samples for detailed examination and analysis, preferably in an appropriate museum, and for the publication of a preliminary report in *Current Archaeology*. The full report, whose cost is always an important element in the budget, may require years to complete. Sometimes the writings of professional archaeologists seem a little off-putting, being full of prohibitions, dire warnings and disparagement of the efforts of clumsy unscientific excavators of the past; however, this is just as it should be. Careless digging can destroy more than it discovers. Nowadays archaeologists are cautious almost to a fault in their interpretations. A report may describe with marvellous precision what has been found but be cautious about its meaning, despite being the medium through which the ordinary person glimpses the lives, beliefs and society of people in the past. The historian takes matters further, daring to speculate from archaeological artefacts, dry bones, stones, buildings and documentary sources on the thoughts and beliefs of people long ago. The percipient researcher studying his neighbours today may also be able to imagine the human faces behind the historic monuments.

Particular experts

At every stage it is worthwhile to consult experts in particular disciplines, including scientists. The historian should never shy away from calling someone in to help out with matters beyond the ability or finances of the generalist and amateur, just as most people are happy enough in their everyday lives to 'get a man in' to service the car or pump out the septic tank. Geographers, soil scientists, stratigraphers, geologists and geomorphologists all contribute to the study of the land and landscape by researching erosion over the centuries or the processes by which blown sand or peat may have encroached upon fieldscapes and farmsteads in prehistoric or more recent times. From patterns of abrasion on ordinary stones these experts show how, over the generations, wind and water have acted upon the environment. Layers of clay and silt, technically known as varve, annually deposited in lakes can be analysed to determine the chronology of glacial sediments. An entomologist identifies ancient insect remains while a malacologist classifies snail shells. Soil samples in an archaeological excavation are usually taken from the different levels and contain wing covers of identifiable species of beetles and the shells of land snails. Different species of insect and snail, of course, occupy particular ecological niches and flourish in a determined environment whose historical climate, pollution and vegetation are amenable to research. The palynologist combines botanical and microscopical skills to analyse pollens preserved in prehistoric soils, providing evidence for ancient flora and land use.

Palaeobotanists analyse leaves, seeds, flowers, twigs, timbers and other plants which can survive for centuries wherever air is excluded. Impressions of seeds and plants may be evident in the clay of pottery or in human excrement rescued from dungheaps, privies, latrines and middens, unequivocal evidence of diet. Even a handful of carbonised grains of barley or wheat recovered by the sieving or flotation of soil samples could be indicative of climate, farming practice and diet. Pollen survives especially well. The botanist identifies remains of plants in peat, tufa and waterlogged deposits, noting significant mixes of flora such as twayblades, wild hyacinth, dog's mercury and wild service, suggestive of old woodland. Botanical skills are recruited for surveying hedgerows, which may be dated by the examination of flora using a crude rule-of-thumb method whereby the number of different woody plant species in a 30 yard (27 metre) sample of hedge suggests the age of the hedge in centuries. This has been challenged because experts disagree on methods of counting. Is the bramble a woody plant? Are the dog rose and downy rose counted as one species or two? Would fieldworkers always distinguish the various *Prunus* species, including such rarities as the wild *Prunus communis*? A single-species newish hedge may replace an ancient one upon a boundary bank first defined in the Bronze Age. An old hedge may have been invaded by a vigorous plant such as elm or blackthorn, crowding out weaker species. Allowance must be made for oak, ash, elm, poplar and other standards planted for timber, possibly all in the same year, which would, on the rule above, denote an old hedgerow.

The geneticist offers tissue identification, genetic fingerprinting and blood-group surveys of bodies, perhaps recovered from church crypt clearances, raising questions about linguistic and social change, immigration, intermarriage and the extermination of native populations. Country burial grounds of disused chapels or monasteries, crypts beneath city churches and urban abandoned cemeteries are prime sites for archaeology. Work has been conducted at Winchester cathedral, London's St Nicholas Shambles and York's St Helen-on-the-Walls. Palaeopathology, the scientific scrutiny of bones and bodies, reveals such aspects of medical history as diet, disease, wounds, deformity and cause of death. The biologist identifies human or animal teeth and bone fragments. The osteologist estimates the age at death of an individual even though only a few bones and teeth have been preserved. Skeletons in Saxon cemeteries are analysed to discover the age structure of village communities when early death seems usual, perhaps resulting in a vibrant young population with few old people to support. This impression might be balanced by evidence from more recent graveyards and church crypts where skeletal data often underestimate age at death as given in registers and coffin plates.

The climatologist offers models for interpreting historical weather patterns. Climate is a key factor, affecting agriculture, settlement, communications, architecture and even religious outlook. Evidence may be gained from analysis of pollen from peat bogs, annual growth rings in trees, bones, insect fragments, snail shells and other animal remains and documents. General climatic conditions endure for centuries interspersed with exceptional episodes of weather such as a flood, blizzard, summer gale or early frost. A coastal parish might be more temperate than an inland parish; a western parish is likely to be wetter than an eastern one; lowland parishes tend to be warmer than highland. Within one parish distinct climate zones may persist, differing for a built-up area, mountain or lake, with a sheltered hollow known as a notorious frost pocket. A south-facing slope receives more sunshine than a slope facing north, with implications for crops grown and the prosperity of individual farms. An average annual temperature change of only 1°C may affect the growing season sufficiently to determine the viability of arable husbandry and thus, perhaps, of whole settlements. Temperature falls about 1°F for every 300 feet (1°C for 200 metres) of elevation. A fall of 0.5°C, if associated with factors such as shade from trees or wind funnelling along a valley, may result in snow lying longer and frost penetrating deeper than elsewhere in the parish, making life on the site rigorous, precarious or impossible at certain periods. Rain, snow, sleet and hail are necessary for growing crops and replenishing ground water, rivers and lakes. Average levels of precipitation over years or centuries as well as particular departures from the normal pattern must be considered. A severe flood could be the spur to the rebuilding of a township or the replanning of a fieldscape. A wet harvest or a single torrential summer storm may destroy a community's grain crop, leading to famine and falling rents, with recovery taking a generation.

Wood from buildings and archaeological excavations may be dated through dendrochronology (Greek *dendron*, 'tree'), a sophisticated procedure based upon the simple principle of comparing patterns of annual growth rings in a sample with an established regional pattern. The Palaeoecology Centre, Queen's University of Belfast, provides a public service, requiring for the purpose a core of timber showing at least one hundred annual growth rings and, for certainty, the last outer sapwood ring formed in the growing season immediately before the tree was felled.

This signpost near Queen Camel, Somerset, contains Latin, Old British and Old English place-name elements. Queen Eleanor held a manor here.

Excavated organic materials such as hair, wood, bone, skin, seeds or textiles may be dated by laboratory measurement of levels of carbon 14, an isotope that accumulates in living tissue during life and decays at a fixed rate after death. Radiocarbon-dating the material gives an idea of the age of the site, though the process can be unreliable for items of late medieval and more recent date. From 1958 the process has provided a scientific basis for archaeology, which previously relied upon comparative chronologies and typologies for pottery, tools, ornaments and weapons. The radiocarbon revolution revealed that earlier chronologies for British prehistory were incorrect, a millennium adrift in some cases. The prehistorian V. Gordon Childe was driven to despair and suicide as his whole life's work was unravelled by the new scientific archaeology.

Place-names

Place-names are studied for what they can tell about former human activity on domestic, sacred and industrial sites, with land use and environment suggested by reference to trees, plants and animals. Place-names hint at the linguistic, racial and cultural heritage of native peoples. The name Avon recalls the Celts, for whom the word meant 'river', and their Bronze Age predecessors, for whom the sound *abh* (akin to *ar*) seems to have denoted 'holiness', as well as 'water'. Kent refers to the Cantiaci people, whom Caesar knew, with their capital at Canterbury; Worcester to the Weogoran Celtic tribe. A place-name on a modern road sign or map is often written and pronounced differently from at first, partly because the way people speak and spell has changed over the centuries. Linguists see these changes as following general and predictable patterns as indicated in documents. The process of place-name perversion in England affected even the humble public house. The inn-name Bag o' Nails derives from the medieval badgers (traders) who patronised the nale (alehouse).

The early form of a place-name generally comprises one or more everyday words which, though readily translated, may not readily reveal their deeper meanings. The place-names Lindow and Dublin share both the British elements *dubo* and *lindo*, which translate into the somewhat banal 'black-pool'. There is deeper significance in these dark waters, for Lindow Moss in Cheshire was a site of Celtic ritual and human sacrifice, its black boggy pools believed to be inhabited by terrible deities.

An excerpt from J. McN. Dodgson's 'The Place-names of Cheshire', 1970 (part 2, page 197).

Cheshire and Ireland were linked, through sacred Mona (Anglesey), with druidical sites across Britain, epitomised by votive deposits of torcs (neck ornaments) wrought in gold from the mountains of Wicklow. The various Blackpools, Blackwaters and Loch Dubhs of Britain may have special significance as places linked to the Celtic water cult, or even as nodes in a druidical network.

Long centuries of English settlement in Ireland spawned a hideous race of toponymical freaks. The rulers, distanced from the language and unsympathetic to the culture of their tenantry, did not trouble to learn the rules of Erse (Irish) syntax and spelling when writing down the place-names, which they did not understand. Anglicised combinations of vowels and consonants flowed easily but meaninglessly from their pens. Béal Atha Bhearaig became Ballyvary; Leitir Mhic an Bhaird became Lettermacaward; Ceathrú Fhiodhghoirt became Carrigart. Anglicisation and standardisation of Celtic place-names throughout Britain and Ireland may also be traced to the work of the Ordnance Survey in the nineteenth century.

Initial research should be checked against the scholarly opinions of experts in E. Ekwall, The Concise Oxford Dictionary of English Place-names (4th edition, Oxford University Press, 1960); the popular Oxford paperback by A. D. Mills, Dictionary of English Place-names (1991); A. Room's A Dictionary of Irish Place-names (Appletree Press, Belfast, 1986) and Dictionary of Place-names in the British Isles (Bloomsbury, 1988); Place-names of Northern Ireland (Institute of Irish Studies, Belfast, 1992, in progress); and J. Field's English Field Names (David & Charles, 1972). The English Place-name Society's county volumes are basic reference sources for parish, field, street, hill, stream and other features. Two introductory volumes by A. H. Smith, entitled English Place-name Elements (Cambridge University Press, 1956), explain 'the final elements (and a good many first elements) which occur in major place-names so far evidenced before the late fifteenth century, whether they be of English, Scandinavian, French, Latin or Celtic origin'.

Fieldwork is indispensable. Gloomy Lochindorb in Moray, with its forbidding ruined castle on an island, has been interpreted as 'loch of grief' from the Gaelic doirbh, 'grievous', appropriate in view of the stronghold's turbulent history; however, the Gaelic doirb translates as 'tadpole', which is less romantic but no less appropriate, for the place is each spring the breeding ground for a prodigious population of frogs. With an observant eye and a botanist, beekeeper, farmer, archivist, oral historian or other expert, the fieldworker can sometimes understand why a place was named 'golden hill', 'barley field' or 'devil's point'. Wild creatures, perhaps now extinct in the locality, are mentioned in place-names: eagles at Garth Eryr; hawks at Moel Hebog; otters at Ottery St Mary; rats and mice at Gortnalughoge; badgers at Broxbourne and Broxted; songbirds at Larkbeare, Thrushelton and Llwyn yr Ehedydd; foxes at Cloonshannagh; and wolves at Breaghva (though Wolvesnewton in Monmouthshire owes its name to Ralph le Wolf, who held the land in 1314). Sheep provided the main element in Sheffield ('sheep field'). Ballynageerach was noted as a 'town of sheep' and Clonmult for its 'meadow of wethers'. Cattle were especially significant, though it is not known why, at Oxley, Oxford, Oxney and Oxton, but not necessarily at Oxted, 'the place where oaks grow', or Oxshott, 'the land of the Englishman Ocga'. The care of Saxon village pigs fell to the young men who watched their grunting charges browse beneath the woodland beeches and oaks at Swanwick, 'farm of swineherds', and Swanscombe, 'pasture of the swineherd'. At Mochdre was a pig farm, at Gortnamucklagh a tilled field reserved for pigs after harvest. Horses grazed in the valley of Coomnagoppul at Killarney. Ballynagore was a village known for goats and Gwaenynog for bees. The produce of the land is reflected in place-names with the elements *ate* (English) and *coirce* (Irish), meaning 'oats'; *bere* (English) or *haidd* (Welsh), meaning 'barley'; *fleax* ('flax'); *whaete* ('wheat'); *ryge* ('rye').

Aerial survey

Townscape and fieldscape look different viewed from above. A convenient high vantage point may be the tower of the village church or the roof of an office block. Alternatively the fieldworker may send a camera aloft by means of a kite or radio-controlled model aircraft. The intrepid researcher might obtain a bird's-eye view by enlisting the services of a flying, ballooning or gliding club, or by taking to the air in a helicopter, hang-glider or microlight. The amateur aerial photographer uses a 35 mm or 70 mm camera (unless he can afford a Linhof Technika 5 x 4), at about 1500 feet (450 metres) altitude, with a black-and-white panchromatic fine-grained ASA 100 film. Colours in the landscape are emphasised in black and white by under-exposing the picture, overdeveloping the negative and printing on paper of high contrast. A second camera loaded with colour negative or slide film captures the subtleties of colour as well as tone. Upstanding monuments and low-relief features are thrown into sharp focus if photographed from the air obliquely with the sun low in the sky, casting long shadows, or under a dusting of snow. Deserted settlements and field systems unrecognisable from the ground are revealed. On the bare soil of ploughed fields, buried features such as banks and trackways should be indicated by a light-coloured soil mark, while the disturbed filling of pits and ditches will appear as a dark-coloured soil mark. Buried remains may be indicated by cropmarks, as the germination and growth of crops, especially corn, are affected by obstructions below the surface. Drought may enhance cropmarks. In the deeper soil of an infilled ditch, seed germinates early, stems grow taller and ripen more slowly, producing a positive cropmark. In the shallow stony soil associated with a buried wall or roadway, growth is retarded,

An aerial survey can be conducted by microlight.

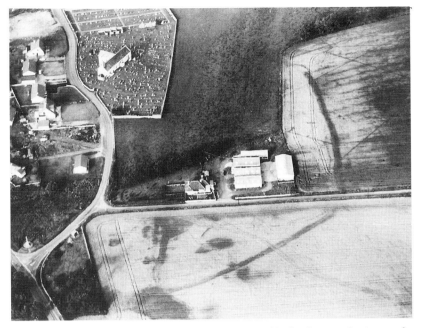

Moray Aerial Archaeology Group was founded in 1984 by three enthusiasts, who between them invested £1000. This photograph of 1985 revealed a cropmark around Old Tarbert church, Portmahomack, Ross-shire, and started a major professional archaeological search for a Pictish settlement.

resulting in a negative cropmark. Cropmarks are, of course, entirely different from the mysterious (or hoax) corn circles which appear from time to time across southern England.

Aerial photography was pioneered by two First World War archaeologist aviators, O. G. S. Crawford and A. Keiller, in their classic *Wessex from the Air* (Clarendon Press, 1928). Other surveys were undertaken in Norfolk by George Swain of Norwich in the 1920s, now available at the National Monuments Record (NMR), and in the Oxford area by G. W. G. Allen in the 1930s, deposited in the Ashmolean Museum, Oxford. The air forces of Britain, Germany and the United States were active in photographing Britain from the air, particularly after the outbreak of war in 1939, the military nature of the enterprise hardly detracting from its usefulness in providing historical evidence. RAF photographs can be consulted at the NMR, with examples also at the Public Record Office and at the Ministry of Defence air historical branch (both London). German Luftwaffe archives were captured by the Americans in 1945 and may be accessed through the national archives of the United States, with examples also at the NMR. The American archive in Alabama holds United States Air Force photographs. The RAF continued to photograph Britain from the air, including views taken directly from above for the national survey of 1946-7. RAF compound images of 1947-53 are at the British Library. Commercial photographic firms such as Aerofilms of Borehamwood flew extensively. Meridian Airmaps Limited's archive of 1952-84 is at the NMR. In 1950 the Cambridge University Committee for Aerial Photography was established to assemble and make publicly available a comprehensive photographic archive covering the whole of Britain, rephotographed periodically to catch fugitive cropmarks and soil marks. The Ordnance Survey began aerial reconnaissance for mapping and archaeological purposes, depositing photographs dating from 1952 onwards at the NMR. Irish landscapes were photographed by J. K. St Joseph during the 1960s and again for the

Geological Survey of Ireland during 1973-7. Collections of air photographs are held in public libraries, university departments (especially geography), archive offices, heritage centres, planning departments and, most importantly, the NMR. A specialist NMR collection of oblique views illustrates architectural, archaeological and landscape features. Collections for Scotland are available in the National Monuments Record, Edinburgh, for Wales at the Welsh Office, Cardiff; for Northern Ireland at the Ordnance Survey in Belfast. Assistance in locating other collections or specific photographs may be obtained from the National Monuments Records and the *Directory of Aerial Photographic Collections in the United Kingdom* (Association of Special Libraries and Information Bureaux, 1993).

Historical Monuments Commission

Building upon foundations laid by the Society of Antiquaries of London, established in 1717, William Morris's Society for the Protection of Ancient Buildings (1877) and the Ancient Monuments Protection Acts of 1882, 1892 (Ireland) and 1900, royal commissions were established in 1908 in Scotland, Wales and England to draw up inventories of 'Ancient and Historical Monuments and Constructions connected with or illustrative of contemporary culture, civilisation and conditions of life of the people ... and to specify which seem most worthy of preservation'. The modern commissions have two major roles. Firstly they record, analyse and assess ancient and historical monuments and buildings. Secondly they compile, conserve and make publicly available national accumulations of documentary information. The commissions identify which monuments are important and for what reasons, but do not normally excavate or conserve them. Records created or acquired by each commission are preserved, listed and made available to researchers through three National Monuments Records, situated at Swindon for England, with a customer service centre in London, as well as in Aberystwyth, for Wales, and Edinburgh, for Scotland. Each National Monuments Record is a significant secondary source, while the primary source is the monument itself. Records are accessed through catalogues and indexes computerised as appropriate for use in the public search rooms, both on-line and in printouts from archival databases. Millions of pictorial and related items are being made available on the internet for school, business and home access.

Architectural records generated by or deposited as a result of each commission's work comprise notebooks, correspondence files and reports of investigating officers, measured surveys of ecclesiastical buildings, historic and vernacular houses and industrial structures such as railway viaducts; photographs taken for record purposes and for use in the various published inventories; building accounts (some from the eighteenth century); excavation reports and drawings by earlier investigators. Outstanding buildings and heritage sites are especially recorded if threatened with destruction. Rural housing of the period 1400-1920 in the Pennines was researched in depth when demolitions accelerated, resulting in three important volumes in 1985-6. The commissions make surveys of domestic and ecclesiastical wall paintings, such as the English and Welsh inscriptions at Eglwys Cymin, Carmarthenshire, and the mural portraits of Church House, Gwehelog Fawr, Monmouthshire. In 1986 the English commission was charged with responsibility for the survey of London, founded 1894, which has published a register of historic buildings in the capital as well as separate volumes dealing with individual buildings and parishes. Homely structures in regional architectural style (vernacular buildings) were more or less ignored by earlier field investigators. Domestic sketch plans were sketchy indeed until the drafting of the report on *Dorset West* in the late 1930s (published 1952) and the researches of Fox and Raglan on *Monmouthshire Houses* (published 1951-4). Since 1945 the commission has emphasised the significance of comparative study of house plans at all levels of structure. This modern theme of function and form has been applied by field inspectors to industrial and

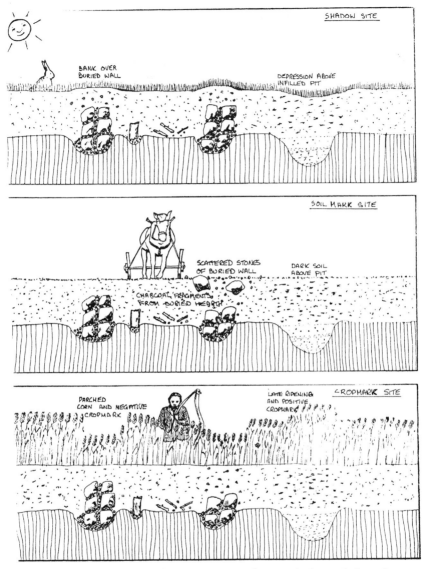

Cropmarks visible in an aerial survey suggest what may lie beneath the soil.

ritual monuments, for instance to investigate the purpose of church aisles, transepts and enigmatic low-side 'leper' windows 'near the west end of the chancel usually on the south side, but sometimes on the north and sometimes on both sides ... occasionally also near the east end of the nave, and in other situations ... No part of our ancient churches has so completely baffled the enquiries of antiquaries' (*Archaeological Journal*, volume 4 [1847], page 314).

The archaeology section of each commission is a repository for files and drawings of its own surveying officers and acquires microfiche security copies of a variety of excavation reports, especially those funded publicly. Field monuments of all dates threatened by afforestation, open-cast mining, housing and agriculture are recorded. The English commission preserves the archaeology archives of the Ancient Monuments Inspectorate, Ancient Monuments Laboratory and the Medieval Settlement Research Group. Following the Serpell report of 1979 the responsibilities of the archaeology branch of the Ordnance Survey were taken over. The commissions acquired microfilms of the Ordnance Survey name books compiled by field surveyors (recording place-names, social and economic information, natural and man-made objects) as well as original maps and aerial photographs. Reports on archaeological sites, whether preserved or destroyed, are presented in the format of the 'national archaeological record card' describing a single site identified by name and national grid reference. Record cards pinpoint find-spots (locations from which significant artefacts have been recovered), and record names for field monuments that were perhaps not recorded on the published Ordnance Survey maps but derive from oral tradition that was already ancient when collected by nineteenth-century surveyors. The cards include, as appropriate, plans of forts, fosses and other monuments, with a miniature photographic record of the site at the time of recording. There is a bibliography of publications by archaeologists and historians who have made significant comment upon the site or monument.

From the voluminous records of the royal commissions, reports are published summarily in parliamentary white papers and in more detail in county volumes. Inventories of sites and monuments published up to the end of 1975, some out of print, are available to researchers separately in microfiche through Chadwyck-Healey of Cambridge. In Scotland summary lists of archaeological sites and monuments have been compiled and published since 1977 for areas where the existing information is inadequate. The commissions also publish reference books on vernacular and industrial buildings as well as field monuments.

There is no royal commission for Ireland, but the Archaeological Survey of Northern Ireland is conducted by the historic monuments branch of the Department of the Environment for Northern Ireland. In the south an equivalent recording and preservation function belongs to the National Survey of Sites and Monuments of Historical Interest and Archaeological Importance of the Office of Public Works. The National Survey set the standard for publication of the *Archaeological Survey of County Donegal* (1983), an exemplary cooperative venture involving ordinary community historians, the County Donegal Historical Society, the county council, Donegal Regional Development Organisation, Bord Failte, the National Museum and the Electricity Supply Board under the overall direction of a professional archaeologist from Ulster. The book describes and illustrates with photographs and plans 1954 separate sites divided into general categories, including crannogs, hillforts, cashels, ring forts, holy wells, ecclesiastical architecture and castles.

Museums

Public museums maintain extensive collections of artefacts recovered from, or otherwise relating to, the researcher's own locality, including biological samples, clothing, furniture, tools, toys, farm implements, weapons and domestic utensils. A few examples may be on display in the public galleries, but the bulk of the collection, held in secure stores behind the scenes, is accessed by means of catalogues and indexes. Museum curators allow researchers, generally by appointment, to examine artefacts from the collections in the museum's own study room. The researcher should arrive fully prepared with paper, pencils (pens may not be allowed), a portable drawing board and a suitable hand lens. Where photography is permitted it will be useful to know in advance what kind of lighting is available and to arrive equipped with film of appropriate speed, a suitable flash and a tripod. Some museums offer a photographic service, though this may involve significant expense. Addresses will be found in the current *Museums Yearbook* and in P. Dale's *Museum and Special Collections in the United Kingdom* (ASLIB/Museums Association, 1993) but time and imagination will be required to identify in directories all the museums with items relevant to a particular project.

The most valuable artefacts in either historical or monetary terms, especially those made of gold or silver or exhibiting outstanding craftsmanship, will probably be lodged in national museums or private collections. Antiquarian and archaeological societies, including the Royal Archaeological Institute (1843) and the Cambrian Archaeological Association (1846), have periodically published descriptions of sites and discoveries, perhaps noting the place of deposit. Computerised museum indexes should locate the current home of most items from a particular parish. The historian can then visit appropriate national museums in London, Dublin, Edinburgh, Belfast or Cardiff to examine the objects and compare and contrast regional artefacts with equivalent items from other localities. The British Museum, London (founded 1753), has acquired millions of artefacts of regional significance, such as flint blades, stone axes, complete mosaic pavements from Roman villas and the regalia of a sixth-century Saxon king of East Anglia (the Sutton Hoo hoard). Definitive collections of dress pins, brooches and potsherds are a basis for dating archaeological sites and identifying cultural influences. The Royal Irish Academy, Dublin, was founded in 1785 'to safeguard and rescue ... natural curiosities relating to Ireland'. In 1890 these antiquities and archaeological finds were given to the National Museum of Ireland, which therefore became the chief repository for Ireland's national treasures and for the physical evidence of history. The gorgeous cross of Cong, the Ardagh chalice and the Tara brooch remind the historian that localities now obscure or depopulated were once powerhouses of culture. In Belfast the Ulster Museum, founded in 1928, holds archives, photographs, maps, estate plans, architectural and landscape drawings, archaeological site reports and ritual and domestic artefacts from prehistory to the present. The National Museums of Scotland, Edinburgh, combine the Royal Museum of Scotland and the Museum of Antiquities, which trace their origin to 1854. The national museums followed the lead of town museums in collecting and preserving medieval and geological artefacts. Curators capitalised on the enthusiasm and expertise of antiquaries by sponsoring investigation in the field and acquiring significant collections for preservation, study and exhibition in the capital. The National Museum of Wales, founded in Cardiff in 1907, holds artefacts and documents relating to the history of Wales. The museum is responsible for the Welsh Folk Museum, a major centre for the study of vernacular buildings; the Welsh Industrial and Maritime Museum; the Welsh Slate Museum at Llanberis; and the Museum of the Welsh Woollen Industry at Dre-Fach Felindre.

In the course of a lifetime the researcher himself accumulates a considerable personal collection of artefacts, such as buttons, buckles, coins, medals, flint implements, craftsmen's tools, pottery, items of furniture, clothing, shoes, bones, bottles and assorted bric-a-brac as well as manuscripts, photographs, rare books, pictures and prints, some perhaps rescued from skips or purchased at auctions and car-boot sales. The whole assemblage constitutes a personal museum which may well be valued as a research resource by future historians. The collection should be preserved, organised and catalogued with the place of origin and the conditions of acquisition (provenance) noted. A museum might accept the accumulation for permanent preservation, if not on loan then perhaps as an outright donation with the consequent right of selection, 'weeding', dispersal and disposal according to policies framed by the trustees or owners. On the other hand, if dignified with a suitable display case in the researcher's own home, the cabinet of curiosities may be treasured as an heirloom by grandchildren and great-grandchildren.

Libraries and archives

The researcher first calls at the public library, where the librarian is a knowledgeable and free resource. The library catalogue of books and special collections may be on card index, microform or computer database. Reference books not held can usually be borrowed through the national inter-library loan system. Library books are generally arranged and classified according to subject, so each bears a class number appropriate to a particular topic, further divided according to place and era, typically devised from the Dewey Decimal Classification system. Library catalogues facilitate a search for books according to author, title or subject. The public library usually holds the British Library *General Catalogue of Printed Books to 1955*, with supplements after that date, listing virtually every book ever published in Britain and Ireland, including obscure and out-of-print regional books. Books may also be traced by author, title or subject through the *British National Bibliography* containing British publications since 1950, now conveniently available on CD-ROM. The Historical Association and Library Association both publish general guides to sources for community history.

Writing about one's own home town has been a popular pastime since the sixteenth century. For most villages and towns at least one history has been written, perhaps still in print, but if not, then available on loan through the library or, quite probably, for purchase at second-hand bookshops and car-boot sales. John Stow's descriptions of London in his *Survey of London ... 1598,* which exists in various modern editions, are an invaluable research source. White Kennett, an antiquarian Church of England minister and expert in languages and landscape, published his *Parochial Antiquities Attempted in the History of Ambrosden, Burchester, and other Adjacent Parts* in 1695; this is now a starting point for modern investigations of this corner of Oxfordshire and Buckinghamshire. Such vintage histories contain a wealth of information derived from archives and reminiscences, perhaps now irretrievably lost, and from landscape features since destroyed. Interpretations offered in early histories may be quite far off the mark, but if transcripts and descriptions are accurate the modern historian may be able to make an educated guess about what a monument or piece of folklore reveals about life both in the author's own time and in the more distant past. The researcher may be fortunate in finding anecdotal history of the type preserved by Richard Gough in his *Antiquities*

The historian should make good use of the public library.

and Memoyres of the Parish of Myddle and *Observations concerning the Seates in Myddle and the Familyes to which they belong* of 1701-2, reprinted with an introduction by D. Hey (Penguin, 1981). Models of village history are Sir Matthew Nathan's *Annals of West Coker* (Somerset), published by Cambridge University Press (1957); W. G. Hoskins's *The Midland Peasant* (Macmillan, 1957), a study of Wigston Magna, Leicestershire; P. D. A. Harvey's *A Medieval Oxfordshire Village; Cuxham, 1240 to 1400* (Oxford University Press, 1965); and R. Parker's *The Common Stream* (Collins, 1975) about Foxton, Cambridgeshire. In *The Fields Beneath* (Maurice Temple Smith, 1977) G. Tindall shows how the medieval landscape affected the growth of London's suburban Kentish Town. In *Fire from Heaven* (Harper Collins, 1992) the Yale historian D. Underdown traces the educational and social history of Stuart Dorchester (Dorset) as a reflection of national events. Sir Francis Hill's four volumes on medieval to Victorian Lincoln (Cambridge University Press, 1948-74) and H. J. Dyos's *Victorian Suburb: A Study of the Growth of Camberwell* (Leicester University Press, 1961) are regarded as standards for urban history. V. Parker's *The Making of King's Lynn; Secular Buildings from the 11th to the 17th Century* (Phillimore, 1971) is notable for detailed structural drawings of houses, while the privately published *The Lead Smelting Mills of the Yorkshire Dales* (Keighley, 1955) by R. T. Clough is equally renowned for engineering plans of old machinery. The publication of J. S. Curl's *The Londonderry Plantations 1609-1914* (Phillimore, 1986) demonstrated that huge tomes of 526 pages and 385 illustrations, priced at £50, are not mere curiosities from the past. However in 1985 the community council of the Shetland capital, recognising that the 'sales of a book about such a narrow subject as Lerwick are inevitably limited, and there is little hope that returns will ever come near to covering the costs of publication', publicly funded J. W. Irvine's *Lerwick: the Birth and Growth of an Island Town* 'for selling ... at a price which will not be prohibitive'.

One of the earliest county surveys containing individual village histories was William Dugdale's *Antiquities of Warwickshire* (1656). Family muniments and official archives are quoted in the county histories of William Lambarde (Kent) and George Ormerod (Cheshire) of the same century. Counties in Britain and Ireland generally have at least one published history. County histories came of age during the nineteenth century in a welter of antiquarian endeavour, culminating in 1899 in 'one of the *greatest works ever attempted* ... a definite finality in English local history', the *Victoria History of the Counties of England* (VCH), comprising, county by county, introductory volumes of general discussion on education, agriculture, geology and industry, followed by studies of individual communities. By 1989 two hundred volumes had been published. Of the 43 counties, thirteen were completed, fifteen partially completed, twelve in progress, but with nothing (up to 1992) for Northumberland, Westmorland or the West Riding of Yorkshire. Northumberland, however, has its own incomplete but monumental annals, published between 1893 and 1940 under the auspices of the county history committee. The tone and content of VCH has been influenced by the changeable climate of historical method and emphasis. Earlier volumes lean heavily on genealogy, heraldry, antiquities and manorial descents, while later contributors concentrate on socio-economic conditions, vernacular architecture, archaeology and population. VCH can be supplemented with such series as the Longman *Regional History of England*.

General histories should provide the background to regional events, as well as referring to issues specific to particular localities from time to time, such as the cooperatives in Rochdale, teetotalism in Preston, Luddism in Leicestershire and boycotting in County Mayo. The classic Victorian national histories, such as *The History of England* in which Thomas Macaulay supplies useful word-pictures of Glencoe (Scotland) and Kenmare (Ireland), should not be neglected. The multi-volume standard *Oxford History of England* is now available at reduced price through book clubs. For Scottish historians the *New History of Scotland* and the

Edinburgh History of Scotland are accessible and affordable paperback series. The *New History of Ireland* is a scholarly and indispensable reference work, but expensive, and so best consulted in the library, while J. Bardon's *A History of Ulster* (Blackstaff, Belfast, 1992) is equally invaluable and in paperback. The multi-volume *Cambridge Economic History of Europe* has chapters on agriculture, settlements, transport, industry, markets, guilds and trade regulation for British and Irish localities. *The Agrarian History of England and Wales* is based on regional sources. Social movements, religious denominations, mining, industries, transport, education, poor relief, prisons, local government and the fisheries have their own national or regional histories, based on archives referring to particular communities.

Public libraries hold back numbers as well as up-to-date copies of professional and telephone directories and yearbooks, with addresses of record offices (archives), heritage centres, national libraries, national archives, specialist repositories, royal commissions, estate offices, lawyers, architects, church officials and company secretaries. The names, addresses and subjects of interest of official and private organisations concerned with archaeology, fieldwork, history, vernacular architecture and various other research areas can be found in *The Directory of British Associations & Associations in Ireland* (CBD Research Ltd, Beckenham), *Whitaker's Almanack* and M. Pinhorn, *Historical, Archaeological and Kindred Societies in the United Kingdom: a List* (Pinhorns, Hulverstone Manor, 1986). Public libraries also compile more localised address files of history and heritage groups, family history researchers, field clubs and antiquarian societies, as well as regional representatives of national organisations such as the Victorian Society (architecture), the National Trust, the Newcomen Society (engineering and technology), the Vernacular Architecture Group, the Society for Medieval Archaeology, the Society for Post-Medieval Archaeology, the Society for Landscape Studies and Medieval Settlement Research Group. The library will usually hold original, photographic or microform copies of old maps, plans, council minutes, valuation rolls, newspapers, parish registers of baptism, marriage or burial, census returns and other documents, all of which saves the researcher visits to national or county archives, where such items are normally accessible.

Pictures of people, buildings and landscapes stimulate the historian through their multi-layered depth of memory and image. Drawings and paintings from psalters, cartularies, memoranda books, church walls or tapestries may be sources of historical information on costume, customs, townscapes, famous events or even industrial developments and machinery. Every picture presents an image, confined in a frame and frozen at one instant, of the artist's own day or of his or her idea of the past. A picture is contrived according to contemporary perceptions of what is decent or required in art, so scenes and portraits conform to the requirements of posture, costume, accoutrements and context set by the person commissioning the picture. Peasant hovels, denuded woodland, roadside beggars or the hilltop gibbet with a body in chains tend to be excluded from the view. Convention may make free with reality in suggesting the perfection of an 'improved' landscape, the glory of a Gothic church, or the gentility of a landowner's face. Any such pictures of the locality are usually catalogued by the public library with references to those held privately or publicly in other repositories. National catalogues include M. W. Barley's *A Guide to British Topographical Collections* (Council for British Archaeology, 1974) and R. Russell's *Guide to British Topographical Prints* (David & Charles, 1979). Items sold in salerooms may be traced through auctioneers as well as in the published catalogues of the art dealers Christie's, Phillips and Sotheby's.

Historical novels may represent the fruits of academic research. Sir Walter Scott was steeped in medieval lore and topography, while E. Bulwer-Lytton's *Harold, the Last of the Saxon Kings* (1848) was based on the author's own fieldwork, 'the obscure MS of the Waltham Monastery', Camden's *Britannia*, and the library resources of the antiquarian Charles Tennyson D'Eyncourt:

On the height called Pen-y-Dinas (or "Head of the City") forming one of the summits of Penmaen-mawr ... reclined Gryffyth, the hunted King ... The central area ... formed an oval barrow of loose stones: whether so left from the origin, or the relics of some vanished building, was unknown to bard and diviner. Round this space were four strong circumvallations ... there, once the Celt had his home, and the gods of the Druid their worship.
Harold, the Last of the Saxon Kings (1903 edition, volume 1, pages 305-6).

The careers of notable people can be traced through the *Dictionary of National Biography (DNB)* and the *New Dictionary of National Biography*. There are also historical biographical dictionaries for specific professions, such as artists, architects, politicians, clergy, labour leaders and businessmen. Lives of past members of aristocratic families are outlined in Cokayne's *The Complete Peerage,* while the pedigrees of peers, baronets, knights and the landed gentry appear in various editions of Burke and Debrett. Family histories recorded during heraldic visitations of 1530 to 1688 have also been published as listed in *Texts and Calendars* (see below).

Surnames were adopted during the Middle Ages. The origin of regional surnames and the mobility of population are studied in the classic *The Homes of Family Names* (1890) by H. B. Guppy and in standard dictionaries such as C. W. Bardsley, *A Dictionary of English and Welsh Surnames* (1901, reprinted Genealogical Publishing Company, Baltimore, 1980); R. Bell, *The Book of Ulster Surnames* (Blackstaff Press, Belfast, 1988); G. F. Black, *The Surnames of Scotland* (New York Public Library, 1946); B. Cottle, *The Penguin Dictionary of Surnames* (second edition, 1978); P. Hanks and F. Hodges, *A Dictionary of Surnames* (Oxford University Press, 1988); E. MacLysaght, *The Surnames of Ireland* (fifth edition, Irish Academic Press, 1980); P. H. Reaney, *A Dictionary of British Surnames* (second edition, Routledge, 1976); and E. G. Withycombe, *The Oxford Dictionary of Christian Names* (third edition, 1976). Definitive collections of information on British surnames include the Erlangen (German) and Lund (Swedish) archives and the Leicester University English Surnames Series. R. McKinley's *Norfolk and Suffolk Surnames in the Middle Ages* (Phillimore, 1975) and G. Redmond's *Yorkshire, West Riding* (Phillimore, 1973) in the English Surname Series and R. McKinley's *A History of British Surnames* (Longman, 1990) provide guidelines for the ordinary researcher learning what family names can teach about community history. The researcher may join a family history society, whose address can be obtained through the Federation of Family History Societies. The Church of Jesus Christ of Latter-day Saints (the Mormons) also has family history centres with addresses in the telephone book and facilities open to all. The Cambridge Group for the History of Population and Social Structure advises historians through its various publications on the reconstitution of families and communities through in-depth study of archival and related sources. The researcher can compile a card index or computer database of the name, age, occupation, marital status and residence of each inhabitant of a town or village for the period under consideration. The index would provide a basis for estimating population or determining social and occupational structure. One project requires a list of the surnames of all inhabitants for a chosen period, with the earliest and latest date recorded. Surnames are divided by category, for instance surnames of specific origin such as Winchester, Bruce (from a place in Normandy), Fleming (from Flanders) or Wallace (from Wales), indicating immigration, and the more general Hill, Marsh or Atwood, possibly originating in the parish itself. Surnames such as Baker, Gow (smith), Steward or Cordiner (shoemaker) are occupational and can sometimes be proved to originate in the parish and perhaps with one individual, particularly when a Tanner's son has become a butcher with the surname Butcher or when estate records show the promotion to the position of butler of a man whose children are henceforth Butlers. Nicknames such as Long, Fox, Grant (grand, big) or Duff (black), diminutives such as Dickens (Little Richard) and patronymics or surnames originally derived from fathers, such as Williamson (son of William) and Bevan (ap Evan, son of John), can provide evidence of racial origins or prejudice. The depth of Norman influence can perhaps be judged from the popularity of their personal names such as Thomas, Robert and Henry, but, while Jews were important to the economy, Jewish personal names such as Isaac were also popular among Christians. Clan or wider family association may be indicated by the Irish *O* and the Scottish *Mac*. Classification is not always easy, for surnames such as Abbot may be occupational, patronymic (though abbots were supposed to be celibate) or nicknames (perhaps from hereditary involvement as abbot in a mystery play). Conclusions from surname research are likely to be variable depending on period, community and archival resources. Moreover one man could have twelve sons who themselves each had twelve, leading one surname to proliferate in a community and unbalancing any statistical survey.

Archive sources in print

Researchers are generally pleased to discover that the public library is the usual first port of call for information from archival sources, albeit in printed versions and translations, as this saves the inconvenience of hunting for dusty documents or poring over the faded ink and unfamiliar scripts of original manuscripts. This has been the work for a century and more of national and county record societies, which the historian may wish to join. Documents in accessible published form may be located through the Royal Historical Society's volume *Texts and Calendars* (1958), updated by *Texts and Calendars II* (1983), both edited by E. L. C. Mullins. *Texts and Calendars since 1982: a Survey* can be accessed electronically through the Historical Manuscripts Commission website. Scottish researchers begin with *Scottish Texts and Calendars* (1987), edited by D. and W. B. Stevenson. An early series of records in print was produced under the auspices of successive record commissions first appointed by royal warrant in 1764. Commissioners encouraged leading scholars of the day to transcribe and translate for publication the most significant archival manuscripts and record series. A special printed typeface was devised to reproduce medieval signs and symbols of abbreviation and so partly to replicate the original text, as in the edition of *Domesday Book* published by A. Farley in 1783. Record commissioners concentrated upon the public records of the nation, for example pleas of *quo warranto,* in which commissioners appointed by Edward I enquired 'by what warrant or right' landowners held their manors and privileges, and inquisitions *post mortem,* in which crown officials investigated the estates and privileges of deceased landowners. Particular places are referred to in the published version of Pope Nicholas IV's *Ecclesiastical Taxation* of England and Wales in 1291 and in records of national financial affairs in the series of *Exchequer Rolls*. Henry VIII's comprehensive survey of the wealth of the church in England was published in folio volumes under the title *Valor Ecclesiasticus* ('The wealth of the Church'). Also from the English public records comes the edition of *Rotuli Scotiae* (the 'Scotch Rolls'), relating to Anglo-Scottish affairs from 1290 to 1516 and including information on estates, castles, churches and towns. Irish record commissioners published the *Annals of Ulster* (431-1540) and transcripts of charters granting privileges to towns and churches. Many documents were subsequently destroyed in civil conflict. Researchers in Wales will not be disappointed by the wealth of evidence in the published series of national records. *The Record of Caernarvon* (1838) is a transcript of documents in the British Museum, especially Harley 696, which surveys lands in the counties of Merioneth, Anglesey and Caernarvon and the diocese of Bangor.

Indexes, transcripts and extracts of archives published by national, county and borough record societies represent the wealth of sources available for a particular history project, which can be researched comfortably and conveniently in the public

Roll of the taxation of the temporal goods, rents and revenues of the religious persons of the Archdeaconries of Oxford, Buckingham, Bedford, Huntingdon and Nottingham (except the Deanery of Rutland) made by Master John Walecote and Master William Steynton in the year 1291 under the reverend fathers the lords O[liver Sutton] by the grace of God, Bishop of Lincoln, and J[ohn of Pontoise], Bishop of Winchester, principal assessors of taxation deputed by the lord Pope Nicholas IV.

Archdeaconry of Oxford
Deanery of Aston

Prior of Wallingford in Chalcford in lands, rents, meadowlands, escheats and perquisites of court	£10	13s	9d
The same has there in bondsmen's labour		36s	9d
The same has in Chennor of rents		31s	3d
The same has in Watlington of rents		20s	
The same has in Chalgrave of rents		48s	
The same has in Cuxham of rents		10s	
Abbot of Abingdon has in Leveknor manor worth annually	£41	10s	3¹/₂d
Abbot of Reading in Adewell in rents		26s	8d

The taxation of Pope Nicholas IV, 1291 (printed by the Record Commission, 1802), concerning the deanery of Aston in the archdeaconry of Oxford, listing the properties of the prior of Wallingford and the abbots of Abingdon and Reading.

library. Also held are transcripts and translations of church records, borough archives, estate papers, charters, probate records and other archives prepared for publication by church ministers, town officials and other knowledgeable researchers in the past – ordinary men and women with a passion for history and a desire to make records more accessible. The preparation of editions of this sort is a worthwhile personal or team enterprise. The British Academy's records of the social and economic history of England and Wales include a survey of the lordship of Denbigh in 1334 and charters of the medieval priory of Bilsington in Kent. The Société Jersiaise has published extents (land surveys) of Jersey from 1274 and Jean Chevalier's important narrative of island events mainly between 1643 and 1651. The Yorkshire Archaeological Society (1885) has published indexes of wills and final concords as well as catalogues or copies of charters, cartularies, visitation returns, court rolls, lay subsidies and civic records. Special interests are served by the publications of societies such as the Canterbury and York societies (specialising in medieval episcopal archives) and the Huguenot Society.

National and regional learned societies periodically publish monographs (articles) on agriculture, town life, industry, administration, health, education, religion, architecture, natural history, landscape and other aspects of history. The articles may result from research by ordinary people in libraries and archives or by means of fieldwork, oral recording and archaeological excavation. References in published articles to archives and archaeological reports point the historian to sources useful to his or her own researches.

Periodicals whose current and back numbers have items of regional interest include *Archaeologia Aeliana* (Newcastle upon Tyne), the *Agricultural History Review, The Antiquaries' Journal, Archaeologia Cambrensis* (Wales*),* the *Archaeological Journal, Archives, Camden Society* (Lancashire and Cheshire), the *Economic History Review, History,* the *Industrial Archaeology Review, Irish Historical Studies, Landscape History, Local Population Studies, Medieval Archaeology, Midland History, Northern History, Past and Present, Post-Medieval Archaeology,* the *Proceedings of the Prehistoric Society, Southern History, Ulster Local Studies,* the *Urban History Yearbook* and *Vernacular Architecture.* There are 124 volumes (published 1851-1994) of the *Proceedings of the Society of Antiquaries of Scotland* (known as PSAS) and 132 volumes of the *Sussex Archaeological Collections* (1848-1994, known as SAC). The Council for British Archaeology publishes an annual bibliography of papers appearing in archaeological journals since 1940, while E. L. C. Mullins edited *A Guide to the Historical and Archaeological Publications of Societies in England and Wales, 1901-33* (Royal Historical Society, 1958). The historian might look forward to receiving at home a subscription copy of the *Local History Magazine,* published by the Local History Press, Nottingham, since 1985, and copies of *The Local Historian* and *Local History News* from the British Association for Local History. As well as the newsletters and occasional papers of his own society, the historian might take out subscriptions to popular magazines such as *History Today* and *Current Archaeology.* Every periodical enhances the researcher's appreciation of the wider world of historical research.

Archives

Archives, strictly, are administrative records created for official purposes but may also denote almost any old document, whether a bound volume or a single page, handwritten (manuscript), typewritten or printed, or indeed the place where old documents are stored. Archives may be the historian's most rewarding source. Even a single document can reveal to the experienced researcher a variety of information which would probably surprise the original compiler. Thousands of documents available for each town or village are the building blocks of history and have the unimpeachable authority of an eyewitness account, written by someone who lived through the period of history concerned. The historian, though, is sensitive to the possibility that writers may sometimes have been inaccurate, tendentious or downright dishonest. As a means of introducing the content and background of forty-eight important types of documents, the researcher can obtain the Historical Association's *Short Guides to Records,* edited by L. M. Munby, revised and reissued 1994-7.

The county or borough record office, archives or heritage centre holds historical documents for public use. Addresses are in the latest editions of J. Foster and J.

Sheppard's *British Archives*, the Historical Manuscripts Commission's *Record Repositories in Great Britain* and S. Helferty and R. Refaussé's *Directory of Irish Archives*. The county record office in England and Wales grew out of the archive of the court of quarter sessions, the administrative and judicial records of the justices of the peace who, from the sixteenth century to 1889, governed the shire. Records of the administration of the civil parish, town council, poor law union, highway authority, river navigation and school board were subsequently deposited along with archives of firms, law practices, architects, estates, manors, charities and families.

The public search room is open to researchers, though it may be necesssary to obtain a reader's ticket and reserve a seat in advance. A policy of closed access locks the entire documentary collection away for security and confidentiality, but researchers readily find their documents through finding aids such as the office guide to resources in summarised form. Catalogues, normally known as calendars because they are arranged in chronological order, may sufficiently describe the content of a document to save the researcher consulting the original at all. Indexes on cards or computerised refer to place-names, personal names and subjects. The researcher requisitions items of interest, ordinarily only three at a time, from the search room supervisor. Pencil, not pen, should be used when making notes, to protect uniquely valuable archives from ink smudges. Documents cannot normally be borrowed, but photocopies can be provided for home study.

Official or public records of national governments are essential sources because communities and individuals, by name or as soldiers or taxpayers, are mentioned. Even the medieval peasant had dealings with the government. Public records are held by the Public Record Office at Kew; the Scottish Record Office, Edinburgh; the Public Record Office of Northern Ireland, Belfast; the National Archives (An Chartlann Naisiunta), Dublin, incorporating the State Paper Office and the Public Record Office of Ireland; and the National Library of Wales, Aberystwyth. There are also repositories in the Channel Islands and the Isle of Man. English records from the eleventh century onwards are introduced through the *Guide to the Contents of the Public Record Office* (1963-8), P. Riden's *Record Sources for Local History* (Batsford, 1987) and the finding aids of the List and Index Society. The National Library of Wales has a *Guide to the Department of Manuscripts and Records* (1994). The Scottish Record Office has *The Guide to the National Archives of Scotland* (1996). H. Wood's *A Guide to the Records Deposited in the Public Record Office of Ireland* (1919) refers to numerous series destroyed in the disastrous fire of 1922. Public records are generally available for research after thirty years. Each office has search room facilities with reference books, indexes and catalogues (calendars). A reader's ticket gives access to the archival treasures of the state.

The Public Record Office, Kew.

Resources are rich and varied, so to ensure that the best use is made of a visit careful planning is required, including advance consultation of various guides and indexes available in the public library. The arrangement of the public records reflects the structure of the civil service at the period in question. Depending on his or her interests, the historian seeks records of the Ministry of Health, the Department of Transport, the Home Office, the War Office, the Exchequer or Chancery. Information on specific people, places and events is located by a patient trawl through general subject files, for example Home Office law and order files concerning Chartist agitation in Newport (South Wales), Birmingham, London and Manchester as well as lesser disturbances elsewhere.

The College of Arms

Armory was a means of identifying individuals in battle, a tournament or the law courts through the display of hereditary devices placed on a shield. Succession to property, marital alliances, bastardy, social status, the right to baronies and honorific titles can all be associated with the right to arms. Royal heralds even conducted visitations from the fifteenth century onwards to determine who might rightly bear coat armour. The College of Arms, incorporated in 1484, functioned as an heraldic and genealogical authority for England, Ireland and Wales. The college holds records of grants of arms and armorials, the heraldic visitations of 1530-1688 (many published by the Harleian Society), archives of the Court of Chivalry and of the Garter King of Arms, papers of individual heralds, and estate, family and antiquarian accumulations, such as the Arundel and Talbot papers. In Scotland the Court of Chivalry, presided over by the Lyon King of Arms, exercised jurisdiction under an act of 1672 over the right to arms and the succession to chiefships or other clan dignities through the registration of arms, bearings and genealogies. Irish heraldry is the function of the Chief Herald. Coats of arms were granted by the monarch as a reward for services. A heraldic achievement comprised a shield, supporters, a helmet, a crest, a lambrequin (mantling) and a motto, as described in J. W. Papworth's *An Alphabetical Dictionary of Coats of Arms* (1874) and J. Fairbairn's *Book of Crests* (1892). A coat of arms may include canting reference to surnames; allusions to the personal qualities of an individual or to the circumstances and origin of the family; and the impaling and quartering of shields, indicating marriage alliances and the descent of manors, estates and titles of gentility, as well as feudal dependences. The language of heraldry derives in part from Norman French. Coats of arms are found in stained glass and on gravestones, memorial brasses and painted armorial achievements (hatchments) in the parish church, as well as on household fixtures, furnishings, napkins, cutlery and the family coach.

National libraries

In 1753 Parliament passed

> An Act for the Purchase of the Museum, or Collection of Sir Hans Sloane, and of the Harleian Collection of Manuscripts; and for providing one General Repository for the better Reception and more convenient Use of the said collections; and of the Cottonian Library, and of the Additions thereto.

The new repository or museum, financed by £300,000 raised through a lottery, opened at Montagu House, London, in 1759. The British Library's Department of Manuscripts is open to readers undertaking research which cannot be undertaken elsewhere. Research begins with a guide by M. A. E. Nickson, *The British Library: Guide to the Catalogues and Indexes of the Department of Manuscripts*, indicating the existence of published catalogues that may be available in public libraries and unpublished catalogues held at the British Library. The index of persons and places published as the *Index of Manuscripts in the British Library* (1984) gives a hint of what may be found for British and Irish communities in this, one of the world's leading archive institutions, and was compiled from indexes to catalogues of the

Additional and Egerton manuscripts (those acquired 1783-1945), the 'special collections' (except Ashley and Yates Thompson), charters and rolls, and the 'foundation collections' of Cotton, Harley and Sloane. The Cottonian collection was accumulated by the historian and antiquary Sir Robert Cotton (1570-1631), whose private library was shelved in fourteen cupboards surmounted by busts of classical figures, whose names later provided the classification system by which Cotton is still arranged. In 1700 an Act of Parliament had confirmed the Cotton family's wish that the library be 'kept in the house at Westminster called Cotton House ... for public use and advantage'. Transferred to Ashburnham House, Westminster, in spite of the family's wishes, the library was damaged by fire in 1731, and the remaining contents were later removed to the new British Museum. There the keeper of manuscripts, J. Planta, commenced a catalogue in 1793, which was published in 1802 by the Record Commissioners. The following are examples of catalogue entries:

Titus, B. X.
[item] 2. An inquisition taken before Arthur Chichester, Esq; and others, at Carrickfergus; concerning some royal domain in the isle of Raghlins. (Lat.) Jan. 3, 1604. [folio] 171.
Cleopatra, E.IV.
item] 75. Wm. Barlow Bp. of St. David's to ... telling of the resort to tapers of "Haverfordwest and Cardigan" and other relicks, and desiring to have the see translated to Kermerddyn. (Orig.) Kermerddyn, March 31. [folio] 117
Augustus I. VOL. II
A large port-folio
1. A plan of Scarborough town and castle. 2. A plan of Bamborough.
9. and 10. Two plans of Dover town, harbour, and castle
20. A plan of Milford Haven. 22. A plan of some lands near Weymouth.

A Record Commission catalogue of the manuscripts of Robert Harley (1661-1724) followed in 1808-12:

Num. 286.
02. Original Letter or Memorial of John Gould Fitz-Stephen ... discovers ... two Mines in

The siege of Enniskillen Castle, 1592. British Library, Cottonian manuscripts, Augustus I, volume II.39.

Ireland; the one of Silver, at Belameir in Carburye; the other of Copper at a Cliffe called Gahynyh-boig in Bantry; both within 36 miles of Corke.
Num. 292
46. A Vewe of the Survey as well of all the Waste Growndes, end longe the Borders or Frontier of the Easte & Middell Marches of England over-againste Scottlande; and a Discripcion of the present state of all Castells, Towers, Barmekins & Fortresses
Num. 4318.
"An account of his Majesties new Docks at Portsmouth...
Setting forth the uncommon properties of the Dry Dock ... Subjoined, are four very accurately drawn draughts ... 1698".

In 1757 George II donated the royal library, including spoils from monastic libraries, accumulated by English sovereigns since Edward IV. The royal library brought the privilege of compulsory copyright deposit of all books published in Britain and Ireland. The royal library was the first of the 'special collections', followed by Lansdowne (1807), Hargrave (1813), Burney (1815), King's (1823), Arundel (1831), Stowe (1883), Ashley (1937) and Yates Thompson (1941). A *Catalogue of the Lansdowne Manuscripts in the British Museum* appeared in 1819:

Num. 110.
1. The inhabitants of Eaton Soken, Bedfordshire, to the Justices; concerning their rights in four mills erected by Mr. John Webster.
10. The irreverend and profane speeches of one Cliberye, Vicar of Halstede in Essex.
11. The inhabitants of Wittresham in the isle of Oxney, in Kent, to the Lord Treasurer; to enable Mr. Genebelli to finish draining the fens.

The two series known as Additional and Egerton manuscripts comprise miscellaneous gifts, purchases and bequests from 1756 onwards. Saxon, Norman and later charters and rolls form a separate series with appropriate catalogues and indexes. Many are printed in facsimile, edited, translated and described at length. There are also estate muniments, plans, surveys, administrative records, drawings, paintings and other pictorial documents.

The National Library of Scotland originated in the collections of the Faculty of Advocates founded in 1682 and was established in Edinburgh under an act of Parliament of 1925 with money from Sir Alexander Grant of McVitie & Price, the biscuit makers. The library is now a principal research centre with family and estate papers, including those of famous Scottish people, political records, newspapers, business records, charters, rentals, correspondence, plans including old and current Ordnance Surveys, photographs, antiquarian papers and archaeological reports.

The National Library of Wales in Aberystwyth was founded in 1907 and serves as a public record office for the principality, holding such records as may be separated from the main English series. The library has diocesan, capitular, parish and nonconformist church records. Estate, family, business and institutional records are extensive, complementing those preserved in county record offices.

The National Library of Ireland originated in the book and manuscript collections of the Royal Dublin Society, which during the eighteenth century became a national centre for the study of Irish civilisation and history. The library expanded its own archives under a policy of acquiring 'everything relating to Ireland or to Irishmen that comes on the market' and is now a major research centre for estate or family muniments, maps, drawings, photographs, ecclesiastical records, archaeological reports and architectural plans.

The Royal Irish Academy (RIA), Dublin, was founded in 1785 for promoting the study of science, polite literature and antiquities by collecting manuscript and other historical sources. The RIA's published *Proceedings* (1836 onwards) are required reading for historians of the Irish sphere of influence that embraced the Celtic lands of mainland Britain. The RIA's medieval manuscripts were the basis of the published *Dictionary of the Irish Language* (1913-75). The library holds the collections of Sir William Betham, herald and Celtic scholar; Edward O'Reilly of Cavan, lexicographer and jurist; John O'Daly and Hodges & Smith, two Dublin book dealers; and the Ashburnham muniments from Stowe, Buckinghamshire, including a ninth-century missal probably copied at St Ruadhán's monastery, Lorrha, County Tipperary. Chronicles, genealogies, surveys, cartularies and other medieval texts have generally been published, usually with an English introduction and translation.

The historian's nearest university will rescue estate, business and official archives relating to a broad hinterland, perhaps in response to the specialised research interests of academic staff. Warwick is a recognised centre for trade union archives, Manchester (John Rylands) for church and estate muniments, Durham for its capitular records, Glasgow for Scottish business records. Trinity College, Dublin, has unrivalled sources for the history of Ireland and Scotland including the historical confection of the *Yellow Book of Lecan* and manuscripts collected by the Celtic scholar Edward Lhwyd (1660-1709), including the twelfth-century *Book of Leinster* from Terryglass, County Tipperary, which mingles saga, genealogy, legendary invasions and lists of provincial chieftains. Trinity also preserves Archbishop Ussher's manuscripts, secured for Ireland by Cromwell, with English saints' lives, documents from the Cottonian collection, the St Albans hagiography of Matthew Paris and annals from Margam Abbey, Glamorgan, for the period 1066-1232.

Leicester is justifiably proud of its department of English local history, whose library is supplemented with manuscripts and correspondence files produced by researchers up and down the country as well as documentary material by such famous teachers as W. G. Hoskins and H. P. R. Finberg. The department of Irish folklore at University College, Dublin, inherited the mantle of the Irish Folklore Commission of 1935, collecting song, music, manuscript and oral sources. The archives are particularly useful for the study of linguistics, onomastics (names), regional buildings, religion, agriculture and domestic economy. The School of Scottish Studies at Edinburgh University is a national centre for the study of oral history and rural life, with photographic and film collections, including that of the anthropologist Werner Kissling (1896-1988), illustrating pastoral, arable and fishing practices, vernacular building, folk customs and traditional occupations. There is a tale archive (traditional narratives), a linguistic survey (dialects) and a place-name survey. Here community history is turned into academic theses. Also at Edinburgh, the Scottish Ethnographic Archive accumulates photographs, drawings, sound recordings and other materials relevant to social history. As wealthy land-owners, the Oxford and Cambridge colleges possess manorial and estate records from many counties. The Bodleian (university library) at Oxford holds collections of deeds, manorial records and papers by local historians, topographers and antiquaries relevant to most parts of Britain. These last include a major portion of the Irish historical collections of the seventeenth-century hereditary *sennachie* (wise man) An Dubhaltach MacFirbhisigh and the collections of the Anglo-Irish scholar Sir James Ware and the 'father of landscape studies', William Stukeley (1687-1765). Cambridge University Library holds church records of Ely, drawings of Suffolk churches, estate muniments from East Anglia, enclosure documents for Cambridgeshire parishes, fen drainage records, topography, art, natural history, journals of travel, title deeds, manorial records, household accounts and terriers from as far afield as Newtown, County Down. Charles Darwin's papers contain reports on the flora, fauna and geology of various British localities.

Location of archives

Documents are usually discovered where good archives should be, in their proper place at home: family papers somewhere in the house, estate muniments in the agent's office, official archives with an official. It can be a lifetime's work to locate the archives for a particular parish, by contacting peers of the realm, company secretaries, famous authors and other owners of documents, though it may involve grimy hours clambering among the rafters of an architectural firm's attics or delving into the damp cellars of the diocesan registrar's office. Such are the usual resting places of archives!

Researchers do not enjoy automatic right of access to historical documents in private hands. A blend of tact and enthusiasm is required when contacting owners and custodians: patience, reassurance, persistence, even flattery and perhaps a little gentle bribery may all be necessary before custodians are infected with the historian's historic passion and the muniments are opened for examination. The search for documents opens up exciting possibilities for travel. The manuscript field notes of Jens Jacob Worsaae describing expeditions of 1842-54, including archaeological sites such as Callanish on the island of Lewis, are available for study at the Nationalmuseet, Copenhagen. The earliest manuscript (1474) of the twelfth-century Latin verse known as the *Prophecy of Merlin* by John of Cornwall, claimed as a translation of an old Cornish original document and a seminal source for the history of south-west Britain, is in the care of the Vatican archives in Rome.

Documentary collections may be located through the London office of the Historical Manuscripts Commission (HMC), appointed in 1869 to inspect and list archival collections. Calendars, lists and edited texts compiled by itinerant inspectors appeared as appendices to the various published reports. The HMC series *Guides to Sources for British History* includes *Records of British Business and Industry 1760-1914* (textiles, leather, metals, engineering; others in preparation) and *Principal Family and Estate Collections.* Important archives have been lost since their original cataloguing, including one of southern Lancashire's most comprehensive collections, belonging to the Bootle-Wilbrahams of Lathom, which was burnt at Blaguegate colliery following the demolition of the family mansion in 1929. Others have been sold to wealthy collectors or to institutions with British research interests, such as the Huntington Library in San Marino, California. Additionally, the HMC maintains a register of manorial documents (MDR) established under the Law of Property Amendment Act of 1924. Also available at the HMC office in London is the National Register of Archives (NRA), which was begun in 1945 'to record the location, content and availability of all archives and collections of historical manuscripts in England and Wales, other than records of the central government, without limit of date'. Scotland and Northern Ireland operate registers on similar lines, held at the relevant public record office. Since 1995 the HMC has made its Internet website *http://www.hmc.gov.uk* the main source of information about its own activities as well as archives in Britain generally, searchable by key words. From the home page the reader can move on to computerised databases of the MDR and NRA and use the ARCHON (Archives On-line) gateway to the websites of British and some overseas archive offices.

The British Records Association (BRA), an organisation unconnected with the government, was founded in 1932 'to develop informed opinion on the necessity for preserving records of historical importance and ... advise on the disposal of papers, deeds and documents of all kinds through its Records Preservation Section'. The BRA publishes the journal *Archives* and the series of pamphlets known as *Archives and the User*.

The researcher should assist whenever possible in the preservation of the archival heritage, beginning with personal and family papers and moving on to business and official archives. This worthy end may be pursued through participation in a group of 'friends of the record office' and by active intervention – scavenging skips for discarded records, soliciting unwanted files from businesses, collecting photographic albums from neighbours, hunting the salerooms for manuscripts. If no suitable public place of safety can be found in the county library or record office then the historian will probably make use of dry storage in a loft or garage, where the documents will at least not be destroyed and may indeed become available for research in the future when circumstances change. The Keeper of the Records of Scotland warns against the desire to preserve everything of an archival nature:

Such a policy is wholly impracticable: archival resources cannot possibly cope with the overwhelming bulk of paper ... produced by the Government, local authorities, institutions, legal and commercial firms and other bodies ... The principle of selection is therefore firmly acknowledged by the majority of the archival profession ... in the long term interests both of historical research and of cost efficiency, an honest selection based on well-judged criteria must be attempted.
A. L. Murray, *Journal of the Society of Archivists*, volume 10, number 4 (1989), page 151.

County archivists may therefore concentrate efforts and resources upon official archives of their authorities. They are understandably cautious about soliciting or rescuing estate, business or family records, which occupy valuable storage space, require conservation, sorting and cataloguing and are likely to be requisitioned only rarely by researchers. Archivists usually select just a manageable 5 per cent sample of a lawyer's or estate agent's ledgers and letter books. There are instances of reduced budgets and staffing where even this sample has been reappraised and whole collections have been disposed of.

In the end the community gets the archives it deserves. Preservation of the documentary heritage cannot be deferred and must not be devolved. Destruction is for ever. Weeded files cannot be recreated. Pulped papers cannot be reconstituted. Dispersed collections are gone for good. As chief user and beneficiary of archives the historian should expect to assume the role of chief guardian ready to campaign, willing to organise archival rescue, conservation and storage, and ultimately even prepared to underwrite the cost personally.

Reading the writing

Palaeography is the study of old handwriting. The historian necessarily becomes familiar with a range of styles in the course of reading archival documents and monumental inscriptions. Palaeographical skill comes through practice with help from primers and also through seminars or more formal teaching, as provided, for instance, under the Cambridge University continuing education series. Palaeography is crucial in dating and authenticating documents and in revealing, through affectations and eccentricities of hand, the authorship of anonymous or imputed manuscripts or, if not the writer's name, at least his official capacity, educational background, regional origin and attitude to work and life.

Writing was introduced to Britain by the Romans in the form of *capitalis monumentalis,* essentially our modern capital-letter alphabet. A freer script, *capitalis rustica,* was developed for formal writings on parchment. The rustic relaxed into a cursive, rapidly written business hand for everyday use. Roman writing may have influenced two other early alphabets used in the British Isles. In Ireland, until the ninth century, a series of straight strokes known as *ogham,* named from the native god of eloquence, was used for memorial inscriptions. In the Anglo-Saxon world some thirty stick-like *runes* were in use and affected English writing in the Roman alphabet, particularly in the use of the runic letter *thorn* (resembling 'y') for 'th', hence the use of 'ye' for 'the' even today, though 'ye' properly means 'you'. Roman letters evolved into a rounded script known as *uncial,* meaning 'inch-high' lettering. Christian Irish monks developed a half-uncial script from the sixth century onwards, for such texts as the *Book of Kells* and the *Lindisfarne Gospels.* Anglo-Saxon writers preferred a spiky minuscule script with letters ascending above or descending below the line.

A neat reformed script, whose letter forms were the ancestors of those in modern print or typescript, was developed by scribes at the court of the emperor Charlemagne and adopted in England from around 960 onwards. Carolingian minuscule script, best known from Domesday Book, was employed for legal and religious writings. Formal inscriptions on memorial stones and literary works were executed in an upright Gothic book or text hand sometimes known as black-letter. Scribes added various flourishes and linking strokes (ligatures) to permit 'joined-up' writing for the requirements of administration and business. From around 1370 business and text hands developed into a current (joined-up) mongrel script usually known as 'bastard', developing into the stylish hands of government courts (departments), which became set in their ways until abolished by act of Parliament in 1731. In practice, though, varieties of court hand continued in use among lawyers for wills, deeds and legal papers into the nineteenth century. The most detailed guide to medieval hands is C. Johnson and H. Jenkinson's *English Court Hand A.D. 1066 to 1500* (Clarendon Press, 1915), which contains tables of individual letters of the alphabet, showing changes over the centuries. The story is continued in H. Jenkinson's *The Later Court Hands in England from the Fifteenth to the Seventeenth Century* (Cambridge University Press, 1927). These two books are now rare, though copies may appear in second-hand bookshops and auctions. Record offices will hold copies in their reference sections; otherwise it should be possible to order through the inter-library loans scheme at a public library.

'Secretary' hand emerged during the sixteenth century as the joined-up business-like, sometimes slovenly handwriting frequently encountered by researchers in parish, court and estate papers. At this period too the humanistic or reformed Carolingian script from Italy became popular. This italic, when mixed with secretary, produced a looped joined-up round hand which remains in use today.

Systems of abbreviation have assisted readers and writers from Roman times to the present day. Abbreviations are used, almost without a second thought, in speech and writing, for example 'i.e.' for Latin *id est* meaning, 'that is [to say]'; 'p' for 'new pence'; 'BC' for 'Before Christ'. Legal writers of Latin within the Roman Empire devised abbreviations known as *notae juris,* 'legal marks', while secretaries used a shorthand named after Tiro, freedman of the orator Cicero. Tironian notes influenced medieval Latin styles of abbreviation as conventional symbols were developed to replace certain groups of letters within a longer word according to definite rules. A common method of abbreviation in old documents is a simple contraction, that is writing just a few key letters of a long word. Medieval clerks might contract *ecclesia,* 'church', to 'ecla'. Another common method was suspension, where the clerk just wrote the first letter or the first few letters of a word, for example 'T' stood for the Latin word *teste* 'with this witness'. The symbol '&' derives from a ligature, or linked form, of the letters *e* and *t* in Latin *et* (English 'and'). Signs might be used in combination with letters: crossed 'l' represented Latin *vel,* 'or'; crossed 'p' stood for *per,* 'through'.

Superscripts were small letters written above a contracted or suspended word to provide the reader with a clue as to what the writer had omitted. Thus J^n indicated the name John. Two guides to abbreviations are: A. Cappelli's *Dizionario di Abbreviature Latine ed Italiane* (Ulrico Hoepli, Milan, 1899) and C. T. Martin's *The Record Interpreter* (1892; third edition, Phillimore, 1982).

Patience is the key to reading documents. Each word is comprehensible if carefully considered letter by letter. Each letter recognised makes the task easier. Each word transcribed increases confidence. Letter forms vary from century to century so consulting examples of letter forms and complete texts illustrated in palaeography textbooks is instructive. From these, and with practical experience of documents, the reader builds up a series of model alphabets. Writing the various letters using a traditional nib or quill (not ball-point) will fix the form of each letter and how it developed over time firmly in the mind. *Examples of English Handwriting 1150-1750* (Essex Education Committee, 1954) by H .E. P. Grieve is a particularly useful short guide, illustrated with photographs of documents from Essex archives and providing parallel transcriptions and translations with helpful footnotes and alphabets. With the assistance of a hand lens, the beginner observes from model alphabets the structure of each letter, whether formed by a series of strokes with a lift of the pen between each, by a single fluid movement, or by involved retracings, crossings, loops and recrossings. Once the particular forms of letters are fixed in the mind, the palaeographer is ready to read a document, preferably a clear photocopy. A knowledge of Latin is a great asset, as it is the language used for many medieval documents. To begin with, it may be wise to choose an example written in English. The beginner should select a manuscript written in the pedantic hand of a careful clerk, rather than a slovenly cursive specimen of a busy merchant's style, and read each word letter by letter, laboriously transliterating each character and then surveying the result to consider whether the word transcribed makes sense. If not immediately and evidently understandable, the word (though ordinary) may be spelled in an unfamiliar manner, represent an abbreviated form of a longer word, or be a legal, technical or obsolete word not in the reader's usual vocabulary. Perhaps there is an error in the transcription: confusion of 'f' and long 's'; miscounting or misinterpretation of the minims of 'i', 'm', 'n', or 'u', which are scarcely distinguished in some scripts. With such points in mind, the palaeographer retransliterates making no assumptions, except perhaps that the expert medieval scribe was less liable to error than the novice palaeographer. Transcriptions published in academic texts, record commission facsimiles and county record office handbooks support the student's practical exercises. Palaeographic practice pieces may be checked against the interpretations of experts, who are themselves not necessarily correct.

Languages of history

The sources of history appear in a variety of languages whose older forms present unfamiliar vocabulary and grammatical rules. The historian can gain a working knowledge of documentary languages with the assistance of a dictionary, primer and literary editions. Professional instruction may also be available. The occasional unfamiliar word may be explained by a friendly expert, librarian, teacher, lecturer, archivist or priest, who may indeed be willing to translate at some length. Courses in relevant languages are offered by some education authorities or university extramural departments. For the true historian there is no more piquant delight than receiving the messages of the past at first hand in their proper voices – Welsh, Irish, Old English or Latin, in all their grammatical subtlety and musical phraseology, undistorted by the garblings of translation, however academic, literal or creative.

English originated among the Angles, Saxons, Jutes and Frisians of the European coasts. Four dialects of Old English emerged as settlers spread across post-Roman England: Northumbrian (Anglian), Mercian, Kentish and West Saxon. Old English was employed in charters, correspondence, chronicles, histories, scripture and literature (poetry, prose, riddles, epics, translations), examples being published by the Early English Text Society. *The Student's Dictionary of Anglo-Saxon* (Clarendon Press, 1896, reprinted numerous times) by H. Sweet is the historian's chief reference.

Middle English emerged during the twelfth century as the spoken and written language of England, continuing to be dominant down to about 1500 and in Scotland to 1700. The vocabulary displays a richness of technical jargon and everyday nouns, verbs and constructions, some of which still survive in dialects, though they have passed out of use in mainstream English. Three chief dialects (northern, midland and southern) are recognised by linguists. Middle English was employed for poetry, romantic epics, hagiography, homilies, chronicles, biblical translation and exposition, charters, correspondence, wills, business accounts, and monumental and other inscriptions. The historian's companion is *A Middle-English Dictionary* by F. H. Stratmann, revised by H. Bradley (Oxford University Press, 1891), with the academic buttress of the *Middle English Dictionary* (University of Michigan,1952, in progress).

Scottish dialect derives its distinctive vocabulary and pronunciation largely from Middle English. Preserved to some extent by rural conservatism, it was also revived by the Romantic writers Burns and Scott and has been nurtured nationalistically by modern nostalgics, notably Hugh MacDiarmid and the Corries. Difficult words are explained in the *Scottish National Dictionary,* based largely on literary and published sources, and W. A. Craigie's *A Dictionary of the Older Scottish Tongue from the Twelfth Century to the End of the Seventeenth* (University of Chicago Press, later Manchester University Press, 1974, in progress).

The most comprehensive collection of English usage and vocabulary is the multi-volume *New English Dictionary on Historical Principles*, known as the *Oxford English Dictionary* (*OED*), which originated in 1857 when the Philological Society was exhorted to search English literature and published records for the form, sense, history, pronunciation and etymology of words. The *OED* was published in fascicles from 1884, with a supplement in 1933 and then a second supplement containing new words and words omitted, including words denied a place in the main *OED* on grounds of decency. A second edition of the *Oxford English Dictionary* was published in 1980, in conventional codex form, followed up by a CD-ROM version. The *OED* is also available and affordable in a microprint version, as well as in an abbreviated form, the *Shorter Oxford English Dictionary*. The complete dictionary may indeed be consulted as an encyclopaedia, explaining each meaning and shift of usage of every English word likely to confront the historian, including archaic, slang, cant, technical, rare, indecent, vulgar, colloquial or otherwise obscure words. All are defined at length, offered in variant spellings and traced, change by change, century by century, through relevant examples selected from a bibliography that reads as a compendium of English culture and historical sources. Peculiarities and unfamiliar usages found in regional documents are usually explained in J. Wright's two volumes *The English Dialect Dictionary* (1896-1905) and *The English Dialect Grammar* (1905). E. Partridge's *A Dictionary of Slang and Unconventional English* (1937) and the abridgement by J. Simpson, *The Penguin Dictionary of Historical Slang* (1972), discuss specially coined words and special senses for ordinary words not found even in the *OED*. The words may be obscene, criminal, fugitive or never before seen in print, though possibly not unknown in unpublished documents and oral history tapes. English continually charms the reader with nice old words such as *fond, sad, still, silly* and *quick* which in their older senses respectively mean 'insipid', 'dignified', 'always', 'defenceless' and 'alive'. The word *fowl* originally meant simply 'bird' and, by extension, any winged creature, including butterflies and bats. Only from the sixteenth century onwards was the word applied specifically to domesticated chickens, ducks and (later still) turkeys.

Old documents also contain words that have entirely fallen from speech, including defunct technicalities such as *infangthief*, an Anglo-Saxon legal term concerned with the right of a lord to try a thief caught within the limits of his manor, and *inexpressibles*, a nineteenth-century euphemism for gentlemen's trousers. When writing history the historian should resist the linguistic inveiglements of jargon and obfuscation when there are plain English alternatives to such phrases as *multisource nominal record linkage, labour force participation rates* or *socio-economic data anomaly.* Jargon is the harlot of history, proffering much, offering nothing. Technical terms should also be employed correctly and explained in the text by context or in a glossary. These include ordinary English words which have both popular and particular meanings, for example *stew* – boiled meat and vegetables, also a brothel; *lavatory* – now generally a water closet, historically a washing facility; *execution* – now popularly capital punishment, technically a legal document narrating the carrying out by an officer of a citation.

Latin, the language of the Roman administration of southern Britain from the first century AD, was adopted by the medieval church, the law, the civil service, the universities, science, manors and business throughout Britain and Ireland. Latin was officially abandoned only in 1733. The most useful dictionary is R. E. Latham's *Revised Medieval Latin Word-list* (British Academy/Oxford University Press, 1965). E. A. Gooder's *Latin for Local History* (second edition, Longman, 1978) is 'a self-teaching manual and guide to the kind of Latin met with in historical records. It had its origin in a course for extramural students of local history who had no Latin

Dreng (dreŋ). *Eng. Hist.*
drengh, 3 drenohe, dringche, 3-4 dring(e, *Sc.*
6-8 dring. [OE. *dreng,* ON. *drengr* young man,
lad, fellow, (Sw. *dräng* man, servant, some one's
' man ', Da. *dreng* boy, lad, apprentice). The
modern word, had it survived in living use, would
have been *dring*; but the OE. and Norse form
dreng is retained by historical writers.] A free
tenant (specially) in ancient Northumbria, holding
by a tenure older than the Norman Conquest, the
nature of which was partly military, partly servile.
See Maitland, ' Northumbrian Tenures ' in *Eng.
Hist. Rev.* V. 632.

a 1000 *Battle of Maldon* 149 Forlet ða drenga sum daroð
of handa, fleoȝan of folmum. 1086 *Domesday Bk.* 269 b,
Hujus manerii [Neweton, Lanc.] aliam terram xv. homines
quos drenchs vocabant pro xv. oris tenebant .. Modo sunt
ibi vi. drenghs. *c* 1100 *Charter of Ranulph* in Murray
Dial. S. C. Scot. 22 *note,* R[anulf] bisceop greteð wel alle
his þeines & drenges of Ealondscire & of Norhamscire.
c 1205 LAY. 12713 Androgien wes þer king ; vnder him wes
moni hæh dring. *Ibid.* 14700 Drenches. *a* 1300 *Cursor M.*
16022 (Cott.) All þai gadird o þe tun, bath freman and dring.
c 1300 *Havelok* 2258 And siþen drenges, and siþen thaynes,
And siþen knithes, and siþen sweynes. 1874 STUBBS *Const.
Hist.* § 96 (ed. 3) I. 262 Lanfranc..turned the drengs, the
rent-paying tenants of his archiepiscopal estates, into knights
for the defence of the country. 1890 F. W. MAITLAND in
Eng. Hist. Rev. V. 628 Under Richard I the thegns and
drengs of Northumberland paid tallage.

b. Contemptuously : A low or base fellow. *Sc.*
1535 STEWART *Cron. Scot.* III. 278 Quhilk is knawin for
ane wrache or dring. *a* 1605 POLWART *Flyting w. Mont-
gomerie* 796 Deid dring, dryd sting ! thou will hing but a
sunȝie. 1799 STRUTHERS *To the Blackbird* ix, The Captive
o' some dudron dring, Dull, fat an' frowsy.

An excerpt from the Oxford English Dictionary, 1933 (volume III, D-E, page 660).

themselves, and it is unique in dealing *only* with the Latin encountered in historical
documents.'

Norman French originated among the Norse settlers in France who learned their
French under the influence of Scandinavian grammar and pronunciation. Norman
French was introduced to England during the eleventh century and to Scotland and
Ireland in the twelfth. The language was spoken in court, castle and church by the
Anglo-Norman aristocracy and ruling class and by their hirelings. It was used in
administrative documents such as charters until the fourteenth century, in acts of
Parliament until the fifteenth century and also for the year books (fourteenth-
century reports of cases, taken most commonly from the *Coram Rege* and *De Banco*
rolls). French was the language of romance, minstrelsy and chivalry and is still used
today in the jargon of heraldry. It contributed greatly to the vocabulary of English
and affected English spelling, for instance Old English *cwen* became 'queen' and
cwic 'quick'. The standard dictionary is R. Kelham's *A Dictionary of the Norman or
Old French Language* (1779, reprinted Tabard Press, East Ardsley, 1978).

Welsh was, and is, used in literary, historical, legal and administrative documents. The researcher in Wales needs, ideally, to understand Welsh and to have
friends to assist with particular linguistic difficulties. The standard dictionary,

Geiriadur Prifysgol Cymru (University of Wales, 1950, in progress), assists with both the medieval and the modern form of Welsh.

Gaelic was, and is, spoken in Ireland and Scotland. Irish is included in the school curriculum in the Republic, so the researcher should have no difficulty in finding bilingual friends to assist with the translation of documents and oral history tapes or the interpretation of place-names. The seminal Gaelic texts are available in translation. In Scotland the researcher will usually find a Gaelic speaker to assist with language problems. The principal dictionaries are N. Ó Dónaill's *Fóclóir Gaeilge-Béarla* (Oifig an tSoláthair, Dublin, 1977), available also in a shorter edition (1981), and E. Dwelly's *The Illustrated Gaelic-English Dictionary* (eighth edition, Gairm Publications, Glasgow, 1973).

Interpreting archival sources

The authenticity and forms of archival documents are the subjects of 'diplomatic' study. Generations of diplomatic scholars have discovered that documents can be dated and analysed according to their content: vocabulary, spelling, legal forms followed in key clauses, handwriting, design and use of seals, styles adopted by witnesses and donors. Standard forms of documents are set out in Thomas Madox's *Formulare Anglicanum* (1702) and E. A. Gooder's *Latin for Local History* (second edition, Longman, 1978). Diplomatic study is relevant because a significant number of sources are forgeries or questionable later copies, as is set out in *Anglo-Saxon Charters* (Royal Historical Society, 1968) by P. H. Sawyer, discussing grants of land to nobles, churchmen and military retainers. Charters can sometimes be proved by diplomatic analysis to be later recopyings of lost originals, writings down of agreements originally made by word of mouth. Certain charters were completely fabricated to set the final seal of approval on the possession of property seized by might rather than acquired through ancient right and legal writ! The priory of St Botolph, Colchester, was the earliest Augustinian community in England, founded about 1095, with primacy over other houses, exempt from the jurisdiction of the bishop and directly responsible to the Pope. However, it lacked written evidence of these claims until in the sixteenth century the house archivist produced a papal bull supposedly written in 1116 but actually composed, diplomatists argue, at some date between 1391 and 1527. Any statement, however false or foolish, acquires an air of truth when written down, and even more so if in print in an official archive or with the authority of antiquity. Following the troubles of 1644-6 the burgesses of Elgin in Moray claimed for goods taken away by the 'common enemy'. Some 220 particular claims were filed, worth tens of millions of pounds in modern value and including much gold and silver. This may be accepted as a comprehensive survey of the possessions of the ordinary citizen and an indictment of the outrages perpetrated by the military forces. At this point the researcher should bear in mind that official documents need not be taken at face value. Elgin burgesses are not evidently wealthy in their tax assessments and probate records. The 'gold and silver' document doubtless describes the style to which the citizens aspired, rendered with all the careful attention to truth and detail normal in an insurance claim.

Downright forgeries are rare and certainly enliven the pages of a history. Few documents, if any, tell the truth, the whole truth and nothing but the truth, despite being old, written on ancient paper or parchment and authenticated with a seal or signature. Just as we ought to take the words of today's newspaper with a pinch of salt, so too should caution be exercised when reading records. A document may omit information not considered relevant to the writer or recipient. *Domesday Book*, although a very significant record of English communities in the eleventh century, ignores many churches that are known from their surviving stonework to have existed in 1086, possibly because they were not taxable property.

A document may add or embellish information, perhaps to help the writer's or recipient's case. Legal papers and particulars of property sales are notoriously

A claim on the government for losses in Elgin during the Civil War, 1644-6.

unreliable. A document may blatantly lie or, more commonly, set out the facts wrongly, perhaps for no more sinister reason than a copyist's error.

A document may be the sole survivor from a larger collection now lost by chance or by deliberate destruction. Owners, custodians, recipients or even archivists may have appraised the collection and disposed of what were considered useless items. One document alone may have been preserved as typical. The character and content of a document may be altered by deliberate removal of a leaf from a codex or of incriminating items from a file. Alternatively the removal may have been effected by natural agencies, such as mouse gnawings, or through administrative misplacings, weedings and clear-outs. A usual archival practice is to keep only a 5 per cent sample of an extensive archive, so altering posterity's image of the locality's history

51

by weighting the evidence. Destruction usually proceeds without record. The historian therefore cannot be sure what documents once existed or what information they might have contained. In these circumstances, what remains is often just a fraction of what once existed. A footnote is called for, recognising that the research has been based unavoidably upon imperfect data or weeded sources.

Restrictions on access for terms of years conceal the content, even the very existence, of documents deemed sensitive. The personal muniments and published works of Peter Anson (1889-1975), artist and historian of the fisher communities of eastern Scotland, are subject to such restrictions. Anson was a founder of the Society of Marine Artists, of the Apostleship of the Sea and of the Scottish Fisheries Museum in Anstruther, and his writings influence the work of subsequent scholars. The folksy portrait of fisher life painted by Anson's published papers will be significantly recoloured by the release of matter contained in the restricted files, illuminative of power struggles among the clergy within the Roman Catholic diocese of Aberdeen and of the homosexual subculture of coastal Banffshire.

The historian soon learns that a document written in the past for one specific purpose may be put to work as a source for a variety of unrelated topics. All kinds of documents contain information on the community, showing significant place-names and the names of people, their marital status, place of abode, age, occupation, literacy level, relationships and status. Documents concerned originally with property may tell something about the way people lived. Documents describing people may shed light upon property and settlement patterns. A document concerned with a man may help us to understand the lives of women. A description of an individual may serve as evidence for the history of a significant social group. Archives of medieval date have been used in prehistoric studies. The *Calendar of Original Rolls in the Court of Exchequer* (1810) refers to buried treasure discovered during the reign of Edward III in the township of Orcheston St George, Wiltshire. The king was interested in the find because he had treasure trove rights over 'gold beneath the earth' (*auro subtus terram*). The historian's interest may be sparked by the reference to gold, perhaps the regalia of a Bronze Age chief. Certainly Wiltshire is a county noted for rich prehistoric graves. The historian in Orcheston St George may be sure that somewhere in the parish is a site worth investigating.

Chronology

Methods of counting years and arranging calendars employed since Roman times are described for historians in C. R. Cheney's *Handbook of Dates* (Royal Historical Society, 1945); the *Handbook of British Chronology* (third edition, Royal Historical Society, 1986) by E. B. Fryde and others (editors); H. Nicolas's *The Chronology of History* (Longman, 1833); and A. Dunbar's *Scottish Kings* (David Douglas, Edinburgh, 1899). National standards were rare. Communities even set their sundials or clocks to indicate noon when the sun was highest in the local sky. This approach persisted until the general adoption of railway or Greenwich time in the nineteenth century. The most familiar chronology is based on the year of grace, the birth of Christ counted as year 1. Years are numbered Before Christ (BC) or after Christ (AD, from *Anno Domini*, 'in the year of the Lord'). The Venerable Bede (around AD 700) is usually reckoned to have been the first British historian counting in this way. Regnal years of popes and monarchs were also used, dating from the accession or coronation. An English source might refer to an event during 'the tenth year of Henry III', which ran from 28th October 1225 until 27th October 1226. A Scottish writer would refer to the first coronation of Henry III of England as having happened during the second year of the Scottish king Alexander II, while Vatican sources dated the event to the first year of Pope Honorius III. A medieval carved stone cross at Lanercost Priory, Cumbria, is dated by an inscription declaring it to have been made 'in the 1214th year from the incarnation and the seventh year of the interdict, Innocent III holding the apostolic see, Otto being emperor in Germany, Philip reigning in France, John in England and William in Scotland'.

Dates within the year were expressed in the form 'Tuesday 22nd March'. Formal legal documents might even show the time of day. Alternatively, writers used church festivals such as Christmas Day, fixed at 25th December each year, or Easter Day, which might fall on any day between 22nd March and 25th April. Writers refer to saints and festivals particular to the neighbourhood. In the diocese of Lichfield a scribe notes the date as *mille martyres*, the feast of the thousand martyrs of Lichfield on 2nd January. Church lawyers prefer the opening or key words of the gospel for the day, referring to the 22nd Sunday after Pentecost, for instance, merely with the words *Reddite que sunt Caesaris Caesari* ('Tender unto Caesar that which is Caesar's). The day before (the eve of) a feast or the eighth day (the octave) following it are also normal dating methods.

The year was taken to begin on various dates, including the day of Christ's birth and that of his conception (Lady Day, 25th March). Bede used 24th September, a Roman imperial convention. During the sixteenth century 1st January came to be widely used in Europe, following an older Roman precedent, and was adopted in Scotland in 1600, but not in England. Documents written by progressive Englishmen between 1st January and 24th March each year might bear double dates, recognising both English and European practice ('22nd January 1592/3'). England, Wales and Ireland came into line with Europe when the day following 31st December 1751 was decreed 1st January 1752.

Because the earth takes approximately 365.2422 days to circle the sun, human calendars written only in whole numbers soon get out of step with the solar cycle. This difficulty was appreciated by the ancients, who periodically reformed their calendars. Julius Caesar inaugurated the Julian or Old Style calendar with the leap year concept in 46 BC and this remained in use during the Middle Ages, though a discrepancy of ten days had accumulated by the sixteenth century. A reformed calendar (New Style) was therefore devised and formally introduced by Pope Gregory XIII on 24th February 1582. The British rejected this Gregorian calendar. Documents written by British businessmen with European connections, Roman Catholic priests or diplomats might bear double dates (Old Style/New Style), written in the form 31st May/11th June 1590. Britain and Ireland were brought into step with Europe in 1752. The accumulated discrepancy, by then eleven days, was remedied by declaring that the day following 2nd September would be 14th September that year. As a result the financial year shifted eleven days from Lady Day to 6th April and, in traditional areas, Christmas to the first week of January.

Weights and measures

The thought processes of people in the past are elucidated in part as the researcher encounters curious and archaic weights and measures. The derivation and usage of such terms as *firlot* or *lippie* are given in the complete *Oxford English Dictionary*. Communities worked to their own standards and requirements, even when Parliament attempted to enforce rules in Scotland in 1661 and in the United Kingdom in 1824-5. Museum collections may include examples of regional weights and measures, permitting the historian to envisage the actual quantities mentioned in documentary sources. Medieval Europeans favoured duodecimal systems which counted by twelves or dozens (Old French *dozeine*, 'twelve'). Larger quantities might be expressed by the term 'gross', meaning a 'great dozen' of twelve times twelve, 144. Counting by hundreds is also encountered. A 'long' hundred of ten dozens, 120, might be preferred for certain commodities such as sawn timber. Attempts to enforce national standards from the Middle Ages onwards culminated in the British Isles in a definition of imperial standard measures by Act of Parliament in 1824. The score (twenty) perhaps originated when herdsmen counted their cattle out loud from one to twenty, then cut (scored) a mark on a stick before counting the next twenty.

The score is met in people's ages, for example 'three score years and ten' (70 years). To a butcher or farmer a score was a weight of twenty (or sometimes 21) pounds (9.072 or 9.525 kg) used in weighing pigs, oxen or large joints of beef and bacon.

The basic unit of distance was based on the Roman mile, derived from *mille passus,* 'one thousand paces'. There were at least twenty lengths for the mile in Scotland alone, and even among those who agreed to use a standard Scots mile of 1976 yards there might be no agreement on the length of the yard. The Irish mile was 2240 yards, hence the complaint of English travellers even in the 1890s that milestones seemed uncommonly few and far between. The medieval mile was divided into eight furlongs ('furrow-longs'), the normal length of a ploughed strip in the open field, eventually fixed at 220 yards.

The yard (Old English *yerd,* 'stick') dates from the tenth century or earlier. The cloth yard was a measuring rod used by medieval merchants. Researchers may have watched old-fashioned drapers measuring dress material with a graduated wooden yardstick. Other units of length include the foot of 'a middling man' divided into twelve inches (Latin *uncia,* 'one twelfth'). King David I defined the Scottish inch by reference to an average man's thumb or as the length of three barleycorns. The ell, varying from 27 to 45 inches, was a measure particularly associated with cloth merchants. The rod, pole or perch (one fortieth of a furlong, $5^1/2$ yards, equal to 5.029 metres) was used as a land measure, though the borough rod was often longer than the rural rod.

Measures of land area generally reflected agricultural practice: the term acre means 'field' (Latin *ager,* 'field'). An acre covered an area one furlong long by four rods broad (4840 square yards), which one team of oxen could plough in a day. There were 640 acres to one square mile. A varying number of acres from ten to eighteen made up an oxgang or bovate. Eight oxgangs were a ploughgate, ploughland or carrucate, basic land measures for taxation purposes. A virgate (from Latin *virga,* 'rod') at around 30 acres was the area of land conventionally reckoned suitable for the support of one peasant family. The usual borough property was one rood (a quarter of an acre) in extent, a typical village plot half an acre.

The decimalisation of British and Irish measures began as early as the seventeenth century under continental and renaissance influence. The standard measuring chain, 22 yards (one tenth of a furlong) in length, constructed from a hundred flexible metal links, was adopted early in the seventeenth century. The link is recorded as representing one hundredth of a chain (7.92 inches) from around 1650. In land surveying, an acre represented an area ten chains long by one chain broad (100,000 square links).

Units of weight ranged from the ton to the tiny grain. The Roman *libra* meaning scales and also a Roman pound in weight, gave the English pound weight its abbreviation 'lb'. The Roman *libra* was divided into twelve *uncia,* anglicised as ounce ('oz'). The medieval ounce varied between one twelfth and one twenty-seventh of a pound. The stone, eventually standardised at 14 lb, varied according to the commodity weighed: a stone of wool weighed 15 lb while a stone of wax weighed 8 lb. The capacity of liquids was measured in gallons. Originally a French measure for wine, the gallon was divided in England into four quarts ('quarters') or eight pints. The pint was defined by the Scottish Parliament in 1425 as the volume occupied by 41 ounces of clear water of Tay. In 1457 the Jug of Stirling became a standard Scottish pint, divided into chopins, mutchkins and gills (Old French *gille,* 'water pot'). The Scottish pint was nearly three times larger than the English, which now equals 20 fluid ounces. Wine and spirits were measured commercially by the tun or hogshead (types of barrel), or in smaller quantities such as the anker, chopin and lippy.

Units of dry measure included the bushel, originally a type of basket, typically for grain, though for tithe, rent and taxation purposes grain might be issued by the boll. This was standardised in Scotland in 1661 by the Linlithgow measure, though individual landowners ignored this. The copper pot known as the Great Boll of Tarbat, kept at the parish church, served the Easter Ross barony for generations and was almost twice the Linlithgow size. The baron took rents and paid debts in numbers of bolls, receiving 'by Tarbat' and selling 'by Linlithgow'! There was trouble in the barony when the Edinburgh authorities sent famine relief by the meagre southern measure. The chalder was a measure used for coal, originally containing 36 bushels, though latterly coal was more usually sold by hundred-weights (abbreviated to 'cwt' combining 'c' for Latin *centum,* 'hundred', and 'wt' for 'weight'). The short hundredweight was 100 lb, the long hundred-weight 112 lb.

The local historian, in tune with the habits of mind of people in the past, tries to understand features in the field in terms of the measuring practices of the past. It is often easier to make sense of the size or weight of artefacts and the dimensions of buildings or fieldscapes if they are measured using historical standards rather than millimetres, hectares, kilograms and litres. The serious fieldworker carries measuring tapes graduated in yards, feet and inches – or even an old-style 22 yard surveyor's measuring chain – as well as the usual metric rule. Older fieldworkers will be familiar with the imperial measures of their schooldays. For younger historians, educated in the metric system, the following table of equivalents may be helpful.

1 inch = 25.4 millimetres
1 foot (12 inches) = 0.3048 metres
1 yard (3 feet) = 0.9144 metres
1 mile (1760 yards) = 1.609 kilometres

1 acre (4840 square yards) = 0.405 hectares

1 grain = 0.065 grams
1 ounce = 28.35 grams
1 pound (16 ounces) = 0.4536 kilograms
1 hundredweight (112 pounds) = 50.8 kilograms
1 ton (20 hundredweight) = 1.016 tonnes

1 pint = 0.568 litres
1 gallon (8 pints) = 4.546 litres

Coinage

Coinage and money are catalogued in standard reference books of the numismatological publishers B. A. Seaby. The *Oxford English Dictionary* and dictionaries of slang and dialect discuss the vocabulary of money including such colloquial expressions as 'tanner', 'bob', 'ducat', 'plack', 'bawbee' and 'dollar'. Gold and silver coins with intrinsic value circulated across frontiers, though debasement created inflation and undermined economies. Scottish coinage was progressively devalued until it was worth only one twelfth of English by 1600. Despite inflation, one penny had considerable value until 1914; it is interesting to discover how ordinary people might purchase one pie from the boy at the street corner or a ribbon at the fair to dress a bonnet for under a farthing (a quarter of a penny), normally the smallest of coins.

Medieval coinage was based upon the silver penny, the word penny being associated with the name of King Penda of Mercia. In Latin writings penny is translated *denarius* and abbreviated 'd'. The half penny (ha'penny) and quarter penny or farthing (meaning fourth part) coins were minted first in silver and later in bronze. Medieval people sometimes preferred to cut their silver pennies into two or four pieces for convenience. Larger denominations included the groat or 'great' coin, worth 4d. A coin worth 12d, known as a testoon or tester, with a naturalistic head (Italian *testone*) of the monarch, appeared in the reign of Henry VII. A subsequent reduction in silver content reduced its value to 6d. From one pound weight of silver, it was possible to make 240 silver pennies, hence the British unit of currency known as a pound (formerly 240 old pennies). Early Norman silver pennies known as sterlings (the origin of this term is much debated among historians and numismatists) were of conspicuous fineness, so the word 'sterling' came to be used for quality and purity in other contexts. In financial accounts medieval writers used the expression *libra sterlingorum,* 'a pound [weight] of sterlings', and the pound sterling is still spoken of today. The '£' sign derives from a medieval Latin abbreviation which used a letter 'L' with a cross-stroke to represent *libra*, 'pound'.

Gold coinage was issued from the fourteenth century in both England and Scotland. The names of coins (angel, crown, noble, rider, double-leopard, unicorn, sovereign) referred to features of the design. Gold coins known as guineas, worth twenty shillings (a shilling, abbreviated to 's', consisting of twelve pennies), were issued from 1663, originally for use by merchants trading with the Guinea coast of Africa (the Gold Coast). The guinea coin rose in value and was fixed at 21 shillings in 1717. Guineas ceased to be struck in 1813, though the term 'guinea', indicating the sum of £1 1s, occurs in many bills of account until the 1970s. Gold coinage reappeared in 1817 in the form of the sovereign, at its original medieval value of twenty shillings.

The shilling was an amount of money for which originally no specific coin was issued. In Anglo-Saxon times the shilling was worth 5d in Wessex and 4d in Mercia, but its value was 12d in Norman England. In medieval Latin 'shilling' was *solidus*, abbreviated to 's'. The English shilling coin dates from 1503. Two thirds of a pound (160d or 13s 4d) was referred to as one mark, though it was not an English coin. A Scottish 'merk' coin, worth 13s 4d in Scottish values, was revalued under Charles II to more than its face value and was therefore known as a fourteen-shilling piece even though it was worth only 1s 2d sterling on account of the unfavourable exchange rate. A Scottish four-merk coin of Charles II, worth £2 13s 4d, was known as a dollar.

Foreign coins circulated when official coinage was in short supply. Silver *rijcksdaler* from the Netherlands, occurring in Britain during the seventeenth century, were referred to in documents as 'rix dollars'. Silver dollars of eight Spanish reales (pieces of eight) were exchanged from the sixteenth century. Under George III, dollars valued at 4s 9d were counterstamped with a tiny bust of the British monarch. The crown (five shillings) was known as a dollar, while the 2s 6d or half-crown coin was colloquially half a dollar.

Shortage of coins, especially smaller denominations, required the issue of local-ised money. During the Civil War simple (sometimes square) coins were minted for such besieged boroughs as Pontefract, Oxford, Truro and Scarborough. Distinctive copper-alloy coins (round, square and heart-shaped) were produced with official sanction by towns and trades under the Commonwealth. Capitalists of the industrial revolution designed tokens for their workers, intended originally for use in company shops but in practice acceptable across a broad hinterland.

Shillings and pennies were abandoned in February 1971. The pound sterling was decimalised, subdivided into one hundred new pence (abbreviated to p, colloquially known as 'new pees'). New denominations of coins were minted. A few old coins continued in circulation, for example the sixpence (valued at $2\frac{1}{2}$p), the shilling (5p) and the two shilling bit or florin (10p), until in due course phased out or replaced by new decimal coins.

From Romans to Vikings
(410-865)

The five centuries following the withdrawal of the Roman legions from Britain after 410 are traditionally known as the Dark Ages, contrasting sharply with the brilliance of classical civilisation. During centuries of disruption, migration and invasion throughout Europe, family groups and whole tribes took up residence in Britain and Ireland by a mixture of peaceful integration or genocidal conflict. The researcher can determine from archaeological, linguistic and written evidence whether a particular parish was affected. The extirpation of Celtic place-names in areas of southern England argues for an overwhelming immigration, though the example of the conquest of Mexico and Peru shows that a mere handful of determined invaders might change a whole country, without necessarily killing all the natives.

Romano-British merchants, administrators and landowners maintained government as best they could long after the legions departed, collecting taxes to finance declining public services and to pay mercenaries, who soon decided that protection rackets were in the end more profitable than fighting. Communities gradually returned to older tribal ways, as evidenced by chronicles and excavations. Abandoned Iron Age hillforts including South Cadbury (traditionally associated with King Arthur, the legendary leader of resistance against the English) were reoccupied. Early in the sixth century the British of Hampshire and Wiltshire, led by Ambrosius Aurelianus, one candidate for the legendary King Arthur, defeated the incomers at Mons Badonicus (Bydon or Badbury) and secured independence for a further generation. Frontiers established at this period were marked with linear earthworks, related in explicable ways to regional military strategies and territories. The Fleam, Heydon, Brent and Devil's dykes in Cambridgeshire, Wansdyke from Savernake to Bath and Offa's Dyke bounding western Mercia were earthen dykes constructed to block natural routes and Roman roads, to defend Romano-British chiefdoms or to consolidate English conquests. Leaders of mercenary forces could, by military coup, take over from the civil power and rule as petty kings in British tribal territories and Roman administrative districts. From the sixth century the area based upon Lindum Colonia (Lincoln) evolved into the kingdom of Lindsey, whose fifth-century ruler, Winta, is recalled in the place-name Winteringham. The researcher who gets out and about here will appreciate the importance of this nodal point where the Roman road crossed the Humber by ferry. Field survey and aerial photographs show the English settlement or royal complex established to control this crucial district.

Place-names indicate that Angles from Denmark colonised parts of East Anglia, while the -sex element in the names Essex, Middlesex and Sussex suggests that Saxons from Germany established these kingdoms. Saxon power expanded along the Thames valley in the sixth century to encompass Gloucester, Cirencester and Bath in 577. The Saxon chief Cudda built his palace at Cuddesdon, Oxfordshire, and was buried under a barrow, demolished in 1261, at Cutteslowe in 584. To the south, Saxon leaders ruled Wessex, which emerged as an independent kingdom under Ceolwulf (reigned 597-611). In the north in 547 Angles under Ida attacked the un-Romanised Britons from the coast and seized Bamburgh as the focus of their territory of Bernicia. The British inland hillfort of Ad Gefrin was converted into Yeavering, an English palace complex of timber halls and even a Roman-style semicircular place of assembly. Angles seized the strategic centre of Catterick around 580, consolidating the kingdom of Northumbria under Ethelfrith (593-617). Subsequent expansion into Strathclyde and Lothian is substantiated by field monuments, stone crosses and place-names. Place-names containing the element *wal,* Old English for 'foreigner', may mark significant pockets of British culture in an otherwise English landscape. The element may also be interpreted as 'a village of (perhaps British) serfs'. There is confusion, though, with the elements *wald,* 'woodland'; *wall,* 'wall' (perhaps a piece of surviving Roman masonry); *waelle,* 'well' or 'spring'; and *Walli* or *Welisc,* an English personal name. The Celtic word for a Briton (*cymro,* meaning 'Welshman' in modern Welsh) was put into place-names by the English in the form *cumbre,* as in Cumberland and Cummersdale. Comberbach, Cheshire, derived from *cumbre-baece,* may represent 'Briton's (or Welshman's) stream', though it may alternatively mean 'stream of the Englishman named Cumbra'. Place-names containing elements from two languages – the first native, the second immigrant – may stimulate discussion as to the implications of this. Crewkerne, Somerset, has *cruc,* British for 'hill', and *aern,* Old English for 'building'. The common British word *ced,* 'wood', is detectable in Chatham and Cheetham, both having the English *ham,* 'village', as their second element. The interpretation 'village near the wood' makes sense and perhaps implies the coexistence or even intermarriage of the British and the English. However, Chetwode, Buckinghamshire, contains the old English element *wudu,* 'wood', and therefore means 'woodwood'. Perhaps this reflects the existence of separate communities who did not understand one another, or maybe an English immigrant pointing to a group of trees and asking a British resident 'What is the name of that *wudu*?' received the (helpful or surly) reply '*ced*' and thence forward knew the *wudu* as *cedwudu.*

From around AD 350 Irish traders and raiders were active in western Britain. The Desi and Liathain tribes from Munster expanded eastwards into Wales and Cornwall, contributing Gaelic elements to the fund of place-names and returning to Ireland with captives and booty. This is attested archaeologically and in legends associated with St Patrick, a Romano-British Christian transported as a slave to Ireland. The Irish word *cnoc,* 'hill', is found in Dyfed place-names in the form *cnwc,* while the name of the kingdom of Gwynedd recalls the Irish Feni, a dynamic people from Connacht, expelled to Wales early in this period of migration. The Gaelic personal name Laigain encapsulated in the place-name Leinster, is also preserved in the name of the Welsh Lleyn (Llyn) peninsula. Also from Ireland the piratical Scotti tribe (Scots) established Dal Riata in western Pictland. Their kingdom of Argyll ('headland of the Gaels') was a springboard for the conquest of northern Britain, known thereafter as Scotland, 'land of the Scotti'. From south-west Britain, perhaps with refugees from the English, British culture was exported to Armorica (Brittany). Around 680, the warriors of Rheged, a British territory south of the Solway, were displaced by the Angles and sailed west to the north of Ireland. They fought for and against the kings of Ulster until 709, when, defeated in the Wicklow mountains, they vanished from written records. Scandinavian Vikings raided and traded for centuries before the deteriorating climate and economy in their homelands encouraged large-scale emigration during the ninth century and the appearance of the first Norse place-names in Britain and Ireland.

Written sources

The period of colonisation was documented at the time in Britain, Ireland and continental Europe by scholars and churchmen. There were archival losses through sectarian vandalism over controversy about the dating of Easter; the deaths of whole religious communities in the plague of 664-5; civil unrest; and Norse invasions – to mention just four of the problems of these four centuries. Manuscripts were written with durable ink on parchment and preserved in monasteries and so have survived the centuries to become the treasured possessions of academic and national libraries. The British Library's Harleian Manuscript 3859 is a miscellany of original texts relating notably to Wales, Mercia, Kent and Northumbria, seemingly put together by monks at St Davids in Wales around 960. The authors wrote in Latin and the vernacular languages from the late fifth century onwards, referring to events of the not-too-distant past. Constantius used recent documentary and oral evidence in composing his life of St Germanus of Auxerre around 480, alluding to the missionary's visits to Britain in 428-9 and 445-6 to combat the native Pelagian heresy, and his information is almost contemporary. Lives of saints generally date from centuries after their deaths so errors and embellishments are a serious critical problem. Fortunately for modern researchers important texts have now been published in translation with editorial notes and indexes and are listed in the bibliographies of standard national histories; in *Texts and Calendars*; in *Arthurian Period Sources* (Phillimore, 1978-90) edited by J. Morris; and in J. F. Kenney's *The Sources for the Early History of Ireland* (Columbia University Press, New York, 1929).

Documentation of this period takes several forms. Religious tracts, epistles and hagiographies refer, not necessarily in a straightforward undiplomatic manner, to such matters as slavery, ostentatious wealth, tensions among Christians of different persuasions and political differences between Roman and native patriotic parties. Trinity College, Dublin, holds the *Liber Ardmachanus* ('Book of Armagh'), compiled at Armagh, perhaps in the early ninth century, to document the fifth-century activities of St Patrick and early missionaries. One important homily on the wages of British sin, *De Excidio et Conquestu Britanniae* ('On the Ruin and Conquest of Britain'), was composed around the year 540 by the cleric Gildas, whose sermon is noteworthy for his grim word-picture of collapsing Romano-British society in western Britain. Gildas was not a remote historian of events, for he was born in the year of Ambrosius's battle of Mount Badon, but his evidence from the fifth century is perhaps unreliable, as he neglects to mention the patriotic ruler Vortigern – another Arthurian-style warlord – by name (unless he be the 'exalted ruler' of chapter 23). Illuminated Christian gospel books or psalters were written in – or relate to – particular localities. Even when they are available in facsimile, there is no substitute for viewing actual manuscripts, either at Trinity College, Dublin – for the books of Dimma, Kells and Mulling, or at the British Library – for the Lindisfarne Gospels and many other English, Welsh and Irish manuscripts. Such treasures indicate cultural influences at work in the community, as exhibited in artistic style. Other contemporary sources are genealogies of Welsh, English and Irish ruling families, providing tenuous but relevant evidence for the development of territories such as Deheubarth. Celtic and English laws provide evidence of social organisation. Those of Kent, written down late in the sixth century, refer to a pre-Christian people, while those of the tenth-century Welsh ruler Hywel the Good, recorded in the thirteenth century, may preserve concepts common to Celtic Britain and Ireland. Examples of brehon, or customary, law tracts preserved at Trinity College and the Royal Irish Academy, Dublin, have been published as *Ancient Laws of Ireland* (Irish Record Commission, 1865-1901).

Poetry is one means through which the historian tries to understand how people thought and acted – what might cause laughter, tears or fear; what social priorities there were, particularly among the nobility and court bards. In *Y Gododdin* of about AD 600, a northern Briton named Aneirin sings in the oral bardic tradition of the royal court of Din Eidin (Edinburgh) of the heroic struggle against the English kingdom of Deira in Yorkshire, culminating in the battle of Catterick. Another northern poet of the same era, Taliesin, was concerned with events in Gwynedd, Gwent and Powys. The Old English poem *Widsith*, of about 600, was copied into an anthology about 975 and later donated to Exeter cathedral by Bishop Leofric. The poet refers to a continental tribe of Rodingas, who may have given their name to the large Saxon territory of Roding, Essex. The famous epic about the hero *Beowulf* provides evidence of the lifestyle of an Anglo-Saxon warlord and his people during the sixth century. Beowulf's father belonged to the Geat tribe of southern Sweden

The Ruthwell Cross, Dumfriesshire, dating from the seventh century, is carved with Latin and runic inscriptions framing biblical scenes. The cross was broken up by Protestant iconoclasts in 1640 but elevated again in the enlightened eighteenth century.

and settled in the vale of the river Deben, Suffolk. The Christianised literary version of *Beowulf* dates only from late Saxon times but arguably rests upon oral tradition of the Geat people. An early Geat leader named Wuffa, whose descendants the historian Bede recognised as Wuffingas ('people of Wuffa'), is thought to have been an ancestor of King Raedwald of the East Angles, who is probably the king buried with his war galley and a cache of grave-goods, including Swedish heirlooms, in one of the Sutton Hoo tumuli. It seems probable that both in Sweden and in East Anglia bards recited the epic to appreciative audiences around the fire in the warlord's hall. A similar setting would have been appropriate for the linguistically refined and often bawdily witty *Riddles of Aldhelm*. The more staid poem known as *The Dream of the Rood*, lines of which are carved in runes on to the Ruthwell cross in Dumfriesshire, shows a characteristic synthesis of pagan and Christian imagery.

Annals compiled year by year are as reliable as any contemporary record can be. Christians required annals to calculate the movable feast of Easter, usually adding newsworthy items in the margins and interpolating information on earlier events as their significance emerged. The Easter annals forming a basis for the *Annales Cambriae* ('Welsh Annals') may have commenced about 450 and continue to about 960, thus providing early evidence of the struggle between the Romano-Britons and the English. *The Annals of Ulster* (Irish Record Commission, 1887-1901) are a source for Irish and Scottish history, allegedly from 431. Histories were written from annals and oral traditions. *Senchus Fer nAlban,* 'the tradition of the men of

Ʞt. Ianaıp.   Œnno ʋomını ʋccc.° Ł.° uııı.° Suaıplec
abbap Œchaıʃ bo, Œılıll banbaıne abbap Ɓıpop, Mael-
coba óa Ƒaelan abbap Cluana uaña, Ƒaelʓup abbap
Roıp cpea, ın pace ʋopmıepunc. Sloʓaʋ mop la hŒm-
laıʃ 7 Imap 7 Cepɓall ı Mıʃe. Rıʒɓal mače Ɵpenn oc
paıč Œeʃo mıc Ɓpıcc, ım Maelpecnaıll pıʒ Ceñpa, 7
ım Ƒeʒʒna comapba Ƥacpaıcc, 7 ım Suaıplec comapba
Ƒınnıo, ıc ʋenum pıʃa 7 caıncompaıcc pep nƟpenʋ,
conıʋ ap ın ʋaıl pın ʋupac Cepball pı Oppaıʒı oʒpeıp
pamča Ƥacpaıc 7 a comapba, 7 conıʃ anʋ ʋo ʋečaıʃ
Oppaıʒı ı n-ʋılpı ppı leč Cuınn, 7 aʋpoʒaıʃ Maelʓualaı
pı Muman a ʋılpı. Maelʓuala pex Muman a Nopʋ-
mannıp occıppup epc. Sečonnan pılıup Conaınʒ, pex
Caıpʒı bpačaıʋe, mopıcup.

1 January 858. Suairlech, Abbot of Aghaboe, Ailill Banbaine, Abbot of Biror, Mealcobha
Ua Faelain, Abbot of Cloyne, Faelgus, Abbot of Roscrea, slept in peace. There was a big
mobilisation of forces into Meath by Amlaiph, Imar and Cerbhall [King of Ossory]. At
Rahugh there was a royal gathering of the nobility of Ireland including Malachy, King of
Tara, and Fethgna, successor of Patrick [Abbot of Armagh], and Suairlech, successor of
Finnia [Abbot of Clonard], confirming peace and concord among the men of Ireland. It was
at the meeting on that occasion that Cerbhall, King of Ossory, pledged obedience to the
religious community of Patrick and successors. And the men of Ossory pledged Conn's
(northern) half of Ireland and Maelgualai, King of Munster, pledged his allegiance.
Maelgualai, King of Munster, was killed by Norsemen. Sechonnan, a son of Conaing, King
of Carrickabraghy, died.

*An excerpt from W. M. Hennessy's edition of the 'Annals of Ulster', 1887 (volume 1,
page 368).*

Scotland', was compiled in the Irish language during the seventh century, though
the surviving version (Trinity College, Dublin) was copied with additions in the
tenth century. The *Senchus* surveys the settlements, armies and genealogies of the
Scots who settled Pictland and is available in W. F. Skene's *Chronicles of the Picts,
Chronicles of the Scots, and other Early Memorials of Scottish History* (Scottish
Record Office Texts and Calendars, 1867). Around the year 730 an English historian,
the Venerable Bede of Jarrow, compiled his *Historia Ecclesiastica Gentis Anglorum*
('An Ecclesiastical History of the English People'), looking back with satisfaction
on the dual advance of his nation and the Roman Christian observance. Here is
Bede, in the translation of J. Stevens (1723; new edition Dent, 1910, pages 132-3),
telling how in 633 the Irish missionary Fursa determined to evangelise the East
Angles by establishing a monastery at Burgh Castle, Suffolk:

> He applied himself with all speed to build a monastery on the ground which had been
> given him by King Sigebert, and to establish regular discipline therein. This monastery
> was pleasantly situated in the woods, and with the sea not far off; it was built within the
> area of a castle, which in the English language is called Cnobheresburg, that is,
> Cnobher's Town; afterwards, Anna, king of that province, and the nobility, embel-
> lished it with more stately buildings and donations.

The *Historia Brittonum* ('History of the Britons'), traditionally compiled or
revised around 830 by Nennius, a Briton of the Welsh marches, uses earlier histories

and oral traditions. From the opposing viewpoint, the scribes of *The Anglo-Saxon Chronicle* began around 880 to use earlier sources including annals from the religious house of Dorchester on Thames, to compile a history of the English from the fifth century onwards. The Everyman paperback edition and translation by G. N. Garmonsway transcribes the various versions in modern English as parallel texts. A chronicle of the rulers or princes of Wales for 681-1282, the *Brut y Tywysogion*, uses annals and oral sources, possibly also mere fanciful scribal embellishment. A document of about 670, known as the *Tribal Hidage*, lists groupings of the English, for instance the Hicca tribe in Hitchin and the Wixan folk of Worcestershire, whose name survives in the place-name Whitsun Brook. This British Library document indicates the relative wealth and territory of each tribe, using the hide as the basic unit; this is a land measure of 60 to 120 acres (24 to 48 hectares), depending on locality, which notionally represents the acreage necessary for the subsistence of one Anglo-Saxon family. The hide remained a unit of taxation, with counties divided into administrative units of a hundred hides known as hundreds.

Anglo-Saxon charters are administrative records dating from the seventh century onwards, which refer to the transfer of land and property, incidentally naming people, noting financial and social relationships and, especially, describing features of the landscape. A few remain in estate and ecclesiastical muniment rooms, though most are now gathered into archival institutions, particularly the British Library. A list of known charters, showing the location of the manuscript with details of published editions, is offered by P. H. Sawyer's *Anglo-Saxon Charters* (Royal Historical Society, 1968). The charter may include a step-by-step perambulation of boundaries where the original donor and recipient of an estate take a tour of landmarks and topographical features. These early parchment charters are, typically, written in Latin but break into English for the perambulation. A knowledge of Old English is not essential because charters are available in translation. The charter below, from Badby, Northamptonshire, translated in *Review of English Studies*, volume 6 (1930), pages 271-83, gives an impression of the landscape a thousand years ago. Even without linguistic ability, the reader will tease out the salient features of an Anglo-Saxon estate march (boundary).

> *Thonne of ðam thornum up on ða lytlan dune middewearde.*
> Next from the thorn tree up onto the small hill keeping to the middle.
> *Thonne of ðære dune east on foxhylle eastewearde...*
> Then from that hill east to the eastern part of Foxhill...
> *Thonne of hindehlypan on thone wylle æt tham lea ufeweardan.*
> Then from Hind's-leap to the well at the clearing's upper part.
> *Of ðam wylle on ðæt heorotsol. Of ðam heorotsol norð on gerihte on ðone beorg ...*
> From the well to the hart's wallow. From the hart's wallow due north to the hill ...
> *Thonne suð on gerihte andlang Wæclingastræt on thone weg to Weoduninga gemære.*
> Then due south along Watling Street on the road to Weedon boundary.

British Library, Cottonian manuscript Augustus II 63, 'A grant of K. Eadmund, of lands at Baddanbyrig, to Ælfric, "pontifici suo". (Lat. with the bounds in Saxon.) A°944', in *Sweet's Anglo-Saxon Reader* (revised by C. T. Onions, fourteenth edition, Clarendon Press, 1959, page 53).

Permanent records of individuals and events were carved on standing stones specially shaped for the purpose, or, as people adopted literate habits of mind, on megaliths belonging to prehistoric cults. The text of inscriptions may consist of no more than a personal name, though some describe events and genealogies. The language and style of lettering may shed light on the racial and religious background of those who commissioned the monument. Different runic alphabets were used by the Anglo-Saxon, Danish and Norse people. Irish ogham inscriptions are found where Gaelic influence spread. Celtic uncial letters derived from Rome suggest a Christian ruling class in the locality. Roman capitals or cursive lettering indicate the survival of Roman culture or perhaps a continuing connection with Rome and Gaul.

The Picts inscribed warriors, hunters and animals on stone monuments and cave walls. A bearded horseman boozes from a drinking horn at Invergowrie; three men walk in dignity at Birsay, Orkney. At Aberlemno in Angus a neolithic holed menhir of pink sandstone was dressed and carved with a Christian cross of fantastic interlace, armed warriors, cavalry and infantry wearing helmets of Anglian type with a nasal bar. The monument may illustrate the Pictish victory over Ecgfrith of Northumbria at Nechtansmere on 20th May 658 or episodes from Celtic heroic myth. A 20 foot (7 metre) monolith at Forres, Moray, in ninth-century style, shows kilted swordsmen, fleeing cavalry, seven headless corpses and a single king enthroned – images perhaps of the subjugation of the Picts by the Scots. In Pictish art there are some thirty core symbols, including a crescent with a broken arrow and a serpent with a broken spear; various animals (boar, bull, wolf, eagle, salmon, sea-monster); and status symbols (mirror-and-comb, bracelet, cauldron). Some symbol stones also include Pictish or Scottish personal names inscribed in ogham characters. For the most part symbols are carved in pairs or groups of four in a manner that seems almost heraldic. The pairing may represent personal names and titles of respect as in English Dark-Age names such as *Ead-weard*, meaning 'prosperity-guard', or perhaps marital alliances in a traditional context of matrilineal descent.

Place-names

Place-names of this period enshrine elements from pre-Celtic languages, even though they were no longer understood or spoken. These elements put the historian in touch with even earlier peoples who occupied and worked the land perhaps seven thousand years ago. Prehistoric elements may be incorporated in such debatable names as Allow, Ayr, Carron, Cart, Elgin, Ettrick, Farrar, London, Ness, Shin, Spey, Tain, Tanar, Tay, Teviot, Thames, Tweed, Wey, Wye; in the river names Aln, Alne, Ayleburn and Ellen, which contain the element *alauno*, of obscure derivation; in place-names derived from *cunetju*, a word with sexual connotations associated with waters (still waters in pools, lakes and bogs; running waters in rivers, streams and springs) such as Kent, Kennet, Cound, Countisbury and Kintbury; in the

A Pictish symbol stone that has been inserted (upside down) in the wall at Arndilly House on Speyside.

element *ar(a)*, 'water', which with the locative suffix *-ina* gives the ubiquitous river name Earn. The element *ben (vin)*, indicating 'height' in the sense of a prominent place of resort, emerged into Gaelic as *beinn*, 'mountain', and into Romano-British as *venta*, 'market' or 'assembly place', as in Winchester, indicating the importance of the site even before Roman times.

Place-names of the period 410-865 are likely to be Irish, Gaelic, British, Old Welsh, Cornish or Pictish, all varieties of an earlier Celtic tongue. Standard textbooks include W. J. Watson's *The History of the Celtic Place-names of Scotland* (1926, reprinted Birlinn, Edinburgh, 1993) and O. J. Padel's *A Popular Dictionary of Cornish Place-names* (Alison Hodge, Penzance, 1988). Celtic place-names in the forms found on maps and road signs include: *aber/inver*, 'river mouth, confluence'; *avon*, 'river'; *ach/iog/es*, 'place of'; *bally*, 'township'; *beg/bach*, 'small'; *caer*, 'fort'; *dal*, 'meadow'; *din/dun*, 'fort'; *glen*, 'valley'; *hen/sen*, 'old'; *kin/pen*, 'head'; *inis*, 'island'; *machar*, 'coastal plain'; *maen/clach*, '[standing] stone'; *mor/fawr*, 'big'; *pit*, 'piece of land'; *tig/lis*, 'house'; *tober*, '[sacred] well or spring'; *tir*, 'land or territory'; *tref*, 'township'; *ystrad/strath*, 'vale'. Rulers or landowners may be recalled in place-names. The descriptive Denbigh, 'small fort', and Dunmore and Maiden, both meaning 'big fort', probably indicate the status of a stronghold and its chief. In Anglesey Pencarnisiog derives from the name Cunogusos, who is actually referred to in ogham script on a standing stone at Llanfaelog. Ben Deargh, literally 'mountain- red', may convey other meanings, because *dearg* was used of rugged mountains where there was danger for herdsmen from the weather, terrain and evil spirits. Other words for hill, notably *ben*, *knock*, *maol* and *sgurr*, each mean something different and specific. This introduces a general problem with place-names. Taken at face value, names such as Loch Buie, 'yellow lake', Strath Glass, 'grey/green vale', and Alves, 'stone place', seem simply banal but may conceal other meanings. Just as we might imply a particular characteristic when calling an acquaintance red (for a communist), yellow (for a coward) or green (for inexperience or environmental activism), so many place-names may contain significant Celtic meanings, some lost, others preserved in archives, legends and folk tales.

Roman place-names derived from British originals were adopted by the English without appreciation of the meanings of the names or the historical origins of the places. Even today scholars do not agree on the derivation of *Londinium*. The standard textbook is *The Place-Names of Roman Britain* (Batsford, 1979) by A. L. F. Rivet and C. Smith. Manchester was known to the English as *Mameceaster*, probably incorporating the British element *mamma*, 'breast-like hill', on which the Roman *castra*, 'fort', stood. The element *mamma* is seen in other hills, such as Mam Tor (Derbyshire) and Maumbury Rings (Dorset). Lost *Mamma* names may also have belonged to the sacred, suggestively buxom hills now anglicised as the Paps of Anu, Pap of Glencoe and Paps of Jura. The Roman *Deva* (river Dee or Dwy) was derived from British *deua*, 'goddess', a divinity present in waters. The word goes back to prehistoric Indo-European roots, meaning 'brilliant', and perhaps relates to the reverence for the sun, moon and sacred waters in the Bronze Age. Roman sites may be indicated by place-names, as at Fawler, Oxfordshire, where a Roman tessellated floor uncovered by archaeologists in 1865 confirmed the name's derivation from *fag-flor*, 'variegated pavement'. Roman remains seen by the Anglo-Saxons, perhaps quarried away for their own buildings, may not be visible to us today, though recalled in place-names.

The English renamed villages, fields, hills and rivers. The decreasing westward impact of their conquest is illustrated by the survival of Celtic names for rivers and hills from central England into Wales. For early forms of names *Domesday Book* and Anglo-Saxon charters are useful, while later tithe and estate plans may provide clues if carefully interpreted. Elements in modernised form include *bury*, 'fortified place', perhaps an Iron Age hillfort; *croft*, 'enclosed land connected to a house'; *den*, 'pasture'; *hirst*, 'wooded hill'; *hay*, 'enclosure'; *ridding*, 'land clearance';

stead, 'place with buildings'; *worth*, 'enclosure for house'. Place-names may provide clues about the date and extent of English settlement. Almondbury near Halifax could be interpreted as 'the fortified hill of Alemanic folk', based upon the older form of the place-name (Almaneberie) recorded in *Domesday Book*. Fieldwork on the site supports the idea of a fourth-century immigrant settlement.

English tribal names are concealed within Ripon (*Hrype*), Jarrow (*Gyrwe*), Tame (*Tomsaeten*) and Ivel (*Gifle*). At Kingston-upon-Thames English rulers were acclaimed at the king's stone, a megalith significant from prehistoric times. *Hlaw*, 'hillock' or 'mound', may indicate a prehistoric tumulus.The name Low Hill is perhaps a clue from Saxon times of the location of a sacred hill whose skyline was dignified with prehistoric burial mounds. These 'lows', recognised by the English as places of power, were adopted as landmarks on estate boundaries or as moot hills. The hundred court of Bucklow in Cheshire met at *bucca-hlaw*, 'he-goat's mound', beside the Roman road known as Watling Street, where three parish boundaries converged. The place-name could refer to the stock of local graziers or to a human inhabitant known as Bucca for some goat-like personal characteristic. As the lows were plundered of their prehistoric grave-goods, tumuli in general acquired a reputation for buried treasure, perhaps protected by terrible guardians, as at Drakelow, Derbyshire, from *dracan-hlaw*, 'dragon's tumulus'. English place-names suggest that deer were significant animals at Darton, Dordon, Derby, Dereham, Dearham and Durleigh. Hindlip, derived from *hindehliep*, 'deer leap' or 'lower place in a hedge where deer might leap', indicates the location of an English thegn's hunting park. Wild boar supplied sport, perhaps also incorporating an element of pagan ritual at Boar's Hill, Boarstall and Boarzell. Salmon (*lax*) were to be found at Laxfirth, Laxay, Leixlip, Laxey, Laxford, Laxdale and at Salt, County Kildare, from *saltus salmonis*, 'leap of the salmon'.

Borrowed Latin words include *castra*, 'fort', in the form 'chester', 'caster' or 'couster'; *strata*, 'street', especially a Roman road; *portus*, 'harbour'; *campus*, 'field', as in Barcombe, Sussex, 'barley-field'. Of slightly later date are names with *inga-*, 'people', and *ham*, 'village', usually linked with a pagan personal name, perhaps belonging to the founder of the settlement. An example is *Snot-inga-ham*, meaning 'Snot's people's village', later corrupted to Nottingham by Normans who found difficulty in pronouncing double consonants like 'sn'. English *ham* was added to Latin *vicus*, 'settlement', to create the widespread Wickham name, generally regarded as among the earliest of English place-names. *Vicus* was joined with an English element where industrial activity flourished, as in Chiswick, 'the cheese-making settlement'. Salt workings acquired *vicus* names, as in Droitwich or Northwich.

Of somewhat later origin, arguably the sixth and seventh centuries, are places ending in -*ing*, 'son of', and *ingas*, 'descendants of','people of', combined with a pagan personal name. Examples are Ealing (Middlesex), from *Gill-ingas*, 'Gilla's people['s place]'; and Iping (Sussex) from *Ip-ingas*, 'Ipa's people['s place]'.

English place-names often contain a person's name in association with a landscape feature, perhaps a property owned by the named individual. Notable elements include *hamm*, 'meadow', usually in a river bend; *feld*, 'pasture'; *leah*, 'grove'; *tun*, 'farmstead'; some of these might be associated with *gemot*, 'meeting', to indicate tribal assembly places, as in Mobberley.

During the seventh century the English settled the wooded northern bank of the river Weaver, Cheshire. Their estate of around two thousand acres was known by a longish name, perhaps *Beornðryðingtun*, representing a founder or early owner, contracted to *Bertintune* by Domesday (1086). By 1150 two physically distinct portions of the estate acquired separate forms of the place-name, variously by loss of the interconsonantal 'r' from *ðryð* and 'n' from *beorn* and by shortening the long personal name before *ingtun*, becoming in the first instance Berthreton (1180), Barthington (1537) and Bartington (1712), and in the second Bertenton (1282), Berneton (1319), and Barnton (1577). In the absence of Saxon charters the etymology of the place-names will doubtless remain unclear, and the historian could argue that Bartington and Barnton had separate origins and histories. The two places were held both before and after 1066 by different men. The name Bartington with 'r' and 't' as significant elements could have developed from *Beorhthereingtun* or *Beorhtgyðingatun*. Barnton with 'n' could have developed from *Beornhaeðingtun*. Such are the challenges the place-name researcher tackles to shed light upon the early history of his township from the evidence of a simple place-name!

The countryside

During the Dark Ages northern Europe enjoyed a phase of settled weather with warm dry summers, cool rainy winters and average temperatures perhaps 1°C warmer than today. Land once fruitful for Bronze Age people was blanketed under raised bog and peat. The dank climate exacerbated the erosion of light soils caused by over-exploitation. Arable cultivation gravitated towards the higher ground of the downs, to heavy clay soils and to drumlin islands away from blanket bog and dense woodland. At the same time, marshland was still a valuable resource, yielding peat, bog-iron ore, fish, thatching reeds and basketry osiers. Managed woodland supplied the community's needs for constructional timber and wood for fuel and utensils. During the fifth century in southern Britain there were villa estates of mixed arable and pasture, sometimes with the addition of market gardening to feed neighbouring urban centres. Fields were large enough for cultivation by the continental heavy plough and ox team. On the plains and reclaimed fenland of eastern Britain, a Roman improvement landscape of rectangular fields in a regular 'brickwork' pattern survived, evident from aerial photography. The land was probably managed by Romano-British or invading English settlers without replanning.

Much of Britain, even Roman Britain, and Ireland was unaffected by Roman farming methods. Arable farming made use of walled, fenced or hedged fields, squarish for criss-cross ploughing or tillage with a spade. Fields were small ($^1/_2$ to 2 acres, 0.2 to 0.8 hectares) and may be identified on Ordnance Survey maps as 'Celtic Fields', though many enclosures date from 3000 BC or even earlier. These landscapes can be viewed today in parts of Cornwall and Connemara. The Anglo-Saxons took over and, initially at least, preserved these fields, as indicated by air photographs and archaeological reports. Archaeologists analyse pollen and carbonised seeds from soils to show that grain crops included barley, wheat, oats and rye, while peas, beans and kale were among other vegetables grown. The size and number of grain storage pits and four-post granaries or corn-rick staddles indicates the success of farmers in overcoming problems. Farming properties of perhaps twenty fields were defined by substantial banks and ditches planted with hedgerows, evident in the landscape even today, perhaps still defining the boundary of an estate or ecclesiastical parish. Features no longer visible on the ground may be identified on the Ordnance Survey, where hedge banks appear as conspicuous narrow corridors of thicket and woodland. Stone markers and place-names with the elements *maere* and *mearc* (usually in the forms *mere* and *march*) tell where significant boundaries ran, possibly still on the trail taken by modern riders of the marches. In Wales, Ireland and Pictland communities maintained extensive areas of open moorland, measuring wealth in bestial (sheep, cattle, horses) rather than corn. Analysis of bones from middens or rubbish dumps indicates that herds of hardy cattle, small hairy black ancestors of the modern highland breed, grazed the hill land. Sheep and goats (not always archaeologically distinguishable) provided meat, milk and wool. Pigs rooted in woodland and fallow fields.

Throughout Britain and Ireland agricultural estates may have passed unscathed from one ownership to another, even through incomers and invaders, though this is a subject much debated. Estates and boundaries survive remarkably well if defined by tradition or by natural features, march stones or earthen banks and ditches. Cantray is a name attached to a variety of farms, hamlets, fields, moorland and a

Celtic *dun* ('fort'), defined by a variety of boundaries reflecting the present division of ownership, spread for 3½ miles (5.6 km) along both sides of the river Nairn just east of Inverness and at the southern limit of arable cultivation below the Cawdor hills. The British name possibly incorporates *cant,* 'border', as in Kent and Canterbury, and *tref,* 'settlement', as in Tresco (Isles of Scilly). Drawing a line on the map round the boundaries of all the Cantray settlements may outline the estate which was in existence when the Gaelic people first settled in the Dark Ages, and long before the Normans constructed their motte as a territorial centre at Cantraydoune.

Defended rural settlements

Defended sites or forts were a necessity in the troubled post-Roman centuries. The researcher is challenged to identify the defenders, the duration of their occupation and the regional significance of the sites. Forts are distinguished by such place-name elements as *cashel* or *dun,* 'defended site', ultimately the same word as 'town'. Forts were built on all types of site, identified on the ground and from air photographs. There are forts on islets in lochs and bays, at least seventy in North Uist alone. To a few the sole access was by boat. Others were reached by a curving boulder causeway, generally now much eroded by rising water levels, though occasionally, as in Loch of Kettlester in Yell, sufficiently preserved to allow walkers access without getting their feet wet. Duns were also perched on rocky outcrops and sea stacks, occasionally linked to the land only by a tightrope of rock above a dizzying natural arch. Most duns are roughly circular, usually of stone, perhaps 150 feet (46 metres) across. There is normally just a narrow entrance with door cheeks and draw-bar slots still evident. Walls might stand 20 feet (6 metres) high and 10 feet (3 metres) thick with parapet walks and breastworks at the top. Stairs and chambers, curved and rounded like souterrains, were built in the thickness of the walls. Timber lacing strengthened walls, with slots in the masonry for lacing beams, now long since rotted away. When timber-revetted and laced walls were burned, the heat of the fire might even melt the stones into vitrified masses. The historian decides whether vitrification is indicative of a particularly warlike or accident-prone region. Perhaps slighting methods have left fewer traces elsewhere.

Fieldwork suggests that some duns may have been roofed over. Elsewhere houses were built as lean-to structures against the walls or free standing within the courtyard. Defences were reinforced with banks, ditches and ankle-breaking pits. A field of *chevaux de frise*, scattered masses of jagged rocks to break up enemy formations and slow the charge, deepened the defences, by some 50 feet (15 metres) beyond the walls of Cathair Bhaile Cinn Mhargaidh, County Clare. At Dunbeg, County Kerry, the designer elaborated his semicircular cliff-edge stronghold with a subterranean sally port connecting the guard chamber and one of the four ditches.

Celtic farmsteads were defended by a stone or earthen rampart, pierced with a single entrance, topped with a fence, thorn hedge or palisade. These defences, perhaps with traces of a roundhouse in the interior, are known in Cornwall as rounds, in Ireland as raths. At least 40,000 raths are identifiable on the ground from cropmarks, circular earthworks, rings of trees, circles of scrub or marsh or from air photographs. At Budure, County Antrim, the old rath is represented by an obscure circular grassy bank 120 feet (37 metres) across, while the new rath with defences crisply defined is thought to be medieval. Farmstead enclosures were normally no larger and no more elaborate or defensible than a substantial sheep stell but sometimes occupied portions of pre-Roman but abandoned forts, as at Dun Lagaidh, Wester Ross, where the narrow humped ridge by Loch Broom was too good a site to forsake. To exploit the food resources of wetlands, lakes and estuaries, Celtic families constructed and inhabited artificial defensible islands known as crannogs, comprising faggots and stones retained by timber piles and jointed beams. Most supported a single roundhouse, though in the Somerset Levels islands coalesced into sizeable villages. Crannogs appear today as round rubbly islets, perhaps also as overgrown mounds in drained fieldscapes. Blackened timbers around the crannog margins provide samples for radiocarbon dating and dendrochronological analysis. A curving rubble causeway connecting crannog to shore may be visible. Timber trackways were also laid across wetlands to link settlements, and King Alfred evaded the Danes through his knowledge of such routes in Somerset.

Villages were usually enclosed with palisades. Clustered clachans (hamlets) of four to six dwellings were the norm wherever native British people survived. Their general outlines appear on estate plans of the eighteenth century and their ruins on air photographs.The fieldworker in a typical English parish should expect to locate the sites of perhaps six self-supporting hamlets, suggested by field names and landscape patterns, indicated by significant concentrations of domestic rubbish and pottery sherds, occasionally with a fortuitous and datable brooch or coin. In the Northamptonshire parish of Great Doddington, seven such concentrations have been recorded and seven settlements are posited. An abandoned settlement may now be indicated by an upstanding monument such as an early Saxon church, a high cross or a runic stele (upright pillar). A trial excavation may determine whether peasant houses clustered close around the monument or stood at a respectful distance. Place-name elements suggest where a village might originally have been established, for example, *bourne* directs the fieldworker's attention to the banks of a seasonal stream rather than to the bogs and crags. The researcher then locates the actual site through field-walking, aerial photographs and trial excavation. A reliable supply of wholesome drinking water was essential, so settlements ranged along spring lines.

Towns

Romano-British town life continued following the withdrawal of the legions. Wroxeter and Verulamium (near St Albans) were still occupied about 450; Silchester until the sixth century; Carlisle into the seventh. Archaeologists suggest that towns were drastically affected by plagues in 443 and 540. The English appreciated cities as centres of trade and government: Canterbury for the Kentish men, Dorchester on Thames for the West Saxons, Winchester for the emergent kingdom of Wessex. During the seventh century the residences of English or native rulers within agricultural estates were occasionally dignified with more typically urban features, such as a minster, a mill, a cemetery, a granary or craft workshops. Winchcombe in Gloucestershire thus developed at the centre of the Roman and English estate of Wycomb. Town planners generally chose ridges of dry ground protected by streams and low-lying boggy land, as at the port (market town) of Wilton, Wiltshire, where the landowner's hall dominated a public market place with a cluster of houses stretching out to the marshy margins. Ports dealing in both foreign and domestic trade, typically containing the element *wic*, were founded on coastal and estuary sites where each lay under the protection of a magnate in a larger town, who controlled and taxed commerce, for example Ipswich under royal Rendlesham and Dunwich under Blythburgh. Hamwic (Southampton) was established by King Ine (686-726) as a seaport for Winchester. Lundenwic, adjoining Roman Londinium, attracted merchants from the coasts of Europe as well as Britain. Industrial centres also received seigneurial sponsorship, for example the Cheshire towns of Middlewich and Nantwich and the potteries of Ipswich. Settlements in Kent, Wessex and Mercia were also fortified, Canterbury as early as 754, perhaps to meet the threat of hostile invaders, and Hereford, the 'army's ford' on the Wye, around 790 for the Mercians against the Welsh. Churches such as that at Lichfield (669) attracted religious communities within the precinct, as well as shopkeepers and farmers in the surrounding lanes.

Houses

Traditional British houses, snugly adapted to the dank climate, were generally circular, some 20 to 50 feet (6 to 15 metres) in diameter, marked as 'hut circles' on Ordnance Survey maps and still evident from high ground and air photographs.

Houses were centrally heated by an open fire on a stone hearth. In timber regions the roundhouse comprised a ring of posts embedded firmly in the ground, supporting walls of wattle and daub and a conical thatched roof. In highland regions stone and turf walls, stone benches and beds, a clay oven and clay loom weights are usual, though internal partitions are not as evident. Straw and rushes, recognised archaeologically, served a sanitary function where half-naked children, senile elders and a miscellany of animals shared the communal space. A cropmark indicates the infilled gutters round the house. A stone habitation with an inner ring of free standing piers supporting the roof is known as an aisled roundhouse while a wheelhouse has piers radiating from the wall. Miniature (7 to 18 feet, 2 to 6 metres) roundhouses are popularly described as beehive huts because their drystone walls corbel inwards to form the roof in prehistoric-tomb style. Huts stood singly or chummily interconnected in warrens within cashels or monasteries. Underground chambers and passages known as souterrains, weems, fogous or earth houses lie beneath dwellings of chiefs, elders or priests. Passages are lined with timber or flagstones and may have served for ritual or storage, or as bolt-holes and hiding places. Collapsed and infilled souterrains appear in air photographs as cropmarks shaped like elongated tear drops.

Rectangular dwellings in continental or Roman style have been recognised in areas of Celtic settlement, though this shape is also an indicator of Anglo-Saxon presence. The houses of these newcomers comprised one rectangular room, usually known to historians as a hall, where the whole family ate and slept. Post-hole evidence suggests that timber-framed houses were made of oak posts and beams slotted and pegged together. Wall panels were of wattle and daub. Roofs were covered with thatch or wooden shingles. Halls sometimes had walls of planks or beams set palisade-wise in continuous foundation trenches. In cruck-framed halls the main structural members were curving timbers (crucks), erected tent-wise, pegged at the apex and linked with a cross-member as an A-frame.

A hall-house was sometimes built on a low raised platform, perhaps representing the general refuse and debris of generations of habitation and rebuilding. This may reflect the stable lifestyle of the immigrants and their regulated method of property transfer and inheritance. House platforms and the cropmarks and soil marks of hearths and the post-holes of the principal timbers appear on aerial photographs. Buildings close to the hall-house may be interpreted as stores, workshops or granaries. Sunken-featured buildings (SFB), once known as *Grubenhäuser* ('pit houses'), consisted of a pit dug into the soil lined with wattle or planks, with vertical posts supporting a thatched roof. One use of SFB was possibly as a weaver's workshop because hundreds of loom weights have been found on sites. Early Viking dwellings, bow-sided in plan, might be occupied as longhouses, where the family dwelt around the hearth at one end while the best beasts were stalled in the unheated end. Family and beasts entered by the same doorway.

Commerce and industry

Mercantile enterprise was facilitated by the issue of coinage, initially imitating Roman and Merovingian (Gaulish) prototypes, subsequently standardised as a silver penny. Moneyers were at work in London and Mercia before 650. Coins typically portrayed an image of the monarch and the name of his moneyer: Abbon at Exeter, Ragnald at Iorvík (York). The historian can identify and date coins from C. F. Keary's *A Catalogue of English Coins in the British Museum* (1887) and its continuation with H. A. Grueber (1893), as well as J. J. North's *English Hammered Coinage* (Spink, 1960-3).

A coin of Offa, king of Mercia 757-96.

An English brooch of about AD 450, inscribed on the reverse 'WODÆN gives this to the lady WINIWONÆW'.

Goods were transmitted as gifts, as bride price and for money. Livestock, hides, salt, metals, grain and illuminated manuscripts were exported to Europe in exchange for Gaulish wine, pottery, weaponry and jewellery. Salt was an important currency – an ingredient in industrial and indeed magical processes, as well as an essential for food preservation. It was produced on coastal sites and at accessible inland brine pits and was distributed as briquettes or packed in pottery vessels which may be found miles from their place of origin. Salt production enriched landowners in Worcestershire and Cheshire.

Manufactures were crafted from raw materials readily to hand. From stone were made spindle whorls, loom weights, saddle and rotary querns for grinding flour and meal. Earthenware bowls, jugs and vases were coarse and plain, though the landowner or cleric might afford glazed and decorated vessels. Iron vessels hung over house fires, bubbling with the staple gruel, broth or brose. Bone was fashioned into weaving combs, dress pins, beads and playing pieces or dice for board games played in the Celtic twilight. Village woodland supplied timber for furniture, tools, utensils, baskets and creels, while wickerwork lined grain storage pits. Water and milk were carried in stave-built buckets and hollowed-out tubs while ale was quaffed from lathe-turned bowls or hollow horns, mounted in silver.

Celtic power was based upon the mystery and mastery of metals. Ores were worked widely in Britain and Ireland, smelted close to the mine for distribution to manufacturing centres. Gold was panned from streams in Wales, Ireland and Scotland while silver was a by-product of lead extraction. Copper was mined in Cornwall and Wales and was transformed into bronze by alloying with Cornish tin and Mendip lead. Gold, silver and polished bronze were fashioned into weaponry, jewellery and other precious objects of conspicuous display, offered as gifts to buy a bride, reward a hero, bribe an enemy or overawe a neighbour, or consigned to bogs, pools and rivers as votive offerings to purchase success, avert disaster or appease the gods. The warriors, feasting from gleaming traditional bronze cauldrons, staggered under the weight of gold jewellery while horses displayed bronze harness trappings. Precious metal chalices, rings, altar pieces and bookbindings glorified the gods and invited the cupidity of marauding colonists. Prestige items for hunters and warriors, such as swords, spears, fighting axes, shield bosses, the single-edged scramasax (a knife), helmets and stirrups were embellished with enamel, gold and silver, perhaps endowed with magical power by means of runic inscription. Wealthy warriors and their wives wore rune-inscribed filigree, engraved and enamelled brooches, later to become evidence for archaeological typologies and chronologies. Women wore festoons of gold, glass and amber, finger rings engraved with the owner's or maker's name, bangles of gold and glass, and, for high-born ladies, jewelled girdles jangling with symbols of rank.

Iron was worked on an industrial scale in the Weald of Sussex and Kent, the Forest of Dean and County Durham. Extraction in the Weald was by opencast pit. The ore was roasted in a trench or circular furnace to slag off impurities and produce a bloom of iron for further refining by heating and hammering. Ruined furnaces and slag heaps, as well as the gentle gradients of cart or packhorse ways and field names, are evidence for the location of the industry, for instance in Gloucestershire around

Cinderford, Coleford and Coalway. As a substitute for coinage iron was carried in the form of ingots to village smiths, whose manly strength implied the favour of the god Wayland. Museums preserve a range of agricultural tools of this period, such as billhooks, saws, knives, chisels, axes, adzes, hammers, sickles and ploughshares.

Paganism

Communities throughout Britain and Ireland honoured pagan deities, observing rituals and frequenting cult sites, whose origins may be sought far back in prehistory. The Isle of Wight in the south and Pictland in the north remained faithful to paganism even when Christian devotion was established elsewhere. Religion and politics intermingled in such centres as Tara, County Meath, where a neolithic stone was associated with the acclamation of Irish rulers. Neolithic and Bronze Age people also venerated the hill enclosure at Emain Macha just outside Armagh. Both place-names may be interpreted as 'hill of Macha', legendary queen and goddess. Here was established the northern Irish capital. Rulers organised feasting for the knights of the Red Branch and displayed the severed heads of enemies in what some archaeologists describe as a communal roundhouse some 130 feet (40 metres) across supported on a central timber originating perhaps as a ritual maypole. Here Cú Chulainn, 'the hound of Culan', defended Ulster against the armies of Ireland led by Queen Medb of Connacht as told in the tale of the *Cattle Raid of Cooley (Táin Bó Cúailgne).* At nearby King's Stables in an artificial pool were deposited sacrificial stag antlers and hounds. The facial part of the skull of a youth was also recovered, cut from the discarded skeleton. At the rath of Tulloghoge rulers of Tyrone were seated on the four stones of *leac na rí,* 'king's chair', in a ritual that continued until the downfall of the Uí Néill in 1602. At the base of the wheel-headed cross of Kildalton, Islay, in one of four hollows, there is a mushroom-shaped cobble which devotees turn three times for luck. Legend has it that this action recalls some prehistoric small-stone cult. In Glencolumbkille, Donegal, pilgrims walk barefoot every June around prehistoric and Christian monuments. The devout formerly paused at one cairn to handle three cobbles, but two have gone missing and are perhaps now mere souvenirs – meaningless when separated from context. Like the cobbles, heritage is often unguarded and thus fragile, totally lost if the historian has not promptly acted to record and protect it.

Sagas, chronicles, annals and field-walking suggest sites of Celtic pagan observance, usually clearly Christianised now with slabs of stone marked with a cross. The place-name *nemeton* indicated 'sacred ground', and *anait* refers to a 'holy place', typically enclosed with a rectangular bank-and-ditch earthwork. An 'oak grove',

doire (derry), and an 'ancient tree', *bile* (ville), associate a ritual place with the druid priesthood. The mother-goddess Anu, a deity of uncompromising sexuality, is recalled in the buxom Paps of Anu hills in Kerry. The Anu cult ultimately merged with reverence for St Anne, the supposed mother of the Virgin Mary who assumed Anu's sexual power. At Carshalton, Surrey, the cult received a further accretion of confusion by association with the spirit of Anne Boleyn! Pagans and Christians reverenced wells, springs and pools. The Celtic goddess Brigid and St Bridget of Kildare were associated with waters granting fertility to the impotent and barren. Wells at Struell, County Down, and Llandrindod, Radnorshire, eased ocular ailments. At Llandeilo Llwydarth, Pembrokeshire, pilgrims still drink healing water from a skull now said to be that of St Teilo. At St Curetan's

A statue of a pagan Celtic deity, perhaps Macha, found at Armagh.

During the annual 'turas' (pilgrimage) at Glencolumbkille, County Donegal, on St Columba's Day (9th June) pilgrims process barefoot around fifteen sites not yet sanitised for the purposes of heritage and tourism.

well, Ross, people bathe diseased or impotent parts with strips of cloth which then festoon the grove's trees and barbed wire fences, having, it is hoped, absorbed the sufferers' ailments. Water sprites and Christian saints are honoured when wells are dressed with flowers, and who can resist the call to drop a coin in a fountain? This compulsion may account for hoards of precious objects, and sacrificed bodies, consigned to earth and water.

At Kildare cathedral, tucked under the rim of a medieval bishop's stone tomb, is a carving of a saucy pagan sheelah-na-gig sprite, erotically symbolising an earthy motherly spirit of Celtic religion whose supposed power persisted into the Middle Ages. Stonemasons put her on a wall of Killinaboy chapel, County Clare; among the bishops of White Island, County Fermanagh; and on a corbel on Kilpeck church, Herefordshire. Carvings of bug-eyed human faces, derived from the Celtic warrior cult of the severed head (*tête coupée*) appear on corbel-tables, capitals and roof bosses throughout the British Isles, most famously at Bakewell, contrasting with the cheery cheeky representations of village people beloved of medieval sculptors. The pagan Anglo-Saxon image of Jack-in-the-green, a human face wreathed in foliage which grows from his gaping mouth and beard, peers from the roof bosses and capitals of many English churches. The nature cult that he represents was particularly popular, deeply rooted in the parochial psyche, and masons have felt compelled to use the image even into Victorian times. Other preternatural and fabulous creatures may, in myth and folk tale, still haunt particular communities, inhabiting the landscape of place-names with *puca* (puck); *hob*, 'goblin'; *dwerg*, 'dwarf'; *thyrs*, 'giant'; or *scucca*, 'sprite'. These elements have been corrupted over the centuries, though the relevant county volumes of the English Place-name Society help to clarify obscurities.

The English and the Vikings shared a belief in a heaven (Valhalla) inhabited by gods and heroic warriors. The names of the principal gods may be familiar because they were adopted for the days of the week: Tiw (Tuesday), Odin/Wotan (Wednesday), Thor (Thursday), Frig (Friday). The cult of the fertility goddess Oestre was so firmly embedded in the popular mind that her name was adopted for the Christian festival of rebirth, Easter. Sites of worship may be identified through place-names.

(Left) At St Gwenfaen's Well, Anglesey, a pebble of white quartzite deposited in the waters is said to cure madness. A belief in the magic of quartzite dates back to the builders of neolithic tombs more than five millennia ago.

(Below) St Curetan's Well, Ross-shire.

73

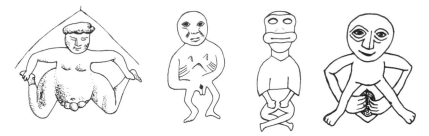

Depictions of sheelah-na-gig sprites, from (left to right) Killinaboy chapel, County Clare; a bishop's tomb in Kildare Cathedral; White Island, County Fermanagh; Kilpeck church, Herefordshire.

Tiw was honoured at Tuesley, Thor at Thunderfield. The cult of Wotan was presumably important at Wednesbury; also at Grimthorpe, bearing his nickname Grim, though this was generally an ordinary personal name used without cultic implications. Old English *hearg*, 'sacred grove', is preserved in sites named Harrow. The place-name Stockton refers to a stump (*stocc*), a coarsely shaped human figure or a phallic object cut from a tree-stump or branch, set up in the open air as a religious focus for a pagan English township. Trees were believed to possess magical properties and might be objects of devotion, so churchyard yews could even have been seeded from parent trees planted for pagan rites a millennium before.

Pagan Celtic burial sites may be inferred from documentary sources and place-names or revealed by archaeology, aerial survey, peat cutting, forestry or building works. Because bodies could be interred with their clothing, jewellery, weapons and food in pottery containers, the investigation of skeletons, clothing and grave-goods provides information on people's age, height, ailments, personal possessions, status, religious customs and cause of death. Celtic graves might be marked with a

The twelfth-century arch from the west doorway of Dysert O'Dea church, County Clare (reassembled in the south wall around 1683), exhibits Norman masks and monsters and a pagan/Celtic cult head.

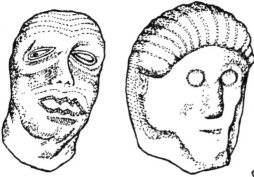

(Left) Pagan Celtic cult heads unearthed during building work at Armagh Church of Ireland cathedral.

(Right) The pagan image of the green man, from a fifteenth-century roof boss in St Andrew's church, South Tawton, Devon.

mound of earth (barrow) or stones (cairn), indicated by the Ordnance Survey with the word 'tumulus'. Aerial surveys occasionally identify whole fields of ploughed-out burial mounds. The challenge is to find the remainder of the population or to suggest on the basis of archaeological evidence how the dead might have been disposed of, whether by exposure to the elements or by cremation and the scattering of ashes, perhaps in sacred running waters, accompanied by gifts of gold and weapons to placate the deities of the stream.

The pagan English preferred the cremation practices of their continental ancestors, the burned bone being buried in narrow-necked globular pottery jars, though eventually the practice of inhumation with grave-goods was accepted in cemeteries associated with sites bearing early place-names such as Mucking in Essex. Thousands of cemeteries have been recorded across England, with a significant number of additional sites in Wales and southern Scotland, as reported in such journals as *Medieval Archaeology* and the annotated list in A. L. S. Meaney's *A Gazetteer of Early Anglo-Saxon Burial Sites* (Allen & Unwin, 1964). At such sites as Finglesham and Updown in Kent, wealthier graves are readily identifiable by the cropmark of an encircling barrow ditch. Humbler burials – the body lying extended in a shroud, cist or wooden coffin – are indicated by simple rectangular cropmarks with perhaps a post-hole for a marker post which stood as a memorial and a focus for mourners. Graves were sometimes covered with a small timber shrine, whose footings may be archaeologically identified. At the royal site of Sutton Hoo the mixture of grave-goods indicates pagan and Christian influences on the daily lives of the wealthy aristocracy. Warrior chiefs were interred with household goods and symbols of power, perhaps under towering mounds, as for Taeppa of Buckinghamshire, honourably interred beneath Taplow barrow. Horses with harness are found in rich burials as at Sedgeford, Norfolk, where the excavation project in 1997 involved primary school pupils, postgraduates and the interested public.

Christianity

Christian worship in certain localities may date from the Roman era, particularly the fourth century when centres of observance were towns and villas. Christianity was carried beyond the borders of the Roman province by merchants and missionaries who travelled in Pictland and across the sea to Ireland.

A principal agent of Roman Christianity was Nyna (Ninian), possibly the son of a British chieftain beyond Hadrian's Wall, who worked in the monastic outpost at Whithorn on the Solway Firth. The focus of the settlement was a chapel built in the Roman manner of stone, white mortared or plastered and so known as Candida Casa, 'the white house'. From this period churches were for the first time dedicated to saints whose relics were not actually preserved on site, and Whithorn was dedicated to St Martin of Tours, whose cult was promoted by Pope Symmachus (498-514). Archaeology puts a date after 500 on Ninian's foundation. The paths of missionaries northwards are traced by dedications to Ninian at Glasgow (from evidence in Jocelin's *Life of Kentigern*), Eccles near Stirling on the Roman road, the promontory fortress of Dunnottar and Arbilot, where a Pictish stone is carved with open books and equal-armed crosses. Ninian's successor, Donan, is commemorated in the place-name Kildonan, 'chapel or cell of Donan', across Scotland as far as the island of Eigg, where he met his death.

Ireland received Christianity from St Patrick and other Romano-British missionaries and from Gaulish evangelists inspired by St Martin of Tours. At Armagh, Patrick buried the pagan idol that had previously commanded the hilltop shrine; a series of idols excavated there is now preserved, though not displayed, within the cathedral. Presumably anathematised idols are buried on Christian sites elsewhere. From the fifth century onwards, Irish (Gaelic) missionaries reintroduced Christianity to Britain, travelling the western sea lanes to found religious settlements, as charted in annals, saints' lives, place-names and church dedications to Maolrubha, Finnan, Ernan, Fillan and Machar. Missionary presence is marked by hoards of gold and silver, as on Ninian's Isle, Shetland, and by sheet bronze or iron handbells, such as the corroded *coronach*, 'dirge' bell, which perches on a window sill at Birnie church, Moray. Travelling preachers erected *leachts* (open-air shrines and altars), such as the jumbled stones of 'St Patrick's Chair', Isle of Man; they religiously ground medicinal herbs and mixed magic potions in *bullauns* (cup-shaped hollows

in rocks still revered in folk tradition); and they reworked prehistoric megaliths into crosses and added the wheel-headed Christian symbol to Pictish symbol stones. Cybi was a typical missionary. Born in Cornwall in the sixth century, he travelled in Ireland before a quarrel among the religious brethren forced his withdrawal to a fortress, now lonely but then a place of power and population. On the Lleyn peninsula in Wales Cybi founded a monastic settlement at Llangybi, site of one of the most elaborate and popular healing wells (Ffynnon Gybi). Irish missionaries evangelised the English in Kent and East Anglia. In Northumbria the island monastery of Lindisfarne was founded by the Irish in 635. Cedd, first bishop of the East Saxons, had been trained in the Irish tradition and

At Thursley, Surrey, is the grove (ley) dedicated to the Saxon god Thunor (or Thor), whose hammer was responsible for thunder.

At Fishbourne, Sussex, a pagan English immigrant burial was found in the ruins of the royal palace of the ancient British king Cogidubnus.

planted his minster in the Celtic manner on a deserted site within the ruins of Roman Ythancaestir (Bradwell on Sea, Essex). Maeldubh, an Irishman from Scotland, established the church, named after him, of Maldulfesburg (Malmesbury) in 650.

Southern Britain was evangelised by missionaries from Rome who campaigned against the powerful but unorthodox Celtic church. Clerics associated in legend, tradition and documentary sources with St Augustine of Canterbury and his successors Laurentius and Mellitus were installed as bishops in minsters or cathedrals, generally in Roman towns. Bishops exercised authority in former imperial administrative centres, now the chief towns of the English kingdoms, including Canterbury with its bishopric established under Augustine in 597, London (601), Lincoln (627) and Leicester (737). The close political and geographical association of bishop and king was a particular feature of the English church and undoubtedly influenced the pace of conversion.

In Pictland Roman missionaries encouraged King Nechtan (flourished 706-29) to expel the Celtic clergy and put his kingdom under the protection of the Pope in Rome in 717. Nechtan sponsored the work at nearby Rosemarkie of a native Pict, educated at Bangor in Ulster, named Curetan, notable locally for his Christianising of pagan cult sites, especially the rectangular earthen embanked enclosures known as *cladh*.

Place-name elements associated with personal names assist in tracing Christian origins. Landulph, Cornwall, contains the British element *lan* ([church] enclosure) and the patron saint Dylyk, while Killaloe, County Clare, has the Gaelic *cill* and St Dalua. Elements of Celtic origin include *aireagal*, 'oratory'; *ceall, cill, kil*, 'hermit's cell'; *clas*, 'monastic community'; *díseart*, 'hermitage'; *donagh*, 'church'; *eclés*, 'church'; *lan*, 'enclosure, church'; *mainistir*, 'monastery'; *merthyr*, 'martyr's grave'; *teampull*, 'church'; *ysbyty*, 'hospice'. Sites of English Christianity are associated with the element *stow*, 'place' or 'special place' of political or religious importance, as in Padstow, Cornwall, meaning 'St Petroc's holy place', and Plemstall, Cheshire, meaning 'Plegmund's hermitage'. Other elements are *rod,* 'holy cross' or 'crucifix'; *bed-hus* (Welsh *betws*), 'house of prayer'; *ecles* (from Latin *ecclesia*), 'church'; *kirk* (Old English *cirice*, from Greek meaning 'house of the lord'). Names and customs

(Above left) A pagan Celtic deity excavated at Armagh Cathedral.

(Above right) A pagan Celtic idol from Tanderagee, County Armagh, sometimes identified as the chieftain Nuadha of the Silver Hand.

associated with holy wells link prehistoric water cults, fertility rites, Christian baptism and church origins. St Non's wells in Brittany, Cornwall and Wales are often in overgrown ditches or muddy fields, though marked by the Ordnance Survey. Non is legendarily the mother of St Dewi (David), and wells adjoin St David sites: for instance Altarnun, Non's burial place, is situated close to Davidstow. Non sites require careful investigation, for St Nunet of the Cornish parish of Pelynt, site of St Nun's well, was in the fifteenth century honoured as a male saint. St Non's chapel and well on the cliffs of Pembrokeshire, near the former monastery of St Davids, may commemorate Dewi's male companion Nonna.

The date at which varieties of Christianity were planted in the locality may be suggested by the style of surviving crosses. Where the Ordnance Survey marks a 'cross' or 'cross-slab', archaeologists and aerial photographers may discover the outline of a walled monastic enclosure with chapel, burial ground, clerical dwellings, garden, midden and arable plots. A simple cross may be incised on a prehistoric megalith or the wall of a cave, presumably a hermit's cell, perhaps originally a pagan cult site. A cross could be carved as a landmark out of a standing stone, as in the case of Fat Betsy on Danby Moor in Yorkshire. The sign of the cross was incised on memorial tablets, for example with alpha and omega signs for the woman Hildithruth at the monastic village of Hartlepool about 679, or embellished with vine scroll, interlace, bosses and biblical pictorial panels. At Wolverhampton the Danes' cross borrowed for its shaft a column from Roman Wroxeter.

A carved stone cross was a central feature of a monastic enclosure. The typical wheel-headed Celtic cross was topped with a stone shrine, perhaps originally containing a holy relic, in the shape of an actual oratory or chapel. Crosses were carved with interlace patterns, birds, beasts and monsters. Biblical episodes interpreted in the native style include Jesus in a kilt at Dysert O'Dea, County Clare, and the apostles with the moon faces of cultic heads at Moone, County Kildare. Memorial stones were written in ogham and Irish script, often with the Celtic

At Clonmacnois, County Offaly, the monastic site is protected by a soaring round tower and a high cross.

formula '*OR DO*...', 'say a prayer for...'

Pagan mythology powerfully affected Christian art. The Gosforth cross, Cumbria, is carved with the image of Thor and the world serpent from Norse myth. At Kirk Andreas on the Isle of Man Christian imagery accompanies a carving of Odin devoured by the wolf Frenir at Ragnarok, the Norse doomsday. The latest Pictish symbol stones (known as class III: rectangular slabs carved in high relief) incorporate Christian crosses, Pictish people and ogham writing in Latin rather than Pictish.

From the seventh century onwards English magnates founded minsters or colleges where communities of religious men and women with servants and followers might live apart from the world (Greek *monasterion*, 'to live alone'). A minster enclosure was protected with a wall or earthwork, whose original line may be traced in modern property boundaries adjacent to a minster. Within the wall was a busy township comprising a principal church, several smaller chapels, houses for the clergy, workshops, a writing room (*scriptorium*), a hospital or hostel, as accommodation for visitors, an infirmary for the sick, barns, byres, latrines, middens and high-standing crosses, whose sculptural style may indicate a date and the cultural background of the community. Male and female communities were founded on an island in the fens at Ely under the royal patronage of Æelðry or Audrey, the twice-married daughter of Anna, king of East Anglia, following separation from her husband, the king of Northumbria, in 672. Bede recounts that Audrey as a young woman loved to wear gaudy necklaces. She died from a throat tumour which she felt was a punishment for her vanity. In her honour the first Norman bishop of Ely established an annual fair, famous for St Audrey laces, plain but showy for the delight of country wenches, hence the derivation of the word *tawdry*. Another royal princess, Cuthberga, a sister of King Ine of Wessex, relinquished a dynastic marriage in favour of education in the mixed-sex community at Barking, Essex, whence she established her own house at Wimborne, eventually with chapels dedicated to St Cuthberga throughout Dorset and Hampshire. Minster priests served a broad territory, coextensive, perhaps, with a secular lordship or region. The minster of Budworth administered some 39,000 acres (16,000 hectares) of central Cheshire, whose thirty-five villages eventually became subject to ordinary parochial government. Priests established crosses and chapels in outlying communities where Masses were sung and converts christened. Smaller medieval parishes may have had as their basis a minster chapelry that remained dependent upon the mother minster and gained full parochial status only in modern times, as evidenced by church archives, township boundaries, field-walking, the style of a carved cross, the absence of a burial ground or a dedication to a saint associated with the mother minster. Landowners established proprietorial or seignorial chapels to serve communities of peasant villagers through a minster's peripatetic priest, who may have provided assistance in estate administration. The chapel usually stood within the enclosure of the chief house. Boundaries of parishes formed from such proprietorial chapelries conform closely to the bounds of the estate as described in charters. In the Isle of Man each secular land division (*treen*) of this era can be associated with a chapel (*keill*).

Churches were generally simple rectangular halls of stone or timber to accommodate only a small proportion of the populace, since attendance was not encouraged except at festivals and fee-earning rites such as baptism. Masonry walls might include squared stones and slim red bricks from nearby Roman ruins. Stones were laid in decorative herringbone courses. Windows were arched with brick in classical style, while the crypt stored relics, treasure and manuscripts. Foundations survive only in special cases, as at Stone by Faversham in Kent, originating as a solid Roman masonry mausoleum. Generally only fragments of walling, incorporated into a later building, are visible to give a clue of an early religious edifice. Churches were founded on sites of political power and pagan observance, sometimes indicated even today by a linear earthwork, henge, symbol stone or standing stone. A circular churchyard enclosed with stout walls (Welsh *lan*, 'enclosure') is typical. Standing stones lost their prehistoric erectile slant when stood up and reshaped into stumpy-armed crosses. Worshippers continued to hold hands through holes in the stone for fertility or to touch a hollow on the surface for luck.

Christians who withdrew from the world emulated the example of the desert hermits Paul and Anthony. Their cells, though known as *deserts*, as at Dysert O'Dea, County Clare, and Dyserth, Flintshire, were in a populous countryside, generally within walking distance of villages and supplies of water. A hermit was

British Christians founded Llanllieni (Leominster) chapel, Herefordshire. This was subsequently developed into a minster by the English. Downgraded by the Normans, the church in 1131 became a daughter house of the Cluniac abbey of Reading, noted for its patronage of the arts of sculpture and architecture. Leominster church offers a sampler of medieval ecclesiastical architecture, from stolid Romanesque to English Perpendicular.

Escomb church, County Durham, was constructed in the eighth century with stones from the Roman fort of Binchester.

generally content with a beehive-shaped hut to live in. For worship an oratory was built, as at Gallarus, County Kerry, where there is a corbelled tent-shaped drystone chapel, rectangular in plan, with a tiny round-headed east window and a flat-headed doorway beneath a large stone lintel. Each Celtic monastic community was a spiritual family under the direction of a *papa* ('father'), who was recorded in such

The oratory at Gallarus, County Kerry.

Skellig Michael, County Kerry.

place-names as Papa Westray, Orkney. The community might retreat from the world to an ascetic round of prayer and privation, perhaps to the middle of a bog, as at Lullymore, County Kildare, or to an uninhabited island such as Inishcleraun in Lough Ree, County Longford. The Irish missionary Columba chose Iona, an island off an island (Mull)! On the jagged rock of Skellig Michael, the ultimate desert, 7½ miles (12 km) west of the coast of Kerry, a dozen devotees founded a huddle of beehive huts on a precipitous terrace 600 feet (180 metres) above the Atlantic rollers. The monks subsisted on seabirds, fish and the gifts of seaborne pilgrims, beguiling the time chipping crude stone crosses from their airy rock.

Monasteries were also planted within the world of men. Clonard, County Meath, became a busy town, expanding outside its walls along streets clearly visible to aerial photography. Glendalough stood as a centre of culture and stability in the Wicklow territory of the Ó Broin and Ó Tuathail. In Wales the *clas*, an abbatial community, cooperated in the construction of a mother church for each administrative *cantref* (hundred) or *cwmwd* (commot). The *cwmwd* of Dinlaen on the Lleyn peninsula was particularly influenced by the unworldly monasticism of Leinster while at St Davids the *clas* actively strove for political and ecclesiastical authority as a cathedral for the whole of Dyfed. At Llanbadarn Fawr in Deheubarth, *clas* property descended in a family of married canons. When Gerald of Wales visited in 1188, the lay abbot Ednywain ap Gwaethfoed maintained an armed bodyguard and paid his sons as priests in the minster church. This not untypical establishment seemed scandalous to Gerald's sensibilities.

Within the encircling walls, a minster was a busy village of barns, beehive cells and guesthouses. Craftsmen applied traditional techniques to the production of gold and silver ritual vessels such as bowls and spoons for libation, chalices and patens for the Mass and reliquaries – for St Patrick's tooth at Killespugbrone and St Bridget's shoe at Loughrea. Jewelled bindings and shrines were wrought for illuminated texts whose laborious manufacture was itself an act of devotion. Oratories multiplied within the walls. Repositories for deceased monastic members were built as miniature oratories but were scarcely shoulder height at the ridge. At the skull house of Cooly, County Donegal, a doorway and window allowed devotees to reach inside and touch the saintly bones.

The Middle Ages
(865-1529)

The Middle Ages (medieval period) span seven centuries between the Dark Ages and the modern era, from the Scandinavian seizure of East Anglia, Northumbria and Mercia in 865 to Henry VIII's summoning of his reformation Parliament in 1529. For background reading, public libraries offer a selection of social and political histories, guides to fieldwork and aids to the location of landscape features. Medieval people themselves wrote prolifically about their own times, the events of previous centuries and the lives of contemporaries and of those long dead, as well as giving descriptions of places at home and abroad. Their books and documents were handwritten in a variety of book and business scripts using parchment, paper, quill and ink durable enough to resist everyday hazards, though not proof against fire, flood, rats or careless custodians. Thousands of these manuscripts are available for research, along with printed books produced from the later fifteenth century onwards. Churchmen, government clerks, lawyers, businessmen, landowners, travellers and poets communicated in Latin and a variety of vernacular languages. In about 1410, for a collection now known as the *Book of Fermoy*, a Roche family genealogist, historians, a priest and medical practitioners all wrote treatises in Erse, a product of that era when the Anglo-Norman conquerors of Ireland were determined to be more Irish than the Irish. On account of their value in monetary terms and for scholarship, such documents are now carefully preserved in national and academic libraries, public and county record offices, estate muniment rooms and cathedrals, where researchers gain access under strict supervision. The *Book of Ballymote*, another Irish language compilation of annals, legends and genealogies of around 1384-1406, was sold in 1522 by its owner at the high price of 140 milch cows.

Medieval people were subject to error and exaggeration when writing anything down, hence expert comment is worth seeking on the reliability and bias of the evidence. Fortunately important documents have been transcribed, translated and edited by scholars for publication and can thus be studied at public libraries. Catalogues of medieval documentary collections may also have been published or, if not, are available in public or county record office search rooms. Published editions are listed in the bibliographies of standard national and regional histories, in J. F. Kenney's *Sources for the Early History of Ireland* (New York, 1929) and in *Texts and Calendars,* for instance under *Chronicles and Memorials of Great Britain and Ireland during the Middle Ages*, issued from 1858 onwards by direction of the Master of the Rolls, and therefore known as the Rolls Series.

Historical writing took various forms. Norse sagas, such as *Harald's Saga*, *Orkneyingasaga, Eyrbyggja* and *Heimskringla*, are secular bloodthirsty adventures of warriors in specific localities. Popular annals were compiled year by year, concerning events known to the author or his or, more rarely, her informants and therefore as reliable as subjective writing can be. There were also chronicles narrating events in date order, notionally without political, religious or racial bias and requiring no literary style. There is no practical distinction between the two forms. Medieval histories can be partisan, inaccurate, selective in the choice of entries and idiosyncratic in comments on people and places, particularly when reliant on suspect oral and written sources. Churchmen were particularly prone to exaggeration about saintly miracles, the wickedness of Norsemen or the extent of their monastic estates, though some of the most detailed and useful regional sources were produced corporately and over generations at such religious houses as Margam, Dunstable, Tewkesbury, Bermondsey and St Edmund's Bury. The fourteenth-century Henry Knighton individually wrote his *Chronicle of St Mary of the Meadows House at Leicester* from 955. The *Anglo-Saxon Chronicle* was compiled annually by monks from around 880 until 1154, eventually at Abingdon, Canterbury, Peterborough, Winchester and Worcester, recounting religious and political events of interest to English readers, who were also an audience for Henry of Marlborough's *Chronicle of Ireland*, 1285-1421. The *Annals of Loch Cé* record Irish historical events for 1014-1590 and the *Annals of Ulster* for 431-1541, while the *Annals of Clonmacnoise* finish in 1408. The *Annals of the Four Masters* were compiled from the perspective of four scholars in Donegal, and the *Annals of Connacht* concentrate on that province for the period 1224-1562. Other historians of note include Orderic Vitalis, whose *Historia Ecclesiastica* continues to 1141; Simeon, a monk at Durham, writing with a particular northern perspective; the twelfth-century William of Malmesbury; the Londoner William Fitz Stephen, describing his native town about 1180; Ralph of Coggeshall; Walter of Coventry; Roger of Wendover; Matthew Paris; and Thomas Walsingham. Compilations by various authors were particularly popular in medieval centuries. The *Book of the O'Kellys* is a mixed bag of history, genealogy and religion written in Irish about 1360-1427 in the vicinity of the river Shannon, while *Leabhar Mór Leacain* from Lecan, County Sligo, of around 1418 incorporated Celtic historical texts and topographical writings from western Ireland.

Travel writing was popular, the best known example being Chaucer's *Canterbury Tales,* set along the pilgrim way from the Tabard Inn at Southwark to Thomas à Becket's shrine in Canterbury. The prologue vividly introduces everyday life in 1387. An earlier traveller with works still in print (Penguin, 1978, 1982) was Giraldus Cambrensis (Gerald of Wales), Archdeacon of Brecon and descendant of the family of Tewdwr and of Norman incomers who settled at Manorbier, Pembrokeshire. In 1183 and 1185-6 he visited his kinsfolk, the Fitzgeralds, in Ireland, and through *The Topography of Ireland* and *The Conquest of Ireland* in 1188 he brought the history, geography, customs and native religion of Ireland to the attention of a wide audience in Britain. In March 1188 Gerald set out from Hereford to help raise men and money in Wales for a crusade. His recruiting party travelled through Radnor and Brecon down to Newport. Gerald then rode around the coastal plain west and north, recording his travels in his *Journey through Wales* (1191) and *A Description of Wales* (1194). At Carmarthen Gerald noticed the Roman walls and princely Dinevor castle, one of only three royal castles in Wales. He described Merioneth as *horribilis*, noting it was a place where men fought with very long spears that penetrated even a cuirass of chain mail. On the northern border of Merioneth Gerald examined the recently constructed stone castles at Deudraeth and Carn Madryn before recounting what he had been told of the longevity of the monks on Bardsey Island. These were Celtic reformers or Culdees. Gerald paused in his travelogue to bring in stories from elsewhere, for example from Howden in the East Riding of Yorkshire. A prominent feature of the old church at Howden was the wooden tomb of St Osanna, a typical Dark Age royal saint, the sister of King Osred of Northumbria. Gerald recounted a tale already hoary with age. The story concerned the wife of a Howden priest. (Clerical concubinage, not unusual in the Dark Ages persisted, though a scandal, into Gerald's time, especially in the Celtic lands.) The Howden woman one day thoughtlessly sat down on Osanna's relics. The saint resented the imposition and the woman stuck fast. Even though she was stripped naked and beaten, her buttocks could not be detached from the woodwork. At last prayer and contrition prevailed and the virtuous saint released the trollop to live more circumspectly thereafter.

King Athelstan and St Cuthbert as depicted in a manuscript of Bede's 'Lives of St Cuthbert', c.934, in the library of Corpus Christi College, Cambridge.

Pictorial sources

Medieval manuscripts were occasionally illustrated. These artistic gems are the prized possessions of private or public libraries and museums. Microfilms, photographs or photocopies of illuminated manuscripts and pictorial sources of regional relevance may be assembled by a public library from originals scattered across the country or in Europe and America. Marginal sketches of ecclesiastical buildings in the cartulary of Lanercost Abbey in Cumbria (Cumbria Record Office MS DZ/1) are a valuable source for the architectural historian. Manuscripts relating ostensibly to one region may in fact originate from and depict a different place. Bede's *Lives of St Cuthbert* (Corpus Christi College, Cambridge, MS 183) was illuminated by an unnamed miniaturist in Wessex for King Athelstan to present to the keepers of the shrine of Cuthbert at Chester-le-Street, County Durham, in the summer of 934. Folio lb shows the king making his donation, humbly bowing to the saint, represented as a tenth-century tonsured priest. The figures stand within a stately edifice. The king is framed by columns supporting a soaring vault. Behind the saint is the coursed ashlar masonry of a church, a slender structure with aisles, clerestory windows and a roof of scale-like tiles. With all this in mind, the historian of Durham or Wessex may attempt to determine whether this image is a useful depiction of the tenth-century shrine or church of Cuthbert; an idealised epitome of English church architecture; or perhaps a stay-at-home southern artist's drawing of his own neighbourhood church at Winchester.

Liturgical manuscripts sometimes record secular activities. Psalters (books of psalms) and books of hours based on a chronology and calendar of devotion often contain decorated initials and marginal illustrations depicting ordinary folk and seasonal pursuits. The psalter made for Sir Geoffrey Luttrell of Irnham around 1340 portrays life on a Lincolnshire manor. The windmill on its motte-like mound is a sturdy post-mill with a tile or shingle roof, guarded by a large dog of fierce aspect and uncertain pedigree, perhaps an Irnham speciality. The watermill is powered by an overshot wheel. Few manors had the wealth to maintain two such elaborate engines. The artist chose to portray sheep folded in a hurdled enclosure for milking rather than being shorn or killed. The harvest is carried home in a two-wheeled iron-tyred Lincolnshire wain, drawn by three horses harnessed in line and driven by a wagoner wielding a long goad from a precarious perch on the shafts. The plough, pulled by four oxen, is drawn in sufficient detail to invite reconstruction and experiment. The Luttrell psalter is also a gallery of characters, including an elderly pinch-faced spinster, a cunning miller, willowy milkmaids colourfully apparelled and Sir Geoffrey's bald and bearded cook, John of Bridgford.

Mural art, stained glass and embroidered hangings made for churches, public buildings and homes are particularly revealing of the tastes and attitudes of the times of composition, though not always of the times depicted. Ecclesiastical frescoes of saints' lives and the day of judgement (doomsday) reflect the fashions of the day – martyrs may be clothed in contemporary dress, set in the artist's own landscape, even modelled on living parochial personalities. Walls and beds were hung with woollen rugs, enriched with embroidery or applied 'lace' braid, cheaper painted cloths and costly woven tapestries from Arras. These hangings are illustrated with scenes generally of regional interest, even if allegedly biblical or mythological. Most famous is the Bayeux Tapestry depicting the Norman Conquest, which illustrates a range of vaulted halls, masonry houses, tiled roofs, towering palaces and motte and bailey castles in Normandy and southern England, as well as ships, cavalry and infantrymen in chain mail and men and women in everyday costume.

King Edmund martyred by Norsemen, in a wall painting at Pickering, Yorkshire.

Medieval textile work can be studied in museums, churches or country houses.

National archives

The archives of national government prove how far the long arm of the monarch's central authority in London, Edinburgh and Dublin reached, through the sheriffs and clerks, into the farthest corners of the kingdom. The monarch needed control over taxation, the judicial system and military recruitment and therefore recorded particular places and people in appropriate detail. Records of the medieval state are preserved in the various national archive offices, though Irish records are sparse. The western isles of Scotland were acquired from Norway only in 1266 and administered from Edinburgh only from 1493 with the forfeiture of the lordship of the isles. Orkney and Shetland were annexed in 1472, earlier records belonging to the Norwegian crown and the feudal rulers. Welsh communities appear in English records from time to time, sometimes separately, but coverage is not comprehensive.

Among early national records in the British Library are the burghal hidages dating from about 890 onwards and recording each *burh* (defensible town) of Wessex. The principal early copy of 1029, destroyed in the Cotton House fire of 1731, may be read in a transcription dated 1562. The county hidage was compiled around 920 for the shiring and tax assessment of the English midlands. Each new shire or county focused upon a defensible town and was subdivided into hundreds (100 hides). The hidage changed periodically according to economic conditions. Northampton's was reduced from 3200 to 2663^1/2 hides in 942 and by the year 1086 was 1244 hides. Cheshire was rated at 1200 hides with twelve hundreds, including two on the eastern side of Offa's Dyke. By 1086 there were only minor changes, resulting from township decay, Wirral hundred being then rated at 97 hides.

Among the most detailed and oldest of the public records is *Domesday Book*, comprising two volumes (now rebound as five volumes) lodged in the Public Record Office. A third volume relating in detail to south-west England (known as Exon Domesday) is held in Exeter cathedral library. Domesday was a survey of English conquered territory ordered by William I at Christmas 1086 and completed by Michaelmas 1087. William required his commissioners to question parochial jurymen concerning landholding, economic and human resources, crown rights and taxation. A printed edition of the *Domesday Book*, in special record type, was prepared by Abraham Farley in 1783. The Exeter volume (Exon) was published in 1816. A photozincograph facsimile of the whole manuscript was published by the Ordnance Survey in 1864. In 1986 the local history publishers Phillimore produced an affordable new edition, arranged by counties, with a translation, a glossary, maps, references and an index. Alecto Historical Editions commemorated the nonocentenary with a magnificent facsimile, with a translation, maps, indexes and introductions. The researcher studying *Domesday Book* will find explanations of precise technical terms in the *Oxford English Dictionary*. The following is a translation of the entry for the royal manor of Marden, Herefordshire: to compare this with the original Latin see illustration on page 88.

The King holds MARDEN. King Edward held it. In that place many hides used to be, but a mere 2 of them are taxable. This land is divided among many people. The King has 3 ploughs in his main farm & 25 villeins, 5 bordars, 2 ploughmen, 4 bondsmen and 4 freedmen; among them they have 21 ploughs. A mill is there worth 20 s and 25 sticks of eels; woodland which returns 20 s. A fishery there is without dues; from the salt-works in [Droit]wich, 9 packloads of salt or 9 d; further, 8 servants of the King have 7 ploughs. William son of Norman holds 3 hides, less 1 virgate, of this manor & Norman Pigman holds ^{1}/2 hide of this manor & Earl William put 1 virgate outside this manor and gave it to a certain burgess of Hereford & Ansketel holds 40 acres, both open land and meadow, which King Edward's reeve leased to his relative. 3 riding men held William son of Norman's land; they could not be separated from this manor. 9 s comes from the produce of this manor's land. In the time of King Edward it paid £9 of blanched pence; now it is assessed at £16.

Domesday is a basic source for place-names, and the name Marden (Maurdine) recalls the English tribe Magonsaete, whose seat of power may have lain there. The Domesday commissioners reported that at Marden crown rights had been eroded by King Edward's reeve and by Earl William. At the time of the survey the manor was managed by two men named William (son of Norman) and Norman Pigman. Ordinary peasant husbandmen (villeins) were in a majority, with four other classes differentiated and a mention of 'servants of the King'. The population might be several hundred souls including women, children and servants, who are usually not counted in official records. The arable farming required 31 ploughs, and there was a a mill, a woodland and a fishery 'without dues'. The village had interests in the lucrative salt industry. Cash sums help in the comparison of communities: Marden's prosperity entailed an increase in tax to £16, paid as a bag of 3840 silver pennies.

The court of Exchequer, the financial arm of government, originated in England during the twelfth century and took its name from the departmental abacus of financial calculation, a chequered cloth upon which various counters, horseshoes and hobnails were moved to aid arithmetic. The Exchequer spread its net across the kingdom, accumulating charters, rentals, manor court rolls and extents (valuations). Clerks of the 'King's Remembrancer in Exchequer' also gathered documents relating, for instance, to the Channel Islands, stud farms, forests, mines in Cornwall and Devon and the lands of the Knights Templar. Sheriffs appeared before the lords and clerks of Exchequer to submit accounts of revenues of crown rents, profits of justice, forfeitures, feudal incidents (income), fines for encroachment on crown lands and trespasses in forests, treasure trove, aids and subsidies. Permanent records were written up on parchment rolls (pipe rolls), which have been published by the Pipe Roll Society. A second archival record was made by cutting notches on wooden tally sticks. When these obsolete records were eventually burned in 1834 the resulting conflagration also destroyed the Palace of Westminster and innumerable irreplaceable state archives. In Scotland royal revenues were sometimes transferred to burghs for a fixed annual payment. Aberdeen's burgh fee was established under Robert the Bruce's charter of 1319 at £213 6s 8d Scots, payable in sterling, which vastly increased the price! The crown granted away £100 Scots of the total, which

An entry in the Domesday Book for Marden (Maurdine).

An excerpt from the Exchequer 'Testa de Nevill' or 'Book of Fees', concerning thirteenth-century tenants-in-chief and their properties in Northamptonshire.

was eventually paid to the bedesmen of the Old Town Hospital as £8 6s 8d sterling (1s Scots was equal to 1d sterling) or £8.33 when finally redeemed on 16th January 1986.

The crown, always keen to maximise revenue, ensured that feudal rights were not allowed to lapse. Edward I, on his return from the crusades in 1274, ordered commissioners to inquire into crown rights across the kingdom. Evidence was collected in each borough and hundred (county division) in ink on parchment; the results were eventually published with indexes by the Record Commissioners in the *Hundred Rolls* (1812-18). A few extracts indicate the variety of information contained in these rolls. In Bideford, Devon, Richard Greville claimed the right to regulate the weight, measure and price of bread and ale, which he claimed had been enjoyed from time out of mind. The abbot of Thame constructed an embankment so that a waterway was diverted into the highway at Bettenale, Buckinghamshire. A royal official at Scarborough scattered oats in the castle ditch to attract the townsfolk's pigs and then extorted money for the stray swine he impounded. When royal justices were next despatched on circuit they were authorised under the Statute of Gloucester (1278) to inquire into crown rights and to demand that the lieges prove *par quel garaunt* (by what warrant) rights were enjoyed. Investigations of franchises are set out in *Placita de Quo Waranto* (Record Commission, 1818). For example, Ralph Basset of Weldon was summoned to Northampton on the Monday after the feast of All Saints in 1329 concerning his claim to have authority over frank-pledge (village peacekeeping), waif (right to abandoned property), the gallows, the punishment cart, the courts, manorial jurisdiction, suit for recovery of stolen goods, the collection of tribute and the right to amerce thieves in the manors of Pighteslee and Weldon. The crown's attorney, Richard Aldeburgh, knowing that only frank-pledge and waif had previously been claimed, stated ominously:

Datus est ei dies coram domino Rege de audiendo judicio.
A day is set when he shall hear judgement in the presence of the Lord King.

Taxation records are significant sources, provided that, as always, allowance is made for evasion, avoidance and deception. English records of scutage (military service), tallage (towns and royal demesnes), hidage and carucage (ordinary lands) begin during the twelfth century. From the next century subsidies were demanded as one tenth or one fifteenth of the value of movable goods owned by clerics and laymen in each community, as here in 1225:

Nicholaus filius petri habet vnam vaccam et valet. iiii. Solidos.
Nicholas Peterson owns one cow worth 4 shillings,
et vnam Iuuencam que valet. xviii. denarios. et unum equm et valet. iii. solidos.
and one heifer worth 18 pennies, and one horse worth 3 shillings,
et. i. modulum ordei. et valet. iii. denarios. et. i. busellum frumenti et ordei et valet. vii. denarios
and one small measure of barley worth 3 pennies, and one bushel of wheat and barley worth 7 pennies.
Summa. xva. vii. denarii et obolus
The sum total of one fifteenth of the above is 7 pennies and one halfpenny.
C. Johnson and H. Jenkinson, *English Court Hand* (Clarendon Press, 1915, plate XIIb)

After 1334 the levy became, in effect, a land tax, requiring a fixed sum from each parish and borough. Periodic reassessment from 1489 of tax income and movables proved unsuccessful, though lists of 1524-5 and 1543 are considered reliable enough. Poll taxes fixed a price on the head (poll) of individual inhabitants. That of 1377 (4d a head) caused disquiet, while 3 groats a head in 1380 conspired with social, economic and political factors to spark off the Peasants' Revolt.

Customs duties in England, levied on imports and exports at London and provincial ports, date from 1275, when Edward I targeted wool, fells (skins) and hides. Collectors' particular accounts, where surviving, name each vessel, its master and owner, the dates of arrival and sailing, the port of origin and the quantity, value and nature of the merchandise, with date and place of shipments. From 1279 there are summaries of total trade at each port with separate figures for wool and wine. Scottish duties were levied from the thirteenth century. To simplify procedures, trade in staples such as wool, hides and fish and the luxuries of wine and wax was supposedly limited to the royal burghs.

Chancery was the nation's civil service, the administrative and secretarial branch of government. The chancellor, as chief officer, used the king's great seal to authenticate documents. English charter rolls (1199-1516) are office copies of royal charters – documents granting lands, offices and privileges to corporations and individuals. Grants may be reiterated in confirmation rolls and the series of *cartae antiquae* (ancient charters). Patent rolls from 1201 contain copies of letters patent documents issued patent (open) for all to see, usually commencing with the words 'to all to whom these presents shall come', concerning land, office, privilege, church dignity, peerage, pension, pardon and royal revenue. 'Letters close' were issued folded, closed and sealed with the wax of the great seal, for opening only by the addressee, concerning such matters as subsidies, family settlements, pardons and the provisioning of royal castles. From the fourteenth century individuals and corporations submitted their own title deeds, charters, bonds and agreements to Chancery, where for a fee clerks would copy the documents on the dorse (back) of the close roll. These endorsements were an insurance against loss, damage or falsification of the originals in the days when houses were insubstantial and even castles were put to the torch through civil unrest. Fine rolls from 1199 detail payments to the crown for borough charters, grants of franchise (market, free warren, fair), pardons, privileges (such as the property of minors or wards) and matrimonial affairs (where property was involved).

Special commissions and inquisitions from about 1220 refer to towns, parks, manors, mills, forests, institutions and charities. Inquisitions *ad quod damnum* ('to what hurt') employed a jury to investigate grants infringing existing rights, especially markets and fairs. Inquisitions *post mortem* following the deaths of tenants-in-chief of the crown investigated, described, valued and drew up extents of the lands, ancestry, heirs, possessions and financial obligations of the leaders of society in the provinces. The heir paid a fee known as a relief to inherit. Those under age were made royal wards and the monarch controlled the affairs of the estate for the time being. An inquisition of 1516 concerned the decay of tillage, the creation of parks and pastures and the desertion of villages since 1488, associated with the growth of sheep farming. Information on this subject has been published in *The Domesday of Inclosures* (Historical Society of Great Britain, 1897, edited by I. S. Leadam). Chancery miscellanea include charters, manorial records, family pedigrees, coroners' inquests, surveys of crown rights in the Channel Islands from the thirteenth century, records of Jews in commerce under Edward I, inquisitions on Irish manors, castles and monasteries, perambulations of forests, notes on guilds under Richard II, captured Scottish documents and returns of lands in Wales. Scottish records in Edinburgh include registers and rolls of the great seal from about 1315. Chancery charters and writs for 1147-1889 are preserved in the Lord Advocate's archives.

Records of the autonomous palatinates of Durham, Lancaster and Chester, with Flintshire from the thirteenth century, include charters, cartularies, manor court rolls, financial accounts, testaments, rentals, leases, land surveys, coroners' inquisitions and inquisitions *post mortem*. Durham's archive, weeded and then rejected by the Public Record Office in 1912, was rescued through community pressure for its

69. **WILL'US DE WALTHAM CLERICUS ET ALII PRO ABB'E ET CONVENTU DE CROYLAND.**
London' unum messuag' et una shopa in venella Sancti Martini Magni in paroch' Sancte Anne infra Aldrichesgate - - } London'.

70. **WILL'US BOSOUN ET RICUS ALBON PRO PRIORE ET CONVENTU DE DUNSTAPLE.**
Dunstaple Luton et Flyttewyke } duo messuag' duo tofta et quatuor acre terr' -
Dunstaple Houghton Regis Sewell et Toturne } quatuor messuag' quatuor tofta 17 acre terr' et 10ˢ reddit' - } Bedford'.
Rokeston et Dunstaple } quedam tenementa et reddit' reman' ·eisdem Willo et Rico -

A catalogue entry (number 69) for an inquisition 'post mortem' for a house and shop in St Martin the Great's Lane, London, belonging to Crowland Abbey. Number 70 refers to Dunstable Priory's lands in Bedfordshire. The date of the original text was 1397-8.

preservation and is now in the public library at Gateshead. Records of the Duchy of Lancaster (which belongs to the Crown) relate to the honours of Bolingbroke, Clare, Leicester, Mandeville, Pontefract and Tutbury and the estates of the earldoms of Essex and Hereford, the Savoy in London and numerous other parishes in England and Wales.

Court records are obvious basic sources for the study of crime, punishment and civil disputes but are also directly or incidentally informative on individuals, occupations, property values, social concerns, beliefs, commerce, industry, place-names and similar matters of record. Even the weather on a specified day may have been subject to comment! Records of the central courts of common law in England commence before 1200. The court of the King's Bench heard cases affecting the king's peace: assault, murder, conspiracy, theft, trespass by force and arms and, by application of a legal fiction, personal actions such as ejectment from freehold property requiring the presence of those nonexistent but ubiquitous pleaders John Doe and Richard Roe. The court also preserved coroners' inquests concerning unnatural deaths and treasure trove. The court of Common Pleas determined civil suits over land and money. Evidential documents include final concords (fines) of 1182-1838 and recoveries of about 1472-1837, resulting from fictitious suits to establish property rights. In company with long-dead litigants, the researcher meets a range of officials such as 'secondaries', 'exigenters' and 'filazers', clerks of the king's silver and the fictitious essoiners Adam Doo and Adam Pye. As a court of law, the Exchequer heard cases concerning church tithes, royal revenue, debts to the crown and personal actions or ejectments. Court writs ran into Wales, the palatinates, the Channel Islands and Ireland. Chancery was also a common law court mainly concerned with family property and inheritance. Scottish central courts analogous to those in England functioned in the Middle Ages, though records are sparse. Acts of the Scottish legal lords of council commence in 1478.

The English crown commissioned judges to hold eyre (itinerant) courts in the shires from the twelfth century. The judges heard cases of murder, manslaughter, robbery, wounding and rape. From 1271 keepers of the peace travelled the country. Their gaol delivery rolls and files continue to 1476. From 1305 royal justices sat in shire courts of oyer (hearing) and terminer (deciding) on civil and criminal business. Professional assize ('sitting') judges travelled a fixed circuit from the thirteenth century, establishing the principal regional court for major trials. From around 1487 until 1700 coroners deposited notes of their inquests at the assizes. In Scotland

An extract from 'Ducatus Lancastriae: A Calendar to the Pleadings &c. in the Reigns of Hen. VII. Hen. VIII. Edw. VI. Queen Mary and Phil. & Mary', Record Commission, 1823.

Hen. VII.			Calendar to Pleadings.			117
No.	Reign.	Plaintiffs.	Defendants.	Premises, and Matters in Dispute.	Places.	Counties.
2.	N. D.	The Tenants and Inhabitants of Glatton and Holme.	Walter Coton, Parson of the Parish of Glatton and Holme.	Claim of Exemption from Tythes.	Glatton. Holme.	Huntingdonshire.
3.	2 Hen. 7.	Margaret Elys. *Et e contra.*	John Lewes.	Disputed Title to Lands.	Powes Land.	Wales.
4.	N. D.	Henry Goodwin.	Sir John Risley, Knight.	Tortious Possession of Lands.	Tottenham Manor.	Middlesex.
5.	8 Hen. 7.	The Tenants of Gretham.	The Tenants and Inhabitants of Bolingbroke.	Disputed Claim to Common of Pasture in the West Fenn.	Gretham. Bolyngbroke Soke.	Lincolnshire.
		H.				
1.	N. D.	William Haigh.	Roger Haigh and Sir Ralph Shirley, Knight, Steward.	Disputed Title to Lands and Tenements.	Biggyng. Duffeld Manor.	Derbyshire.
2.	N. D.	John Harrys.	The Abbot of Crowland.	Disturbance of Possession of a Farm, of Water, and Fishing and Fowling thereof.	Purfounte.	Lincolnshire.
3.	N. D.	Richard Higham, and Ann his Wife.	John Higham and others.	Disputed Title to Lands and Tenements.	Higham. Gayfeley. Cavenham. Baroo.	Suffolk.
4.	N. D.	The Tenants and Inhabitants of Higham Ferrers and Rushden.	Sir Thomas Cheny, Knight, and others.	Disputed Claim to Right of Fishery, and Destruction of Mill Dam at White Willugh.	Higham Ferrers Lordship. Rushden Lordship.	Northamptonshire.
5.	N. D.	The Tenants of the Wapentake of the High Peake.	King's Officers of the Toll.	Claim of Exemption from Toll.	Burgh and Chapell in the Frith.	Derbyshire.

In p̄ns of þe lordꝭ of confale Williaɱ mētetħ of þe kerß
Archibald of mētetħ his broß alex̄r mētetħ for thaī
ß kyn and frendꝭ oñ þe tapte / ꞇ robert broiß of
Artħ Alex̄r broiß lucas broiß robert broiß for þaī ß
brethir kyñ and frendꝭ oñ þe toßpte / Ar bundin and
oblift to ftand and abid / at the deliůance and ordi-
nance of thir lordꝭ vnd'writtin / tuiching þe making
all accioñs vnkyndnes ꞇ difpileſſore doñe be þe faid
of amēdꝭ for þe ꝼauchꞇ of vmquhile Johñe þe
Williã archibald alex̄r ꞇ ß frende to þe faid robert alex̄r lucas robert ß kin or frende
broiß-of-artħ ꞇ tuiching þe making of amite luf

This judgement of 28th January 1488/9 seeks to establish amity, love and tenderness in place of a blood feud between the Monteaths and the Bruces of Airth, Stirlingshire; from 'Acts of the Lords of Council in Civil Causes A.D. M.CCCC.LXXVIII. - M.CCCC.XCV.', Record Commission, 1839 (page 101).

justice eyres were also despatched to the provinces, though surviving court books under this system cover only the period 1493-1575. During the fourteenth century the chancellor in England formalised the procedure for hearing grievances by rules of equity and conscience, making it possible to initiate suits by simple and supposedly affordable petition in what was notionally a poor man's court. From about 1440 pleas (bills) were submitted in English rather than Latin or Norman French. Among miscellaneous business, Chancery dealt with coroners' inquests. Despite good intentions, Chancery became a byword for tardy and expensive justice.

Parliament

Medieval parliaments in England, Scotland and Ireland met irregularly, as circumstances required, to transact business that might affect the whole kingdom or relate to some particular region. The archives of the English parliament are publicly available at the House of Lords Record Office within the Victoria Tower of the Palace of Westminster and are described in M. F. Bond's *Guide to the Records of Parliament* (HMSO, 1971). Acts of Parliament refer to borough liberties; to powers and privileges in respect of trade, lands, harbours, monopolies or fishing; to charitable institutions, such as hospitals and almshouses (bedehouses); to bridges, roads, rights of passage and waterways; to trading standards, weights and measures and product quality; and to industry, for instance coal miners in the Forest of Dean and tin miners in Cornwall. Statute 3, chapter I, of 31, Edward III (1357) ordains that 'all the Ships called *Doggers* and *Lodeships*, pertaining to the Haven of *Blackney* ... shall deliver or discharge their Fish within the Haven of *Blackney* only, betwixt *Benord* and *Hogfleet*'. Chapter VI of 9, Henry VI (1430) ordains that 'the Burgesses of the Borough of *Dorchester* shall not be disturbed of their Right, to use their weighing by twelve Miles round the same Borough'. Parliamentary language was for a long time Norman French as in 3, Henry VI, chapter V (1424), regulating the river Lee, 'une des grandes rivers qi sextende de la ville de Ware jesqe al eawe de Thamise' ('one of the big rivers which stretches from the town of Ware to the river Thames') 'en les countes de Hertf' Essex' & Midd''; the document was 'pur surveier redresser & amender toutz les defautes en la dite eawe pur le passage des niefs & batelx' ('to survey, redress and amend all the defaults regarding the said river for the passage of ships and boats').

Acts of the English Parliament from 1235 are printed in volumes entitled *Statutes of the Realm*, also known as *Statutes at Large*, usually available in public libraries. Repealed and obsolete sections of medieval acts are often omitted from later editions. Each volume has a chronological list of acts. Further sources are the *Chronological Table of the Statutes* and the *Index to the Statutes in Force*.

The original rolls of acts of the medieval Irish parliaments were destroyed in 1922. A selection culled from various sources has been published, but unpublished acts can also be studied in private and ecclesiastical archives. Scottish acts were printed by the Record Commissioners in twelve lavish volumes, *The Acts of the Parliaments of Scotland* (1814-75), including charters, royal ordinances and miscellaneous writs from 1124. The Scottish Record Office holds original manuscript rolls, minutes and acts from 1293 onwards.

Town and county administration

Records of town and county administration are scarce until about 1400 and fragmentary even down to 1500. Space and cost limitations militated against the preservation of extensive series of minutes or deeds, and many were disposed of, particularly if faded or illegible. There were few burgesses' votes in archives: most old documents were destroyed in periodic flurries of 'weeding' and modernisation. London's muniments were better cared for than most; the compilation *Annales Londonienses* ('Annals of London') for 1194-1330 (Rolls Series, 1882) is evidence that access for research was possible.

The variety of town records: Elgin burgh charters of 1268 and 1396; an Act of Parliament of 1785; and the Guild of Hammermen's design for an iron cage for an executed murderer, 1810.

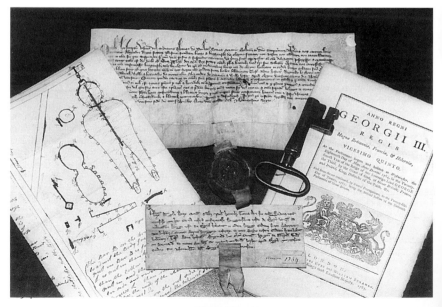

Borough foundations are evidenced by charters on parchment, granted perhaps as early as the twelfth century by the monarch or another sponsor to ensure the community's monopoly over trade within a broad hinterland and ownership of common-field arable, pasture and moorland for the common good. Charters permitted and protected annual fairs, weekly or more frequent markets, fisheries, mineral rights, peat cuttings, courts and the raising of rates. In his charter to Inverness of about 1179 William I promised to construct earthen embankments on which the burgesses would maintain a good palisade. Legal papers, petitions, correspondence and official reports provide glimpses of some daily problems and challenges of medieval urban living.

Borough courts of law and administration heard a range of cases, making new burgesses, measuring building feus (see below), fixing weights, measures and prices, repairing prisons, punishing crime, meting out capital punishment, and deciding commercial and neighbourly disputes among the townsfolk. There is often a concurrent set of records relating to the activities of representatives of the burgesses in council. Minute books set out decisions on community administration, public health, management of common lands, regulation of building works, sanitation, water supply, weights, measures and trading standards. Title deeds, perhaps collected in cartularies, refer to community property. Financial accounts relate to public buildings, market dues, official salaries, educational provision and public works. Rate books indicate the comparative value of houses and shops owned by named individuals.

Medieval people tended to rely on memory and sworn testimony in property disputes. Title was transferred by public ceremony in the presence of witnesses, involving tangible objects such as a handful of earth, a stone, a piece of wood, a handful of corn (tithes), or a mechanism from a mill. From the thirteenth century onwards people became accustomed to written evidence and developed means of keeping their parchments safe. One way of achieving this was by paying a lawyer or notary to copy title deeds into a record book known as a cartulary or to pay for a formalised statement or protocol to be written out in an official book. A borough court book was a safe place to record private business. Copies in public archives are more likely to survive than originals that were kept at home, so registers are worth locating for any study of people, property, enclosure, family settlements and business relationships.

Merchant burgesses associated together as a guild to protect their interests and to regulate trade. Archives are held by present-day successors of the guild merchant if not integrated with town council records. The guild charter is sometimes regarded as the founding deed of a borough. The charter of William the Lion about 1180 to

Punishment for a dishonest baker, from a marginal illustration in 'Assisa Panis' of 1266, concerned with the price and quality of bread in the city of London.

townsfolk along the shores of the Moray Firth provides evidence of Norman burghal organisation in Macbeth's former territory as early as David I's reign in 1124-53:

> *Burgensibus meis de Aberdeen. & Omnibus Burgensibus de Morauia. &*
> To my burgesses of Aberdeen and all my burgesses of Moray and
> *Omnibus Burgensibus meis ex aquilonali parte de Muneh manentibus*
> all my burgesses staying north of the Grampian Mountains
> *liberum ansum suum Tenendum ubi uoluerint. quando voluerint.*
> whose free guild should be held where and when they wish.
> *Ita libere ... sicut antecessores eorum tempore Regis Dauid ... habuerunt.*
> They should enjoy this as freely as their predecessors in the time of King David.
> Aberdeen City Archives, A1 1, charter of William I, about 1180

Incorporations to promote the interests of glovers, smiths, tailors, tanners, wrights and other craftsmen created registers of members and also of weights, measures, product quality, apprenticeship and indigent members.

Manorial muniments

A manor was a territory held in fee (feu), meaning that it was held conditionally, on the performance of some military, religious or financial service for a superior who in turn owed fealty to his lord, and so on upwards through the hierarchy to the monarch. The essence of the feudal land law was that every piece of land had a lord or lady; no individual could be a lord without holding land in fee. The practice of intermediate or *mesne* lordship (also known as subinfeudation) can only be investigated by reference to the archives of the particular manor as well as those of any superior lords. A royal manor did not have these complications, being held directly by the king or queen. A manor might consist of a single compact village or of scattered parcels of land where the lord carved out a demesne or home farm based on the manor house. Even the demesne was not necessarily a compact block of arable and pasture land but was intermingled with tenant holdings. A wealthy landowner usually owned several manors scattered across the country, visiting regularly to collect profits and consume the contents of barn and cask. The manor was the main agent of community administration in England and Wales until the seventeenth century, but manorial customary and copyhold tenures were not abolished legally until 1925. In Ireland and Scotland the barony was the unit created by incoming Norman settlers.

Manorial records narrating the history and ownership of the land may remain in the possession of the present landowner or the estate agent, if not deposited in a record office. Archives contain the *valor,* an indication of the worth of holdings; property rentals; terriers showing the location and extent of holdings; custumals setting down in writing the rights and duties of lord and tenants; and jury verdicts as precedents on matters of manorial administration. By the fourteenth century medieval landowners and their agents were beginning to write financial accounts; inventories of agricultural stock; specifications for estate improvement; and business correspondence, even family letters, examples of which have been published. The entertaining and informative letters of a Norfolk gentry family have been edited by J. Gardiner and published as *The Paston Letters* (1904). Other collections include the *Stonor Papers* from Oxfordshire (edited by C. L. Kingsford, 1919), the *Plumpton Correspondence* from Yorkshire (edited by T. Stapleton, 1839) and the *Cely Papers* from a family of merchants (edited by H. Ellis, 1824-46). Among the most numerous and informative of documents are various types of title deed, particularly charters. The usual conveyance transferring property from one person to another was written in Latin on parchment, authenticated with a wax seal and, from about 1280, dated. Published transcripts or summaries are usually available for collections publicly deposited. Deeds are a basic source for following parochial land transactions, revealing not merely the names but also the residence and status of sellers and purchasers, whether they were gentry, ecclesiatics, yeomen, lawyers, aristocracy, widowed heiresses or impoverished dowagers. Property owners were active in enclosing common fields, depopulating hamlets, building churches and manor houses, and introducing new agricultural methods. Historians contrast the open village, comprising a number of small landowners or even dozens of peasant proprietors, with the closed parish owned by one family. Title deeds provide a list of conditions of purchase, usually in a common form, but indicative of regional customs:

> *Reddendo Inde annuatim domino capitali de barton vnum denarium argenti*
> Giving hence annually to the chief lord of Barton one pennyweight of silver
> *et mihi et heredibus meis vnum clauum Gariofri ad festum assumptionis beate marie virginis*
> and to me and my heirs one clove of gillyflower at the feast of the assumption of Blessed Virgin Mary
> *concessi eidem cecilie homagium bermani de neuham & heredum suorum.*
> I have granted to the same Cecilia as her feudal servant the Porter of Newham and his heirs.
> Barnton Heritage Collection, charter of Roger, vicar of Eccles, to Cecilia of Eccles, his ward, about 1260.

Charters contain perambulations or guided tours of property boundaries, which are a means of learning about the landscape and economic activities of the area.

> *Incipiendo ad stockenford usque ad divisas ricardi le Rimur ... vsque pomarium ...*
> Beginning at the ford of logs, continuing as far as the bounds of Richard Rimmer's land ... to an orchard ...
> *ad quamdam quercum ... vsque ad magnum lacum qui descendit in milnebroc ... vsque in Caldebroc ...*
> to a certain oak tree ... as far as the great lake which leads into Mill Brook ... as far as Cold Brook ...
> *via regali iuxta fossatum quod se extendit uersus neuham*
> the king's highway adjoining the embankment and ditch which extends to Newham

Property was described without a map but with reference to adjoining owners, as here in an extract from a quitclaim of 10th April 1439, referring to a typical strip within the furlong (carucate) of a common field:

> *unam acram terre cum pertinenciis in carucat' de Eskyr in campo vocato mayneskyr.*
> one acre of land with appurtenances in Eskyr ploughgate in a field called Mayneskyr.
> *quequidem acra iacet in latitudine inter terram Iohannis lang ex parte orientali*
> This acre lies in breadth between John Lang's land on the east
> *& terram nuper Thome Alford ex parte occidentali*
> and the land lately Thomas Alford's on the west
> *extendit se uero in longitudine a terra dicti Thome Alford ex parte australi*
> extending in length from the said Thomas Alford's land on the south
> *usque terram Iohannis peickeston ex parte boriali.*
> as far as John Peickeston's land at the north
> National Library of Ireland, Sarsfield Vesey MSS, D3330, deed 2

Title deed bundles may contain a variety of documents such as final concords and recoveries to establish a proper written title in court. Feoffments to uses avoided feudal obligations because the legal owner supposedly held for the benefit or use of another. Marriage settlements protected property rights when estates merged in dynastic marriages. Entails ensured that the estate passed to specified heirs. Disputes over land, rents, crops and customary services created work for lawyers and thousands of documents for the modern topographer and genealogist. In 1510 Griffith, son of Meredith, son of David, made an arbitration award concerning the hay crop held by John, son of Griffith, son of Belyn, in *ywern vawr*, 'Big Meadow':

> *yn amod ir Res ap Iankyn ap ll' ap thomas adv gwair*
> on condition that Rhys Jenkinson Llywelyn Thomason relinquish the hay
> *ysydd yn ywern vawr yn llaw Iohn ap gruff ap belyn*
> which is in Big Meadow in the hand of John Griffiths Belyn

i Ieuan ac i yncharad derym vi bylynedd am ddyledion oedd ar Isabel Vz gruff ap Ieuan.
to Evan and Angharad for the term of six years for the debts of Isabel, daughter of
Griffith, son of Evan.
National Library of Wales, Coed Coch, Denbighshire, 573, arbitration

As with the boundary walks of the charter, a manorial extent or *extenta manerii*
(description of the manor) offered a word-picture of the manor and its customs,
valuations, tenants' rights or duties, boundaries, fields and commercial assets. The
modern historian supports archives with fieldwork, stepping out with a map and a
translation of the charter to trace the hedgerows, embankments, standing stones, old
thorn trees and tumuli – the types of landmark that may have served the Roman or
neolithic territory. Medieval maps, drawn mainly in the course of legal disputes, are
rare. Features are usually represented pictorially or as bird's-eye views rather than
as accurate ground plans. A useful guide for the historian is *Local Maps and Plans*

*The manorial extent of the lands of Llwyngwril, Merionethshire, 1419, from 'The
Record of Caernarvon', Record Commission, 1838 (page 272).*

---

272   EXTENTA COM' MERYONNETH'.

LLOYNGWRIL'.

In eadem Villa est vnū Wele terr libe Et sunt hered dei Wele Jeuᵃn ap
Gruff ap Mad dd ap Hoell ap Joż dd ap Jeuᵃn ap dd ap Eigñ lloid
Jonkus lloid ap Jeuᵃn ap Gruff & alii & dant inde Dño Princ quolibt
ʼtmino &c. ijˢ. viijᵈ.

Et oñes hered & tenent dei Wele debent Sect ad Hundr tantū pℓ Jeuᵃn
ap Gruff ap Mad qui debt Sect ad Coñi & Hundred Et debent Sect
ad Molendinū Dñi Pⁱncipℓ de Llanegryñ Et soluent xˢ. de Releū xˢ.
de Gobr & xˢ. de Amobr toc quoc acciderit Et est in eadem Villa
quedam pcella terr extent voc terr dd ap Kevynvryd & dat Dño Princ
p Annū   xxiijᵈ. ꝑut extenditʳ ab antiqū soluend ad festa Pasche
& Sēti Michis equalitᶜ

σ Smᵃ xjˢ. iijᵈ.

LLOYNGWRIL
In the same township there is one gwely [lord's allocation to one family] of free land. And the
inheritors of the said gwely [through a gravelkind subdivision known as *cyfran*] are: Evan son
of Gruff son of Madoc David son of Howell son of John David son of Evan son of David son
of Eignon Lloyd Jonkus Lloyd son of Evan son of Gruff and others. And they give thence to the
lord prince [of Wales] at each term etc. 2s 8d.

And all the inheritors and tenants of the said gwely owe customary service only at the hundred
court, except Evan son of Gruff son of Madoc who owes customary service at both the county
and hundred courts. And they must send their grain to the lord prince's mill at Llanegryn. And
they pay 10s as feudal relief; 10s as prize money payable by a girl's father to the lord on her
marriage; and 10s for a bondswoman's marriage or incontinence, as often as it shall fall due.
And there is in the same township a certain parcel of surveyed land known as David son of
Kevynvryd's land yielding annually to the lord prince 23d proportionately as it is surveyed
from old times to pay in two equal instalments at the feasts of Easter and St Michael.
Sum total 11s 3d

from Medieval England (Oxford University Press, 1967) edited by R. A. Skelton and P. D. A. Harvey, along with photocopies of maps accumulated and indexed in public libraries.

The lord or lady of the manor governed through a manorial court where such officials as reeves (administrators), constables, haywards, aletasters and beadles (court officers) were appointed. Disputes were decided, miscreants punished and communal regulations enforced by the lord's steward. The steward also carefully compiled and preserved various parchment rolls recording decisions reached in the manor court. The manorial lord exercised an authority that extended to many aspects of the villein's life. A manorial tenant, for instance, paid a fee for permission to reside outside the manor.

> *katerina filia Iohannis Kentyng' alias Candelman nuper vxor Iohannis Corte*
> Katherine daughter of John Kentyng, also known as Candelman, formerly wife of John Corte
> *de Stalham vidua est nativa domine de sanguine ...*
> of Stalham, widow, is a serf of the lady of the manor by blood...
> *que debet dare domine de cheuagio, vi d.*
> who owes the lady for permission to reside outwith the manor, 6 pennies.
> Norfolk Record Office, MSS 6020, 16 B 5, presentment, Antingham, 17th September 1438

The peasant relinquished his land only to the manor court. The heir gained entry following the payment of a fine. Copies of relevant entries in manor court records are known as surrenders and admittances. Land so held is referred to as copyhold because the peasant was given a copy of the court roll entry to prove the right of tenure. Considerable acreages reverted to the manor following famines or plagues, notably the Black Death.

> *ista tenementa remanent in manibus domini ... Tenementa que fuerunt Simonis MeleWard'*
> Those tenements remain in the hands of the lord ... tenements which belonged to Simon Meleward,
> *videlicet vnum messuagium et dimidia Wista terre in Blachyngton*
> that is to say, one messuage and half a wista of land in Blachyngton ...
> *quod nullus post mortem tenentium tenementorum predictorum proeisdem sequebatur.*
> because no one fulfilled the duty of attending the manor court following the tenants' deaths.
> East Sussex Record Office, SAS G18/6b, presentment, Alciston, 13 June 1349

The court enjoyed ultimate authority over all villein land transactions.

> *Iohanness Story vendidit Ricardo hodgekyns I acram dimidiam terre in ij petiis I*
> John Story sold to Richard Hodgekyns one acre and a half of land in two portions
> *in Antyngham sine licentia curie Ideo preceptus est seisire etcetera ...*
> in Antingham without court licence. Thus the tenement is ordered to be seized &c.
> Norfolk Record Office, MS 6020, 16 B 5, presentment, Antingham, 17th September 1438

The manor court maintained the peace through the system of frank-pledge, and the guilty were punished by flogging, the stocks, mutilation or fines. The lord also sat as coroner. In the manor of Alciston, Sussex, the court heard cases from the busy hinterland of Seaford. An accidental death on the sandy ridge known as the Links in the tithing of Blatchington on 1st October 1288 could be properly investigated only when the discoverer of the corpse, his neighbours (as witnessses), the jury of twelve and the court officials had finalised their itinerary and timetable of investigation.

> *Accidit per Infortunium ... quod quidam Willelmus miles accessit ad quemdam locum uocatum*
> It happened through a mischance ... that a certain William Miles went to a certain place called
> *Lynkes iuxta hospitale sancti Jacobi de Sefford et ibidem fodiit in quodam puteo (ac in fodiendo*

the Lynkes next to the hospital of St James of Sefford. He there dug in a certain hole and, in digging,

per terram desuper ipsum cadentem subito oppressus fuit per quod obiit ... ideo datus est dies ...

was suddenly crushed by earth falling upon him so that he died.

Therefore a day was appointed ...

East Sussex Record Office, SAS G18/3, presentment, Alciston, 11th November 1288

A parishioner in the stocks, punished perhaps for theft of the pig around his neck or for selling a diseased animal, from a bench end in Grimston church, Norfolk.

The Church

The Christian church influenced the lives of everybody in Britain and Ireland from the cradle to the grave – and beyond. The conversion to Roman Christianity of the pagan kingdoms, the extirpation of rival, particularly Celtic, forms of worship and the establishment of Catholic liturgy, doctrine and ecclesiastical government were achieved through the missionary and pastoral endeavours of the Roman pontiff and his court. The medieval church was centralised around the office of Bishop of Rome (the Pope), who through a hierarchy of princes, prelates and parsons corresponded as appropriate with any parish priest, parishioner, congregation or society within the obedience. The papal monarchy was concerned with every aspect of ecclesiastical life, even at parochial level, appointing to benefices, financing the rebuilding of churches or hospitals, suppressing disorderly convents, offering indulgences, licensing notaries, manipulating the politically and economically influential classes, and corresponding about revenues, abuses, consanguinities, appropriations, divorces, dignities and offices. Papal archives are thus of crucial significance for the study of religion in medieval Britain and Ireland, for an understanding of the causes of religious dissent and for the history of the survival or growth of church organisations – and are relevant even to the remotest parish.

Research might begin with L. E. Boyle's *A Survey of the Vatican Archives and of its Medieval Holdings* (Pontifical Institute of Mediaeval Studies, Toronto, 1972). Various published editions, transcripts and indexes should next be sought through a public or university library. Petitions, licences, correspondence, dispensations and bulls from the sixth centry onwards are the building blocks for a history of parish, monastery and diocese in Britain and Ireland. The work of making records available to British and Irish researchers was begun in 1823 by Marino Marini, prefect of the Archivio Segreto Vaticano. His forty-eight volumes of transcripts were deposited in the British Library (Additional MSS 15, 351-401). In 1864 Marini's successor, A. Theiner, published a book of Vatican sources of Irish and Scottish history, which seems to have encouraged the British government in 1872 to appoint the Scottish antiquary and scholar the Reverend Joseph Stevenson to seek 'all the materials illustrative of the history of Great Britain' in the Vatican. Stevenson's successor, W.

H. Bliss, published the first volumes of *Calendars of Entries in the Papal Registers relating to Great Britain and Ireland* (Public Record Office, 1893; still in progress but since 1961 the responsibility of the Irish Manuscripts Commission). In 1934 the Scottish History Society began its programme of publishing the *Calendars of Scottish Supplications to Rome.*

The technologies of microform, computerisation and the internet are now being used to make actual records accessible to researchers. Those planning to visit Rome to consult original unpublished series of records will require palaeographical and linguistic skills (Italian for negotiating with officials and Latin for reading the archives).

The papal secretariat filed or registered copies of documents despatched to cardinals, bishops, abbots and priests across the whole Roman Catholic sphere of influence and preserved supplications and communications received at the Lateran or Vatican palaces. Pope Innocent III (1198-1216), like his contemporary kings John in England and William in Scotland, reorganised the administration of departments and the creation of records. The papal chancery initiated the systematic registration of documents as one means of facilitating permanent preservation and ready access. Fascicles of registered records were immediately bundled together in parchment folders. One main series known as *Registra Vaticana* dates from the thirteenth century onwards; another, *Registra Avenionensia*, is from the period of the residence of the Popes in Avignon, France (1309-77); and *Registra Lateranensia* dates from after 1378. The registers were rebound in the eighteenth century, when extensive indexes were also first provided by the archivists: Pierre de Montroy's index occupied eighty-five tomes, summarising letters, arranged alphabetically, diocese by diocese.

The archives of the archbishoprics of Canterbury and York are available at Lambeth Palace Library, London, and the Borthwick Institute of Historical Research, York, respectively. Archbishops exercised administrative and judicial power over belief, morality, appointments, taxation and church buildings, down to parish level. Provincial courts of audience, courts of prerogative to prove or validate testaments or wills and courts of appeal maintained records of proceedings affecting individuals and whole communities.

Scottish and Irish records are few and far between. Advice on sources may be sought through the Scottish Catholic Archives and the library of the Representative Church Body in Dublin.

A large measure of autonomy was enjoyed by royal free chapels, such as St George's Chapel, Windsor; minsters and collegiate churches, such as Beverley and Southwell; such cathedrals as Bangor and London, which did not have monastic establishments attached; and several thousand religious monastic communities. In Ireland and Scotland most cathedrals were non-monastic (secular). Governed by a chapter of canons (clerics) who began each meeting by reading a chapter of the rules, each institution accumulated wealth in manors and rectories. Capitular records are deposited in national or provincial research centres, including record offices. The chapter minuted in act books decisions on such matters as the appointment of staff, building programmes, liturgy, property speculation and manorial administration. Charters concerning church land were registered in cartularies, which also contain records of law suits, pensions, ordinations, vicarages and charities. Many collections have been edited for publication.

illud mesuagium quod vocatur mulleberyhall in Stayngat ... cum omnibus domibus superedificatis ...
that property known as Mulberry hall in Stonegate ... with all houses built there
iacet in longitudine a Regia strata de Stayngat ante vsque ad venellam que vocatur
stretching lengthwise from the king's highway of Stonegate at the front as far as a passageway called
Grapecuntlane retro. et in latitudine inter tenementum Prioris sancti Oswaldi ex parte
Grapecuntlane at the rear; and breadthwise between the holding of the Priory of St

Oswald on the
occidentali et tenementum Ricardi de Seleby ex parte orientali
west and the holding of Richard of Selby on the east
York Minster Library, M2/4g folio 26 verso, capitular register, 4th February 1342/3

Financial records show outgoings on building projects and the upkeep of religious services. The chapter was concerned with a range of regional matters such as bridge tolls, estate administration, stipends for clergy and reports on goods ordered from parish suppliers for capitular purposes. The chapter from time to time received grants of additional authority, for instance to prove wills, record marriage bonds and allegations and even administer the surrounding county division known as the hundred.

Records of religious houses of monks, nuns, friars and hospitallers survive mainly within cartularies or registers, which are more difficult to tear up or burn than individual parchments or papers. Most of these collections have been edited and published for record societies. The cartularies of Beaulieu and God's House, Southampton, concerning lands in Berkshire, Hampshire and Cornwall are published in the Southampton Records Series (1974, 1976). The cartulary of Missenden (Buckinghamshire Record Society, 1939-62), comprising charters, court papers, papal bulls, pedigrees and final concords, relates to properties in the counties of Buckinghamshire, Bedfordshire, Huntingdonshire, London, Middlesex, Oxfordshire and Suffolk. The deeds of the hospital of St John the Baptist in Dublin for about 1290-1486, written into an official register, were published by the Irish Manuscripts Commission in 1936, while deeds registers for St Mary's Cistercian abbey, St Thomas's Victorine canons and Holy Trinity Augustinian priory, all in Dublin, have also been published.

The bishop's records are usually deposited in a designated diocesan record office, in England often the county record office. Survival of Irish and Scottish diocesan records is patchy. Most likely to survive and to be available in published form are cartularies containing copies of charters, surveys and rentals.

Registers of the bishop's pronouncements and regulations, known as acts, survive from the eleventh century onwards (Chichester from 1075, Llandaff from 1140) and may also be available in published editions. The core business was the institution of clergy. The *Register of Edmund Lacy, Bishop of Exeter, 1420-1455*, edited by G. R. Dunstan jointly for the Canterbury and York Society and Devon and Cornwall Record Society (Torquay, 1963-7), includes the following:

> tithes from Pottington and from John Chichester's meadow ... called Hollyforde (11th October 1435)
> replacement of the belfry and bells at Little Torrington, destroyed by lightning (11th February 1438/9)
> alienation by the prior and convent of Plympton of their properties in Plymouth ...
> some were intact, others were in ruins, having been burned by the Bretons (11th January 1439/40)
> Vincent Clement ... chancellor of Lichfield cathedral, resigned the benefice of St Ewe on the grounds
> that he could neither speak Cornish nor keep personal residence (30th July 1450)

The bishop inspected parishes in periodic visitations, armed with presentments from churchwardens, which brought out matters requiring remedy either in the fabric of the church or in the conduct of the clergy. The bishop's courts heard cases involving moral lapses, matrimonial disputes, slander, property, inheritance and charities.

The court of audience for sensitive cases involving the moral lapses and relapses of the clergy, as well as matrimonial disputes, was presided over by the bishop in person, or an auditor under the prelate's close supervision. This work is documented variously in general or specific registers. The consistory court, presided over by a dignitary known as an official, heard cases of a more mundane nature, involving property, money, slander and wills. Summary correction of such offences as sabbath-breaking, arising from information or accusation, perhaps received during a visitation, involved a decision by the 'mere office of the judge' and a fine, a penance or public contrition. Procedure by plenary jurisdiction was initiated for cases involving opposing parties, whose written submissions were filed and recorded in act books. The medieval church was frequently concerned with the inheritance of property. Possessions normally passed smoothly, under the supervision of a feudal lord, to a person's heirs without the need for written documentation, though for wealthier families written testaments were encouraged. These were validated or 'proved' by church officials, who retained copies in the diocesan archives. The surviving testaments of the prerogative court of Canterbury date from 1384 onwards and can be researched through the Public Record Office family records centre in London.

Medieval testaments from Scotland and Ireland rarely survive. A testament might contain bequests to the church, perhaps paying a priest to chant masses for the soul of the deceased in a chantry chapel within the parish church. There might be bequests to servants, family and friends, with references to manors, houses, stock-in-trade, craftsmen's tools, furniture, clothing, bedding, armour, farm animals and stored crops. The testament might include an inventory of contents in the house or workshop, with accounts of debts owed and shares in ships and business undertakings.

The medieval parish was governed by a meeting of responsible men assembled in the vestry (robing room) of the church. Minutes and accounts of the vestrymen may survive from the fourteenth century onwards, lodged perhaps in a church strongbox (parish chest) or record office. The vestry compiled registers of land and houses as a basis for fixing a cess or rate. Two vestrymen, acting as churchwardens, took responsibility for, and kept records of, parish treasures, including gold and silver plate, precious manuscripts, vestments and relics. The vestry monitored contracts for building works which may enable the researcher to date precisely any additions and alterations to the parish church.

Place-names

During the period 865-1050 settlements of Scandinavian immigrants were established and consolidated. Place-names were coined in the immigrants' native tongues. In some districts Scandinavian names almost wholly supplanted their English or Celtic predecessors. This raises questions about the nature of the settlements, their extent, the number of immigrants in each, the political influence of the newcomers and the fate or subsequent status of the native people.

Danish families settled particularly in eastern and central England. Danish place-name elements include *by*, 'village'; *eng*, 'meadow'; *haugr/hoe*, 'mound'/'tumulus'; *hulm/holm*, 'island'/'water-meadow'; *kirkja*, 'church'; *thorp*, 'farmstead'; and *toft*, 'house-site'. Families from Norway and Sweden settled in the northern isles and all around the coastal regions washed by the Irish Sea. Their vocabulary survives in many modern words, including 'field', 'beck' (stream) and 'fell' (hill). Typical place-name elements include *bolstathr/bister/bost*, 'dwelling place'; *brekka*, 'hill'; *buth/ both*, 'shelter/house'; *by/ber*, 'village'; *dalr/dale*, 'valley'; *erg*, 'hill pasture'; *ey*, 'island'; *fjall/fell*, 'hill'; *fjörðr*, 'firth'/'bay'; *gata*, 'road'; *nes*, 'headland'; *sáetr/setter*, 'hill pasture'; *thveit*, 'clearing'; *thing*, 'regional folk assembly' – as at Tingrith, Bedfordshire, and Tynwald on the Isle of Man. Fieldwork and archaeology may be an essential adjunct to place-name studies. Freswick in Caithness is etymologically identified with Thrasvik in *Orkneyinga Saga*. This literary source recounts the launch of Norse longships, bent on trade or plunder, from Freswick beach around 1154. The topography of modern Freswick – a secret cove with an Iron Age fortress above it – conforms to the saga description. Archaeological excavation in the 1930s uncovered a Norse settlement, comprising bow-sided halls and longhouses with a barn, a corn-drying kiln, a smithy, a storehouse and a sauna grouped defensively around a common courtyard.

English place-names underwent further change during the period 865-1050.

During Viking invasions powerful Anglo-Saxon landlords reorganised their estates, granting lands to their retainers and dependants. Usually these new owners, who might be relatives, servants, warriors or priests, gave their own names to the manors. Occasionally there is documentary evidence to prove the point. A particularly clear example is Wolverhampton. The evidence here is an authentic charter of 985. This granted an estate, known until then simply as *hea-tun*, 'high farmstead or township', to a certain lady with the Saxon name Wulfrun. Her name was prefixed to the existing place-name to give *Wulfrun hea-tun*, subsequently corrupted to *Wulfrunehanton* in the Pipe Roll for 1169. Such documentary evidence may be rather rare. Even so, the historian is challenged to think carefully about local place-names, perhaps seeking the advice of linguists and other experts in the absence of archive sources. A name of the Wolverhampton type may have been coined during the late Saxon or early medieval period. From such a place-name the researcher may perhaps infer a transfer of ownership of the township at this date. Fieldwork may show that the hedge-banks bounding the estate date from about the same time and that the parish church was rebuilt in the course of improvement of the estate by its new owner. The place-name may reveal the name, racial origin or linguistic background of the earliest named inhabitant of the locality.

Manors belonging to important people, notably the king, bishops, noblemen and sheriffs, became known as king's town, bishop's farmstead or sheriff's acres, for example, while the subservient settlements of peasants might be Carlton, Charlton or Chorlton, from *ceorl*, 'churl'/'peasant'. If charters or other documentary evidence survive it is sometimes possible to discover which king or bishop was referred to, and even the name of the place before the change of ownership. Edward the Confessor's queen Eadgyth gave her name to a favourite village in Rutland, subsequently known as Edith Weston.

The Normans entered into possession of a land fully settled and were generally content with the addition of their family surnames to vernacular or existing place-names: examples include Newton Blossomville, Buckinghamshire (de Blosseville family); Kingston by Sea, Sussex (corrupted from the name of Robert Busci who held the manor in 1199); Kingston Bagpuize, Berkshire (originally *cinghaema gemaere*, renamed by Ralph de Bachepuz, whose surname was from Bacquepuis in Normandy); Ashby de la Zouch, Leicestershire, held by Roger de la Zouch in 1200. The Normans added the diminutive suffixes *el* and *et* to certain names, for instance Cricket Malherbie, Somerset, from *cruc-et malherbie* 'hill-little-Malherbe (family)'. Some newly established settlements received fully French names, though usually the conquerors limited their contribution to a few descriptive words, notably *beau*, 'beautiful, and *mal*, 'bad', as in Beauly, Ross, and Beaulieu, Hampshire ('beautiful place'), and Malzeard, Yorkshire (from *mal-assart*, 'wretched clearing').

Climate

During the period 865-1200 a benign climate benefited agricultural production. Average temperatures may have been as much as 1°C higher than today. Crop yields were enhanced by a slightly longer and less stormy growing season, some crops being grown on land now considered marginal or inappropriate for grain production. Vineyards were planted in sheltered localities in southern England. Monks were traditionally famous for their grapes and wines. Upland areas were colonised by communities of arable husbandmen.

The population increased until around 1320, despite the onset during the thirteenth century of drier summers, colder wetter winters and unpredictable episodes of gale and flood. Average temperatures dropped by perhaps 1.5°C, a crucial and disastrous change for communities on marginal lands.

Milder but wetter conditions prevailed during the period 1320-1490 – the era when the Black Death (bubonic plague) depleted British communities. Upland arable lands became unworkable. Settlements whose populations had been reduced by plague and weakened by famine were abandoned. Hill lands were devoted to sheep farming, and the wool trade became the basis for prosperity. Around 1490 two centuries of severe cool weather commenced, known as the 'little ice age', characterised by cold winters, late snows, hard frosts and short cool wet summers.

Towns

Fieldwork and archaeology in the old centres of modern towns may reveal aspects of the medieval origins and plans of the settlement. During the period 865-925 the West Saxon and Mercian monarchs founded new towns and replanned existing settlements throughout southern England as one aspect of the response to disruptions caused by Danish invasion and settlement. The siting, planning, size and shape of each town was determined by regional political factors, financial resources and the manpower available for the defences. Each new town was an administrative centre and defensible settlement, strategically sited perhaps at a river crossing, as were Cricklade, Wareham and Witham. A town on open land was defended by earthworks and palisades and thus described as a *burh*, 'enclosure', 'defended place', giving rise to the modern word 'borough'. The extent of the defences and the area of the original town may be traced on the ground or from air photographs. Defensive circuits can still be traced in the town plans of Maldon (secured about 916), Towcester (917), Thelwall (919), Manchester (919), Bakewell (921) and Clwydmouth or Rhuddlan (921). Fieldworkers assess the relationship of the measurable length of defences, the town taxation (hidage) and the manpower required to defend the town according to the ratio 4:3:3. Winchester's palisades stretched 3280 yards, assessed at 2400 hides for 2400 soldiers; Lyng, Somerset, rated 100 hides for defences 140 yards long. Each town was ideally laid out as a rectangle, with an outer ditch, a palisaded earthen embankment, an internal paved walkway and a single broad rectangular market place or thoroughfare, as at Langport ('long market'), Somerset. The new rectangular *burh* of Bedford cut into an older town on the site. Prehistoric and Roman forts were recommissioned and repopulated as urban centres, including Old Sarum near Salisbury, Chichester and Exeter. In Cheshire the forts of Eddisbury and Halton guarded the Dee and Mersey estuaries, securing Saxon advance against Scandinavian incursions west from the Wirral, as indicated distinctly in place-names. Elevated spurs within crooks of rivers or in marshland were natural defences for new towns such as Lydford, Shaftesbury and Twyneham (Christchurch). Towns attracted and boroughs monopolised trade within a broad hinterland. Exotic goods such as wine, silk, spices and cloth were landed at the town's own quays, perhaps on the coast some miles away. Following the reforms of King Aethelstan (924-39), the minting of coins was a privilege of favoured boroughs and a boost to trade, for example in Rochester, Lewes and even Horndon (Essex).

Scandinavian defences are occasionally traceable archaeologically or along later property boundaries. Danish trading communities were sometimes planted as suburbs of older English towns sited along main roads and navigable waterways, as at Wigford beneath Lincoln and Huntingdon outside Godmanchester. Parish churches were dedicated to the favourite Danish saint, St Clement, as in London at St Clement Danes. Stamford St Michael developed, under the protection of the Norsemen's favourite warrior saint, to outgrow the older English *burh*. In Ireland Scandinavians founded urban settlements at Cork, Limerick, Wexford and Youghal. At Waterford their early tenth-century defensive ditch, 23 feet (7 metres) wide, is still identifiable in places. Excavations since 1974 on Dublin's Liffey waterfront have uncovered quays, warehouses and workshops of around 900.

A coin of Eric Bloodaxe, the Norse king of York 948-54.

Scandinavian settlers were banished from Dublin to the 'eastman's town' (Oxmanstown) north of the river after the Anglo-Norman invasion of 1170-1. The Normans established boroughs as centres of commerce and administration, havens of civilisation for continental immigrants. Towns were planted on undeveloped sites or on land from which native settlements were forcibly cleared, and also as extensions to existing towns. In proud medieval boroughs an earthen bank, a ditch and a palisade or stone wall with projecting bastions defined the area where burghal privileges applied. Access was controlled by officials stationed at gates where taxes were levied on goods brought to market. Gypsies, criminals judicially branded or mutilated and pregnant women – potential burdens on the community – might be refused entry. Sites of gates may be identfed from place-names containing the element *porte*, 'gate'; those containing *gate* derive from the Norse *gata*, 'street'. At Alnwick and St Andrews fortified ports still mark the town bounds.

A royal or baronial castle was a usual feature of a medieval borough. Castle and town might form two elements of a single ground plan, as at Caernarfon, Denbigh and Chepstow. In such schemes the siting of the castle was given priority, with its walls and baileys perhaps affecting the clearing of old properties, the line of streets and the shape of feus. In later centuries the growth of the town around, in or into the castle site depended on the castle's subsequent legal status. The Welsh border towns of Cefnllys, Dolforwyn and Skenfrith were confined within the baileys and did not prosper. The historian may infer the extent and shape of a vanished castle from the position of lanes, property boundaries, humps and bumps as well as from house names and site descriptions in old title deeds.

Norman towns were often planned along a single rectangular street or market place. Elaborations of the linear plan included rear access lanes skirting the borough boundary and perhaps also one or two streets running at right angles to the axis leading to the mill, a religious site, common fields or neighbouring communities.

Towns were also laid out around a rectangular, triangular or oval central market place. The shape might be determined by natural features such as streams, bogs, pools or hillocks which may not now be evident. There may have been man-made structures, such as a circular monastic enclosure or a castle with its outer wards and baileys. Plans might be determined by a pattern of roads converging on the market

The medieval town walls of Tenby, Pembrokeshire.

The town defences of Rye, Sussex, a port from which the sea retreated.

place, as at Alnwick, or simply by the inexplicable whim of planner and patron.

A pattern of streets incorporating grid-like features appeared in about one in ten new towns, including Winchelsea, Ludlow, Stratford-upon-Avon, Clun and New Radnor. One block of the grid was usually reserved as an open market place. Most notable of medieval grids was the plan of the thirteenth-century city of Salisbury, which replaced an older *burh* established within an Iron Age hillfort at Old Sarum. The bishop planned his new town on open meadow land beside the Avon, with five streets aligned north-south, crossed by six streets aligned east-west.

A borough's original market place should be identifiable, perhaps still as the commercial heart of the community, perhaps sidelined or infilled and constricted by subsequent development. Here goods from town and country were bought and sold, initially in the open air. When the defensive function of a fortified settlement had ceased to be important, commerce often rescued the economy, as indicated by the name Market Harborough ('market army town') or by the prefix Chipping (from *ceap,* 'commerce') added to the town's name. A high cross was often erected in the market as a reminder of the duty of honesty. At the stocks or pillory petty criminals and dishonest traders were punished. A public weighing machine with the borough's standard weights was known as a steel yard or 'trone', hence Trongate. A metal rod one yard or one ell long was built into a convenient wall as a check on individual measures. A guildhall, town hall or 'tolbooth' in the centre of the market-place served as the council offices, treasury, courthouse and archives.

The prison was shared by borough and shire. As merchants brought further prosperity in the thirteenth century, additional market places were sometimes established, usually functioning on a different day from the principal market, perhaps sited in suburbs dedicated to the commercial St Giles. Temporary stalls erected on market days might in due course be established as permanent booths and elaborate dwellings around or

The community seal of Tiverton, Devon, showing the defensible church, castle and bridges. The woolsack indicates the basis of the town's prosperity.

Ludlow, Shropshire, was replanned soon after 1066 along a broad high street and was enlarged during the twelfth century with three wide parallel streets.

infilling the market place – a type of development documented in borough archives, as burgesses paid fees, fines and feu duties for their encroachments. Alleys off the market place took the names of particular crafts, such as that of the skinner, the cooper (barrel maker) or the cordwainer (shoe maker). Butchers established a 'shambles', where animals were slaughtered in the street. Chapmen set up in Cheapside, while Haymarket and Old Poultry indicate areas allocated to specific trading. The gibbet was sited beyond the boundary on a hill, perhaps called Gallows Hill, within the jurisdiction of the county sheriff, possibly at a Shermansbury farm or Shirewood. A pond, perhaps identifiable by the name Ordeal, was used for the trial by ordeal of alleged witches and the ducking of shrewish wives, scolds and rumour-mongers.

Along the market place were pegged out house plots known as burgages, initially all of equal breadth. The fieldworker measures frontages in the modern town, calculating averages and explaining discrepancies with reference to title deeds, early maps and plans to reveal the breadth of the medieval plot. Research

The market place of Dumfries with the burgh tolbooth containing the town administrative offices, courtroom and gaol.

may prove that there was a relatively small number of original house plots for the restricted group of merchants who were first encouraged to settle. In Forres, Moray, there were just ninety-six burgages, half on each side of the rectangular market street, for the pioneering Norman, Breton, Flemish and English families. Archives suggest that burgages might have been marked out with the standard measuring rod 16 feet 6 inches (5.029 metres). A favourite breadth was 1½ rods (24 feet 9 inches, equal to 7.544 metres). Plots along Scandinavian Dublin's Fishamble Street were just under 23 feet (7 metres) broad while Alnwick's were 1½ or 2 rods wide. Each burgage plot extended for perhaps 400 feet (120 metres) from the street frontage to the borough boundary ditch. A property owner thus received a long, slender tenement. The marking out of side boundaries, which were, and still are, typically curved and kinked, suggests some other means than a straight pole, perhaps a ploughed furrow. Evidence from the countryside indicates that the ploughman's furrow followed a graceful reversed-C or S course – exactly what is seen even today in urban property boundaries. Particular studies have been conducted into the twelfth-century royal burghs of Inverness, Nairn, Auldearn, Forres, Elgin, Cullen, Banff and Aberdeen, showing there was remarkable consistency in planning. A plough was possibly used in marking out the plots, because an extra 9 inches (229 mm, the width of a furrow) was added to each plot, which therefore measured one rood (a quarter of an acre or 0.101 hectare) in extent. Discrepancies may be attributed to inaccurate measurement by modern researchers or medieval planners or perhaps to changes in the length of the regional inch – three barleycorns long in medieval times – over intervening centuries.

When new towns and suburbs or borough extensions were later developed, straighter boundaries were the rule while burgages were perhaps narrower or smaller than the standard rood. These properties were measured with chains and pegs specially purchased, recorded in the archives.

Each burgess defined his boundaries with a line of boulders, fence posts or walls of turf and stone. Some boulders have remained in position to this day, usually preserved by being incorporated into subsequent house walls. Big walls rebuilt and heightened over several centuries are also a feature of medieval towns and are generally significant in fieldwork, rewarding detailed investigation. They were very

Newark, Nottinghamshire, was planned for the Bishop of Lincoln about 1123-48 around a rectangular market place, reduced by encroachment to its present size by 1710. Brick and classical façades mask vernacular and timber-framed medieval structures.

The medieval town of Cullen, Banffshire, as drawn by a professional surveyor for the landowner in 1762. All the houses were later cleared.

practical in deterring neighbourly encroachments and have ensured that many medieval property boundaries remain clearly defined. Trespassing by even a single inch would have been sufficient for a law suit, as indicated in borough court records, which incidentally contain a wealth of information on the shape, delineation, ownership and history of plots.

Property boundaries should not be confused with other delineations. These might include early municipal boundaries, the swathe of ground cleared between a borough and its castle or the division between the town and the minster or cathedral.

Within the rood, each burgess's house was sited according to town planning regulations. On narrow urban properties, the house typically stood with its gable facing the street. A private alley, gated for security, gave access to the open ground behind the house. Usually planners insisted that every house should be orientated the same way. The main door and window opened on to the owner's close. In certain towns rear house walls were statutorily blank. This sensible regulation ensured that there was no window for spying or emptying chamber pots into a neighbour's property.

At the foot of the blank back wall of each house a gap, typically 9 inches (229 mm) wide, was maintained. This 'eavesdrip' or 'eavesdrop' belonged to the householder whose rainwater dripped on to it. Medieval statutory gaps may be best observed today from the rear of town properties.

Householders made their own sanitary arrangements. Cesspits, privies and middens (dung heaps) may be identified archaeologically and are a prime source of information about intestinal parasites, diet, health and lifestyle. Sometimes dung heaps were sited on ground owned by the householder on the street front, for ease of removing to the town's fields. Middens might obstruct the street drain and so be noted in court records. Water was drawn from a private well within the house plot or from a public well in the market place.

As populations grew, servants' dwellings, workshops and cottages were erected behind each house. On narrow urban roods this resulted in a snaking row of buildings, kinked and bent to fit the curve of the burgage.

By the fifteenth century business premises faced the street, perhaps (as here in Burford, Oxfordshire) built astride the access alley to the original family dwellings gable-on to the street. These tacked-on frontages invite investigation of the earlier structures behind.

Each merchant was allowed to erect a stall on the street in front of his house. This might be rebuilt with permission, or on payment of a fine (set down in borough archives), as a permanent shop or forebooth perhaps, with an unglazed window to the street. The top half of the shutter opened upwards as an awning, while the lower half descended as a counter. Hinges, bolts, slots and surviving shutters may be evident. For this reason, in prosperous towns, building lines tended to move forwards into the market place, which nowadays may be much narrower than when originally laid out.

Villages

Vulnerable villages were transplanted and replanned from around 865 onwards as a defensive measure in response to Norse attack, as well as around 1070 following William the Conqueror's genocidal harrying of northern England. Rural populations were also relocated from time to time by landowners as a result of demographic or economic change. The researcher should be aware that even the remotest and apparently most unplanned settlements required some kind of systematic planning. Celtic townships known as clachans appear as undisciplined clusters of huts, but order exists in the form of a communal green, even if much encroached on, and stable property boundaries. Corbel-roofed beehive huts might have been clustered together, even interconnected, regardless of individual wishes, in response to communal planning regulations. Retainers of the feudal landowners of Scotland and Ireland were housed in turf and wicker huts within the bawn (defences) of the lord's castle, according to arrangements made by officials. The varieties of township plans and the process of making planning decisions are thus prime concerns for the historian.

Ickleton village green, Cambridgeshire.

The typical medieval village was planted around a broad communal space, sometimes rectangular like a market place, perhaps in such instances indicating a town that failed to thrive and grow. Other villages were set out around a triangular or circular area, probably then, as often now, under grass. At the head of the village green, typically, stood the manor house and parish church: secular and clerical authorities standing shoulder to shoulder to govern the community. Medieval public amenities may survive on the green. The sites of others may be identified through fieldwork, archival research and place-names. A public well supplied drinking water. A pond watered cattle and was home to flocks of geese. Trials by ordeal and judicial ducking of scolds took place there. The stocks and the pillory stood prominently as a deterrent. The pound or pinfold was an enclosed area where stray cattle were folded.

Village properties usually retain their original squarish, broad-fronted shape, some occupying plots of half an acre (0.2 hectare) – very different from the narrow-fronted, slender quarter-acre urban roods. Village houses usually stood fronting on to the green, rather than gable-on as in the case of town houses. The extent and shape of house plots may indicate a founder's intention as to an urban or rural future for a settlement. The linear green of Barnton, Cheshire, may be paced out with the aid of the tithe map. Set along the route of a salters' way, the green was 794 feet (242 metres) long, widening from 143 feet (43.6 metres) at the south to 221 feet (67.4 metres) at the north, where the manor house and a cleared pre-tenth-century village stood. The east and west margins were each pegged out as five tofts of half an acre (0.203 hectare). One toft can still be identified, though subdivided and occupied by housing, and retains its pre-Domesday dimensions of 156 feet (47.5 metres) by 130 feet (39.6 metres) or nearly half an acre (0.203 hectare).

Colonisation of the countryside is suggested by the element 'new' as in New

At Chastleton, Oxfordshire, the manor house and parish church stand together. The manor was sold to Walter Jones, a Witney wool merchant, in 1602. He rebuilt the house in Jacobean style, and the family also reconstructed the church tower. The medieval village was removed.

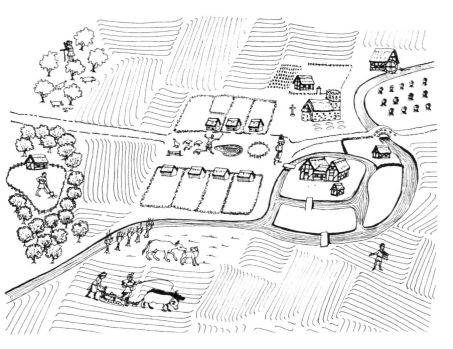

A lowland village scene.

Lynn, the parent place-name becoming Old Lynn, though care is needed as Oldcoates, Northumberland, means 'cots inhabited by owls'. Daughter settlements are implied in the names *New*ham, *Little* Neston, Ashton *Parva* (from Latin, 'small') and Bally*beg* (Gaelic *baeg,* 'small'). Decolonisation is indicated by the thousands of decayed or deserted communities. Sources include estate and legal records and air photographs. The researcher looks out for tell-tale hedgerows around the village site, footpaths leading apparently only to rough pasture, an isolated or ruined church, hollow or sunken roads, the humps and bumps of rectangular house foundations or the village pond marked seasonally with sedge or cotton grass. Some place-names containing the elements *ton* or *baile*, both meaning 'township', may now be attached only to an isolated farmhouse, probably on an old village site, while such field names as Oldtown or the Gaelic equivalent, Shenval, could be further clues. Deserted townships may have been surveyed by an archaeological field club, the Ordnance Survey, English Heritage or the Medieval Settlement Research Group, though much work remains for the field-walker, who may identify such natural processes as landslip or bog flow as the agents of disaster. Old Winchelsea was inundated by the sea in 1287, and its successor was later stranded when the ocean retreated. Kenfig, Glamorgan, was destroyed by sea and sand storms, leaving a ruined castle and church along with a lake and a rabbit warren. Plague certainly depopulated the Oxfordshire villages of Standelf, Tusmore and Tilgarsley. Elsewhere climatic change conspired with pestilence in a more subtle long-term process to seal the fate of villages on marginal sites and soils: Caldecote ('cold cottage') is a typical name associated with deserted places. Desertion was sometimes the result of military action, as at Athassel, County Tipperary, burned by a Norman baron in 1319 and again by the Irish a decade later; humps and bumps are still visible in pasture land in the shadow of the Augustinian abbey, which was itself burned in 1447, later repaired and finally dissolved about 1550. Villages were removed to make way for parks, chases, warrens and forests; at least twenty for the expansion of

The isolated church of St Twynnell, Pembrokeshire.

the New Forest by William I. Successive agrarian reorganisations cleared numerous settlements in the interests of progress and enclosure. Cistercian monks initiated improvements for sheep ranching during the twelfth century, removing houses, hedgerows and paddocks and relocating peasant populations. Secular landlords maximised the productivity of estates by evicting surplus population; at least twenty-seven villages were destroyed in the Isle of Wight for late medieval prairie sheep farming.

Agriculture

Communities evolved systems of agriculture appropriate to regional terrain, soil type, labour force and social organisation, as evidenced through estate archives and field-walking. In Devon, Connemara and Breconshire small squarish fields were worked in landscapes planned perhaps before 1500 BC. These systems are sometimes referred to as Celtic fields, though they predate the emergence of Celtic culture. Fields were enclosed with hedges or walls of turf and stone and are sometimes associated with winding sunken roads. Agricultural operations were managed from a single house or hamlet, perhaps sheltering two or three families with dependants and servants.

In regions of marsh or native woodland, small areas of arable land and pasture, indicated by the elements *assart, stubbs, royd* or *newland*, were created to support a single family. These small-field ancient landscapes occasionally survived into the modern era and may be recognised from air photographs and maps, for instance in Kent, the Lake District and central Wales.

At the time of the social revolution that began during the struggle between Saxons and Danes, tenth-century English kings and landowners reorganised agricultural landscapes and imposed new conditions of tenure. This feudalisation of rural society was subsequently carried into Wales, Scotland and Ireland as part of the cultural baggage of the Normans during the twelfth century. Medieval-style open field landscapes can still be visited on the Hebridean island of Berneray and at Laxton, Nottinghamshire (altered in 1908 and described with plans in the classic survey by C. S. and C. S. Orwin: *The Open Fields,* published by Clarendon Press, 1938). The arable land of the village and borough was defined as two or three extensive common fields, each of perhaps 200 acres (81 hectares). The hedgerows, banks and ditches bounding these open fields may remain evident. Each field was subdivided

Berneray, Outer Hebrides. Women work unfenced strips in the open field in a scene redolent of medieval agricultural practice but photographed in 1982. The high ground of the island, corrugated with ancient ridge-and-furrow and later potato 'lazy beds', is now grass-covered, unfenced common grazing for the island's sheep and cattle.

into brakes, 'shotts' or furlongs ranging in size from 2 to 10 acres. Furlongs might preserve Celtic field boundaries and were defined by untilled weedy baulks consisting of stones cleared from the ploughland. The furlong was the unit of cultivation, its crop rotation, manuring, fallowing and grazing being determined by the manorial court. Furlongs within an open field could be variously planted with wheat, rye, barley, oats, peas, beans, flax, vetches, brassicas and root vegetables.

Each furlong was further divided into long narrow strips for individual ploughing. Each strip might be around 1½ to 2 rods (24 feet 9 inches to 33 feet, or 7.5 to 10 metres) wide, extending the full length of the furlong. The peasant's virgate (holding) was notionally the acreage required to support one family over and above rent, taxes and tithes but varied according to regional circumstances, soil, climate and tradition. Typically the holding consisted of about thirty strips scattered through the fields. In the 157 acre (63.5 hectares) Townfield of Barnton, Cheshire, according to the 1843 tithe map, the Near Furlong (5 acres, 2 hectares) contained eight 'loonts' held by five different tenants. In certain villages strips were allocated in the same order as houses around the communal green. This arrangement is evidenced in manorial records and estate plans at Wharram Percy, Yorkshire. A heavy iron-shared wheeled plough, communally owned and pulled by up to eight oxen, heaped soil inwards into high broad ridges, two or more to each strip, perhaps to assist drainage. Corrugations of 'ridge and furrow' are the most immediately obvious evidence on the ground of the extent of an open field and can also be studied from air photographs and estate plans. Strips, ridges and furlongs curved in reversed-C or S shape, perhaps resulting from the movement and turning of the unwieldy ox team approaching the head baulk. Baulks formed sinuous access ways, perhaps 8 inches (457 mm) high and 40 feet (12 metres) broad, and are sometimes still visible in low sunlight as relief features. Corn lands of the highland zone were also organised on communal lines with arable land known as the infield bounded by a stone or turf head-dyke. Additional breaks of infield were scattered across the rough moor ('scattald' in Shetland) and were mucked and also abandoned from time to time. Strips in the arable land were allocated and cultivated with the foot or ox plough depending on village prosperity.

The heavy ox-drawn wheeled plough, essential to medieval agriculture, from a manuscript in the British Library, Cotton Tiberius BV part I, folio 3.

Waste land beyond the village arable land provided common grazing for cattle, goats and sheep in both lowlands and highlands. The numbers of beasts were regulated and documented in administrative and court records by the landowner. Animal husbandry in the lowland zone was relatively unimportant. In the highland zone the grassy upland moor was reserved for cattle, peat cutting, quarrying, rabbits and game birds. The outfield grazing stretched for miles into the hills, where subsidiary or temporary settlements, known as summer 'shielings' in Scotland, *hafod* in Wales and *buaile* in Ireland, were established. Transhumance facilitated the exploitation of poorer pastures, such as the milking place with sixteen stone shelters that can still be visited at Bunowen Booley near Achill Head, County Mayo. Water meadows may be evidenced by sluices and channels to control the flooding of low-lying areas and encourage the growth of grass. Fuel was a vital resource for domestic cooking and heating and industrial processes. Wetland and bog, preserved for peat cutting year after year, may now be identifiable only through the place-name elements *bog, fen, marsh* or *mere*.

Communal open-field systems were attacked by agricultural reformers. 'Improvement' generally entailed the creation of fenced-off enclosures for exploitation free of the communal constraints of common-field regulations. Whole fieldscapes were thus reorganised. New fields were generally small in size if intended for crops, larger if for sheep ranching.

In districts of medieval enclosure, for example areas of East Anglia, villages can be few and far between. Former fields may be evidenced by such names as Old Town Field, Longshotts ('the long arable strips') and West Loonts. Open areas, once village greens, may be identifiable, though now with only an isolated church or a single farmhouse where once there was a whole township.

From the fourteenth century, occasionally even earlier, far-sighted landowners reorganised common fields and unenclosed grazings into a series of discrete holdings usually described as 'farms' because they were farmed out for cultivation. The farmer divided his holding into rectangular fields enclosed with hedges, walls of turf and stone or fences. The new fields sometimes followed old furlong boundaries and were consequently curved to a reversed-S profile. New enclosures might completely redraw the fieldscape so that old cultivation ridges now ran under newer hedgelines.

Piecemeal enclosure was achieved by enterprising peasants acquiring several adjacent strips in a furlong. The peasant might then, with the landowner's permission, fence his block of strips and cultivate the field regardless of the needs of neighbours. These engrossments fit into the general pattern of ridge and furrow but are enclosed with hedges proved to be medieval by a count of the species in them. Common land, woodland and waste were also subject to piecemeal enclosure. A peasant might create a smallholding by assart, that is, breaking in and cultivating underexploited land. This may be identified by the elements *ley, hay* or *thwaite*. The assart supported a single cottager, hence the place-name Cottarton, or if on the parish bounds, a community at an *end, bottom* or *top.*

Woodland, forest and park

Broadleaved woodland was vigorously managed and regenerated to supply the community's building timber, firewood, fencing and charcoal. Black poplar, sycamore, oak, ash, hazel, lime, elm and birch were felled, sawn in pits, dressed in joiners' yards, pegged and carved, then carted as kits for erection as a house or barn. Acorns and beechmast fed swine. Peasants gathered fruits, herbs and fungi in season, trapped songbirds for the pot and poached deer and rabbits that belonged to the manorial authorities. Medieval woodland is identified by surviving boundary earthworks, stools of coppiced trees, top-heavy pollards (their crowns of new growth above the reach of browsing animals) and clumps of wild flowers such as dog's mercury and wood anemone.

Kings and noblemen set aside tracts of countryside as forest, including woodland, heath, hill pasture and open fields. Forests were governed by a distinct code of laws to preserve the landowner's interests. Relics of forest law survive, for example, in the Forest of Dean. Here special courts meet and foresters enjoy particular privileges and the benefits of certain constraints. Legal forests were not depopulated hunting reserves but vibrant communities complete with fields and grazings.

Forest law once regulated village life throughout the shires of Cornwall and Essex and also in Amounderness, Arden, Bleasdale, Braden, Cannock, Galtres, Huntingdon, Inglewood, Kingswood, Knaresborough, Lonsdale, Pickering, Rockingham, Sherwood, Shotover, Wirral and Wychwood. Henry III set aside forests in eastern Ireland: Obbrun and Slefco (near Dublin) and Cracelauh (possibly Carlow). Scottish kings established some ninety forests for commercial profit and princely indulgence, yielding constructional timber, wood from pollards and coppices, venison, rabbit and pork for the court, fines from poachers, rents for assarts and licences for emparking (creating a park by fencing and enclosure). The cost of enclosing a forest can be appreciated through fieldwork, for instance by walking the long miles of the deer pale of the forest of Kincardine, which survives as an impressive grassy ditch and heathery bank.

Private parks and chases were created by noblemen and lords of the manor. *Domesday* records a park of woodland beasts at Borough Green, Cambridgeshire, where a linear earthwork can still be inspected. Embankments and ditches were so arranged that deer, boar and other beasts could enter relatively easily but escape only with difficulty. Fallow deer were introduced during the eleventh century and became favourite beasts of the chase in lowland areas, while native red deer were hunted elsewhere. The cony (rabbit) was introduced under Norman influence. Rabbits bred in designated warrens, such as at Stackpole in Norman Pembrokeshire, or under artificial mounds which may still be evident, perhaps referred to as Giant's Graves. Park boundaries along Bank Street in Bishop's Waltham, Hampshire, and at Ongar Park, Essex, seem to predate parish boundaries. Elements of place-names indicating a park include *laund*, 'open grassy glade', and *pele*, ' fence'.

Paganism and superstition

Even among communities of Christian Celts and English a variety of pagan habits and beliefs persisted. Ordinary folk and indeed their masters accorded a high place in their rituals to superstitions and omens inherited from the pagan Iron Age and more distant predecessors. The 'green man' and associated foliage were accepted elements in ecclesiastical stone carving. Celtic heads were worked into corbel stones supporting timber roof trusses in churches or carved on to beam ends of baronial hall roofs. Pagan well rituals were encouraged but reinterpreted as Christian healing or baptismal rites. Danish and Norse immigrants of the ninth century brought with them pagan traditions akin to those of earlier Germanic migrants, such as the Yule log, roast boar and the use of holly and ivy for decoration. A sense of the mystery and power of pagan practices can be gained by observing or, better still, participating in ceremonies of ancient origin. Midwinter fire festivals with bonfires, torches, drinking and carousing cannot fail to impress and are probably Scandinavian in origin. The Moray ceremonies can be proved to be medieval, but the Viking Uphellya pageant in Lerwick took its spectacular form only in the twentieth century as Shetland people asserted their affinity with Scandinavia. Burial sites and associated finds are evidence of the lifestyle and beliefs of pagan Norsemen. Burials might be marked with settings of stones in a boat shape or even a modest megalith carved with runic lettering. Bodies were sometimes buried in boats, in many cases perhaps just a rowing skiff rather than a glorious dragon-prowed longship. The archaeological excavation of such burials uncovers the shape of the boat, with the timbers entirely rotted away but clearly outlined by rows of rusted nails in the soil. Norse bodies might be crouching or extended; most were equipped in pagan style with goods for the afterlife – a woman might have domestic utensils, a craftsman tools and a warrior weapons. Horses with harness equipment have been found in rich graves as at Sedgeford, Norfolk, where the excavation project in 1997 involved a range of helpers from primary school pupils to postgraduates and the interested public. The fighting farmers of the Isle of Man were conspicuously well endowed for eternity. At Balladoole in Arbory a warlord was interred with his boat, treasure, horse harness and female companion; a Ballateare man was buried under a tumulus with his shield, sword, three spears and a woman – his wife, concubine or slave – killed just before burial by a slicing axe or sword cut to the skull.

Churches

The Christian church was organised by bishops, each exercising authority over a wide geographical area known as a bishopric, diocese or see. The bishopric might be coextensive with a secular territory or Dark Age kingdom; Bangor diocese, for example, for the princedom of Gwynedd. At the heart of each bishopric was the church where the bishop established his throne. This church was known as a cathedral from the Latin *cathedra*, 'throne or chair of state'. From the ninth century onwards the territorial power of the bishop was developed and consolidated with royal encouragement, beginning in the English south, thence north and west, and finally under Norman protection into the Celtic lands. In some cases a bishop shifted his *cathedra* from older Dark Age sites into a town or borough, particularly after Archbishop Lanfranc's decree of 1075. Sherborne and Ramsbury were united, then removed to Old Sarum in 1078. The bishop of East Anglia moved his throne from North Elmham, first, in 1072, to the commercial town of Thetford and thence to Norwich about 1095, though Elmham remained the manorial chapel and hunting lodge of the bishops. When the last old-style Gaelic bishop of Clonard died in 1191 a foreign prelate was imposed to shift the cathedral to Newtown Trim. Bishops in Moray were enthroned in small chapels on Celtic sites at Kinneddar, Birnie and Spynie, which stood on defensible islands and headlands amidst bog and marsh. In 1224 the aristocratic Norman bishop Andrew moved his cathedral to a site adjoining the defences of the royal burgh of Elgin, though Spynie remained a fortress-palace of the diocese until the abolition of the episcopacy late in the seventeenth century.

Bishops divided their territories into the basic ecclesiastical units known as parishes. This was accomplished during the late twelfth century, and the general parish map then remained remarkably stable until the Reformation. The boundaries of the parish were chosen with care, perhaps to coincide with those of a landed estate or Saxon minster, themselves possibly descendants of a Roman villa property or even a prehistoric territory. Boundaries followed watercourses and watersheds and, where necessary, were marked by march stones and hedge banks. Church officers and parishioners periodically rode the marches and beat the bounds to check the position of stones and note encroachments. Small boys might be ceremonially flogged at strategic intervals to impress the route on their memory, so that they could give evidence on oath when required in the future. The historian is also well advised to set aside time to walk the bounds, equipped with copies of charters and Ordnance Survey maps to consider the topographical, political, administrative or even religious reasons determining the route. Typically each parish was served by one principal church with a graveyard and by one or more priests. Parishes varied in area. In a prosperous borough a parish might consist of just two or three streets whose merchant inhabitants could afford their own church and clergy. Rural parishes, especially in northern England and the Celtic lands, were enormous, sometimes including twenty or more townships or villages dispersed over hundreds of square miles. In some of these outlying settlements a limited range of service was provided in a chapel of ease, perhaps once an important early Christian site, though lacking that indicator of parochial status, a graveyard.

Church dedications may illuminate the processes of reform under Norman influence. Continental saints elbowed aside Celtic and English missionaries who might have originally brought Christianity to the district and served as resident priests. The Norman burgesses of Forres adopted the popular Spanish St Lawrence, a third-century deacon of Rome, for their parochial patron. The old chapel of Maolrubha of Bangor, just beyond the burgh boundary, was rebuilt in Gothic style and rededicated to the Frankish nobleman Leonard, a hermit of Noblac near Limoges and the protector of captives and pregnant women. The siting of the parish church usually tells the historian something useful, providing a correct interpretation of the landscape is achieved. The church was usually erected in a prominent though not necessarily elevated position, respecting perhaps a site sanctified from prehistory with standing stones, a henge, a burial tumulus or a pagan Celtic well. A circular churchyard suggests an earlier stone circle, ring fort, druidical grove or defended residence of a converted chieftain. Typically, the church was located prominently in the medieval market place or village green, close to places of contemporary power – the landowner's residence or the royal castle. The church might take over an existing Saxon or Celtic hermitage or monastery or a seignorial chapel. The building was aligned by the sun and stars to permit the priest at the altar in the chancel to face east, the direction of sunrise at Christ's resurrection, though certain Saxon churches are said to be orientated towards sunrise on the patron saint's day. This can be verified locally. A church was difficult to relocate once established, even if the entire village was deserted or replanned.

Historians may profitably devote years to researching, documenting and describing the structure, features and fittings of the parish church, supplementing work already done by Nikolaus Pevsner in his Buildings of England series, the Royal Commissions and previous generations of antiquaries. Church building was big business, with international ramifications. Projects demanded industrial methods of quarrying stone, felling timber, transporting materials, hiring skilled labour in distant regions, paying for goods abroad, insuring against theft or misappropriation and raising and safeguarding money for the project over decades. The researcher may wish to consult ecclesiastical and national archives in addition to undertaking extensive walking of the sites. Architectural ideas and style travelled fast. Parochial masons copied styles employed for high status churches elsewhere, usually a cathedral or a nobleman's chapel (which is likely to be well researched, with published material available). By looking carefully at architectural features the researcher can compare and contrast and ascribe approximate dates to the various sections of a church.

Archaeological investigation, documentary research and architectural style may suggest that the parish church was wholly demolished and reconstructed several times over the centuries. Various kinks, bulges and out-of-plumb walls require investigation as possible indications of piecemeal restoration, extension or repair –

(Left and below) Marnoch church, Banffshire, is situated within a prehistoric stone circle on Cairnhill, a sacred pagan high place, but significantly lacks a graveyard. This has been a church site since only 1797. The medieval church and village (Kirktown) lay at St Ernan's Well, where the parish graveyard still remains. (Map: Ordnance Survey, Banffshire, second edition, 1904, sheets XV.16 and XVI.13).

processes perhaps resulting in a lopsided ground plan, so familiar to ecclesiastical surveyors and to students of church architectural plans. Archaeologists at St Pancras, Winchester, have revealed at least eight successive plan-forms with walls, aisles, piers, doors, windows and transepts occupying significantly different positions on each occasion. A crucial aspect of the plan of any church was the ritual division of nave and chancel, usually marked by a change in floor level and slots in the walls for securing the carved rood

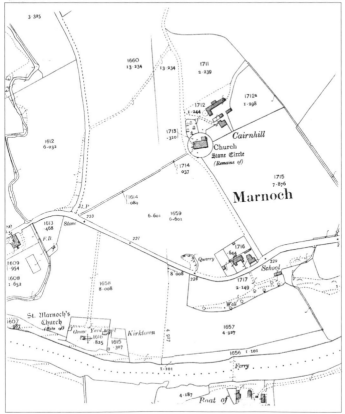

At Sompting, Sussex, the slender flint tower of about AD 1000 is capped with a shingled roof in European style known as a Rhenish helm. The bell openings (west) are Saxon; the two-light openings with central shaft (south) are Romanesque. The nave was remodelled following the gift of this church to the Templars in 1184. After 1306 the church was granted to the Hospitallers, whose north-eastern extension is visible as a ruinous gable attached to the tower.

(crucifix) screen. Liturgical factors may have stimulated rebuilding. The popular cult of the Virgin Mary suggested to wealthy parishioners a new transept or lady chapel. The acquisition of a famous holy relic may have attracted pilgrims and donations to finance additions in the latest style. Population growth necessitated an overflow aisle or gallery.

The most prominent feature, the tower, should be surveyed and photographed, and expert advice should be sought. The walls and foundations of earlier towers and bell-towers may be detected beneath the body of an extended nave, in the crypt or confused in the masonry of walls and piers. As research progresses the historian may be emboldened to ask why a church should have a tower at all.

Earlier Saxon builders preferred a narrow chancel, perhaps with a semicircular apse at the east end. The typical Saxon nave, tall and narrow without aisles, had a narrow round-headed public entrance in the south wall. Towers were square with an unadorned high belfry opening. Windows were round-headed, narrow and splayed, perhaps incorporating slim tile-like Roman bricks. A later Saxon church tended to be more ambitious, with side chapels off the nave and an underground crypt to store treasure or the shrine of a saint. Decorative strapwork and low-relief pilasters embellished the exterior masonry. Belfry openings were enhanced with a baluster or stumpy column. The plain stone lintels of older structures were replaced with round-headed doorways. Round towers with splayed porthole windows are a feature of flint structures in East Anglia.

Saxon and Celtic churches were regarded by the Normans as primitive and reminders of alien religious practices. Buildings were immediately improved by the insertion of new round-arched doorways and windows, with the voussoirs (the stones of the arch) decorated with fierce beasts, staring pagan faces and chevron carving. The Normans entirely demolished hundreds of old churches and minsters. The Norman style of about 1050-1200 is stolid, with stout stone walls, square buttressed towers, plain round columns and round-headed arches.

The Gothic style of about 1200-1450 is characterised by pointed arches, sinuous curves, slender lancet windows (thirteenth century) and elaborate decorative tracery (fourteenth century). During the period 1450-1530 parishes prospering on wool and cloth adopted the Perpendicular style, typified by slender columns supporting fan-vaulted ceilings and tall broad windows of rectilinear tracery.

A brilliant cacophony of painted stars, stripes, comic-strip hagiographies, stained glass, gilded statuary, shining brasses, altarpieces and perhaps a doomsday representation and a sculpted reredos was surveyed from the rafters by a heavenly host of wooden angels or a range of pagan masks carved on to corbel stones, brackets and beam ends. Among fixtures and fittings the font for baptisms may be the oldest

(Left) At Castle Rising, Norfolk, the church was built by William d'Aubigny, Earl of Sussex, following the demolition of an earlier structure during the construction of the castle. A village community relied on the landowner to provide a church of this style and opulence.

(Right) Norman architecture at Castle Acre Priory, Norfolk.

(Below) Plumpton, Sussex. Archaeologists trace settlement at Plumpton back to the Bronze Age, while archivists know that there was a church here during the reign of Alfred. The fieldworker notes the thirteenth-century flint tower and the shingle and tile roofs of a church spared extensive subsequent renovation.

church feature, perhaps salvaged from an earlier structure on account of its liturgical significance. Research into fonts shows links with the import-export business, financial credits and capital investment by churchmen in industrial enterprises. There was a bulk supply of Tournai marble fonts brought to England in the 1160s by Henri de Blois, Bishop of Winchester, while another import of the same period, the font of Brookland, Kent, intricately cast in lead, has a duplicate at Saint-Évroult-de-Montfort in Normandy. In the chancel priests and choir perched discreetly on tip-up seats known as misericords (from Latin *misericordia,* 'mercy' or 'compassion'), carved with playful caricatures of parishioners and everyday scenes. Jolly carvings in similar style may be worked on to bench or beam ends. Worshippers stood, though the weak 'went to the wall' to perch on a moulded stone string course. Bells and clocks may be inscribed with dates, places and the names of makers. Weathervanes, sundials, spires, parapets, timber work and gargoyle waterspouts all merit attention. Lofts, galleries and enclosures were constructed by guilds and landowners. Side chapels were each fitted with an altar dedicated to a particular saint, whose relic might be accommodated in an altar reliquary, while in a chantry chapel masses were chanted for individual souls.

Outside the church the charnel-house contained bones periodically dug up from the churchyard, particularly important where the church occupied a restricted site in a market place. Despite occasional clearances the debris of centuries of burials has often raised the level of the church site appreciably, sometimes leading to its erroneous interpretation as an earlier prehistoric tumulus or defended homestead. Bodies were buried shrouded in linen, usually without a coffin or headstone. Parts of modern churchyards and their environs are excavated for new paths, drains and pipes, providing a marvellous opportunity to record the extent of the medieval burial area while rescuing concealed grave slabs and fragments of carved stone. Always willing to call in an expert when required, the dedicated historian reports observations to the county archaeologist, who may investigate while the ground is opened up. One particular study concerns the shape and condition of bones, analysis providing data on dietary deficiencies, age at death, genetic traits, deformities, injuries and subsequent healing. Leg bones may have been affected by squatting rather than sitting, while neck bones can be deformed from carrying loads on the head. Medieval leaders of society often demanded burial under the floor of the church, beneath slabs (throughstones) or brass plates inscribed with their names, titles, coats of arms and stylised portraits.

A medieval dentist at work, from a bench-end in Grimston church, Norfolk.

Ruined monasteries are conspicuous landscape features. Numerous minor sites, especially in the Celtic lands, have been only partially excavated and incompletely described and interpreted. Various monastic rules were current, though each monastery fitted into a wider religious landscape. Native communities survived where protected by a conservative environment, in Scotland partly through adopting reforms of the Culdee brotherhood in the tenth century. Irish monasticism flourished also, suggested by the construction of expensive slender round towers with conical stone-tiled roofs, so stoutly designed as to have survived to the present. The round towers of Ireland (examples also in Scotland – for example Abernethy) served as places for retreat and contemplation and also perhaps as places of refuge from bandits and invaders. Power politics and ecclesiastical fashion favoured continental Benedictine orders from the tenth century onwards, at the expense of Irish customs. At Mungret, County Limerick, St Nessan's sixth-century foundation survived attacks by Vikings, Normans and Ulstermen until its two churches were donated to the diocese in the twelfth century. Then the austerity of its anchorite (hermit) and the irregular activity of its travelling preachers were exchanged for a strict regime of parochial duty. In the royal hunting forest of Pluscarden, St Ernan's cell at Incharnoch survived until about 1230, when the Normans planted French Valliscaulian brothers to civilise the troublesome men of Moray.

The earliest Cluniac house in England was St Pancras at Lewes, founded by William de Warenne in 1077; Paisley in Scotland dates from 1163. The origins of the Augustinian, Austin or Black Canons may be traced at Colchester, Huntingdon and Canterbury to the last years of the eleventh century; in Scotland at Scone, the Celtic power base, to 1114. The Augustinians were the largest of Irish orders, and each house could adopt its own version of the order's liturgical practices, architectural style and monastic site layout. The Black Canons were providers of hospitality, and a reminder of their work with the sick is supplied by the London hospitals of St Bartholomew and St Thomas, both former Augustinian houses. Cistercians chose rural and potentially valuable lands, for instance at Waverley in Surrey, 1128-9, and in the Yorkshire dales (Rievaulx, Fountains, Kirkstall). The order was introduced to Ireland in 1142 at Mellifont, County Louth, and its thirty-three houses exercised great influence on agricultural improvement as well as on religious reformation. About 1131 Gilbert, a priest at Sempringham, financed an extension to his parish church for a few pious women, who were eventually joined by laymen and clergy. This revived the concept of a mixed monastery, though women were later removed from all but eleven of the Gilbertine houses. In 1143 the Premonstratensians were established at Newhouse in Lincolnshire. The first English Carthusian house (Charterhouse) was founded in Somerset at Witham in 1175-6. The earliest house of the military order of the Knights of the Hospital of St John of Jerusalem was established at Clerkenwell about 1110. The rival order of the Knights Templars received Cressing in Essex and Cowley in Oxfordshire in 1137-9. These orders of crusaders acquired extensive estates in Britain to finance their holy ventures in the east. Their churches were sometimes circular, as at the Temple in London, in imitation of the Holy Sepulchre in Jerusalem.

There is formality and consistency in the arrangement of buildings in a reformed continental-style monastery. The historian can construct plans of abandoned sites from air photographs, archaeological reports and archives, though full investigation may involve archaeologists and geophysicists. A religious house expected the best in contemporary planning for the convenient administration of a populous community of clerics, lay people and their guests. The site was chosen in consultation with the owner or donor to ensure space for development, an adequate reliable supply of drinking water and a powerful watercourse through the grounds for drainage, sewerage and washing purposes. This was not always feasible in towns, hence the periodic resiting of urban religious houses. Stone conduits, reservoirs and lead piping (a Franciscan speciality) improved sanitation and water supply on difficult sites. The grandeur and floor area of the monastery buildings probably bear some relation to the roll call of monks and the contents of the treasure chest. A patron's taste and the regional economy will be reflected in the fabric and style of the monastic architecture, which would be refurbished when money flowed in or became dilapidated when favour was withdrawn. The church was orientated east–west and constructed on a cross plan with north and south transepts. The lady chapel and other buildings to the east of the eastern high altar were normally added later, perhaps in the fifteenth century. Monastic accommodation was sited to the south of the church. A covered walkway or cloister around a garth (garden) gave access to the first-floor dormitory (dorter) and latrines (reredorter), with the warming-room below. A stairway took the monks down into the church for their night-time services. The refectory was above the lavatory (from the French *laver*, 'to wash'), where the monks washed. Kitchens lay nearby, in a separate building to minimise the risk of fire. In the *scriptorium* documents were composed or copied – a time-consuming but occasionally profitable enterprise if the products could be sold. The infirmary offered the sick, the aged and malingerers warmth, fresh drinking water, comfortable latrines, washing facilities, plentiful food and the opportunity for conversation. Illness and the common practice of blood-letting required days of recuperation, so communities generally restricted the number of annual health cures permitted. The abbot or prior was not so restricted in his own lodging, often sited west of the church, where his entertainment of important guests, including the royal family, could proceed unhindered. The abbot's dwelling, perhaps of three storeys with a parlour, a bedroom, a dining room and guest accommodation, was occasionally preserved at the Reformation as an ordinary home, and some are identifiable today.

North of the church was the burial ground, where monks were interred in simple shrouds or stone coffins. These sites were generally grassed or built over following the Reformation, so bones are still dug up from time to time. In monastic infirmary middens and drains archaeologists have uncovered spectacular data in the form of faeces, bone, pottery and even remains of flesh and blood from which DNA can be extracted and studied. The entire monastic complex was surrounded by a high wall with an elaborate gatehouse containing administrative offices, a schoolroom and perhaps even a prison. A busy community of lay workers inhabited the immediate vicinity of the gatehouse, perhaps with their own church, as at St Margaret's, Westminster. Beyond the walls of the monastery were monastic agricultural holdings with tithe barns, a granary, a bakery, a malthouse, a brewery, a smithy and stables. Monastic ownership is still recalled in place-names containing such elements as *abbots, fratrum* ('brother'), *canons, maiden* ('sister'), *prior, white lady, austin* and *grange*.

Following rules of behaviour devised by St Francis of Assisi and St Dominic in

At Kells, County Kilkenny, big walls alert the historian to a site of importance. Here the Augustinian canons kept their treasures secure against the greed of a lawless countryside. An irresistible target for a penurious tyrant, the monastery was suppressed by Henry VIII and granted to James, Earl of Ormond.

the early thirteenth century, friars were clerics committed to preaching and teaching, owning no property and subsisting on begging. Friary churches were usually built just beyond the limits of towns, identified in such place-names as Blackfriars, alluding to the dark habits worn by Dominicans, and Greyfriars for Franciscans. Lesser orders included the Hermits of St Augustine (Austin friars) and the Carmelites (White Friars), whose schools at Oxford were notable. The Crutched Friars were canons regular with Augustinian rules who established hospices for the sick in numerous towns.

As time passed, friaries began to include residential quarters, kitchens and storerooms. British friary buildings have generally been demolished, their sites having fallen into the hands of town councils and laymen, though the extent of a friary may often be traced in modern property boundaries. In Ireland St Saviour's Dominican priory church, Limerick, was founded by the king of Thomond in 1227. Excavation in 1975 revealed that the friars were not uncomfortable and had imported wares from France, Germany and England. Ireland's upstanding friaries, with slender tapering towers and intimate cloisters, date mainly from the era of Gaelic resurgence in the fifteenth century. Typical is that in Sligo, rebuilt for the Dominicans in 1416 with support from the antipope John XXIII. Moyne, County Mayo, founded in 1460 by the landowner Barrett of Tirawley for the Franciscans, was sufficiently remote to shelter friars until the death of the last one in 1800.

Military constructions

Estate owners built fortifications to safeguard their possessions in troubled times, as happened at Hallaton, Leicestershire, where a motte-and-bailey castle was raised, probably during the civil war of Stephen's reign (1135-54). Military construction also often followed the acquisition of an estate with inadequate or outmoded defences, as at Peveril, Derbyshire, where Henry II built a stone keep about 1176 following his seizure of the estate of William Peverel, the poisoner of Ranulf, Earl of Chester. The military architect favoured a site with the natural defences of a river, gully, bog or hill and access to drinking water. A Nairnshire legend explains the selection of a site for the thane of Cawdor's castle. In this whimsical tale the thane put his treasure chest on a donkey's back and loosed the animal to wander the countryside. Where it stopped, there Cawdor would construct his stronghold. Fortunately the donkey had a strongly developed strategic sense and rested at last beneath a thorn tree by a rock, which stood like a natural fortress, surrounded by

Fifteenth-century buildings at Ross Errilly Franciscan friary, County Galway, occupied by the brothers until 1753.

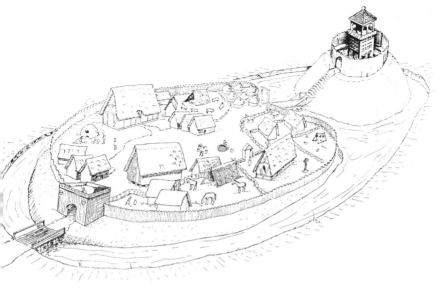

A motte and bailey.

rushing torrents and overlooking the populous and fertile Strathnairn.

Motte-and-bailey forts formed the bases from which the Norman conquest of England was accomplished, and they extended across Wales, Ireland and Scotland. The motte consisted of earth and rubble skilfully rounded to a pudding shape by a military engineer. At Thetford, Norfolk, the mound rose 80 feet (24 metres) within a Celtic bank-and-ditch fortress. In Ireland mottes were built upon native raths or earthwork forts. Elsewhere natural features such as a river bluff, a drumlin or a promontory were sculpted into a motte shape. The motte was crowned with a palisade which protected a timber watchtower or hall-house. Wooden structures might later be replaced with masonry walls, though even these have usually now been demolished, ploughed out or shrouded in trees, leaving the motte difficult to locate. Historians play a game of hunt the motte using estate maps, air photographs and exploration on foot in the vicinity of a successor mansion or castle. A motte without a successor house or a castle without an earlier motte demands special investigation. A place-name such as Castlehill or Torchastle might betray the site of a motte. The bailey was an area of perhaps 10 acres (4 hectares) at the motte's foot, enclosed with earthworks and walls, where soldiers, servants and hangers-on lodged. The extent of the bailey may be determined from modern property boundaries. Despite its central location the bailey of the royal castle of Forres, Moray, was not municipally owned until 1933 and not built on until 1955 because it had remained for centuries under the sheriff's control. An awkward kink in the road pinpoints the junction of bailey and burgh lands, while a big wall and a green lane followed the line of the bailey earthworks.

A square stone keep with sheer walls and narrow window slits represented the best in Norman military architecture, for instance at the royal residences of London, Rochester, Carlisle, Chepstow and Dover. The entrance to a keep was at first-floor level, protected by another building in front. The ground floor of the keep was used for storage, with perhaps a pit for prisoners. Upper floors housed the family and retainers. Accommodation for the wealthiest families can still be studied at Castle Hedingham, Essex, built about 1138 in flint rubble and faced with Barnack stone.

A motte-and-bailey castle at Castle Acre, Norfolk, secured the estates of the Norman William de Warenne; the stone curtain wall was added during the anarchy of Stephen's reign.

Norham, Northumberland, was home about 1157-74 to the princely bishops of Durham. Keeps appeared in Ireland, from Carrickfergus (1200-14) in Ulster to Athenry (1235-50) in the far west. A round keep (*donjon*) was the strong point of the coastal castles of Dundrum, County Down, and Penfro (Pembroke). The keep loomed over one or more wards with masonry walls, moats and ramparts. At Portchester the outer ward was a rectangular Roman fort. Round or polygonal towers, resistant to stone-throwing siege artillery and undermining (sapping), projected from curtain walls and allowed defenders to aim their crossbows more effectively. From timber galleries (hoards) projecting from the battlements missiles were dropped on enemy sappers. Beam slots show where hoards were attached. Round towers and bastions buttressed square keeps, particularly in Ireland, from Ferns, County Wexford, around 1204, westwards to Ballinafad, County Sligo, around 1590, where the four angle towers dwarfed the keep. At Nunney, Somerset, built under licence by John de la Mare in 1373, the towered keep was protected by a moat.

Bronllys, Breconshire, was seized by Bernard de Neuf Marché in the twelfth century, securing the conquest with a motte and bailey, subsequently rebuilt in stone on the original site and plan. The motte was noticed by Gerald of Wales on the journey from Brecon to Abergavenny.

The motte of Ruthven secured the Norman conquest of upper Speyside and was later a residence of the Bishops of Moray. The baronial courts of the lords of Ruthven met at the nearby 'standing stones of the rath [fort] of Kingussie', a prehistoric place of power. The present ruins are of Hanoverian barracks.

During the thirteenth century concentric castles increased fire power, offering defence in depth, the inner curtain wall – with bastions, turrets, hoards, shuttered crenels (archers' spaces in the battlements) and merlon loops (stretches of parapet between two embrasures) – towering over an outer curtain. Outer earthworks and moats, as at Caerphilly, Glamorgan, begun 1271, extended the defences. From such fortresses the conquest of Wales was accomplished. By the fifteenth century comfort was balanced with defence. Walls were pierced with airy mullioned windows and extended to accommodate corbelled garderobes (latrines). Masonry chimneys rose above the battlements. Bodiam, Sussex, licensed in 1386, had thirty-three fireplaces and twenty-four privies. Raglan in Monmouthshire was a sumptuous

palace, but the Herbert family's detached hexagonal yellow tower of Gwent, with its own moat, suggests there was still a need for security in the troubled marches. Gun-loops were slapped through existing walls, while special gun towers were commissioned for modern artillery.

At lower social levels security was achieved and status proclaimed by means of a water-filled moat surrounding the family home and outbuildings. Ducks and geese swam, cattle drank and the latrines emptied in the moat. Numerous sites are still occupied, though the medieval house may have been rebuilt and the moat filled in. A deserted site can be identified as a squarish boggy or sedge-

The coastal castle of Dundrum, County Down, features a round keep.

129

(Above left) Portchester's medieval square keep is protected by Roman walls.

(Above right) Caerlaverock Castle, Dumfriesshire, has thirteenth-century curtain walls, round towers with machicolations, a gatehouse and a moat. A sizeable peasant township flourished at the castle gate.

filled depression surrounding a raised house platform. The Ordnance Survey indicates sites, which are densely occurring in such counties as Norfolk and Suffolk where moats conserved scarce water supplies. Crannogs supporting island residences or castles also remained popular in the Celtic lands and may now be investigated by underwater archaeology. Research is facilitated by the drainage of lakes and bogs, exposing domes of rubble with tufts of scrub or birch.

A tall structure known as a towerhouse, pele, bastle or strength was the proper setting for a landowner in the highland zone and was also popular in boroughs and cathedral closes. In Ireland an Act of 1429 offered £10 for any pele raised at least 40 feet (12 metres) high in town or country. Towerhouses and defensible first-floor halls or bastles proliferated in the contested land of the Anglo-Scottish border, while in Scotland itself fifteenth-century gentry or lairds expressed their growing power and prosperity in 'strengths' that safeguarded both person and property. Towerhouses were of stone

The keep at Threave, Kirkcudbrightshire, is situated on an island in the Dee and is further protected by outer walls and towers.

At Dunnottar, Kincardineshire, the Pictish fort may be the Dun Fother mentioned in the 'Annals of Ulster', stormed in AD 681 during the wars of King Brude against the Gaelic invaders. The present gatehouse, curtain walls, keep, barracks, chapel and palatial residence date from the period 1360-1650. The castle was demilitarised following the Jacobite rising of 1715 and restored during the 1930s.

and were usually square on plan, rising three or more storeys in height with a single vaulted room on each floor. There was one turnpike (spiral) stair, in a projecting turret or within the thickness of the wall. The ground floor was reserved for storage. The entrance at first-floor level was protected by machicolations and murder holes, which enabled defenders to drop missiles on attackers. A stout wooden door and an iron yett (gate) barred the entrance. A bawn protected the animals and the servants' shanties.

Houses

In Scotland and Ireland circular houses were built during the medieval period. A wigwam of poles and timbers rising from a circular base of drystone walling was covered with turf or clay thatched with heather or straw. Another style comprised stone courses without mortar, stepped inwards towards the roof in corbel construction and beehive shape.

Rectangular houses of timber or stone, with walls bowing out in a boat shape, were a Norse speciality, as excavated on Dublin's waterfront, where the single-roomed halls were around 26 feet (8 metres) long. The roof with timber shingles rose highest in the centre, above the central hearth. Such dwellings are recorded in

The bastle at Low Leam, Northumberland, offered a defensible hall and chamber on the first floor above a ground-floor byre and storage area.

The towerhouse at Cashel, County Tipperary.

sagas and also clearly reflected in Norse hog-backed tombs, shaped as houses in miniature. Archaeologists discover pottery, clothing, jewellery, clay crucibles, vitreous objects and bone combs to fill out a picture of domestic life.

The rectangular hall-house was the basic medieval plan; it was a single room in which the whole family lived. The wealthy landowner also inhabited a hall centred on an open hearth, as at Stokesay and Penshurst, sharing the space with servants and guests, though he and his lady separated themselves from draughts and the churlish crowd by taking seats on a raised platform at the far end of the hall.

Across a yard or passage stood the kitchen, brewhouse and latrine. As a defensive measure, and for comfort, the hall might stand at first-floor level above a ground-floor storage room, as depicted in the Bayeux Tapestry and exemplified by the Jew's House, Lincoln. Larger halls were aisled, as at the fourteenth-century Tiptofts, Essex. An extended hall or longhouse (in Wales *ty hir*) accommodated the family at the upper end (*y pen uchaf*) and beasts in the lower (*y pen isaf*).

Medieval halls were sometimes improved by the addition of a two-storeyed transverse wing at the upper end, containing a solar (private apartment) above a pantry or storeroom. The solar with garderobe at Old Soar, Plaxtol, Kent, dates from about 1290. The upper floor might project (jetty), a structural feature that is today – as also, doubtless, in the Middle Ages – admired for its decorative effect. Double-ended halls were created by adding transverse wings at each end of the main hall, perhaps one at a time, perhaps contemporaneously as in the Wealden houses of the south-east.

Houses were constructed from materials available in the region. Timber, especially oak, was favoured for crucks, posts, beams and other load-bearing members (native pine was used in Scotland). Wall panels were of wattle and daub, internal partitions and floors of sawn planks. For visual effect, some timber-framed houses had close studding (close-set timbers) or decorative framing at the front but cheaper practical wide framing to the rear. Stone, typically random rubble, was favoured where timber was scarce.

The remains of turf houses may be recovered archaeologically or detected as cropmarks and low-relief features during field-walking and aerial surveys. Cruck-framed turf halls were built until the later eighteenth century, so visible remains may not be medieval, though perhaps occupying ancient sites. Cob (mud and clay), common in south-west England, lent itself to stout thick walls and deep-set windows and required broadly overhanging thatch, as well as plaster weatherproofing. Bricks were manufactured for prestigious building projects, such as Wenham Hall, Suffolk, constructed around 1270.

Timber houses were either cruck-framed or box-framed. Crucks or couples were stout curving timbers, leaning against each other in pairs and pegged at the apex to

At Monks Eleigh, Suffolk, this yeoman's timber-framed medieval hall is situated between two-storeyed wings of different builds. As a village rather than town dwelling, the house faced the street.

support the roof covering. They could be stabilised with a longitudinal ridge pole and cross members, forming an A-shape. Two pairs of crucks for a simple house enclosed a space or bay of about 16 feet (4.9 metres). A box frame consisted of stout vertical posts set in foundations and stabilised with longitudinal wall beams and cross-beams. This created a rectangular box of timbers. Roofs comprised pairs of rafters joined at the apex, each reinforced with a horizontal collar to make an A-frame, strengthened with longitudinal purlins and a ridge beam. From around 1280 (1460 for yeomen), a chamfered decorative polygonal crown-post rose from a tie-beam spanning the hall. This supported a collar purlin (crown plate), which ran the length of the house connecting the collars of the A-frame rafters. A central vertical king-post added strength to the low-pitched stone-tiled roofs of northern halls from around 1450. Roofs were covered with thatches of straw, reed and heather, gathered from the manorial waste; stone slabs and slates, if they were available from nearby quarries; wooden shingles manufactured by village craftsmen; or rectangular clay tiles baked in clamps and kilns on the building site from the fifteenth century onwards. The size of the tiles was fixed at $10^{1}/_{2}$ inches by $6^{1}/_{2}$ inches by $^{1}/_{2}$ inch (267 by 165 by 13 mm) by law in 1477.

Many medieval houses survive, though altered and improved, perhaps converted into museums or farm outbuildings. Rebuilding or alteration usually accompanied regional prosperity. Yeomen in Kent and Sussex rebuilt from the profits of Wealden iron, wool and grain during the fifteenth century; Burford merchants as a result of the woollen boom of about 1470-1560. The process of dating and describing a house can be learned from textbooks on vernacular architecture. Additionally, the floor plan, elevations, roof structure, building materials, coping, mouldings and general aspect should individually be compared with those of other houses in the vicinity of similar appearance and date. A dendrochronological analysis of timbers can be commissioned, comparing patterns of growth rings in timber samples against established sequences. Leading specialists in this field include Queen's University, Belfast, where a commercial service is offered.

The foundations of successive structures on a site can be examined most easily when a house is being gutted or demolished. Any original features, including those hidden behind plasterboard or above ceilings, should be surveyed for evidence of the size, style and domestic arrangements of the dwelling. This demands the skill of mental dissection, whereby all post-1530 additions, such as slates, brick chimney stacks and bow windows, are stripped away in the imagination. Abbots Court farmhouse at Deerhurst, Gloucestershire, when so dissected, gives evidence of having originated in a religious structure, Earl Odda's chapel of 1056. The homestead of Littywood in Bradley, Staffordshire, does not appear at first glance to be medieval but has a moat, which indicates an interesting past. The three-storeyed brick extension at the east, with cellar and oven, is clearly date-stoned 1790, and a cellared outshut of 1800 may also be ignored. The two-storeyed timber-framed extensions seem antique, and the carpentry, general aspect and documentary evidence prove a date of about 1580. Perhaps a couple of decades later are the fireplaces with brick flues and chimneys and the brick infilling in the structural timbers. Various internal partition walls of wood, wattle and plaster are later insertions, as is the whole of the upper floor. What remains, then, after modern additions have been mentally stripped away, is an airy medieval hall-house of two bays with a solar at one end.

Industry, commerce and travel

Researchers should consider the range of raw materials and manufactured items available to the medieval consumer. Goods made in the home are revealed as archaeologists excavate habitation sites, workshops and middens. The beams and posts of houses, furniture, chests and platters are examined, testifying incidentally to the use of the drill, lathe, wedge, axe, adze, saw and chisel. Microscopic examination reveals the type of timber preferred for particular products, while

Synyards, Otham, Kent, was built for a fifteenth-century yeoman, announcing its owner's prosperity by the inclusion of jettied ends and costly displays of close-studded timbers. Around 1600 the open hall was divided into two storeys, and brick chimneys and stone fireplaces were inserted. The attic floor was created in 1663, according to the date painted on its prominent gabled dormer. During the early twentieth century the house was renovated according to vernacular revival taste.

counting annual growth rings shows the year of felling. Carts were built locally by cartwrights; wheels by wheelwrights. Blacksmiths sought ironstone or bog iron in the neighbourhood for blades, buckles, nails and other useful tools, while whitesmiths dealt in tin. Peasants made their own hoe handles of ash wood and besoms of birch. Urban craftsmen smelted gold and silver, or polished precious stones brought along the silk road from the mysterious east, for the lucrative personal jewellery business, as well as embellishing ecclesiastical manuscripts and other books, altar pieces and triptychs. Timber for the church roof and rood screen could be grown in the neighbourhood and felled, sawn, dressed, pegged, carved, transported and erected by village craftsmen. Stone was an abundant raw material, used by fishermen for net sinkers and masons to repair the church. Stone for the castle was quarried, worked, transported, raised and mortared into position using estate labour and a hired windlass, tread-wheel or pulley. Kilns for drying grain were normally dug into sloping sites, with flues to maximise and draw the heat from peat fires. Quern stones were purchased or manufactured for the domestic grinding of grain, perhaps in violation of manorial rules concerning the lord's mill. Bread was baked in a communal oven, whose circular foundation and paved floor can often be plotted. Coarse pottery was a village product, contrasting with imported decorative pieces, datable from archaeological typologies. Evidence of cooking and diet may be found in the butchered bones, human faeces, seeds, native plants and imported spices of middens. A knowledge of dict, foodstuffs, herbs, cooking facilities, pots and traditional recipes may inspire the researcher to do some cooking over a fire, the final product perhaps giving an actual taste of the past!

Salt was an essential ingredient in preserving and cooking food. Sea water was concentrated in salterns or shallow ponds and then evaporated over coal or charcoal fires at such villages as Budleigh Salterton and Saltram, Devon. Inland brine deposits at such places as Salt, Staffordshire, were reached by shafts whose subsequent collapse pocked the landscape with flashes (lakes) in Worcestershire and Cheshire.

Wool was produced in prodigious quantities, particularly in lowland villages, whence woolsacks could be transported by packhorse or boat to the coast for export or to one of the cloth fairs. In the thirteenth century Winchester fair attracted merchants from Spain, Flanders and Normandy. Wool was used in every community for clothing, rugs, wall hangings and bedding. Wool shears, stone loom weights, rocks (distaffs) and spindles are among the most frequent finds on domestic sites. Households added to their income by manufacturing woollen goods for travelling middlemen employed by wealthy clothiers. The fine, double-width but plainly woven black broadcloth was a speciality of south-west England, while the tough yarn from Worstead in Norfolk typified the East Anglia cloth, known as worsted. Coarse narrow-ribbed cloth from long-staple wool, named after Kersey, Suffolk, was a product of the West Riding of Yorkshire. The fieldworker may identify sites of fulling mills, where cloth was cleansed and thickened using fuller's earth and quantities of water. More readily appreciated are associated structures, such as the wool merchants' guildhall, packhorse bridges, wool-pack inns and the soaring Perpendicular wool churches of East Anglia and the Cotswolds.

A Norse silver penannular brooch.

The corn mill was usually a profitable manorial perquisite, to which families were thirled (bound). The simplest Irish or Norse mill was a drystone structure, stone-roofed or thatched, astride a watercourse. Wooden turbine blades turned millstones, into which grain was jiggled from a wooden hopper and shoe, by means of a clapper. The distinctive busy sound of the wooden mechanism gives the name 'click-mill' to

A spinster spinning with the muckle wheel, from the Luttrell Psalter (British Library, Add. MS. 42,130) of about 1340.

northern examples that have been commercially milling within living memory, for example, Huxter Clack Mill, Shetland. Few watermills were driven directly by a natural stream, because of the irregular movement of the water. Instead, the undershot, overshot, pitch-back or high-breast wheel was turned by water in a lade, fed through sluices from a pond, which itself took supplies from natural streams. In this way, pairs of stones were driven to grind grain into flour or meal. An alternative power source was the windmill, which pivoted on a post and was turned by the miller into the wind to activate sails and grindstones.

The mining of metals was generally by opencast methods, as in the Mendips, the Pennines and Montgomeryshire, where lead operations have raked hillsides with controlled flooding to strip the topsoil and expose ore-bearing bedrock. Lead was particularly valued for roofing and piping. From the thirteenth century, coal was mined from shafts sunk vertically to a seam, from which galleries were driven outwards. Collapsed or backfilled shafts or bell pits appear as doughnuts of rubble. Coal was a valued fuel, and its production supplemented monastic incomes from

A weaver at his loom around 1250, from Trinity College, Cambridge, MS. 0.9.34, folio 52 verso.

An overshot watermill of about 1320, with fish and eel traps set in the lade, from the Luttrell Psalter (British Library, MS. 42,130, folio 181).

wool in Yorkshire and the marches of Wales. Ironstone was extracted by opencast methods, and iron was smelted in stone furnaces situated in woodlands, where charcoal fuel could be manufactured. An air blast from water-powered bellows produced a red-hot bloom. Slag driven off by hammering and reheating may be revealed by an electromagnetic survey. Iron was processed by smiths into all kinds of weapons and domestic tools. The preponderance of the surname Smith indicates the importance of the trade. Place-names in *smith* (English) and *gobha* (Gaelic), for example Smeaton and Balnagowan, identify the site of forges, foundries or smelters. Tin was dug in Cornwall and alloyed with copper from Anglesey, Cumberland and Cheshire to form bronze, and with lead from Yorkshire to make pewter. Both were valued for domestic utensils and ornaments, sold far and wide by tinkers and cairds with laden pack-horses.

Byways, literally 'village-tracks', connected the community's fields, mill, church, meadows, moor and woodland, tracing easy routes uphill, following the reversed S of ridge and furrow, curving round bogs and buildings. Their surfaces were generally of compacted gravel, though perhaps worn into muddy puddles or impassable morass during inclement weather or when repair work was beyond what the community was able (or willing) to afford. Special attention was given to the maintenance of roadways to the mill, market place, church or other places of social or economic importance. Byways were much frequented and were therefore walled, hedged or embanked when threading through open arable land or pasture. Road works were financed and organised by the community, perhaps assisted by charitable donations, with stone quarried, carted, broken and laid by manorial or parish workers. Many byways are still used as public footpaths, bridleways or lanes; others appear as cropmarks in air photographs or as depressions in vegetation in low winter sunshine. Roadside embankments of earth and rubble, typically about 3 feet (914 mm) high and 33 feet or 2 rods (10 metres) apart, are best preserved within early modern timber plantations or sheep pastures that were formerly open fields.

Cross-country routes were byways joined end to end, usually with an awkward kink at the shire or parish boundary. Air photography should reveal the swathe of cleared ground that flanked roads through woodland where bandits lurked. Travellers on the king's highway enjoyed legal rights and protection. Where the highway became rutted traffic was allowed to stray on to firmer ground alongside it, creating distinctive braided 'holloways' (sunken paths) climbing a hill or traversing a mire. Trade routes are evidenced in place-names containing such elements as *salter*, *drove*, *weg* and *gata*. Abandoned routes may be inferred from surviving clues in the landscape, such as bridges, fords, hedges, wayside crosses, shrines or holloways and

The fieldwork of roads leads to places best reached on foot or by bicycle. A north–south route crossing the river Rede at Woodburn, Northumberland, continued as a highway with a stately two-arched bridge until abandoned around 1792 in favour of a revised road layout and a new bridge a mile to the south. The old route remained a byway and a drove way for Scottish black cattle, declining by stages to a green lane, its fine bridge barred by a farm gate.

from careful reading of Ordnance Survey maps. The names Stanway, 'paved road', Broadway, Greenway and Broomway describe the appearance of particular main roads. A community prospered from traffic through the market place, so bypasses were hardly encouraged; indeed, roads were constructed or diverted to lead directly to the town gates. The authorities in Bicester, Oxfordshire, ensured that market days were busy by stopping up a section of the Roman Akeman Street and diverting traffic into the town. Ermine Street bypassed Caxton, Cambridgeshire, until the landowner relocated the whole town, except the church, on the main road some time after 1247. Newborough, Staffordshire, was founded about 1120 where two trade routes crossed. In this instance, however, merchants began to use another road (now the A515) because the town offered few facilities and levied heavy tolls. The nascent town of Slepe was economically stifled in about 1110 when the Abbot of Ramsey diverted the highway across a new causeway to his own newly established town of St Ives, Huntingdonshire.

Travellers preferred to cross waterways at a maintained ford paved with flat stones, as indicated by names in *ford*. Bridford ('bride's ford') in Devon possibly refers to the goddess Brigid's ford, crossing sacred waters. Fords may still be evident where a footpath leads to and from a river, though crossing today is often impracticable. Waterways were crossed by commercial or charitable ferry boats, as at Ferriby on Humber. The boatman was summoned by lighting a beacon. Place-names in *ferry* and *boat* are obvious clues. Bridges also appear in such place-names as Bridgnorth, though care is needed, as Bridport, Dorset, is the port (or borough) of Bredy.

Bridges were generally of timber, and their remains may be recovered archaeologically or indicated in such names as Salterhebble, Yorkshire, meaning 'salter's footbridge'. Masonry bridges were not uncommon, and a considerable number remain in use. Parapets were unusual on small bridges. The abutments of destroyed bridges can be excavated out of river banks. Round or pointed arches, ribs and mouldings were commissioned according to the taste and engineering practice of the day, and some bridges also comprised a chapel (Bradford-on-Avon), a gateway (Monmouth) or even multi-storeyed dwellings (Lincoln). Medieval boats and barges with shallow draught carried bulk cargoes far inland on waterways now considered unnavigable. Numerous inland villages therefore enjoyed bustling waterfront activity,

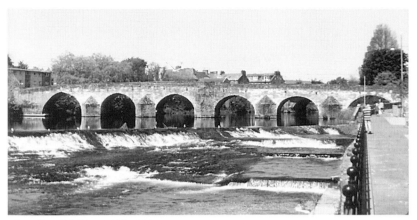

A medieval bridge at Dumfries.

with timber quays, warehouses and merchants' dwellings. Inland towns also established harbours on the coast where borough bylaws, weights, measures and freedoms applied. Sea-going ships were designed to beach and unload on open shores, so coastal and estuarine communities prospered on seaborne traffic and a monopoly of trade within a defined hinterland granted by royal or baronial charter. Waterways sometimes changed course or narrowed, resulting in successive waterfronts; the waterlogged timber or stone foundations of those that became redundant sometimes underlie modern streets, as in Dublin, London and Bristol.

People travelled regularly to buy and sell at their nearest market town. Distant fairs were annual attractions for particular wares. Cattle were driven to market along designated tracks, such as the Welsh Way to London, still marked on the Ordnance Survey. Wool, woollen cloth, silks, wine, spices, hides, grain, metalwares and rare timbers were imported or exported through seaports attended by merchants and chapmen, whose packhorses rested on commons perhaps now indicated by an inn with the woolpack sign. For security against outlaws people travelled in groups, resting at wayside monasteries, hostelries and camping grounds. Weddings, funerals and pilgrimages took families on foot, on horseback or by cart or carriage to distant churches and shrines, along corpse roads or pilgrim ways marked with stone crosses. Pilgrims' mislaid souvenir badges are occasionally discovered in ditches and molehills. Imported and luxury items may be examined on site; they include the gleaming white Caen stone and the polished limestone known as Purbeck marble that were transported across country for prestige structures. In some communities medieval stained glass, silken vestments, vellum books, gold and silver, dyed materials, painted pictures, bronzework and weapons of war may still be preserved.

$\mathcal{T}$he modern era
(1529 onwards)

The ecclesiastical reforms initiated by the English Parliament of 1529 accompanied a redefinition of government structures and services at parish and national level. During the ensuing four centuries British and Irish communities experienced civil conflicts; the advent of popular politics; the reorganisation of rural life; the growth of towns and population; industrial, commercial, technological and transport revolutions; and the emergence of new attitudes to work and leisure. Immigrants introduced skills, alien languages and forms of religious observance, with attendant social problems. People migrated within the British Isles and overseas to colonise an expanding British cultural zone. Imperial expansion, international trade and world wars affected every region of Britain, enriching, impoverishing and decimating. These changes attended a paper revolution. Literacy became a necessity in commerce, technology and bureaucracy. The modern era is an age of archives. The story of the community is told directly through documentary records compiled by successive generations of officials, as well as by ordinary people in diaries and private letters whose words may complement or contradict public records. Historians theorise, analyse, speculate and form opinions which also become part of the documentary record.

Maps and plans

Documentary research begins with the general overview offered by maps and continues with larger-scale plans, as suggested by D. Smith in *Maps and Plans for the Local Historian and Collector* (Batsford, 1988) and P. Hindle in *Maps for Local History* (Batsford, 1988). The public library or archives hold original drawings on paper and linen as well as copies of items held in other repositories of regional relevance. Published catalogues of university and national collections include the British Museum's *Catalogue of the Manuscript Maps, Charts and Plans, and of the Topographical Drawings* (1844, reissued 1962) and *Catalogue of Printed Maps, Charts and Plans, complete to 1964* (1967) in fifteen volumes, with supplements from 1965; *Maps and Plans in the Public Record Office, 1. British Isles c.1410-1860* (HMSO, 1967) and *Descriptive List of Plans: Scottish Record Office,* published periodically from 1966. The Public Record Office of Northern Ireland publishes *Maps and Plans c.1600-1830* for each of the six counties. Maps commissioned by Henry VIII, detailing coasts, estuaries, harbours, forts and other strategic localities with their hinterlands, proved useful enough for the government to survey the entire kingdom. The task fell to Christopher Saxton, whose county maps show settlements, havens, castles, parks and woodland at a scale of around 5 miles to 1 inch (1:316,800). The maps were printed 1574-9, then revised and reworked until around 1770 by such map makers as John Norden, who added roads, and William Smith. Timothy Pont's manuscript maps of Scotland of the 1590s, reproduced in J. C. Stone's *The Pont Manuscript Maps of Scotland* (Map Collector Publications, Tring, 1989), were amended somewhat inaccurately for publication in Jan Blaeu's *Atlas Novus* (1654), which also included regional maps of Ireland. John Speed published county maps in *Theatre of the Empire of Great Britaine* (1611-12). John Ogilby's *Britannia* (1675) comprised geographical and historical descriptions of England and Wales, accompanied by strip maps of the countryside on both sides of the main roads. Admiralty coastal surveys were initiated in 1681. Irish counties and

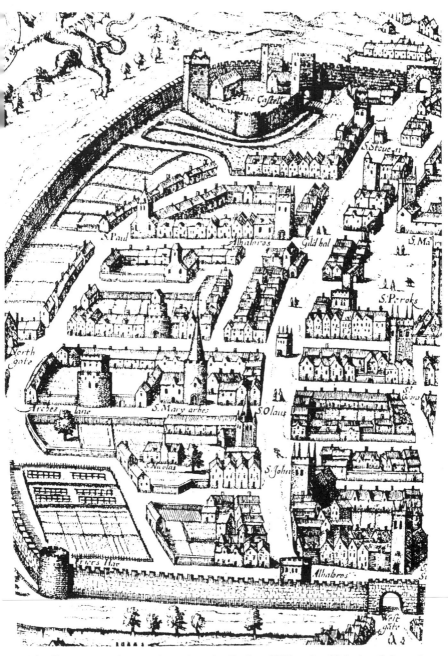

A bird's-eye view of Exeter drawn by John Hooker, 1587, and published at Cologne in Braun and Hogenberg's 'Civitates Orbis Terrarum', 1618, volume VI number 1.

towns appeared in *Hiberniæ Delineatio* of 1685. Parliament subsidised John Adair's hydrographical and county maps by an Act of 1686, and his atlas, *Descriptions of the Sea Coasts and Islands of Scotland*, was published in 1703. Lewis Morris surveyed the Welsh coasts from 1737, and Murdoch Mackenzie northern Britain and Ireland from 1749. County maps, such as Joel Gascoyne's *Cornwall*, were published during the eighteenth century at scales of 1 or 2 inches to 1 mile (1:63,360 or 1:31,680). Grand juries administering Irish counties commissioned maps for their own purposes, for example Wicklow in 1760 and Queen's in 1763. During the years 1776-96 Charles Vallancey, an army engineer, surveyed Ireland at scales large enough to reveal the detail of landscape, settlements and military roads. Francis Beaufort's classic Admiralty charts were prepared from 1829 in the national interest of coastal security. British counties were mapped during the early nineteenth century, generally for use in atlases, by C. & J. Greenwood (35 counties, 1817-34), Swire & Hutchings, Bryant and Thomas Moule (*The English Counties Delineated*, 1837).

Towns and villages were shown panoramically from the late fifteenth century onwards, as in Wijngaerde's picture of London dating from 1543-4 now in the Ashmolean Museum, Oxford. A bird's-eye map of London, made before 1497, was copied for Henry VIII in 1539 and is now in the British Library (Cotton MSS. Augustus I.ii.64). London was surveyed from the 1550s onwards, illustrating the developing street pattern, public buildings, markets, privatised religious houses, churches, bull and bear baiting centres, archery fields, orchards, gardens, mills and riverscape. A large but incomplete bird's-eye map perhaps drawn by Wijngaerde and engraved on copperplates about 1553-9 depicts, on one sheet now held by Dessau Art Gallery in Germany, old St Paul's with the high spire which crashed in a storm in 1561. Horses were watering in the shallows of the Thames at Bridewell by the Fleet outfall. This copperplate was apparently copied for a woodcut prospect of London formerly attributed to the land surveyor Ralph Agas. G. Braun and F. Hogenberg included London in the six-volume atlas *Civitates Orbis Terrarum* (1572-1618). A French woodcut map of the capital dates from 1575. London and other towns were also shown as insets in the margins of estate and county maps, for instance by John Norden in the 1590s. The now conventional street plan was favoured by surveyors from the seventeenth century onwards, for example that of Bristol published in 1673. The rapid urban expansion may be traced as streets and factories spread across agricultural land in plans of Birmingham dated 1731 and Manchester (1746). The French surveyor John Rocque completed a plan of London in 1746 before turning to various Irish towns. The growth of London is depicted in successive editions of John Cary's 1787 plan (6^1/$_2$ inches to 1 mile or 1:9748). Richard Horwood mapped London at 26 inches to 1 mile (1:2437) in 1792-9, with updated versions appearing in 1807, 1813 and 1819. Scottish towns were surveyed by John Wood for an atlas published in 1828. The population explosion ensured that updated town plans were in constant demand. Leeds was mapped twenty-nine times before 1800 and 339 times during the nineteenth century.

Military mapping followed the Jacobite rising of 1745-6. In 1747-55 William Roy supervised surveying teams for a map of Scotland at a scale of 1:36,000. Roy was interested in antiquities, and his maps emphasise a medieval pattern of settlement and land use which within a generation would be subject to clearance and radical replanning.The original coloured maps are in the British Library, but most major public libraries have acquired transparencies of relevant regional sheets. In 1784, for the Board of Ordnance, Roy's baseline in southern England initiated a national trigonometrical survey which was published from 1801. This was the beginning of the modern Ordnance Survey (OS). By 1844 all of Britain south of Preston had been surveyed. In Ireland detailed written parish surveys were prepared from 1809 onwards for maps at 6 inches to 1 mile (1:10,560), the first published (1833) being of County Londonderry. A 6 inch mapping of England began in 1840,

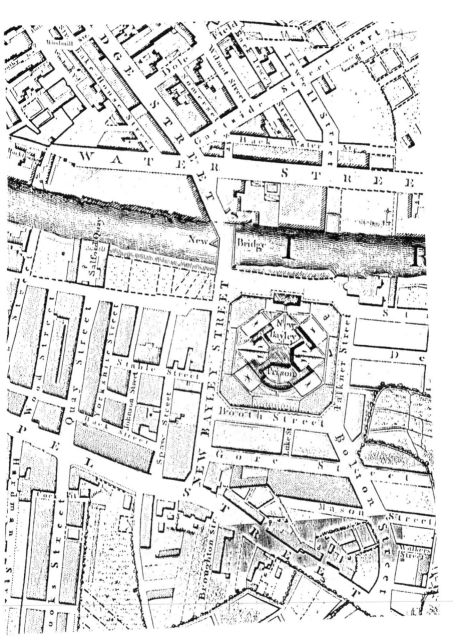

A topographical plan of Manchester and Salford 'shewing also the different allotments of land proposed to be built on', by C. Laurent, engineer, 1793.

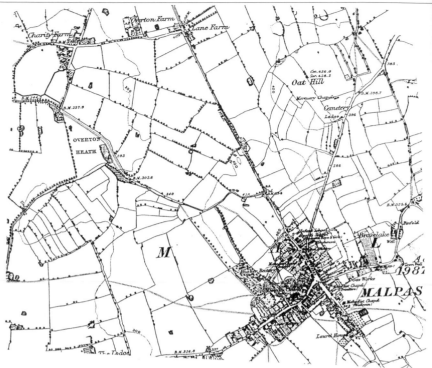

A first edition Ordnance Survey 1:10,560 (6 inches to 1 mile) plan, Cheshire sheet LX, 1881-2, showing medieval arable strips and a straight Roman road. Malpas grew up around a Norman motte and castle.

of Scotland in 1843. Mapping at the larger scale of 1:2500 (25.344 inches to one mile, popularly known as the 25 inch map) commenced in Durham in 1853 and eventually covered much of Britain and Ireland. Coloured printed maps with individual properties numbered and marked with acreages were accompanied by printed books of reference, indicating land use and field names. The 25 inch map shows individual buildings, roads, railways and fields. The 6 inch and 25 inch maps have been revised several times, providing a series of cartographical snapshots of the changing landscape. OS maps indicate archaeological sites and find-spots, many not now evident on the ground, by such labels as 'Stone Coffin and the Barrel of a Gun', 'Sword Blades, Buckles and Pieces of Tartan found A.D. 1864', 'Roman road (site of)' or 'Danish camp'. Researchers may know that recent scholarship suggests the 'Stone Coffin' is a Bronze Age burial cist; the 'Roman road' a bypassed stretch of Hanoverian military or turnpike road; the 'Danish camp' an Iron Age hillfort. To facilitate this work the Ordnance Survey compiled the National Archaeological Record cards with plans, photographs, bibliographies and miscellaneous notes on sites marked on maps. This record is available in public libraries and at the three Royal Commissions.

In Ireland town plans were produced by the Ordnance Survey, beginning with Derry in 1827 at a scale of 24 inches to 1 mile (1:2640). The earliest were not printed but may be available in manuscript at Oifig na Suirbheireachta Ordanais (the Ordnance Survey office) in Dublin. In Britain printed town plans at 1:500 (10.56 feet to 1 mile) and 1:1056 (5 feet to 1 mile) began with St Helens in 1843. At these large scales property boundaries can be measured as one means of discovering the

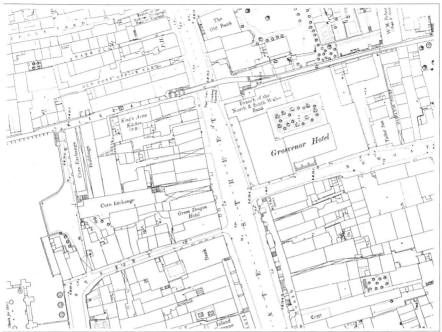

An Ordnance Survey 1:500 (10 feet to 1 mile) plan of Chester, Chester sheet XXXVIII.11.18, surveyed 1872.

underlying medieval town. The ground-floor plans of buildings perhaps long since demolished are shown, as are the positions of street furniture, drains, wells, antiquities and footpaths. Subsequent revisions, often commissioned by local authorities and executed by local land surveyors, might be superimposed upon older plans and are like archaeological layers going back through the decades of rapid change.

The unpublished archives of the Ordnance Survey, centralised in Southampton, were largely destroyed in a wartime fire. The Public Record Office holds parish acreage lists, place-name books and maps of commons in the vicinity of London in 1865. The Irish Oifig na Suirbheireachta Ordanais preserves correspondence files and field and town name books. The Royal Irish Academy has extracts, inquisitions and correspondence relating to the surveyor John O'Donovan, as well as Ordnance Survey memoirs on parish topography, families, trade, industry, place-names, customs and antiquities in nineteen counties, mainly in the northern part of Ireland, in 1830-7. Memoirs on Carrickfergus amounted to four volumes. Lisburn's reports included interesting data such as coach fares, dwellings insured with Sun Fire and the daily rum consumption of the oldest inhabitant. The OS memoirs have been published in affordable paperback volumes by the Institute of Irish Studies, Queen's University of Belfast.

The Geological Survey (1845) published 1 inch drift and solid geology maps with memoirs based on data available in the libraries of the Institute of Geological Sciences and set out in the series *British Regional Geology*. Mapping the chemistry and fertility of the soil was pioneered in Dorset in the nineteenth century and continued by the government Development Commission in Wales from 1925. The Soil Survey (1939) issued land capability maps, soil maps with memoirs and surveys at 1:25,000 of much of lowland Britain, describing the environment in which families created history.

From the sixteenth century landowners employed professional surveyors to draw

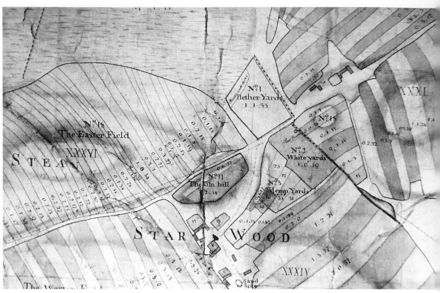

Part of a 'PLAN of the Lands of ROSEISLE as they now ly in Runrigs', drawn by Alexander Taylor, land surveyor, in 1773-5 for the five principal landowners of this area of Moray, prior to reallocation, division, enclosure, clearance and improvement.

up large-scale plans of estates, villages, fieldscapes, woodland and industrial sites, perhaps with schedules showing tenants and acreages. Such plans often coincide with ambitious estate projects for park landscaping, factory construction, building a new town, altering land tenure arrangements or reorganising the open fields. Commercial and political considerations also required large-scale surveying. Following the Jacobite rising of 1715-16 the York Buildings development company in London commissioned a large-scale plan of the land use, mineral resources, harbours, estates, roads and waterways around Inverness and the Moray Firth not previously exploited by the resident and disaffected gentry. Estate plans are held at the estate office if not officially deposited in public archives. Plans and awards in connection with the enclosure of open arable, common or waste land in England and Wales were deposited with the clerk of the peace and in individual parish chests from about 1750 onwards. Plans prepared by estate agents or auctioneers in advance of property sales were accompanied by books of reference describing tenure, land use and types of building, which are particularly useful for dating urban housing schemes. From the eighteenth century onwards architects drew detailed plans of houses, steadings, public buildings, warehouses, factories, churches and other features of the built environment with written specifications, schedules and correspondence. Architectural plans, specifications, bills of quantity and correspondence are usually preserved by the firm, its successors, the record office or the public library. Each town and county council commissioned and preserved plans showing public property including streets, bridges, houses, schools, sewers, water supply, gas works, harbours, tramlines and industrial zoning. Plans of houses, factories and shops that had been constructed or renovated were also deposited with the council by individual applicants, under public health, building control and planning regulations. Church tithes could be paid in kind, for example one piglet from each litter, until legislation in 1836 permitted a money rent charge shared among property owners. A surveyor drew up a large-scale plan of the parish, numbering each building and parcel of land, whose owner, occupant, acreage and state of cultivation were specified in an apportionment. Tithe documents should survive among parish, diocesan and public records. Irish tithe applotment books of 1823-37 in the National

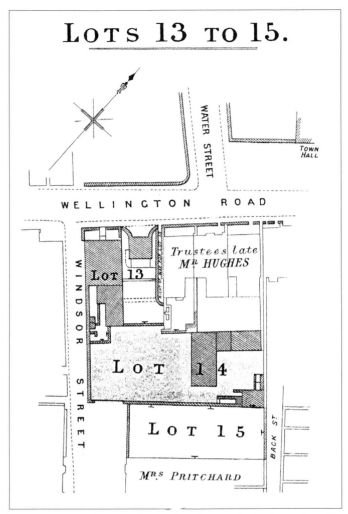

LOTS 13 TO 15.

The plan accompanying the particulars and conditions of sale of a portion of the estate of the deceased Joseph Evans esquire of Haydock, 'comprising valuable freehold residences, houses, cottages, building sites, accommodation lands and an excellent farm, all situate in and near the town of Rhyl, to be offered for sale by public auction by Messrs W. Dew & Son at the town hall, Rhyl, on Thursday the 7th day of August 1890 at 12 o'Clock noon: solicitors Messrs Robt. Davies, Sharp, Kirkconnel & Co., Warrington; surveyors, Messrs Williams & Son, Salop House, Oswestry'.

Archives comprehensively survey rental, property value, owners, occupants, soil type, antiquities, place-names and natural resources:

There was a Danish Rath on this Holding but which is now nearly levelled (Knockanaphibole)

a small Flour Mill on this Holding (Upper Kilshane)

Ruins of a Castle said to have been built by Ulick and John Bourke (Knockanacurra alias Castlecurra)

National Archives of Ireland, TAB27s/30, tithe applotment, Kilshane parish, Emly diocese, 8th March 1834.

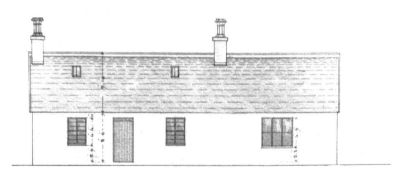

SOUTH ELEVATION

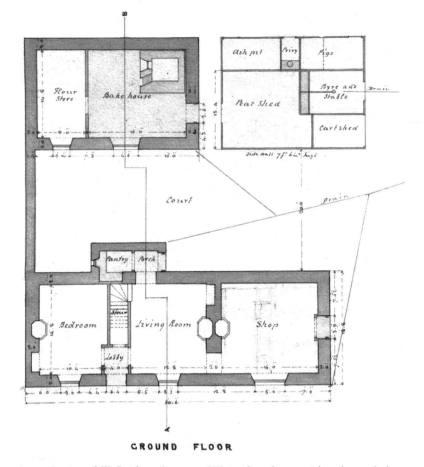

GROUND FLOOR

A design by A. and W. Reid, architects, of Elgin, for a house with a shop, a bakery and offices, to be erected in the new planned estate village of Tomich, Inverness-shire, about 1860.

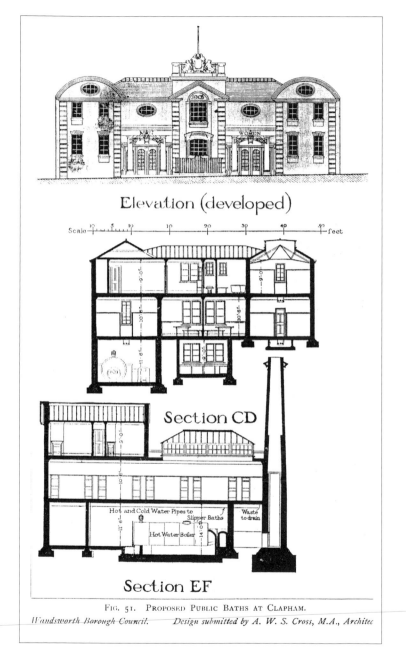

Elevation (developed)

Scale

Section CD

Section EF

Fig. 51. Proposed Public Baths at Clapham.

Wandsworth Borough Council.   *Design submitted by A. W. S. Cross, M.A., Architec*

Hot and Cold Water Pipes to Slipper Baths

Waste to drain

Hot Water Boiler

An illustration from A. W. S. Cross's 'Public Baths and Wash-houses', London, 1906 (page 68).

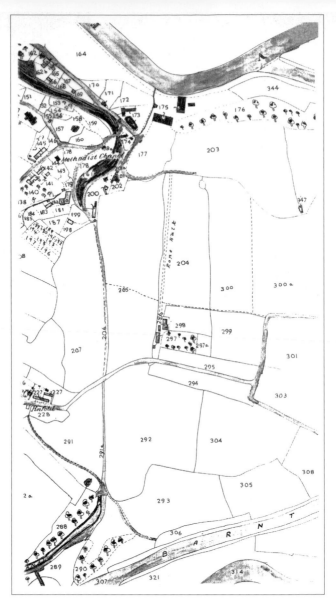

A plan of the township of Barnton in the parish of Great Budworth, Cheshire, 1843,
'made for the commutation of the tithes ... copied from the ... 1st class plan made by
John Beckett for Henry White, Landsurveyor, Warrington'.

Pictorial sources

People and places appear in paintings, prints, drawings and tapestries – at ease in
their own homes or at work in the landscape. Tapestry, embroidery and other
decorative textiles may show houses, schools, villages and genealogies. Valued as
fine art, high-quality oil paintings or watercolours may be found far from the place
depicted, usually in a national gallery or even overseas. Humbler pictures may be
located through the bush telegraph: family portraits at the rectory, watercolour
landscapes on living-room walls. The work of the Lossiemouth artist David West

The agricultural counties of Elginshire and Banffshire supported quarrying, limekilns, coachbuilding, hotels and a hydropathic establishment, as portrayed on company stationery.

(1868-1936) was liberally scattered through the community during the artist's days of penury as traders accepted pictures in payment for goods and services. Originals or reproductions are often accessible through a public museum, library or art gallery.

Business correspondence and tradesmen's bills are often embellished with decorative letterheads illustrating an appropriate shop, factory, machine or product. Pictorial sources may be biased, particularly if a patron wanted his estate immortalised as an idyll of rural prosperity, ignoring the hard life of his servants and husbandmen. In political propaganda the artist may deliberately have exaggerated squalor or wealth. Historical scenes commissioned by official bodies, though apparently well intentioned, are suspect if not misleading. In Glasgow's ebullient town hall of 1883-8, against romantic scenic backdrops, a procession of worthies from St Mungo onwards strides purposefully towards an age of material affluence. Nowadays the panorama seems rather an ironic comment upon subsequent chapters of economic stagnation, industrial decline, architectural decay and incipient social collapse.

Paintings, drawings and sketches by artists at all levels of ability are sought by researchers. Watercolour, oil, pastel, charcoal, pen and ink and chalk have been used for a range of artwork, including the theatrical set-piece, the miniature in a locket and the doodled marginalia of a diary. From the late seventeenth century the improving landowner often commissioned a portrait of his mansion and environs, as in the anonymous images of Stradbally, County Leix, and haymaking at Dixton Manor, Gloucestershire, as well as Jan Siberecht's prospect of Bifrons Park, Kent. A recognisable landscape usually forms the background to a portrait of a prize bull or pig, the objects of much community pride and perhaps the progenitors of a famous breed or blood line. Fine art sources, particularly from artists of national repute, are available in print; examples are Constable's 'Haywain' and 'Flatford Mill', sources for the buildings of East Bergholt, Suffolk. The Suffolk landscape of the next generation was depicted by Frederick William Watts. Particularly relevant are scenes sketched at the time on the spot, for instance John Sell Cotman's 'St Benet's Abbey, Norfolk' and Peter de Wint's 'Old Houses on the High Bridge, Lincoln', both pre-dating photography. The painter John Varley (1778-1842) was influenced by a comfortable suburban upbringing in Hackney, whence he would sally forth in search of the picturesque, with the topographical draughtsman and engraver J. P. Neale, to Tottenham, Stoke Newington, Hoxton and other villages in north London. Varley's sightseeing was reflected later in his work on English and Welsh towns, the suburbs of Millbank and Lambeth and the countryside of Wales. Among the talented and saleable artists famous enough to have their pictures in print is John Linnell (1792-1882), a London painter who specialised in Surrey scenes and with William Mulready depicted Bayswater townscapes of 1811-12. The Irish artist Jack B. Yeats (1871-1957) painted the fairs, races, boxing booths and inns of Devon. The genre paintings of the nineteenth century (those showing scenes of everyday life) are firmly rooted in regional landscapes, for example W. P. Frith's 'Life at the Seaside', depicting holidayers at Ramsgate. William Mulready's 'The Last In' preserves an image of an Irish school, while S. A. Forbes's 'Health of the Bride' depicts identifiable residents of Newlyn, Cornwall.

Woodcuts, etchings, engravings, mezzotints, lithographs and photomechanical blocks were printed in quantity as book illustrations or framed for display from the sixteenth to the nineteenth century. Most renowned are the grotesque social commentaries of Hogarth, the grim cityscapes of Doré and the social and political lampoons of Gillray, Rowlandson and Cruikshank. Among early illustrators of town and country was Johannes Kip (1653-1722) in *Britannia Illustrata* (1708). John Slezer (died 1714) abandoned his army career around 1678 'to make a book of the figures, and draughts, and frontispiece in Talyduce of all the King's Castles, Pallaces', towns and other notable places in the kingdom belonging to private subjects; which resulted in *Theatrum Scotiae*. Slezer shows public buildings, ordinary dwellings, mills, roads, bridges and an adjacent treeless countryside of ridged and furrowed common fields. Samuel and Nathaniel Buck engraved views of towns, abbeys, mansions and castles between 1720 and 1753, which can be sampled in *Buck's Antiquities* (1774) and the more recent *A Prospect of Britain* (Pavilion, 1994) edited by R. Hyde. During the first half of the nineteenth century John and Charles Buckler drew pictures of towns, schools and churches, of which some were

The village of Minchinhampton, Gloucestershire, from Johannes Kip's 'Britannia Illustrata', 1708, showing a broad market street, regular feus and well-defined boundaries.

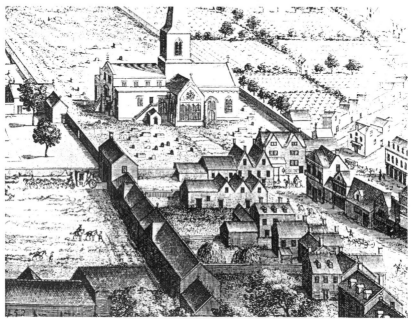

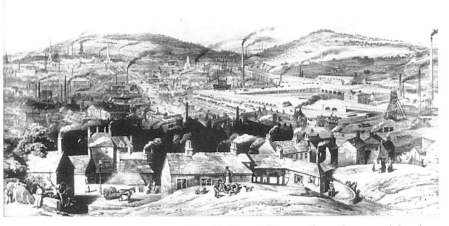

Sheffield in the 1850s, engraved by William Ibbitt, a silver chaser and local councillor.

printed while others are preserved in manuscript in the British Museum.

Photography was popularised during the 1840s. Within a generation most towns supported a professional photographer and a legion of enthusiastic amateurs. Anyone with the money, time and skill to use the equipment and the brawn or servants to carry it around could take up the art. Julia Cameron did so at the age of fifty in the 1860s, using the collodion wet-plate process, and became one of the medium's pioneering experts. Early portraits show people stiffly posed, in formal dress, perhaps with a few studio props, though the bourgeois opulence forming the backdrop may be as insubstantial as the subject's pretensions. More informal full-length photographs, as well as head-and-shoulder *cartes de visite* (visiting cards), became quite a craze in the 1860s. Naturalistic images were sought outdoors. People were photographed at leisure, taking tea, playing croquet, catching a train, cutting down a tree. The background may be the earliest visual record of a particular street, bridge or promenade. In an official photograph the barefoot boys who push to the front or the buildings forming a backdrop could be as historically informative as the dour gravity of the principal actors. Early photographers tended to focus upon the quaint, unusual, innovatory or old-fashioned. Their views may be distorted, skewed anachronistically away from ordinary activities, street scenes, factories and shops. Townscapes, landscapes, public events, sporting scenes, transport, beauty spots, factories, even domestic interiors captured using flash lighting or long exposures were the subjects of specialised photographers, such as G. W. Wilson (1823-93) of Aberdeen. Studios sold albums of picturesque countryside scenes and pairs of identical prints mounted on cards for home entertainment using a stereoscopic viewer. During the 1890s Paul Martin, a London engraver, took candid pictures of people and street scenes. Frank Sutcliffe of Whitby made a photographic record of his seaport town at the turn of the nineteenth century, inspiring disciples up and down the country to photograph people out of doors at their daily labour and recreation. Francis Frith (1822-98) made his fortune in grocery by the age of thirty-five, laid aside his apron and took up the camera. Published prints of Egyptian scenes established his reputation, and in 1860 he set up business in Reigate as a photographic publisher of 'realistic records of scenic attractions'. He commissioned work from a network of photographers, whose views were sold in a variety of formats, including picture postcards. Over 50,000 photographs were accumulated in the company archives by 1914 (300,000 by 1970), representing over four thousand places in Britain and Ireland. When the company closed in 1975 the archive was preserved, relaunched the same year as the Francis Frith collection and selectively published in 1988 on microfiche in sixty-seven volumes. Picture postcards were

Brentford's high street gracefully curves in medieval fashion, lined with individual properties of equal breadth. When this photograph was taken around 1888 some timber-framed houses with tiled roofs were still evident, though masked by early nineteenth-century façades of brick and stucco. Respectable working men, wearing hats rather than cloth caps, pour out of the Bull. A policeman on foot patrol is also present. Women are conspicuously absent. The International Tea Company, founded at 339 High Street, eventually evolved into the Gateway supermarket chain. (London Borough of Hounslow: Chiswick Library Local Studies Collection – 725.72/5149)

also issued by the leading Scottish publisher James Valentine of Dundee and by J. P. Gibson (1838-1912) of Hexham, who specialised in photographing landscapes, architecture and antiquities.

The public were introduced to silent moving pictures through Edison's kinetoscope in 1893. Recorded sound with moving pictures was demonstrated in 1896 and colour ten years later. The extensive preserved footage of film and video provides a comprehensive visual coverage of communities since the 1890s. By such means were created countless thousands of pictures of ordinary buildings, popular customs, work, leisure, home life, domestic interiors, costume and public events, now available for study in family collections, public libraries, record offices and such national collections as the Victoria and Albert Museum, the National Film Archive and the National Museum of Photography, Film and Television, Bradford.

Newspapers

The modern newspaper originated in Civil War propaganda sheets of the 1640s. Titles are listed in the *British Union-Catalogue of Periodicals of the World ... in British Libraries*, the British Library's *Catalogue of the Newspaper Library* and *The Times* of London's *Tercentenary Handlist of English and Welsh Newspapers, Magazines and Reviews, 1620-1919* (1920). Public libraries hold original or microfilm copies of regional newspapers, while the British Library's files are national and regional. The *London Gazette* (1665) is the official source for government contracts, army appointments, imprisonment for debt, bankruptcies, sales of debtors' property and people gazetted for creditable or disreputable reasons. For regional events worthy of national coverage *The Times* of London is the standard reference, accessed through Palmer's index from 1790, supplemented by *The London Daily Post & General Advertiser,* 1734-94, and the *Gentleman's Magazine,* 1731-1883. Files of the *Worcester Post-man* from 1690, the *Stamford Mercury,* the *Norwich Postman, Williamson's Liverpool Advertiser* and the earliest Irish paper, the *Belfast News-letter* (1737), are useful when seeking detailed information on community events, obituaries of prominent citizens or forthright reports on public or council meetings. In 1890 most newspapers screamed 'Outrage in Tipperary' when 'a brutal crowd' physically attacked the daughter of a Presbyterian minister out shopping alone. The Nationalist MP John Dillon wrote privately in measured tones to offer an alternative view:

> Miss Holms ... ordered goods from a man named Rutherford, who is one of the shopkeepers boycotted ... two young girls met her and charged her with buying in the boycotted house ... they did not further molest her ... some little children shouted after her, and grown persons who were present immediately checked them. This was the whole assault.
> Trinity College Library, Dublin, Dillon papers 6816/1/5, letter 2nd July 1890

From 1842 the *Illustrated London News* carried reports from all over the country, with drawings by artists who were usually, though not always, on the spot at the time. It also accepted advertisements for manufactures, building tenders and situations vacant:

> A GENTLEMAN FARMING one of the Best STOCK FARMS in East Suffolk has an opening for a companionable gentlemanly YOUTH who is desirous of studying Practical Agriculture. To save trouble, terms 150 guineas per annum. Address, "Agricultura", Post-office, Ipswich.
> *Illustrated London News* 14th March 1863

Advertisements relate to schools, shops, transport, religious services, sports and theatres. Tenders requested from masons, joiners, plumbers and slaters may fix building dates. Property sales may be described, as here in the case of the Spreadeagles, Wrexham, sold on 22nd December 1777 in eleven lots:

> 10. A Dwelling-house, in the holding of Mr. Edwards, Silversmith, standing at the corner of the High-street, near the Market-hall; containing a commodious shop, fronting two streets, a large dining-room, a parlour, kitchen, pantry, scullery, and a cellar, five lodging-rooms, with garrets over.
> *Chester Chronicle* 5th December 1777

Ships, cargoes and destinations are reported, sometimes in special daily bulletins known as *entry lists.*

Directories, guidebooks, memoirs and novels

Printed directories appeared from the seventeenth century onwards, setting out the names and addresses of merchants, craftsmen, landowners, clergy and householders alphabetically or by trade or profession. Churches, schools, societies and public institutions with the names and addresses of officials, are similarly recorded in the comprehensive directories of Baines, White, Pigot, Slater, Bagshaw, Holden, Kelly (*Post Office London Directory*) and Oliver & Boyd (*Edinburgh Almanack*). National Telephone Company directories of before 1914 indicate those organisations and individuals then at the cutting edge of communications technology. Reference books include P. J. Atkins's *The Directories of London 1677-1977* (Mansell, 1990), J. E. Norton's *Guide to the National and Provincial Directories of England and Wales ... before 1856* (Royal Historical Society, 1950) and G. Shaw and A. Tipper's *British Directories: A Bibliography and Guide to Directories Published in England and Wales (1850-1950) and Scotland (1773-1950)* (Leicester University Press, 1989).

From 1793 the Board of Agriculture sponsored county surveys of agriculture,

NEW ASYLUM FOR FEMALE ORPHANS AT BEDDINGTON, NEAR CROYDON.—SEE PAGE 617.

(Above) An engraving of an orphanage at Croydon, from the Illustrated London News, 30th June 1866.

(Left) Advertisements on the front page of a Scottish newspaper, 13th October 1891.

INVERNESS AND LEITH STEAMER.

THE STEAM SHIP,

DUKE OF RICHMOND,

CAPTAIN CAMPBELL,

Will leave LEITH and ABERDEEN, for INVERGORDON and INVERNESS, on

TUESDAY the 3d March;

And will continue afterwards to Sail Weekly, from

Leith, every Tuesday Morning,

AND FROM

Inverness and Invergordon,

Every FRIDAY Morning, as formerly,

Calling at all the usual places.

Passage Fares, and Freight of Goods and Live Stock, at the former Low Rates.

The Proprietors of the DUKE OF RICHMOND have made arrangements, at a very considerable expense, to land and embark their Passengers, at all times of Tide, at

GRANTON PIER

Without the inconvenience of Small Boats; and Live Stock will always be landed at the Pier immediately on arrival.

Aberdeen, 28th February, 1840.   AGENT AT FINDHORN—THOs. DAVIDSON.

D. CHALMERS AND CO. PRINTERS, ABERDEEN.

A handbill from the archive of the Forres Gazette.

known as the *General Views,* which were revised and republished in 1805-17, complementing the unofficial *Annals of Agriculture* of 1784-1815. Scottish parishes are surveyed in the three series of published *Statistical Accounts* of 1790-8, the 1840s and the 1950s. From the eighteenth century publishers compiled and periodically reissued gazetteers or descriptions of towns and villages with notes of population, industries, ancient monuments, agriculture, fisheries, charities, schools, public services, churches and landowners. Examples are D. and S. Lysons's *Magna Britannia* (1806-22); N. Carlisle's *A Topographical Dictionary of England* (1808), and similar directories of Wales (1811), Ireland (1810) and Scotland (1813); S. Lewis's *A Topographical Dictionary* covering all four countries (1840-7); and the *Ordnance Gazetteer of Scotland* (1882).

> Llanidan, a parish in Anglesey ... contains the village of Brynsiencyn, which has a post, money order, and telegraph office under Llanfair (R.S.O.) Acreage, 4398; population,

1209. Llanidan House is a seat of Lord Boston. The parish is notable both for large connection with the ancient Druids and for military operations of the Romans; it formerly had many remains of both, which have disappeared; and it still retains ... Tre-'r-Dryw, the spot where the Archdruid resided.

J. H. F. Brabner (editor). *The Comprehensive Gazetteer of England and Wales* (William Mackenzie, 1894-5), volume 4, page 67a

Guide books for visitors were produced as knowledgeable residents or enthusiastic incomers wrote about their favourite places. The poet William Wordsworth wrote a classic guide to the Lake District for inclusion in a longer work published in 1810 but its popularity justified separate publication for use by tourists and residents as excursions became popular and, later, the railway age dawned. Reference works, notably *Chambers's Encyclopaedia,* the *Encyclopaedia Britannica* (particularly the 1911 edition) and *The Globe Encyclopaedia of Universal Information* (J. S. Virtue & Company 1876-81), provide such regional information about people, places, industries and agriculture as was publicly available at the time of publication. Travel writing may be located through G. E. Fussell's *The Exploration of England: A Select Bibliography of Travel and Topography, 1570-1815* (Mitre Press, 1935). Examples are the *Itinerary* of 1536-43 by John Leland, Henry VIII's librarian; William Camden's *Britannia* (1586); William Smith's *Particuler Description of England* of 1588; Fynes Moryson's *Itinerary* of 1598, embracing Ireland and Britain; Martin Martin's writings about Scotland (1697); Celia Fiennes's account of her travels on horseback in England (1698); Daniel Defoe's *Tour thro' the Whole Island of Great Britain* (1724-6); the complementary accounts of Boswell and Johnson on their Scottish expedition (1773); and John Hassell's account of the

A page from The Gentleman's and Citizen's Almanack, Dublin, Samuel Watson and Thomas Stewart, 1778.

Grand Junction Canal of 1796. Cultural matters were noted by L. Simond, a French visitor in 1810-11; Dr S. H. Spiker, the king of Prussia's librarian, in 1816; and A. Pichot's *Voyage Historique et Littéraire* of 1816. The agriculturalist Arthur Young recorded his travels in the 1760s; John Wesley his evangelical missions of 1735-90; Dr D. C. Otto from Copenhagen his medical observations in 1825, published in German; and George Borrow his romantic 1854 walk in *Wild Wales* (1862; new edition, Collins, 1955). J. M. Synge published his own photographs in *The Aran Islands* (1907: reprinted by Oxford University Press, 1962). J. G. Kohl's *Reisen in Irland* (1843), describing his travels in Ireland just before the famine, generalised that the people of Kerry were scholarly but rustic; those of Limerick handsome and agreeable; those of Dublin courteous; and those of Cork incisively witty.

Reminiscences, autobiographies, memoirs and even private diaries, whether in manuscript or published, are first-hand descriptions of people and places. Classics include the Reverend J. C. Atkinson's *Forty Years in a Moorland Parish; Reminiscences and Researches in Danby in Cleveland* (second edition, Macmillan, 1891); E. M. Sneyd-Kynnersley's *H.M.I.:Some Paragraphs in the Life of one of H.M. Inspectors of Schools* (Macmillan, 1908); and R. Roberts's *The Classic Slum: Salford Life in the First Quarter of the Century* (Manchester University Press, 1971). Donald Macleod's *Gloomy Memories* (1857), originally written for the *Edinburgh Weekly Chronicle,* has powerfully shaped perceptions of the Sutherland clearances. His family was burned out from their home in Rosal some time between 1814 and 1818, though archaeological excavations in 1962 failed to find the evidence. Sutherland estate muniments refer in 1808 to thirteen families who were in due course offered improved allotments with four years' notice. The diary of the hedge-school teacher Humphrey O'Sullivan of Callan, County Kilkenny, refers to cholera on 28th June 1832:

Tá tuí chum leapan dá tabhairt amach gan a hú do bhochtaibh Challainn
Straw for beds is being granted free of charge to the impoverished people of Callan
agus na seansoip agus na dreancaidí dú gcaitheamh amach.
and the old pallets complete with fleas are being chucked out.
Tá gach carn aoiligh agus gach bréanóg dá glanadh.
Every dung heap and every midden is being cleared away.
Do rinne eagla an Ghalair Ghoimhideach Ghorm an méid se maitheasa dúinn.
Fear of the biting blue sickness has brought us that much good.
Cin Lae Amhlaoibh (An Clóchomhar Teoranta, Dublin, 1970), page 101

Those with a strong urge to write – aspiring poets, novelists and playwrights – are likely to have recorded their thoughts on their neighbours, the landscapes, the institutions and the scandals of their own place and time. Much remains in manuscript among family papers, though some regional novelists and poets, such as Maria Edgeworth of County Longford, John Galt of Irvine, Jessie Kesson of Elgin and Charles Kickham of Mullinahone, had their work published. Major writers, including Jane Austen, the Brontës, Joyce, Kingsley, D. H. Lawrence, Richardson, Sillitoe, Dylan Thomas and Anthony Trollope also describe actual localities. Tobias Smollett in *Humphrey Clinker* (1771) involves his characters in a journey through Britain in which landscapes and society are clearly depicted. Elizabeth Gaskell and Charles Dickens provide eye-witness accounts of social and industrial conditions in particular regions, while Thomas Hardy describes life and landscapes in 'Wessex' (south-west England). The poet George Crabbe gives an account of the labouring life in Aldeburgh, Suffolk, in *The Village*. Brentford, Middlesex, is viewed derogatorily by the poets Gay and Thompson. Conversely, the seventeenth-century bard William Myddleton would brook no criticism of the bathing rooms and waters of St Dyfnog's healing well near Llanrhaeadr yn Cinmerch, Denbighshire: '*Ffynnon Ddyfnog, ffein iawn ddefnydd*' ... 'Dyfnog's well, very good stuff!'

XVIII.

Cork.

Die Kerry=men sind, wie gesagt, gelehrt, aber arm und in ihrer Sitte etwas bäuerisch, die Limerick=people sind schöne und artige Menschen, die Dublin=people sind besonders zuvorkommend und gastfreundlich und die höflichsten und feinsten von allen Irländern. — „Und wie sind die Cork=people?" fragte ich meinen Reisegefährten, der mir dieß Alles im Commercial=Hotel, in welchem wir abgestiegen waren, des Breiteren auseinandersetzte. „Rather sharp!" (mehr oder weniger etwas spitzig!) antwortete er. „Sie machen sich gern über Andere lustig und sind vor allen Irländern durch ihren eigenthümlichen moquanten Witz ausgezeichnet. Sie merken schnell die schwachen Seiten anderer Menschen und verfolgen sie oft unbarmherzig mit feinen, aber schneidenden Sticheleien." — „Haben denn die Cork=people selbst keine schwache Seite?" — „O ja! hm!" — indem mein Freund noch darüber nachsann, was er mir darauf antworten wollte, brach unter unserem Fenster eine der furchtbaren Musiken los, welche die Temperance=Banden, die des Abends in den Straßen von Cork herumziehen, zu machen pflegen, und es folgten ihnen, da es gerade ein Sonnabend war, so viele Menschen nach, daß ich wohl einsah, wie eine der schwachen Seiten der Cork=people in die Nähe des Ohres fallen müßte, da bei ihnen so schreckliche Ohrenschmäuse von ihrer Polizei nicht unter die das ganze Publicum beleidigenden Katzenmusiken gerechnet werden.

The Kerry men are, as I said, scholarly, but poor and somewhat rustic in their manners. The Limerick people are handsome and agreeable people. The Dubliners are especially extrovert and hospitable, and the most courteous and the most cultivated of all the Irish.
'And what are the Cork people like?', I asked my travelling companion who elaborated upon all this in the Commercial Hotel at which we were staying.
'Rather sharp!', he replied. 'They like to make fun of others, and their characteristic mocking wit sets them apart from the rest of the Irish. They are quick to notice other people's weaknesses and often pursue them relentlessly with subtle but cutting gibes.'
'And do Cork people themselves have any weak side?'
'Oh yes indeed!'
While my friend was considering how to answer me, there broke out under our window one of the dreadful musical performances which the temperance bands (parading the Cork streets of an evening) were in the habit of inflicting. And since it was a Saturday, they were followed by so many people that I could well see that one of the Cork people's weaknesses lay in the vicinity of the ears – because such frightful musical treats were not considered by the police to be caterwauling offensive to all bystanders.

Page 344 from J. G. Kohl's 'Reisen in Irland' ('Travels in Ireland'), 1843.

Church archives

Established church records in England and Wales are normally at the county or diocesan record office; important collections are also held in national archives and specialist repositories. D. M. Owen's *The Records of the Established Church in England excluding Parochial Records* (British Records Association, 1970) and the Church of England Record Centre, London SE16, are starting points. At national level, the central archives of the provinces (archbishoprics) of Canterbury and York are at Lambeth Palace Library, the Public Record Office and the Borthwick Institute of Historical Research in York. The records of the two faculty offices, created by Henry VIII in 1534 to assume the Pope's licensing powers, refer to plurality (priests holding several charges and incomes), marriage licences, the ordination of clergy and *fiats* ('let it be done') petitioning for such action as rebuilding a church.

Capitular records relate to the administration of cathedrals and their estates by deans and chapters, who owned valuable properties in developing towns of the industrial north. The prince-bishop of Durham was early faced with the unpleasantness of environmental pollution:

> the whole north end of the town of South Shields has been built upon saltpan rubbish, making a part of the rubbish hill now on fire ... such is the nature of their rubbish that ever since it has been thus wantonly and wilfully set on fire, the air of the whole town of Shields is infected in a very great degree, when the wind brings that sulphureous stench and smoke over it...
> Durham University, Department of Palaeography and Diplomatic, Durham Dean and Chapter, loose papers box 5, proceedings relative to the fire, 20th April 1793

Diocesan and archdeaconry records concern the work of a bishop and his deputy the archdeacon, for example licensing marriages, schoolmasters, midwives, surgeons, dissenting meeting houses and absentee clergy, or regulating by faculty the building and renovation of churches, schools and parsonages, perhaps following presentments on their condition set out in inspection journals. The bishop's court of audience heard matrimonial and morality cases while the consistory court considered property, money, slander, probate and other mundane affairs. Procedure by plenary jurisdiction, involving written submissions, was recorded in act books. Under canons (regulations) of 1571 and 1604 in England and Wales, glebe terriers (territorial inventories) were required from parishes, describing the priest's glebe, the vicarage, the school, church farms, fees, tithes and valuable plate in the strongbox.

> The Parsonage ... a Four Square brick house three stories high besides cellars containing four rooms in each story ... a necessary in the Garden with a pigeon house over it ... There are no lands Tithe free in this Parish ... all sorts of grain, pulse, hemp & flax are paid in kind ... one penny for the smoke of every house ... Easter offerings is Three pence for a man & his wife...
> National Library of Wales, SA/TERR/535, terrier, rectory of Worthenbury, Flintshire, 13th August 1778

The bishop periodically visited each parish. In advance of a visit questionnaires were despatched. Answers formed a basis for the prelate's investigation of the physical condition of property and the moral condition of the parishioners. Following his progress the bishop filed a report on 'things found out'.

> Moyvile The parishe Church hath certeine ruines of old walles not fitt to be built upon. But there is a chappell built up and slated albeit not fully finished in a place most commodious for such Englishe as doe inhabite in the saide parishe...
> Trinity College Library, Dublin, MS 550 (formerly E.3.6.), the state of Ulster dioceses, 1622

Among diocesan archives at Lambeth Palace, the William Salt Library (Stafford) and county record offices are returns to the religious Compton census of 1676, named after the bishop of London at the time, estimating the parochial strength of Anglican, Roman Catholic and Dissenting congregations. The returns for the Canterbury and Worcester dioceses and the Nottingham and Leicester archdeaconries are the most extensive while parishioners were actually named at Bispham, Broughton (Preston), Clayworth and Goodnestone-next-Wingham. The census was edited by A. Whiteman for the British Academy (1986).

From the sixteenth century prosperous yeomen, craftsmen, merchants, some women and even labourers made wills, particularly after 1540 in England, Ireland and Wales when for the first time landed property as well as goods could be specifically devised. The church administered the probate (authentication) of wills and inventories until 1858. Wills proved by the archdiocesan authorities of York are held at the Borthwick Institute, York, while those for Canterbury are held by the Public Record Office but available at the Family Records Centre, London EC1. Also at the Family Records Centre are the death duty registers of the Estate Duty Office, detailing wills proved and administrations granted 1796-1858. Wills proved by diocesan courts and peculiars (districts exempt from diocesan control for historical reasons) are generally held by county record offices, indexed and located through J. S. W. Gibson's *Probate Jurisdictions* (fourth edition, Federation of Family History Societies, 1997). In England and Wales from 1858 one principal and a number of district registries administered probate and provided copies of wills. In Scotland reformed secular commissary courts replaced medieval dioceses in 1563 until superseded by sheriffs in the nineteenth century. Records are held in the Scottish Record Office, Edinburgh. An inventory or will not officially proved may be found in collections of papers accumulated by the family or estate lawyer. Wills contain the wishes of the deceased concerning body and soul, which, sensitively interpreted, may indicate the individual's religious affiliation and depth of faith. Charities, schools or hospitals may be founded:

> I bequeath the sum of Twenty Thousand Pounds Sterling, for the Establishment of an Hospital in the Town of Elgin ... near the Pansport, formerly the property of my family...
> Will of Dr Alexander Gray, proved Fort-William, Bengal, 29th July 1807

Friends, business partners, servants, family relationships and tensions are recalled:

> the most abandoned and deliberately infamous Wife that ever distinguished the annals of turpitude ... a Sister, whose foolish marriage to a man who never had the prospect of supporting a family ... has occasioned all my domestic misery...
> Will of Dr Alexander Gray, proved Fort-William, Bengal, 29th July 1807.

Wills dispose of houses, mills, farms, ships, slaves, cattle and other property:

> All those my Four Meadows situate, lying, and being on the East Side of, and adjoining to Saint Bees Powe [creek] ... to the School of Saint Bees, and commonly called ... Walton Dykes...
> Cumbria Record Office, will of William Skelton of Lowkrigg, Cumberland, yeoman, proved 16th October 1741

An inventory of personal possessions might be compiled for tax or debt purposes by appraisers who walked round the house or estate, writing down and valuing pots, pans and hams in the kitchen, furniture and floor coverings in the reception rooms; beds, bedding, bedpans, bed hangings and chamber-pots in the bedrooms; also books, papers, pictures, clothing, curtains, stock-in-trade, craftsmen's tools, farm animals, stored grain, haystacks, cash, arms, armour, silver plate and debts. Inventories and wills indicate the extent to which the industrial revolution was financed through the investments of farmers and craftsmen as well as from profits of estates and slaves in the British empire.

The reformed church in Scotland consisted of a legal hierarchy of the General Assembly, the synod, the presbytery and the kirk session, each court creating minutes, accounts, correspondence and title deeds. The presbytery's concern with churches, manses and school buildings resulted in periodic visitations:

> There is also a Jacobite meeting-house in the town of Huntly, wherein Mr James Allan (depos'd by the Synod of Moray for error) serves, which is much frequented and encouraged
> Scottish Record Office, CH2/342/5, minutes, Strathbogie presbytery, 1736

Kirk session records of discipline set out parochial evidence of misdeeds in breaking the Sabbath, slander, cursing, witchcraft, superstitious customs, abortions and sexual delinquency:

...a verie sinfull miscarriage in some people in East Alves the last week, viz, the ringing of a Millen-bridle (as they call it) upon ane aged and diseased poor woman called Margreat Anderson thereby to hasten her to death as they conceived ... at ... her own desyre ... they shall be censured with sackcloth...

Scottish Record Office, CH2/11/1, minutes, Alves kirk session, 15th and 22nd March 1663

Wrongdoers were fined, put in sackcloth or shamed on the stool of repentance before the congregation. In Scotland poor relief remained the responsibility of the kirk session until 1845. The minutes, accounts and correspondence of heritors (inheritors) – the landowners responsible for the maintenance of church buildings and graveyards – date from the eighteenth century onwards.

Nonconformists in certain parishes outnumbered members of the established church, for example Methodists in north Wales. In Ireland Roman Catholics outnumbered Anglicans. The central archives of nonconformist sects are available at national headquarters; Quaker (Society of Friends) records at Friends House, London; Methodist records at John Rylands University Library, Manchester; Scottish Catholic Archives at Columba House, Edinburgh. Records of town or village chapels are usually retained by the congregation, with others in the public libary, the record office or even a lawyer's muniment room. Nonconformists were active philanthropists and educationalists, as indicated in congregation minutes and correspondence. Quaker records are eloquent in describing the 'sufferings' of members, arising from prejudice and persecution.

Registers of baptism, marriage and burial are basic sources for the study of demography and family reconstitution. The historian can find out about marriage alliances, the distances over which spouses were sought, the number of children

The parish chest at Grimston, Norfolk, for the secure storage of registers.

resulting from each union, the class and employment structure, changes in population, life expectancy and causes of death. Registration began in England and Wales in 1538, in Scotland during the 1560s and in Ireland during the seventeenth century. In England and Wales a copy of each parish register annually lodged for safety in the diocesan archives is known as a bishop's transcript. Registers of sects outside the established church were brought into official custody when national registration began in the nineteenth century. English and Welsh records can be studied at the Family Records Centre, London EC1; Scottish records at Register House, Edinburgh. Access to records through microfilms is facilitated by the microfiche index compiled by the Church of Jesus Christ of Latter-Day Saints (Mormons), issued as the International Genealogical Index (IGI), available in public libraries or at Mormon genealogical research centres worldwide. D. J. Steel edited the *National Index of Parish Registers* for the Society of Genealogists from 1968, and this is complemented by C. R. Humphery-Smith's *The Phillimore Atlas and Index of Parish Registers* (1984). Academic research on registers and associated sources is conducted by the Cambridge Group for the History of Population and Social Structure.

The vestry meeting of the English and Welsh parish administered church property, charities and services; compiled property assessment rolls and lists of inhabitants; and chose parish officers, including churchwardens; who kept inventories of treasures:

> In primis iiij chalycys, a pyxe of syluer, a bason of syluer, a pax of syluer coper, a crosse with v stons yn yt, a canape clothe, iij Dyaper towells one Dyaper awter clothe newe,
> a chercher to cover the crosse, v grete surplusses & one for the clerke...
> East Sussex Record Office, PAR 414/9/1/1a, Lewes St Andrew's churchwarden accounts, 14th September 1540

The vestry answered queries sent out by Parliament concerning, for instance, charities in 1816 and 1819-37. Lists of inhabitants compiled by the vestry detailed males of military age, householders, taxpayers and paupers, as shown by surviving documents from Ealing (1599) and Stafford (1622). Following an Act of 1836, the poor law commissioners could require corroborative property surveys, perhaps with maps, which the vestry may have preserved. The vestry supervised schools and social welfare:

> Quarter-land of Clegnagh ... towards the *erection & endowing* a Charity School at Ballintoy ... for the teaching of the Children of the poor Inhabitants of ... Ballintoy of all Religious Denominations whatsoever to read & write...
> Public Record Office of Northern Ireland, T679/68, vestry minutes, Ballintoy, County Antrim, 31st March 1777

The minutes and accounts of parochial officials such as the sexton, the beadle, the horse pinder (responsible for impounding horses) and the hedge supervisor, are known collectively as town books; originally stored in a triple-locked parish chest, they are now usually available at the county record office. The constable kept watch and ward and also supervised the trained band and militia. From 1555 onwards the supervisor of highways required people to work a few days annually on the roads, which might be commuted to a money payment. From 1572 until 1834 in England and Wales the parish administered poor relief. Paupers were supported with a dole of food, money or clothing in their own homes or else given board, lodging and useful employment in the workhouse. The overseer of the poor began as an almsgatherer and supervisor of rogues, vagabonds and sturdy beggars. The Poor Law drew little distinction between the genuine unemployed, victims of economic circumstances and the wilfully idle. Bundles of apprenticeship indentures (agreements) show how pauper children were placed in employment, perhaps to learn a useful trade or perhaps as cheap factory hands for industrialists. Travellers described as Egyptians (gypsies) and seamen who had been shipwrecked or had escaped from pirates were among the people constantly on the move through the parish. The historian will investigate whether these travellers seeded the community with foreign ideas, money or, perhaps by interbreeding, with surnames – and genes.

County, parish and social welfare

The modern administrative history of a community is researched among records of the borough, barony (Ireland), county commission of supply (Scotland from 1667), grand jury (Ireland), improvement commission, quarter sessions, police commission (Scotland from 1833), Poor Law union (England and Wales, 1834; Ireland, 1838), parochial board (Scotland, 1845), board of health (England and Wales, 1848), highway board (England and Wales, 1862), urban and rural sanitary

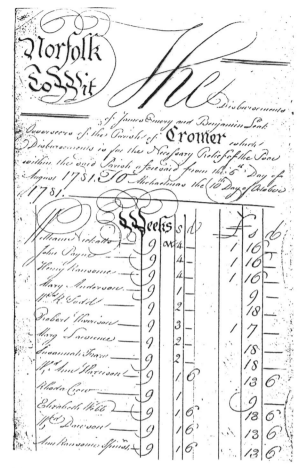

Cromer parish over-seer's accounts, 1781. (Norfolk Record Office, PD 523/128)

district (England and Wales, 1872), county council (England and Wales, 1888; Scotland, 1889; Ireland 1898), parish council (Scotland, 1894), urban and rural district and civil parish (England and Wales, 1894). Councils exercised authority over the built environment, common lands, commodity prices, education, elections, gas supply, highways, lighting, markets, paving, police, poor relief, public health, sewerage, valuation, water and many other social concerns, often operating policies of, and reporting on economic and political conditions to, the national government. The clerk of an authority occupied a pivotal position in public affairs, managing information through agenda notes, the ordering of business and the minuting of decisions. He typically contrived a bureaucratic blandness in council records, with the result that historians learn as much from newspaper reports. Clerks were usually clever lawyers, though a few were simply incompetent. In 1803 the town clerk of Forfar was a boy of twelve, later medically diagnosed imbecile, who could not readily be removed from office because the appointment was for life.

Bylaws regulated neighbourly behaviour on behalf of the community in such matters as slaughtering animals, the condition of dung heaps, noxious trades, building works, roofing materials for fire precautions, the siting of windows, sanitary arrangements, ventilation, the curfew (literally 'cover-the-fire'), traffic control, furious driving, planning, development, libraries, the parking of carts, public open spaces and street trading. Minutes formally summarise the transactions and decisions of a council and its committees on such public services as water supply, town lands, the gaol, finance, public health and market trading. Police committee minutes and reports trace officers around their beats on foot or horse-back, their notebooks giving details of crimes, disturbances, vagrancy, disorderly alehouses and even constables themselves, periodically 'found on the public Road in a State of beastly intoxication'. At the police station were maintained incident books and records of constables and inspectors:

> A Mrs Anderson Spirit-dealer Kinloss ... lodging indifferent companies paid her a visit learned from herself that Constables Glass & Taylor were sometimes in the habit of drinking there ... severely reprimanded her ... at the Findhorn Toll Bar ... found two carts & horses standing in the middle of the road without a guide challenged the Toll Keeper ... if they were drinking in the house, which was denied, when I immediately alighted stepped into the House and found the two drivers viz a Male a Female drinking.
> Moray District Record Office, minutes, Elginshire constabulary force committee, 22nd August 1840

Police information papers among council archives concern violent or sudden deaths, accidental fires, breaches of bylaws and various incidents not reportable as crimes. Individuals and groups petitioned the council, highlighting some of the problems of the community. Petitions were carefully noted and filed, even though little practical help could be offered for lack of resources or will, as when the Old Mortality of Elgin cathedral, a particular butt of the city's blades, begged the town clerk of Elgin for protection as Auld Hallowe'en (11th November), traditionally a night of riot and mischief, drew near:

> John Shanks Keeper of the Gate of the Elgin Cathedral ... lives on the north side of the gate of the Cathedral, and on the south side are two establishments for the gratification of the carnal passions – That these establishments are frequently attended, and as often has your petitioner been aroused from his nights repose by these attendants, who thunder at his door, and frequently drive it up, to the great alarm ... of ... his tender spouse ... That wednesday night being halloween your petitioner dreads a similar attack, and he therefore humbly prays – That it may please your Honors to set a guard on his house.
> Stewart & McIsaac, solicitors, Elgin

Courts heard criminal and civil cases. A few towns preserve records almost as old as the community itself, for example Kilkenny, 1223-1537. Court books contain bylaws, charters, rolls of freeholders and suitors, burgess acts, arbitrations and financial accounts. Detailed narratives of law cases are provided by the claims, petitions, replies, duplies, accounts and correspondence retained by the court clerk. Disputes arose from affairs of everyday life, such as animals straying across the unenclosed common fields, the shifting of boundary markers, the cursing of merchants in the authentic dialects of the people, dung-heaps, noxious trades, smoking chimneys. Actions for debt indicate the type and prices of goods manufactured and traded, the management of credit, the circulation of coinage and the availability of imported or luxury items. Courts protected consumers, providing information on weights, measures, quality of manufactures and range of foodstuffs. Criminal cases of theft, burglary, pickpocketing, mugging, assault, riot, arson, witchcraft, poaching and disturbance of the peace were heard:

> Patrick Cantley wes upon ... the mercat even of Saint James Fair... Challenged ... for the stealling ... of Tuo pair of pleads, tuo pair of Linnen sheits, Tuo coads and ane Chamber pott ... being Searched and Dankered ... taken reid hand with the Fang ... wes found guiltie ... Ordained ... to be Immediatly taken to the pillar in the fish mercat ... and ther his louge to be nailled to the Trone by the hand of the hang-man ... goods and gear to be escheat ...worth nyne or ten thousand merks for the use of the common good...
> Moray District Record Office, ZBEl A329/698/1, decreet of preference and declarator, 21st January 1698

Punishments included fines, confiscation of goods, banishment, flogging, branding, ducking, the stocks, the pillory, the joggs, ear marking and various forms of mutilation. Imprisonment was unusual because expensive. The court might indicate how far the authorities considered contemporary punishments fitted or deterred crimes in the locality.

Title deeds to council property may date from as early as the twelfth century. As landlords, councils have accumulated plans, surveys, cartularies, rentals, leases and other estate records. They have maintained registers, mainly under national legislation, for instance in connection with highways, planning, building control, pharmacies, explosives stores, council housing, slum clearance, war comforts funds, driving licences, motor vehicles, caravan sites, dairies, shops and quarry employees under silicosis and asbestos schemes. Papers accumulated during elections include periodically updated lists of voters. Before the introduction of secret ballots, poll books proved how each elector voted. Election papers are especially voluminous for the period following the Reform Act of 1832. Financial records such as cash books, ledgers, rentals, accounts of charge and discharge, annual abstracts of accounts and associated correspondence refer to rents received on council property, expenditure on the poorhouse, prison, orphanage, school or slaughterhouse; and salaries paid to the beadle, schoolmaster, gaoler, county clerk and scavenger. Voucher bundles comprising invoices, bills, final demands, receipts and statements for a single year refer to such matters as repairs to the market cross, claret consumed at a council meeting, the fee of the executioner for scourging a criminal, the master's salary at the song school, the shambles, petty customs, paper for official archives, the purchase of standard weights and measures, representation on joint boards and borough dues paid to Exchequer. Revenue was raised through a tax (rate) calculated in relation to property values. Valuation, assessment, cess and extent (or 'stent') rolls, usually in book form, comprise a list of taxable property (house, shop, chapel, workshop, garage, factory, hotel) with the annual value and the names of owners and occupiers. Records may be found from the sixteenth century onwards. Parish vestry rate books in England and Wales should have been preserved following an Act of 1744. Irish valuation records survive from reforms of 1838 and 1852. Scottish valuation was modernised in 1855. A property in an old valuation book can be traced forward year by year to discover the buildings, families and businesses successively occupying the site. By finding a property in a recent valuation, the researcher can follow back annually the description of the site and its occupants. Noting the properties on either side at the same time is a useful way of checking.

Officials have produced correspondence in prodigious quantities. Letters sent and received may be available in single-subject files or bound chronologically with indexes, or perhaps tied up with string just as the clerks left them decades ago. Incoming letters were typically folded lengthwise, endorsed with a date, the subject and the writer's name, then stored in chronological bundles. The correspondence file of the town clerk of Buckie, Banffshire, reminds us that the design of the heraldic achievement for that very religious fishing burgh was agreed over a dram in the 'Huntly Hotel (upstairs lounge), Huntly, Thursday, 27th April 1950 (between 11.30 am and 12.30 pm)'. Suggestions for the town motto were solicited publicly. The author Eric Linklater wrote in with 'PIETAS ET PISCES' (piety and fish). The town clerk replied on 20th July 1950:

> The motto suggested seems to be a very apt and attractive one.
> P.S. The only trifling flaw that occurred to me after reading it was that the graceless youth of our countryside, seeing the phrase in public places, might conceivably find a ribald assonance in the first syllables of the first and third words.
> Antons, solicitors and estate agents, Buckie

The clerk, treasurer, librarian, borough surveyor, sanitary inspector, medical officer of health and other paid officials submitted annual reports on their work, which might be copied into council minute books, filed by the officials concerned or printed for public information about the work, finances and concerns of the

THE
W.V.S.

The Nottingham Branch of the Women's Voluntary Service was formed in April, 1939, with Miss Lavinia C. Talbot as City Organiser. The following is a brief summary of its main activities.

Recruiting : The W.V.S. recruits for all the Women's Civil Defence Services e.g. Nursing Services, A.R.P., Ambulance Driving, etc., as well as enrolling volunteers for war-time service of all kinds. Although a number of volunteers have since left the City, or have been obliged to resign for personal reasons, over 4,000 women have been enrolled in this way since the Branch was formed.

Canteen Work : Three Canteens in the City have been organised and staffed by the W.V.S.
1. At the Headquarters of the City A.R.P. opened almost immediately after the outbreak of war.
2. At Locksley House for the City A.R.P. Report Centre.
3. At the Victoria Station for the use of H.M. Forces. This was opened in October, 1940.

At the request of Lady Trent helpers have been sent to the Canteen at the Regional Commissioners H.Q.

Queen's Messengers : The City Branch, together with the County W.V.S., has had the honour of being asked to staff the local unit of the Queen's Messengers' Convoy.

Comforts for H.M. Forces, & Civil Defence Personnel : The W.V.S. administers the wool for the Lord Mayor's Comforts Fund. Up to July, 1941, 31,500 garments have been sent to the Council House, and £1,350 has been contributed to the Fund.

Salvage : At the request of the Local Authority the canvassing of the City was undertaken, and nearly 80,000 housewives have been interviewed. This work is being extended and developed.

community. Reports by the borough surveyor, medical officer and sanitary inspector may build up a dossier on housing conditions. Reports by the roads surveyor may be trawled to date the construction of a bridge, the diversion of a highway, the replacement of the county's signposts or the growth of motor traffic. Miscellaneous documentation only obliquely relevant to the day-to-day business of administration, such as private title deeds, marriage contracts and wills, was accumulated by clerks in the course of business and accepted for safe keeping. Officials collected trade catalogues when budgeting for future projects, and these are now a colourful source for the social historian. The council may have accepted records of meteorological societies founded in the 1850s to make daily observation of the weather regionally and to send telegrams to the capital where forecasts were compiled.

> 13 May 1860 Night foggy; sky overcast all day; corn crake first heard
> 3 October 1860 Night blowing a gale; Stormy all day with wind & rain ... between the hours of 7 and 9, it raged with such violence, that chimney cans were blown down, and houses stripped of their slates and thatch. The barometer fell ... 0.66...
> Moray District Record Office, DJJ 593/1, meteorological register kept at Forres

The corncrake is not now heard in Moray, having fallen victim to the early cutting of grass for silage. Temperature, precipitation, wind-speed and barometric pressure fill out a picture of a changing regional ecosystem, perhaps presaging the dramatic social and environmental developments of the late second millennium AD.

Secular provision for the support of the old, infirm, disabled, orphaned, unemployed, feckless, idle and poor dates from the nineteenth century. Documentation, usually in the county record office, dates from 1834 onwards (England and Wales), 1838 (Ireland) and 1845 (Scotland), when elected boards of guardians (parochial boards in Scotland) began to administer poor relief. The authorities levied rates to

A bookmark from Inverness Library, about 1930.

relieve the poor of each union of parishes indoors in a workhouse or outdoors by dole in their own homes. Minutes of meetings of parochial guardians, registers of applications for relief with biographical details, inspectors' pocket visiting books and voluminous correspondence about paupers with legal settlement elsewhere are essential sources for the social scientist. The following concerns Jane Taylor, hawker, aged 58 when admitted to the poor roll in 1878:

> [She] was married over 30 years ago to David Audsley who deserted her about 18 months afterwards. She is a most worthless drunken character and renders abortive all the efforts of her relatives to assist her to live honestly and decently. She is now chargeable through having fractured her leg by falling out of a Van at Peterhead.
> Grampian Regional Archives, ZPKe A5/102, register of the poor of Keith, 1855-99

Punishment books were maintained by officials of the poorhouse or workhouse:

> Elspeth Gow 30 Using obscene language. Ill treating her child. Bringing in whisky and refusing to work when the bottle was taken from her. Also with threatening to stab a servant. Porridge milk stopped for two days.
> Moray District Record Office, ZUMm 5/1 2nd April 1899

Minutes, correspondence, applications, letter books and registers of claims were created by old-age pensions committees set up in 1909 for people aged seventy or above.

Philanthropic, charitable and pressure groups were responsible for good works in the community. Archives are held by the organisation's lawyer or secretary or by the descendants of ordinary members. Care of the aged, the mentally ill (lunatic is the usual term in documentary sources), the sick and the orphaned in institutions was, in general, the concern of private charities, whose records include foundation charters, title deeds, registers of inmates, correspondence, minutes of governors and financial accounts. These may be held by the organisation's lawyer or by the county record office. The prescription books of pharmacists indicate the diseases of individuals from the 1830s onwards and how these complaints were treated. The patient registers of hospitals and dispensaries offer evidence on community health, sanitation, working conditions, injuries, occupational diseases and diet, as here in the house governor's book of General Anderson's Institution, Elgin:

> 1837. June 18th. Mrs. Wright died this day at ¼ to 4 o'clock, of suffocation by a lump of beef.
> 1853. April 26. Mrs. Donaldson died here this afternoon between 4 & 5 o'clock. She sunk under the gradual decay of nature ... Her death was sudden – she had just partaken very heartily of some soup ... a few minutes afterwards, she was lying in the bed quite dead ... In her youth she had addicted herself to guilty pleasures, and was a great sinner.

Education was organised in uncoordinated fashion through institutions, for the most part independent of central government. The famous public schools were, in many cases, founded early in the modern era to provide schooling free to promising poor boys and for a fee to those who were more affluent. Grammar schools catered for the sons of merchants, gentlemen and professional men. Orphans and the children of 'distressed gentlemen' might attend charity schools such as Christ's Hospital, London (1552). Bishop Maule's Green Coat charity school in Cork became one of Ireland's leading Protestant establishments. Schools for the lower classes proliferated during the nineteenth century, notably those promoted by altruistic landowners and such societies as the Society for Promoting Christian Knowledge (SPCK), founded 1698; the British and Foreign School Society (1807); and the National Society (Anglican), founded 1811. School records are preserved by the schools themselves or their lawyers, if not centralised at the charity's headquarters or lodged in the record office.

> the Committee of Management ... are decidedly of the opinion that a *Female Teacher* will not be able to maintain a sufficient degree of authority over boys ... to keep up that discipline which forms so distinguishing and essential a feature in the Lancasterian system ... therefore Resolve ... to place a *middle aged man* as Teacher ... *Mrs. Don's services, as Teacher, will be dispensed with.*
> Stewart & McIsaac, solicitors, Elgin, minutes of Elgin Education Society, 3rd February 1824

The middle-aged man was, however, observed several times about town 'in a state of inebriety' and dismissed before even taking up his appointment. Registers of such institutions provide the names, ages, parentage and residences of scholars, with comments on their characters: 'trifling ... sly ... dull & dogged'. James Thompson was dismissed for absconding twice from General Anderson's Institution, Elgin, in 1854. The background to the case emerged only in 1870 during public education debates when a radical divinity student, the boy's former classmate, informed the sheriff that James ran away after being stripped naked and whipped by the governor, the Reverend John Eddie, a man 'of an exceptionally sensitive temperament' (*Elgin*

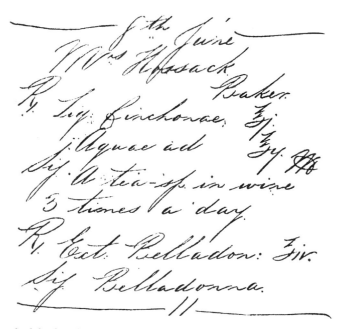

A record of the fact that Mrs Hossack, the baker, was given belladonna for an upset stomach, 8th June 1879, from the prescription book of John Innes & Company, Elgin.

Winchester College, founded 1382-93, was built in monastic style around two quadrangles and a cloister.

Courant, 18th February 1887):

> Nearly all the boys that were in the Institution in my time were stripped ... we could not well see the performance, except when the victim, creeping under the lash, moved too near ... the School door ... If we did not see we heard well, and more than that we have seen the marks of the strap black and blue on the skin of the victim ... Mr John Stalker, watchmaker, High Street, Dingwall on the 24th of October last: – "I was stripped five, if not six times. It is a little severe but very wholesome."
> Stewart & McIsaac, solicitors, Elgin, letter from Donald Simpson, 21st November 1870

The activity of public boards of education, established under an Act of 1870 (in Scotland 1872), is recorded in minutes, accounts and correspondence files. Each school also maintained its own standard records, such as registers of admissions, withdrawals and attendance, confidential files on individual pupils and log books (diaries) of ordinary daily events. The log of Drainie school for 1883 comments on one pupil who later became prime minister:

> J Ramsay Macdonald has passed well, but should attend to History.
> Grampian Regional Archives, ZCMn SRDr79/1

Quarter sessions

Justices of the peace operated at county level, meeting four times a year in formal courts of quarter sessions under a qualified lawyer, the clerk of the peace, but also exercising personal summary jurisdiction in courts of petty session. Records are usually deposited in the county record office. Scottish and Irish records are in the relevant national archives. Following an Act of 1461 quarter sessions were given much of the legal work previously carried out by the sheriff. Justices investigated law breakers indicted by village constables and other officials for theft, highway robbery, burglary, assault, rioting, drunkenness, profane swearing, refusing to attend church and publicly denigrating the authorities of church and state. As landowners, the magistrates were particularly zealous in protecting property through laws against the poaching of fish, game and deer, the cutting of estate timber, the burning of moorland, encroachment on the manorial waste and rick-burning.

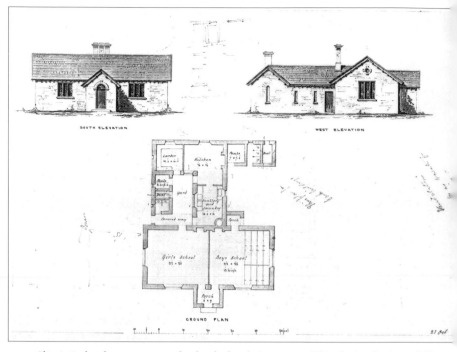

Altruistic landowners erected schools for their tenants. This design by A. and W. Reid, architects, of Elgin, dated 23rd October 1860, was intended for children of the estate village of Tomich, Inverness-shire.

Magistrates could imprison, fine, transport and flog offenders.

> Thomas Mason hyrer in Forres ... pressed to enlist for a soldier ... turned me Crazie in the head ... ventured to go to the Castell Yard and carry away corn and straw ... to suport my horse. The Baillies ... appoint his hands to be tyed behind his back and a Label put on his Breast with these words in Capital Letters A NOTORIOUS THIEF ... put in the Joggs ... drummed thro' the Town with a sheaf of Corn & Straw on his back
> Moray District Record Office, ZBFo B3/773/1, petition, 16th April 1773

The JPs also heard cases of debt, settled disputes between neighbours and resolved differences between master and servant:

> Bell Thomson ... three weeks absent from my service under pretence of illness On Monday ... unwell ... On Tuesday ... worse ... On Wednesday ... speechless ... On Friday ... put on the thin and airy dress of a Bridegrooms maid ... attended the Ball in the Evening – danced – and remained there all night
> The Justices ... Declare her wages for the current halfyear to be forfeited, Fine ... her in the Sum of One Pound one shilling ... for behoof of the poor...
> Moray District Record Office, ZJMm FoB32/836/3, process, 1836

JPs took advice from men of skill in assessing claims for loss or damage, particularly in commercial disputes. On 21st January 1785 Joseph Forster, master of a canal boat, loaded at Newton, Cheshire, 692 bushels of white salt for home consumption, paying the crippling duty of £150 15s 6d then in force. Forster travelled along the Trent and Mersey navigation:

> Barnton Tunnel being an underground Passage the said Vessel being heavy laden ... Suddenly Sunk and went to the bottom of the said Canal or Trunk, being nine feet deep, whereby the said Salt being in Bulk, was intirely Lost ... through suction or wake of

another Vessel passing just before and a high Wind abaft or astern...
Cheshire Record Office, QJF 224, file 1, number 36

The magistrates accepted the loss as accidental and permitted refund of duty.
JPs undertook a number of administrative responsibilities in county government.
Their clerk of the peace accepted for safe keeping personal wills, title deeds,
marriage contracts and (from 1536) deeds of bargain and sale. The clerk registered
victuallers (from 1552), cattle drovers and travelling dealers in foodstuffs (1563).
He was involved in the removal of paupers back to their native parishes (or other
place of legally defined settlement) from 1662. He registered hearths (1662) and
windows (1696) for taxation purposes, useful also for the historian of housing. The
clerk registered dissenting chapels (1689), jurors (1696), diversions of highways
(1697), election poll books (1711), Roman Catholic property (1715), trees planted
in Ireland (1765), land taxes (1780), Roman Catholics (1791), plans of public
undertakings such as canals (1792), friendly societies (1793), men for military
service (1795), inland navigation boats (1795), parochial charities (1796), freemasons
(1799), savings banks (1817), road, gas and water works (1819), nonconformist
sects (1829) and electors (1832).

Estate and family muniments

The archives of estates and families may be available in the estate office, the
family home or a lawyer's office. Title deeds and charters describe property and its
development. Deed bundles might include mortgages, arbitration awards, wills,
house plans and other legal papers, with site plans added from around 1800. In 1574
Thomas Huyck, a lawyer, paid £40 for

> the whyte lyon scituate and beinge in the strete called St Johns strete withowte the
> barres of west Smythfelde in the suburbes of London and in the parishe of St Sepulchre
> withowte newgate of London nowe or late in the tenure or occupacion of margarett
> Hollingeshedd widowe ... also all shoppes cellers sollers buyldinges roomes yardes ...
> mynymentes ... to be delyvered ... within the nowe dwellinge howse of the said Thomas
> Huyck within a greate messuage called the Arches howse and sometyme called
> Mounioye Place in the parishe of St Bennett next Powles wharf in London
> Clwyd Record Office, Nercwys MSS, D/NH/882, bargain and sale by Robert Wyncott,
> 2nd July 1574

J. Cornwall in *How to Read Old Title Deeds, XVI-XIX Centuries* (Birmingham
University, 1964) explains how to understand what legal documents are saying
(rather than how to decipher their handwritings). Accounts of income and expenditure include bills for work on estate buildings and statements of the reinvestment of
rental income in improvements. Personal and household account books are in effect
priced lists of furniture, clothing, food, utensils and other goods daily purchased or
sold. From around 1550 word surveys name each parcel of land, perhaps with rental,
crops, value, occupier, former tenant or possibilities for improvement.

> One close of pasture called Hobb Ridinges abutting north on the lands of John
> Richardson, south on Barnton townfeild 5 acres 2 roods 10 perches One parcell of
> arrable called Dichland in the Common field abutting northeast on Oxhay, being the
> land of Mr. John Venables, John Varnor on the east side, Judge Warberton on the west
> side 0 acre 2 roods 32 perches ...
> C.L.S. Cornwall-Legh of High Legh, Swynehead cartulary, survey of demesnes in
> Barnton, Cheshire, 1620

The professional surveyor usually recommended improvements:

> The Arable ground is Generally good and fitt for wheat, barly, oats and pease ...
> improovable ... if any pains weir taken to fence and Inclose the Arable ground then
> might Great herds of Cattel be easily kept in the spacious mountains and valleys ...
> thire is suposed to be some rich minerall, becaus of the shineing of the Clay ... Their are
> no woods ... Aghnehow seshagh £9 06s 00d ... but if it have A Market & trade and be
> well planted it will be of thrice that value.
> National Library of Ireland, Leslie papers, MS 19,786, Thomas Knox's survey, lands of

Termond Magraagh, County Donegal, 1682

Estate letter books and journals refer to the conditions of employees or tenants, the improvement of park landscapes, crops, the requirement for machinery, fences, grass seed, plantations, pedigree beasts, plough horses and other necessities, work in the kitchen garden and the weather:

> April 14 Different sorts of seeds sown Viz Irish Golden beet. Best red beet. Altringham carrot ... Florance Coss Lettuce, black spanish Lettuce ... London Leek Salsafy & Scorzonera 47:56:50 Very fine
> June 30 Ice got for the first time this season out of the new Ice house 54:60:59 Stormy
> Barnton Heritage Collection, daily journal of Richard Yarnold, gardener, Knowsley, 1820

Some landowners preserved records of their visitors, sporting bags and daily weather from the seventeenth century. Personal letters and private diaries survive in their tens of thousands, and many collections of notable people have been catalogued, edited or published in full. The journal of Giles Moore, rector of Horsted Keynes, for the period 1655-79 has been transcribed in parts for the Sussex Record Society (1971). The Royal Historical Society, Camden third series, has published (1961) the diurnal (daily journal) of Thomas Rugg for 1659-61, a miscellany of personal observations, correspondence, news and the 'conversational grist of his fellow Londoners'. The correspondence of the Constable family of Everingham estate for the period 1726-43 has been edited for the Yorkshire Record Series (1976). Most letters and diaries, though, remain unpublished and await research in family homes, lawyers' offices and public archives to bring alive ordinary people whose opinions are recorded nowhere else. The handwritten diary of James Allan, a Presbyterian preacher, passed from family to family until 1978 when it was at last deposited in a record office. The diary commenced in December 1689 when the young man wrote:

> [I was] sore disquieted & tormented in my sleep wherby I was shortly awakened & thought I found something severall times stirring the cloaths, which I apprehended to have been the devill ready to appear to me in bodily shape.

Allan did not mince his words about the wickedness of certain places:

> the great wickedness & abominations of that sinfull place stonehive [Stonehaven] cam in to Edinburgh, which was a very strange like place to me & my heart was as if I had been entering a wilderness full of venemous beasts.
> How soon we passed Spey I looked on all ye countrey befor us twixt yt & dundee as ye devills bounds ...

Although Allan travelled throughout the country, in all weathers and with Jacobite armies on the rampage, he encountered few problems greater than an inconvenience in crossing the Moray Firth by the Ardersier ferry, which plied the narrows where Fort George was later built:

> ... when I cam to ye ferrie I was much hindred befor ye boat cam over & yet when I went over, tho I kindled no smoak, they forced me to pay a shilling sterling which haveing chod a litle with them, put me all out of frame ...

From Cromarty to Stonehaven (145 miles, 230 km) it was easier to take the regular – but sometimes slow – sea route:

> we embarqued that night & went off next day I was very sick & sore distressed all the time I was in ship which was six dayes haveing got only one stool but many vomites ...
> Moray Council Libraries, DBL 79/1, memoirs of James Allan, 1689-91

Family and business often mingled when a member was also an industrialist or public figure. In 1890 R. P. Gill, an architect, was involved with the New Tipperary Tenants' Defence Association:

> ... several stores stables and workshops are being constructed – structural alterations in the arcade are in progress, besides the completion of the sewerage system ... The heaviest work in hand at present is the building of Nine large 3-storey masonry houses with shops ... erected by the express direction of Mr John Dillon M.P. ... the complete

Geological research among the Old Red Sandstones at Tarbat Ness, Ross-shire, from the sketch book of the Reverend George Gordon of Birnie, about 1850.

transfer of the people & their business to New Tipperary is what is being effected ... Trinity College Library, Dublin, John Dillon papers, 6816/2/53, letter, 10th November 1890

Business records

Commercial expansion and industrialisation are evident from the sixteenth century, particularly in England. The city banker, urban craftsman, railway promoter and village shopkeeper appreciated the need for accurate records, whose location is nowadays a matter of priority for the historian intent on making a valid survey of commercial and industrial activity. Business records may be preserved by the present representatives of the individual, family or company concerned, or possibly in the record office. Obviously the small firm even today preserves little documentation, but the larger company may hold an old business prospectus, a partnership agreement, minutes of the board of directors, a register of shareholders and financial records of raw materials, products, wages and factory machinery. Legal files and letter books facilitate the study of customers, markets, commercial expansion, competition, pollution and takeovers. Title deeds, site plans, engineering drawings, trade catalogues, product samples and stock lists may be available.

Among the most significant and extensive of business records are those accumulated by lawyers. Since a legal accumulation may be the single most productive historical source for community history, and for certain projects may provide the entire documentation required, the archive is worth diligent pursuit. Annual legal

The diary of James McGregor, farmer, Whiteacen, Elginshire.

APRIL—1877

SATURDAY.

SUNDAY.

MONDAY. Lady Day Fire Insurance ceases.

TUESDAY.

WEDNESDAY.

THURSDAY.

directories provide a means of tracing names and addresses of partnerships over the generations. Access is a privilege, though simple if collections are already deposited in a record office. In an average town the researcher should expect to find two or three old-established legal firms, each with an Aladdin's cave of documentary treasures. In the Scottish burgh of Forres the firm of Davidson and Leask was a relative latecomer to the legal scene, commencing business only in 1851. The firm's own archive, deposited in the public archives in 1975-6, centred around a series of indexed books, including legal drafts (1887-1969; 293 volumes), business ledgers (1851-1950; 65 volumes), in-letter books (1894-1969; 579 volumes), out-letter books (1851-1969; 295 volumes) and business diaries (1854-1975; 83 volumes). About one million additional documents belonged to hundreds of ordinary families. There were records of estates; of traders like Thomas Davidson, a banker and ship owner with connections in the Baltic; and of insurance, banking and hotels including the hydropathic establishment patronised by film stars, foreign aristocrats and the *nouveaux riches*. Records of industry (the water, gas, building, bobbin and shoe companies) and transport (Findhorn railway, Findhorn toll bridge, the Moray Firth and London Steam Shipping Company) were stored in metal travelling trunks next to documentation on angling, commercial salmon fishing, farms, market gardens and agricultural nurseries, including pioneer growers of Moray seed potatoes, raspberries and fir trees. Leask held archives of the court of vice-admiralty, of the police, burgh and county and of the Conservative Association, parish heritors, the United Associate Congregation (from 1756), the guildry and the Society of Wrights (from 1789). The papers and architectural plans of Peter Fulton were preserved when the firm was wound up. The partners corresponded with landowners, visitors and august former residents, including Sir Alexander Grant of National Library of Scotland fame, head of the biscuit manufacturers McVitie & Price, Donald Smith, founder of the Canadian Pacific Railway, Sir Arthur Conan Doyle, Baden-Powell,

Service industries, including show business, visible in the documentary record but elusive in the field, were central to the social and cultural life of the community.

NEW CIRCUS.

NORTHWICH.

The Gentry and Inhabitants are respectfully informed that by request of several Families of the Town and Neighbourhood, the Company will have the honour of prolonging their Stay for One Week more, when an entire

Change of Performance

WILL TAKE PLACE.

On MONDAY, the 23rd July,

And every Evening till further notice.

The Amusements will commence with the

RUINS OF PALMYRA,

Or Animated Architecture.

By the whole Troop, shewing in different Forms and Positions the Manner of the Ancients Scaling the

WALLS OF TROY.

YOUNG McINTOSH, the Youthful Highlander,

WILL PERFORM SEVERAL CURIOUS

FEATS OF HORSEMANSHIP,

IN A STYLE PECULIAR TO HIMSELF.

Master of the Ring Mr. BROTHERTON.

Clown to the whole of the Amusements, **Mr. USHER.**

THE GRAND

TURKISH CAVALCADE,

Of Eight Horses Exhibiting their Eccentric mode of Warfare,—attired in the Splendid Costume of Eastern Grandeur.

MISS ALLEN,

Will on this occasion particularly exert herself, and introduce her extraordinary and unequalled Evolutions on the

SINGLE HORSE.

For the First Time **Mons. CLARITUS,** will introduce his Comic Extravaganza, entitled the

EQUESTRIAN BOOBY.

MISS USHER will go through her admirable Performance on the

SINGLE TIGHT ROPE,

And will perform many Astonishing Feats which have never been attempted by any person but herself, various Tricks with One and Two Hoops, pass herself through Two Hoops at once with such velocity as will puzzle a quick eye to discern how it is accomplished—she will also introduce an Admired

SOLO ON THE FLAGELETO,

And exhibit her WONDERFUL EQUILIBRIUMS in attitude on a

SINGLE LEGGED TABLE,

with other arduous Feats which the Limits of this Bill will not admit of expressions.

PAUL PIETRO,

Will introduce his Courtship Scene on his Rapid Courser, entitled the

PAGE TROUBEDOUR.

TAILOR'S DISASTER,

Or, Brentford in an Uproar,

In which more Sagacity will be exhibited by the celebrated Horse Timour in his repeated attacks on Mr. BUTTON—seizing his apparel, pursuing, and ultimately throwing him off his back and driving him from the ring.

Billy Button, Mr. Henderson.

B. oxes 2s.---Pit 1s.---Gallery and Standing Places 6d.

Tickets of Admission may be had of Mrs. Carnes, Printer, Northwich, where places
may be taken.---Doors open at Seven performance to begin at half-past.

N. B. The Public will be pleased to observe that the Horses will parade through the Town on Monday and Market day.

Carnes, Printer, Northwich.

Lord Roberts, Earl Haig, Lord Salisbury, Arthur Balfour, Lloyd George, Ramsay Macdonald, W. E. Johns (Biggles), Hugh Trenchard (RAF), Lord Reith and Charlie Chaplin. The collection was made available to the public through a summary catalogue of no fewer than 1396 pages.

Fire insurance was a thriving business from the seventeenth century, when lead fire-marks attached to buildings told the fire crew which company insured the building. The Hand-in-Hand, founded in 1696, and the Westminster (1717) restricted their cover to London properties. Companies operated in London, Bristol, Edinburgh and Glasgow by 1720. Registers describe the construction, contents, heating and lighting of buildings; hazardous goods in production; machinery on the

The archive of J. and H. W. Leask, Forres, Moray, was saved during the winter of 1976-7. Some 2.5 million documents were rescued from damp cellars and leaky garrets, together with a motley collection of dead pigeons, mouse corpses, rats' nests and one unexploded bomb.

site, the name, status, occupation and address of the proposer or tenant; and the reputed value. Companies may hold their own records or may deposit them in record offices. The Guildhall Library, London, has indexed the archives of over eighty firms, including the Hand-in-Hand (1696) and the Royal Exchange (1720), and has

TO BE
SOLD BY AUCTION,
AT THE HOUSE OF MR. HUMPHREY ADAMS,
The Crown Inn, in Northwich
IN THE COUNTY OF CHESTER,
On FRIDAY the 24th DAY of MAY, 1822,
AT THE HOUR OF FOUR IN THE AFTERNOON,
Subject to Conditions that will be then and there produced.

Thirteen Parts or Shares
(THE WHOLE BEING DIVIDED INTO FORTY)
OF AND IN A
Rock Salt Pit
And Close of Land,
ntaining about 1A. 3Q. 3P. Cheshire Measure, situate in Marston, in the said County of Chester, held by Lease for a Term Years, which will expire the 25th Day of March, 1835, at the Yearly Rent of £62.

Together with the like Shares of
A STEAM ENGINE,
Twelve Horses Power, upon the principle of BOLTON and WATT's late Patent, and of the Buckets, and other Utensils, and ierials, now in use at the said Pit.

And the like Shares in
Two Flats,
CALLED THE
Howe AND Active,
ith their small Boats, &c. now navigating the Rivers Weaver and Mersey

 Premises are most eligibly situated a short distance from the Navigable River Weaver. The Pit and Buildings are substantially made and built. The Engine and Machinery are all in good order, and capable of delivering any quantity of Rock Salt that can be disposed of.

he said Sum of £62. is the only Rent the Landlord is entitled to, which is £200. per Annum less than is paid for any other Rock Salt Pit in the Neighbourhood,

Further Particulars may be had by applying to Mr. BARKER, Solicitor, Northwich.

CARNES, PRINTER, NORTHWICH.

A handbill from the archive of Chambers & Company, solicitors, of Northwich, Cheshire.

Insurance company plaques.

made them accessible in microform through public libraries. Sun Fire policy registers covering the years 1710-1863, accounts of 1728-1903 and agency records of 1768-1908 show that by 1792 about half of the business came from the provinces; there was a network of agencies in King's Lynn, Norwich, Swaffham and Yarmouth for East Anglia alone.

Parliament

The supremacy of Parliament in political affairs was gradually established during the modern era. Parliaments in England, Ireland and Scotland met irregularly, the members establishing no effective systems for the permanent preservation of records of proceedings. In 1621 clerks of the English House of Lords began to maintain an archive of journals, petitions, bills and related documents in the moated Jewel Tower of the Palace of Westminster. Here the records remained, suffering from damp, vermin, neglectful keepers, periodic weeding and finally the great fire that swept through the Palace in 1834. The archives of the Lords and the Commons were eventually rehoused in the House of Lords Record Office, though certain manuscript and printed records, for instance the Marylebone election papers of 1837, remained in the parliamentary libraries, all as set out in M. F. Bond's *Guide to the Records of Parliament* (HMSO, 1971). Also deposited are papers of public interest such as those of the Commons and Footpaths Preservation Society, referring, for instance, to Epping Forest (1720-1882) and Medmenham, Buckinghamshire (1778-1898). Before the Scottish and English parliaments were united in 1707, the Scottish legislature comprised a single chamber in which the three estates of prelates, barons and burgesses met to impose taxes, devise legislation and administer justice in consensus with royal policy. Records are the responsibility of the Scottish Record Office. Surviving Irish records are lodged in the library of Dáil Éireann, the National Archives or the National Library, all in Dublin. From 1494 until 1783 Irish legislators passed only Acts approved by the English Parliament, and English legislation also applied in Ireland. In 1801 the Dublin legislature was abolished, and

Irish members then travelled to Westminster.

The journals of the English Houses of Lords (1510 onwards) and Commons (1547) indicate how closely members could be involved in the mundane affairs of communities, particularly if there were also personal or financial considerations in relation to such issues as the enclosure of common land, the desertion of villages and the wholesale replanning of landscapes. The journals have been printed and indexed and may be held in record offices and public or university libraries. Using the indexes, the researcher identifies subjects, people and places, perhaps also looking under general headings for unindexed or unexpected references.

> ACCOUNTS OF ... the West India Dock Company .... to the 1st of February 1805; also a Statement of the Progress of the Works ... at the Isle of Dogs .... and ... of the East India Company at Blackwall
>
> BILLS ... Concerning Sewers in the Port of Southampton, rejected 32o Die Parliamenti. [26th February 1509/10]
>
> CLEVELAND in Yorkshire, a Petition of the Gentry, &c. for a happy Reformation, and a just Execution of the Laws against Papists read, 10th February 1641
>
> LEIGHTON BROMSWOLD Barony. The Lady O'Brian's Petition claiming a Right ... 8th January 1673
>
> *Calendar of the Journals of the House of Lords,* 1810, pages 387, 10, 27, 231

Parliamentary sessional papers accumulated in their thousands, including returns in response to an order of one of the Houses or following an address to the monarch, papers presented by command of the monarch, reports of royal commissions, annual reports of public organisations, private or public Bill papers, and the documentation of committee reports, Church Assembly measures, house resolutions or standing orders. Also held are the protestation returns of 1642, an archive of certificates collected in English parishes of males subscribing the oath of protestation, swearing to 'maintaine & defend ... ye true Reformed Protestant Religion expressed in ye doctrine of the Church of England ... ye power & Priueledges of Parliament. The Lawfull Rights, & Liberties of ye subiect'.

The command paper of 1873, known as New Domesday, sets out the name and address of every owner of one acre and upwards in the kingdom, with the acreage and annual value of each person's holding, together with the total number of owners of less than one acre plus the gross value and acreage of land. Sessional papers have been printed since 1660. Bound collections from 1801 onwards are held in eleven major libraries in Britain as well as at Westminster. Larger public and university libraries hold microform editions as well as 1112 volumes of reprints, accessed through Luke Hansard's *Catalogue and Breviate of Parliamentary Papers, 1696-1834* (facsimile edition, Blackwell, 1953) and P. and G. Ford's additional breviates into the twentieth century, published by the Irish University Press, Shannon. When Parliament investigated such matters as the poor law, trade, factory hours or transport, evidence was written down as a dramatic dialogue of questions and answers, often involving ordinary people who, prompted by MPs, lawyers or clever administrators, gave accounts in their own words, which were recorded verbatim, though with the normal hesitations omitted. Below, as an example, is the evidence of Bartholomew Lyons, grave-digger at St Ann's church, Soho, London. In 1842 he was called before the House of Commons select committee on the improvement of the health of towns. The committee was concerned at this stage with the health hazards arising from over-full urban graveyards and interments beneath church floors.

> I dug a grave on a Sunday evening on purpose to get ready for Monday ... and when I went to work on Monday morning I finished my work, and I was trying the length of the grave to see if it was long enough and wide enough, so that I should not have to go down again, and while I was in there the ground gave way and a body turned right over, and the two arms came and clasped me round the neck; she had gloves on and stockings and white flannel inside, and what we call a shift, but no head.
>
> 1071. The body came tumbling upon you? – Yes, just as I was kneeling down; it was a very stout body, and the force that she came with knocked my head against a body

underneath, and I was very much frightened at the time.
1075. [Mr. Vernon.] What depth were you down when this body fell upon you? – About nine feet.
Report of the Select Committee on the Improvement of the Health of Towns: effect of interment of bodies in towns, 1842 (327) x.

The activity most commonly associated with Parliament is that of making laws or statutes of the realm. The legislative process, initiated by the government in the public interest, concerns such matters as economic policy, taxation, crime, poor relief, health care, factory inspection, hours of work, wages, trade unions, military camps, militia, illegal organisations, roads, canals, harbours, railways, water, gas, pollution, planning, development control and ancient monuments, mostly affecting specific localities and enterprises. A legislative proposal was brought before the Commons or the Lords in documentation known as a Bill which was discussed (debated), amended, voted on, rejected or approved (passed) as a statute of the realm. Acts of Parliament are dated by regnal year and year of grace and are numbered in the order of receiving royal assent; for example, 4 George III chapter XXXVII (1763) is an Act arising out of the particular circumstances of Winchelsea's textile industry. It has a *long title*:

> An Act for the better establishing a Manufactory of Cambricks and Lawns, or Goods of the Kind usually known under those Denominations, now carrying on at Winchelsea, in the County of Sussex; and for improving, regulating and extending the Manufacture of Cambricks and Lawns, or Goods of the Kind usually known under those Denominations, in that part of Great Britain called England.

This Act is usually referred to by its *short title*, 'the Manufacture of Cambricks Act', and is classed as a public statute, relating to the whole of England and Wales. Each Act usually commences with a *whereas* clause, explaining the background and reasons for the Act. Winchelsea's Act has a six-hundred word preamble on the financial and legal circumstances as well as the necessity to define the terms *lawn* and *cambric*. Public Acts may be found through index volumes available at reference libraries, the *Chronological Table of the Statutes* (HMSO), using short titles, and the *Index to the Statutes in Force* (HMSO), arranged chiefly by subject but with some places listed. Each published annual volume with the full text of the year's statutes is also indexed. There are other cumulative indexes in various published collections of statutes, though these may be chronological listings rather than alphabetical indexes.

The authoritative text of Acts was enrolled by Parliament in England from 1497. Printed sessional *black letter* (from the style of lettering) volumes of Acts appeared from 1483, including certain private Acts, though these are rarely found outside the archives of Parliament. Texts of public Acts are available in the Record Commission's *Statutes of the Realm* (1235-1713) held by public libraries. Repealed or obsolete sections and repetitive annual Acts, omitted from certain published editions, can be read in the enrolments at Westminster or in printed annual volumes from 1713. *The Acts of the Parliaments of Scotland* are printed up to 1707. The original rolls of Irish Acts were destroyed in 1922; the printed Acts of 1310-1800 are incomplete, though some missing ones are preserved as copies in private archives. Parliament's legislative business included proposals arising from independent sources, usually termed *private* or *local and personal*. These arose from petitions by town councils, corporations and individuals for laws about such matters as agricultural reorganisation (enclosure), tithes, estates, charities, transport (road, rail, canal or harbour undertakings), municipal waterworks, divorce and naturalisation, for example.

> An Act for the establishing of the Lands given by John Bedford's Will to the perpetual Repair of Highways at Ailesbury
> 39 Elizabeth I chapter 12 (England and Wales, 1597)
> An Act for repairing the Road leading from the Green of Kilcullen, in the County of Kildare to the Town of Athy ... thence through the Town of Stradbally to the Town of Timoko
> 9 George II chapter XXIII (Ireland, 1735)

An Act for building a Bridge over that Part of the River Rumney which divides the parish of Rumney, in the County of Monmouth, and the Parish of Roath, in the County of Glamorgan

45 George III chapter lxxiii (1805)

From 1792 organisations proposing such public works as docks, waterworks, railways, bridges, tramways, canals and turnpike roads were obliged to deposit with Parliament drawings, maps, plans and explanatory books of reference with duplicates despatched to the relevant county clerk. Deposited plans are supplemented with reports among sessional papers. From 1571 onwards the titles of private Acts were included in volumes of sessional papers as well as in series of public statutes of the realm. Published indexes to private, local and personal Acts may be consulted in the *Index to Local and Personal Acts* (HMSO), relating to the period from 1801 onwards, and the *Analytical Table of Private Statutes* (1813, 1835), which are held in public libraries. *The Chronological Table of Local Legislation, 1797-1994* (Law Commission and Scottish Law Commission, 1996) contains the titles of some 26,500 private, local and personal Acts. R. Devine's *Index to Local and Personal Acts, 1850-1995* (HMSO, 1996) supplies subjects, personal names, place-names and short titles. The text of private Acts was sometimes included in sessional papers from the sixteenth century but more consistently from 1798. Some of those not published in the local and personal series concerning enclosures, tithes and estates were collected in special sessional volumes entitled *Private Acts*. Individual volumes of private Acts are also available from 1798; only from 1876 are all Acts included. Because private, local and personal Acts are significant for any community history, it is worth enquiring of lawyers, estate owners, town clerks, company secretaries or any other legal descendants of the original promoters of the legislation.

Public records

The extent of modern public records reflects increasing levels of state control over every community, dating from administrative reforms initiated by Edward IV in the 1470s. As the secretarial arm of government, Chancery impinged on ordinary people's lives, for example in regulating agricultural enclosure, property transactions, trade, prices, coastal shipping, religious affiliation, bankruptcy, specifications

Brimstone.

1. May be imported, 16 *Car.* 1. *c.* 21.
2. To what Duties liable, 2 *W. & M. fesf.* 2. *c.* 4. § 51.

Bristles.

To what Duties liable, 4 *W. & M. c.* 5. § 2.

Bristol.

1. Silver how to be touched and marked in *Briftol, Chefter, Exeter, Newcaftle upon Tyne, Norwich* and *York, &c.* 2 *H.* 6. *c.* 14.   12 *&* 13 *W.* 3. *c.* 4.
2. The Under-fheriff, *&c.* of *Briftol* fhall continue in Office in like Manner as in *London,* 6 *H.* 8. *c.* 18.
3. Penalty on calling Ballaft in *Kingrod* Road, *&c.* leading to *Briftol,* 34 *&* 35 *H.* 8. *c.* 9. § 2.
4. Corn fhipped in the *Severn,* to be brought to *Briftol,* 34 *&* 35 *H.* 8. *c.* 9.
5. In what Cafes *Briftol* Merchants may ufe Strangers Bottoms, 1 *El. c.* 13. § 5.
6. The Streets of *Briftol* how cleanfed, paved, lightened and watched, 11 *&* 12 *W.* 3. *c.* 23.   22 *Geo.* 2. *c.* 20.   28 *Geo.* 2. *c.* 32.   29 *Geo.* 2. *c.* 47.
7. Brokers in *Briftol* how admitted and regulated, 3 *Geo.* 2. *c.* 31.   *For other Matters, fee* **Gold and Silver, Highways, Paving.**

5   **Britifh**

Brimstone, Bristles and Bristol: entries from O. Ruffhead's 'A Complete Index to the Statutes at Large from Magna Charta to the Tenth Year of George III', 1772.

The first page of the pioneering Bristol Workhouse Act, 1696.

of patent inventions, militia, registration of title deeds and other personal legal documents. The monarch's privy (private) council considered such matters as church property, public health, education and national security, usually in terms of specific localities. The subsidiary Court of Star Chamber until 1642 heard cases of abuses by landowners. The Court of Requests expedited poor men's causes and heard riot, forgery and admiralty cases. The state papers of the principal secretaries of state appointed in 1540 for home and foreign affairs continue to 1782. Their subject matter, which is extensive, includes coastal forts, education, highways, agriculture, paupers and public order. Scottish state papers begin in 1505. The Home Office, created in 1782, was concerned at various dates with internal security, political dissent, riots, industrial disputes, militia, police, prisons, internment camps, bomb damage, health, transport, fisheries, agriculture and the census of church attendance of 1851. Law and order in Ireland was the responsibility of the Chief Secretary, with records of a similar nature to the British for the period 1778-1924. Series of 'outrage papers' highlight rural unrest during the period 1832-52.

(3)

Anno feptimo & octavo

Gulielmi III. Regis.

An Act for erecting of Hospitals and Workhouses within the City of BRISTOL, *for the better employing and maintaining the Poor thereof.*

WHEREAS it is found Preamble. by Experience, That the Poor in the City of *Briftol* do daily multiply, and Idlenefs and Debauchery amongft the meaner Sort doth greatly increafe, for want of Workhoufes to fet them to work, and a fufficient Authority to compel them A 2 thereto,

> ... as the fair of Killsalaghan was drawing to a close, a fight commenced between two Parties, one calling themselves Sackmen, and the other "Billysmiths" ... I charged the mob and made four of the ringleaders prisoners, the principal ringleader ... who resides generally at Swords and who is a very noted character in this district, Escaped thro. the tents ...
> National Archives of Ireland, State Paper Office, Dublin, outrage papers, Dublin 9/69; statement of chief constable, 27th May 1838

Records from 1878 refer to Fenians and the Land League and National League and other nationalist movements.

> In the month of March 1884 Henry Young and his son Denis Young, of Glin, took a farm of seven acres at Tullyglass, near Glin, from which the former tenant, Stackpool, was evicted by the Knight of Glin for non-payment of rent ... On the 11th May 1884 ... notices were posted ... calling on the people to boycott the Youngs ... The house of Denis Young was attacked ... a cow ... was killed ... In February 1886 Denis Young surrendered the farm ... was then admitted a member of the Glin branch of the Irish National League. His customers returned to him, and he is now working at his trade as boot and shoe maker.
> National Archives of Ireland, State Paper Office, Dublin, INL 1884 1/277, report, 1886

The financial department of government, the Exchequer, impinged on communities

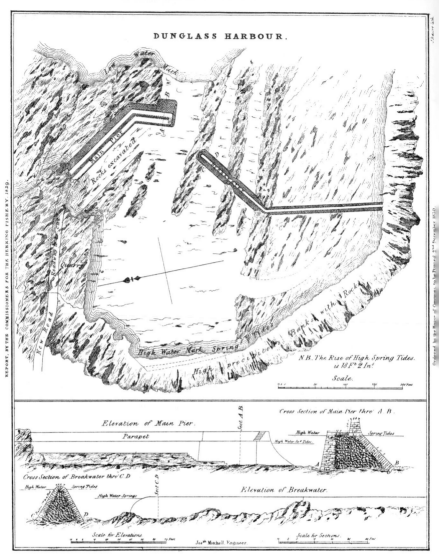

*National governments promoted economic development in the regions by overseeing
and promoting public works. Designs for harbour works at Dunglass, Berwickshire,
by Joseph Mitchell, engineer to the board of commissioners for the herring fishery,
were published in the board's report for the year ending 5th April 1830.*

through its taxation responsibilities and the recording of goods and shipping in
individual port books until 1798. The Exchequer was responsible for crown estates,
accumulating charters, deeds, court rolls and surveys of properties confiscated by the
state. The Augmentation Office administered lands of the dissolved monasteries as
well as of the Duchy of Cornwall. The King's Remembrancer's archive documents
royal forests, stud farms, mines in Devon and Cornwall and the Hackney Coach
Commissioners (1672-1753). During the sixteenth century the Treasury emerged as
the chief financial office of state, holding records on localities and individuals, such as
the London house duties series for 1698-1778, the Holyhead harbour commission
accounts (1810-23), the apprenticeship registers (stamp duty), the inhabited house duty

and land taxes. Individual tax returns under the New Domesday of 1909-10 usually survive with the title deeds in private hands, while Treasury files summarise these by district.

Extensive tracts of countryside and economic assets belonged to the crown despite sales under the Commonwealth and William III. From 1760 crown property was surrendered to Parliament and administered by the Crown Estates Commission. Records of money, lands and assets from churches, chantries and religious houses dissolved after the Reformation are initially studied through published volumes of the survey *Valor Ecclesiasticus* (1535). The Surveyor of the King's Works, eventually the Ministry of Works, maintained and preserved documentation about individual properties throughout the kingdom, such as castles, royal lodgings, ordnance factories, naval dockyards, army bases, ancient monuments, strategic roads, bridges (including the Menai Bridge) and prisons (including Brixton). A Board of Public Works Commissioners (1817) facilitated the construction of harbours, housing, roads, waterworks, hospitals and other council projects.

The seventeenth-century redistribution of land in Ireland from native Catholics to planted Protestants is documented in the Quit Rent Office records, though most originals were destroyed by fires in 1711 and 1922. The Down Survey of lands forfeited under Cromwell and described and mapped by William Petty is held by the National Library of Ireland. Volumes for Antrim and Tyrone are in the Public Record Office of Northern Ireland. The Quit Rent Office holds Ordnance Survey sheets with Petty's maps superimposed. Petty's barony maps, now in the Bibliothèque Nationale, Paris, were reproduced by the Ordnance Survey in 1908. A derivative atlas, *Hiberniae Delineatio,* prepared by Petty, was reprinted in 1968 and 1969.

The valuation of Ireland for rating purposes began in 1809, requiring a national property survey. Each field, dwelling and commercial building could then be measured and assigned a notional value. Valuators drew up maps, useful if predating Ordnance Survey or estate maps for authentic place-name spellings. House books describe individual dwellings and business premises, with comments on improvements and state of trade.

Wibrants Olphirt Esq Flax Mill Length 22ft 6in Breadth 18 - 0 Water Wheel Diameter 13 - 0 Fall of Water 7 - 0 No. of Bucketts 48 ... Has water & Employment for 9 Months in Each year at 12 Hours per day.
National Archives of Ireland, OL 5.0827, houses in Ballyness, County Donegal, 19th July 1855

Field books record the uses and condition of land. Record of tenure books show the acreage, rental, tenure, occupier and immediate lessor. The commissioner Richard Griffith's standard valuation of 1847-65 was printed for wide circulation, showing lessors, occupiers and annual values. Agricultural crises in Ireland from 1815 onwards highlighted problems arising from restrictive entails and family settlements. The Landed Estates Court (1849) assisted the sale of encumbered estates through the publication of descriptions and plans of property. The Irish Land Commission (1881) acquired and documented land redistributed among smallholders. The Congested Districts Board (1891-1923) assisted people in western Ireland to acquire viable holdings or disperse through emigration.

Following the Jacobite risings of 1715 and 1745, commissioners were appointed to administer estates forfeited by rebel landowners. Agents reported on social conditions, improvements, clearance and enclosure. Statistics and reports on the annexed estates culled from commission archives were published in 1973 by the Scottish Record Office.

English administrative reforms (1550-72) designated legal quays for foreign trade, where daily statistics were kept of imports, exports and revenues. A Board of Customs was established for England and Wales in 1671 and embraced Scotland from 1723 and Ireland from 1823. Board minutes (1696-1885) are supplemented by correspondence with collectors in the outports, establishment records, commercial

MIDD'.

Valet in firm' fcit' priorat' prediĉt' cum le court yerde et divs' domibus ac ortulag' et gardin' fcituat' infra precinĉt' prefat' priorat'.

N' que refvatur in man' diĉte dne prioriffe et convent' ejufdm et null' profic' inde proven'.

Valet in reddit' affis' cum at reddit' et firm' tenenc' in divs vitt hameletts et perochijs videlt.

		£ s. d.
Tam in civitat' London' quam in fuburb' ejufdem	jᶜlxxij xix iiij	
Iflyngton - - -	xv v —	
Holway - - -	— xxxiiij ij	
Mufwell - - -	— cviij ij	
Et Edelmeton - -	— lxxiiij viij	
Langforth - - -	— xxx —	
Eltwode - - -	— xxx —	
Wanfted - - -	— xiij iiij	ijᶜxxij iij j
Et Tottenham - -	xvij iij iiij	
ut patȝ diĉt' valor' inde faĉt'		
Gyngmountney - -	— v j	
Orfett - - -	— xl —	
In toto -	—	

	£ s. d.
Valet in bofco ibm infra diĉt' dnia vitt hameletts eftimat' fore in valore cõibus annis ut fequitur videlt In Mufwell x acr' precij acr' xijᵈ	— xviij —
x —	
Edm'ton viij acr' precij xijᵈ - viij —	

		£ s. d.
Valet in oblacõibus et decimis cõibus annis in ecctia poch de Clerkenwell -	liij ij ob'	
Mufwell - - -	— xl j ob'	iiij xvij iiij
Pens' magrī Wittmi Bryges rector' Beate Marie Staynyngs -	—. iiij —	

(Left) 'Valor Ecclesiasticus' (here seen in an edition by the Record Commission, 1810, volume I, page 395) appraises the possessions of the priory of the Blessed Virgin Mary of Clerkenwell, showing interests extending far beyond the immediate village into Essex, Kent, Sussex and Dorset

(Below) Easby Abbey, Yorkshire, founded in the twelfth century for Premonstratensian canons, was dissolved in the sixteenth, the ruins offering a romantic prospect for the lay landowner who took over the estates.

data and reports on specific ports from the 1830s. Excise duties raised money from goods produced for home consumption, such as whisky. The Board of Trade originated in a Privy Council committee in 1621, concerned with colonial trade, but following Pitt's reforms in 1786 the regulation of commerce and industry was assumed, including factories, alkali works, joint-stock companies, trade petitions and disputes, coal mines and pit disasters, railways and train crashes. The regulation of merchant shipping and seamen under Acts of the period 1786-1854 created records relevant for the history of individual ports. Customs officials registered ships and fishing boats, requiring the names of owners, a description and the name of each vessel, the date and details of its construction, its previous history and its current registration, with annotations relating to subsequent developments, such

King's Lynn customs house, 1683.

as when it was broken up, wrecked, seized by privateers or taken for smuggling. Registers may be among the public records or deposited in a county record office. Seamen's agreements, official log books from 1850 and lists of crews from around 1747 (arranged by port and ship) are held by county and public record offices, the National Maritime Museum and the Memorial University in Newfoundland.

The Board of Trade's Statistical Department from 1832 published reports on regional economies, which were also covered in detail by papers on industrial reconstruction following the two world wars. The Patent Office registered, enrolled and published specifications of patent inventions from 1853, though eventually the printed volumes for its own and public libraries referred back to 1617. The public registration of designs was also initiated with the preservation of original or pictorial representations of textile patterns and other articles from 1839. Economic development in Scotland, especially the linen industry, was fostered by the Board of Manufactures (1727-1927). Rural communities are documented in files of the Board of Agriculture (1793), the Tithe (1836), the Copyhold (1841) and the Enclosure Commissioners (1845), the Cattle Plague Department (1865) and the Board (later Ministry) of Agriculture (1889, with fisheries added in 1903). The Forestry Commission was created in 1919, taking over the archives of manors and royal forests, compiling forest histories (from 1951) and conducting censuses of woods and hedgerows.

From the 1830s a national system of education was developed, consequently creating files in national archives. Commissioners were appointed in Ireland (1831), where their one-roomed national schools are a feature of rural communities Minutes and reports of a Privy Council committee for England and Wales refer to expenditure on parish schools. From 1870 (Scotland 1872) central government supervised a national and bureaucratic system of compulsory (subsequently free) education. In the supervision of poor relief, interpretation of public health legislation and the implementation of national policies in respect of particular social groups such as single parents and the disabled, voluminous Local Government Board files complement county, parish and borough archives. Ministry of Housing and Local Government files complement town and county records on such matters as housing and industrial estates, especially from 1919 onwards. Records of the departments of Development and Economic Planning document the strategies determining regional prosperity.

Regional prosperity might be boosted by selling food to the army or servicing a naval dockyard. From the sixteenth century Commissioners of Marine Causes (Navy Board) shared responsibility for the navy with the Admiralty. Registers, reports, correspondence, ships' log books, personnel musters, description books and victualling accounts are available for the historian of Chatham, Dartmouth, Devonport, Portsmouth and other naval bases. The recruiting, mustering, stationing, manoeuvring and discharging of troops throughout the kingdom are referred to in army records from a variety of departments including Board of Ordnance from 1570, Secretary-at-War as financial administrator from 1661, Commander-in-Chief, whose earliest letter book is 1765, Secretary for War from 1794, Judge Advocate General, Commissary General, Board of General Officers and Adjutant General. The military were concerned with works at Hull (1660-84); powder mills at Ballincollig, County Cork; king's works at Purfleet (1793-1834); the musketry school at Pendine, Carmarthenshire; royal hospitals at Chelsea and Kilmainham; the depot at Lymington; alehouse billets; Chartists; Sinn Feiners; strikers; and the obliteration of a whole community for a fort or airfield. The Air Department of the Admiralty was formed in 1910 for work at Cardington, Bedfordshire, on lighter-than-air machines but expanded during the war of 1914-18 into an independent flying service under the Air Ministry (1918). In addition to defence department files at the Public Record Office and with historical records branches of the services, researchers will also find exhibits and documents at the Imperial War Museum, in London, the National Maritime Museum (Greenwich), the National Army Museum (Chelsea) and the Royal Air Force Museum (Hendon), as well as regimental museums throughout the country. The following unofficial transcript of an air accident record card summarises an official inquiry which is at odds with oral evidence, that the pilot was heroically heading *away* from the town to avoid a major tragedy:

> Aircraft flying at about 1200' when the nose dropped and aircraft went into a steep dive from which it did not recover. Engine running normally. Aircraft crashed into two houses ... not engaged on exercise requiring flying over Forres town where pilot's wife lived 250 yards from crash under path taken by aircraft and where wife of one of Sgt pilots lived facing crash. Dive intentional; left recovery too late.
> Royal Air Force Museum, Hendon, Archives, transcript of form 1180 (Whitley N1440), 7th November 1940

In England and Wales parish censuses can be located in church chests, borough muniments and diocesan archives. Ireland has census information from 1652 (County Dublin), 1659 (national) and 1766 (religious). The Irish census proper began in 1813.

Scottish researchers benefit from Alexander Webster's *Account of the Number of People in Scotland* (1755), prepared by parish ministers and the Scottish Society for Propagating Christian Knowledge and published in *Scottish Population Statistics* (Scottish Academic Press, 1975) edited by J. G. Kyd. Since 1801 a census has been taken in Britain every ten years (except 1941). From 1801 until 1831 the government published statistics and destroyed individual household returns. From 1841 onwards, household returns were retained, showing each inhabited house and the name, age, occupation and native parish of every individual including lodgers and visitors on census night, a snapshot of family life and social structure of the community. Enumerators completing forms for illiterates or making fair copies of untidy returns inevitably caused errors. The disaffected gave misleading information while burglars, prostitutes, adulterers, moonlighters, brothel-keepers, sweat-shop owners, unlicensed publicans and illegal immigrants kept low profiles, distorting the modern researcher's view of the neighbourhood considerably. Census returns are most easily accessed on microfilm in the public library or record office, though documents are closed for one hundred years to preserve confidentiality.

From the Middle Ages authorities attempted to establish registers for title deeds and other legal documents. The Scottish register of sasines concerning transfers of heritable property began in 1599. From 1617 each sheriffdom maintained a particular register with a general register in Edinburgh; both are lodged in the Scottish Record Office. English county registers began in Middlesex and Yorkshire from 1707-35 but were eventually superseded by national registration originally conceived in 1862. A national Irish registry was created by an Act of 1707 for formal agreements, wills and title deeds, though not leases for less than twenty-one years, the sole tenure available to Roman Catholics. During the nineteenth century statistical registers under government control were introduced. District registrars recorded and issued certificates of births and deaths, also performing secular marriage ceremonies at the registry office, from 1st July 1837 in England and Wales, and from 1855 in Scotland and 1864 in Ireland. Registration was free but compulsory. Copies of all registrations were despatched to the relevant Registrar General at the General Register Office. Certificates can be obtained for a fee from the district and national registrars. In England and Wales the Family Records Centre, London EC1, facilitates personal searches of the records. Where registers have been made available for statistical analysis, historians can reconstitute families and compile data on the age structure of populations, age at marriage, second marriages, illegitimacy, longevity, causes of death, occupations, social class, family mobility and the number of people in a family.

In England, Ireland and Wales the central common law courts of Common Pleas, King's Bench and Exchequer heard criminal cases and civil disputes until the reform of 1873-5. Assize judges toured the country in fixed circuits as the principal provincial court until this was merged with quarter sessions in 1971. Coroners deposited inquest findings at assizes from about 1487 to 1700. At the National Library of Wales are records, deeds, inquisitions, plans, enclosure awards and financial accounts – and the archive of the Ruthin lordship – from the Court of Great Sessions for 1542-1830. Estates of bankrupts were administered by commissioners from 1571, though the Court of Bankruptcy records are most useful from 1710. As a court proceeding by rules of equity and conscience, Chancery was notionally a refuge for poor pleaders escaping from the common law.

> ...compleyneth ... Owen o Ryordan & Mahowne o Ryordan ... of the Towne & lands of Bohernefoyny ... that Mortagh mcBryen of Castelltowwne ... disseysed your supplyants of two third parts ... in as much as your supplyants are verry poore and unhable to try right vith the said mcBryen ... a man of greate alyance & kinred ... with whom your supplyants can hardly have anny indifferency of tryall by ordenary cowrse of common lawe ... to graunt ... wrytt of subpena to be dyrected unto the said mcBryen
> National Archives of Ireland, C198 (IC.2.146), Chancery bill, after 1604

Chancery gained exclusive jurisdiction in respect of trusts and the rights of married women, infants and the mentally ill or disabled. The law courts of the palatinates of Durham, Lancaster and Chester acted independently of the national courts until the nineteenth century. In Britain and Ireland regional Admiralty courts determined cases involving merchandise, salvage, piracy and spoil.

The highest Scottish court of first instance and appeal, the Court of Session in Edinburgh, heard civil cases, for instance of property or debt. From the sixteenth century the court created general and particular minute books of cases, serving as chronological indexes; registers of Acts and Decrees; and files of relevant case papers known as processes. From 1554 personal legal documents such as title deeds and business contracts could be copied for security into registers of deeds known as books of council and session. Commissary courts from 1563 dealt with executry, slander, aliment and marital causes. The Exchequer court dealt with smuggling, illicit distilling and other revenue matters. The High Court of Justiciary in Edinburgh, with circuit courts, was the supreme criminal court, creating books of adjournal and minute books. Written reports of witnesses from 1812 onwards are in Lord Advocate's records:

> Alexander Gillan ... you followed Elspet Lamb ... a girl under eleven years of age, herding her Father's Cattle ... through a Plantation to the moor ... you did, wickedly and feloniously assault ... barbarously murder the said Elspet Lamb, and beat out her brains
> Scottish Record Office, JC26/344, Court of Justiciary, Inverness, porteous roll for Elgin county, September 1810

Gillan was eighteen. His case is further documented in county archives. The executioner, William Taylor, was borrowed from Inverness and on his arrival in Elgin was lodged in gaol and liberally supplied with food but only moderately with ale. Nevertheless he somehow became inebriated and as a result botched the execution. Law reports in newspapers are accompanied by accounts of young Gillan's execution:

> ... he [Gillan] attempted to address the spectators ... but his agitation of mind rendered him unable to proceed ... he became more tranquil, ascended the ladder with a firm step, and awaited his fate ... He was detained in this state of awful suspense too long, by the unskilfulness of the executioner but at last, when the drop gave way, so great was the fall, that he yielded his spirit without a struggle. Having hung an hour, he was cut down and put into irons; and he now remains suspended from the gibbet, a shocking example of the dreadful effects of unbridled passion.
> *Aberdeen Journal* 21st November 1810

Archives of the Incorporation of Hammermen provide a sketch for Gillan's cage of chains with a note that he 'was taken down in the dead of night by his friends in a furtive manner and interred in the Wood'. Gillan's grave is marked by the Ordnance Survey, and his chains are preserved at a neighbouring farmhouse. Correspondence among officials in Inverness and Elgin provides a sequel to the case, the murder of executioner Taylor by two Elgin apprentices, for which they were sentenced to transportation.

Sheriffs recorded civil and criminal cases of slander, debt, assault and theft through minutes, act books, diet books, processes and registers of decrees. Registers of deeds (legal documents) were also maintained. Sheriffs could impose the death penalty:

> James Gray ... commonly bruted for a loose man & common thief ... did steall ... ane young Cow and did ... kill her & did Eat & make use of the blood ... with which Fang wholl & Inteir, Skein & birne, hyd & horne ... Red hand apprehended ... to be takin upon Fryday nixt ... From the prison of Cullen ... to the Clune hill theroff & Gibbitt standing theron, betuixt the hours off tuo & Four aclocke in the afternoon & therupon hang'd up by the neck by the hand of the Common executioner til yee be dead.
> Antons, solicitors and estate agents, Buckie, inquest and judgement, 10th and 13th March 1699

Cases concerning the removal of tenants date chiefly from 1756 onwards and show the process of agricultural clearance and enclosure, involving forty days' notice given by the sheriff officer to the tenants:

> ... to flitt & remove themselves wives Bairns servants subtennants Cottars & all heil goods & Gear Furth & from their respective possessions at the term of Whitsunday next ...

Notice was delivered by the officer:

> ... this I did by delivering ... full writen Copies in their own hands subscribed by me personally apprehended Excepting the said Donald Grant in Mains of Relugas whose Copie I left in the Lock hole of the most patent door of his house after giving severall knocks at the said door with acquainting his wife of it in order to be given him because I could not personally apprehend him ...
> Stewart & McIsaac, solicitors, Elgin, court process, 1766

The Scottish Land Court and Crofters' Commission archives from 1886 are sources for highland and island communities.

From time to time the government answered public concerns by means of a royal commission, public inquiry or judicial inquiry. Reports may be published and are available with original statements of evidence in government departments, national archives or university libraries. At Trinity College, Dublin, are preserved depositions of 1641, gathered in the course of official investigations into alleged robberies, rapes and massacres of Protestant settlers in Ireland. These contain special pleading, myth, propaganda and falsehood:

> Alice Gregg the Relict of Richard Gregg late of Loughgall ... farmer ... deposeth ... the Rebells ... stripped att one tyme above 300 of them, of all their clothes & then drive them like sheep into the Church of Loghall. And then & there the grand Rebell Doghertie publiquely sayd to his bloudy and Rebellious crew That all theis (meaning

the protestants soe imprisoned) shall be putt to death ... and left them there naked ... And with their skeanes sett upon this deponent and her husband & children ... & gave her eight wounds in her head: and devided & cutt her soun John Gregg whilest he was alive into quarters & threw them att his fathers face ... forced about fourscore protestants into the water off the bridge of Callon nere Mr Fairfax howse & there drowned them ...
Trinity College MS 836, formerly TCD F.3.7, 21st July 1643

Commissions and inquiries were especially favoured by nineteenth-century governments as a means of gathering data and demonstrating official concern over such contemporary issues as working conditions in mines and mills, public health in towns and housing for the working classes. Modern inquiry records include papers on the Brixton riots of 1981 and on Sizewell B nuclear plant (1983-5).

Post Office archives trace the beginning of the inland postal service in 1635. Initially private contractors retained records, though those of Roger Whitley for 1672-7 were later given to the archives. Financial records (from 1677), letter books (1686), reports (1790) and minutes (1794) document the careers of officials, the use of mail coaches and the opening and closing of post offices. More recent services are described in the periodical *Post Office Guide* from 1856, a weekly Post Office circular from 1859, annual reports to Parliament from 1854 and *Post Offices in the United Kingdom from 1884*. Documentation on coaches and mail contracts dates from 1786 in England, supplemented by reports and letters of the administrator John Palmer. Charges varied according to distance, the recipient generally paying. A London penny post was initiated in 1680; in Dublin and Edinburgh not until 1773; in Manchester in 1793. Official records are supplemented by the journals, minutes, correspondence and autobiography of Rowland Hill, the founder of the penny post throughout Britain, for the period 1836-79. Drivers, guards and postmasters are documented from 1691, though detailed records of salaries, pensions and ridings begin later in the 1760s. The Post Office telegraph service was established under Acts of 1868 and 1870, with private telephone companies commencing operation in 1877. The United Telephone Company served London from 1880. Municipal telephone services were established, for example in Glasgow, Hull and Brighton. Telecommunications services, amalgamated into a national government monopoly, are researched at the British Telecom Archives, London WC1, where records of telephone companies, early directories and correspondence are held.

Records of nationalised rivers, harbours, docks, canals and railways are held in national and county record offices, though industries, such as coal and steel, established their own repositories and research centres. Records of predecessor private companies were taken over at nationalisation, though in certain instances the reversal of that policy has led to records being dispersed. In practice the bulk of older documentation always remained in the possession of clerks to the companies, either in their own headquarters or with their lawyers, and in some cases was later deposited in libraries or archives. Records of gas companies taken over at an early date by town councils are usually now in the county record office. Useful information is often found in the periodical *Gas World*. Transport undertakings were also managed by county or town councils. In Cheshire the trustees of the Weaver Navigation were landowners who as magistrates also ran the county, so the records found their way naturally into county archives.

Oral history

Oral history is the collection and recording of people's reminiscences of the recent past and their thoughts too on their community's earlier history and oral traditions. An elderly person recounting an episode learned as a child at a grandfather's knee spans a century or more of experience. As a journalist Charles Dickens investigated the Fleet Street district of London by interviewing the residents. In *Oliver Twist,* Fagin's well-managed business doubtless kept good records of income and expenditure, enforcing performance indicators in respect of youthful workloads. For Bill Sikes's branch of the business Dickens relied on uncorroborated oral testimony. Nancy's trade might be documented through court records, directories or memoirs, though generally prostitution was an underground but not illegal business. None of the pimps, rent-boys, retired whores, streetwalkers, gigolos, courtesans, madams or clients would admit knowledge or past involvement, except to the most adventurous or discreet of oral historians. A pioneer of oral history was George Ewart Evans, whose numerous books include *Where Beards Wag All: the Relevance of the Oral Tradition* (Faber, 1970) and *The Days That We Have Seen* (Faber, 1975). The techniques were then formalised through the writings of Paul Thompson of Essex University's oral history unit in such works as *The Voice of the Past* (Oxford University Press, 1978) and in the publications of the history workshop of Ruskin College, Oxford. The journal *Oral History* keeps the researcher abreast of developments. For his book *Speak for England* (Secker & Warburg, 1976) the writer Melvyn Bragg interviewed seventy Wigton people, whose reminiscences provided a history of Britain as seen through Cumbrian eyes from 1900 to 1975. Listening to people talk by the fireside or in the pub is obviously a natural means of gaining information. Peig Sayers (1873-1958) in her cottage on the island of Great Blasket recounted in Gaelic the legends and history of the wild Kerry coast. Her spontaneity was somewhat distorted when her son wrote down her memories later in life, but his action did mean that her stories were preserved. Mary Kennedy further honed the reflections for publication as *Machtnamh Seana Mhná* (1939), while a translation (Oxford University Press, 1962) took yet another step away from Peig's words.

Today, reminiscences are collected on tape, video or disk, or simply in typescript by libraries, record offices and the National Sound Archive in London. Posterity may be grateful also to the historian who has not neglected to tape his or her own reminiscences, write a diary or compile autobiographical notes for preservation by the family or at the public library as an intimate documentary source for future researchers. For actual recording a portable cassette recorder preserves the maximum of information with the least trouble and expense. At the beginning of each tape the name of the interviewer and informant, the date, the subject and the place and time of the conversation should be recorded, and the same information should appear on the cassette and cassette box. In the absence of a tape recorder, shorthand may be used, though manuscript notes can seldom reproduce an individual's quirks of emphasis and inflection. Another option is the camcorder, though this can make the informant too self-conscious to speak freely. The first task of the interviewer is persuading the subject to speak. An informal setting and a comfortable chair, perhaps before a warm fire in the subject's own home, are recommended. Informants may be old, frail in body and weak in mind, tedious, evasive, incoherent, obscene, obtuse, enigmatic, ironic, vindictive or rude! They may tell lies or fabricate missing details. The process of remembering is sometimes more creative than truthful, as the imagination conjures up what the historian seems most anxious to hear. Informants will be disconcerted by severe questioning and unlikely to recall incidents concisely or to date them accurately. The researcher is not in any position to apply the thumbscrews to extract the truth, the whole truth and nothing but the truth. Questions should therefore be carefully framed. A structured questionnaire may be helpful. Questions should be suited to the informant's personality, intellect and experience, comprehensible but not patronising, penetrating but not impertinent. The informant may choose to speak frankly, in which case the interviewer must be prepared to listen patiently, without appearing shocked or critical. Tapes should be carefully preserved, accurately transcribed and not edited, because the significance of an apparent irrelevance may emerge later.

Oral information is quite often all the researcher has to rely on, at least in the first instance. On 7th November 1940 a Whitley bomber crashed on houses in Forres, Moray, killing the crew of six. Reports of the incident were not permitted in the newspaper or town council records, and families were ordered not to speak, but there were rumours that the pilot saved children's lives by refusing to land on the school field. Numerous people were happy to theorise:

> There was an almighty bang. It shook all windows. I ran out and just followed the people who were running ... When we got to Fern Villa Mrs Bethune was throwing her clothes, fur coats and best clothes and other items out of the window. We could see the flames and smoke from the plane. Mr Miel, an Italian who owned a fish and chip shop, was hero of that night. I can still see to this day the men taking the stretchers out with 'heaps' on the stretchers, it really made us sick ... During that time there was an awful lot of planes crashing and the local people were saying, 'It's sabotage. The Irish are putting sugar in the petrol' and we all believed that.
> Information from Jeanie Ross of Forres, 1978

Board of inquiry papers suggest the pilot flew over Forres against orders and buzzed the town to impress his wife of six weeks. The historian must decide on the evidence available, which explanation – pilot error or sabotage – best fits the facts.

The historian, who should be fluent in the language of the area, gathers as much evidence as possible on which to make a judgement. While the informant speaks, the historian listens and learns to relish any humour, popular prejudice, regional pride or even downright racism. Talking to people may be the best means of accessing poorly documented history, such as the black market and black economy, Romanies and travelling folk, the production of hallucinogenic potions, philtres and poisons by herbalists, the supply of opium as laudanum by Victorian physicians or the fuelling of youth culture with cannabis and LSD in the 1960s. This secret world can be investigated by asking the living gangster or businessman about supply networks during his active lifetime and by interviewing surviving users. Despite its central role in human history, sexual behaviour is one of the most difficult subjects to research; surprisingly informants may be more willing to talk about abnormal practices, such as bestiality, paedophilia, abortion, pornography and homosexuality than 'normal' sex in the marital bed. Few communities have not at some time served as a seedbed or sanctuary for dissenters. Information about counter-cultures is often inaccessible, unless they have attracted community sympathy. People might then reminisce or recall an oral tradition about a thriving Satanist cult, a coven of witches, a Blackshirt training camp or an Irish Republican Brotherhood cell. Without people willing to talk, recent community history can be a closed book.

Industrial archaeology

The fieldwork of the modern era begins with the physical remains of the industrial landscape, along with equipment and products. Supported by research in libraries and archives, the study is known as industrial archaeology. Standard textbooks by Bracegirdle, Buchanan, Burton, Cossons, Major, Pannell, Raistrick and Trinder refer in their bibliographies to studies of individual sites and industries. Books in the Longman Industrial Archaeology series cover the principal industrial subjects, such as textiles, shipping, crafts, building materials, iron, coal and farm machinery. Short accounts with numerous illustrations are supplied by many titles in the Shire Album series. Modern industry was born in the towns and rural parishes of Britain and Ireland, where the researcher may discover record-breaking events or features, such as the earliest adoption of a certain process, the largest example of a particular monument or the oldest example of a machine or product. Famous inventors, engineers or entrepreneurs may have been natives of the parish. The historian investigates the existence of particular skills in the workforce, the availability or mobility of labour, sources of power, capital and raw materials, improvements to transport networks and links with suppliers and markets. Industrial monuments are normally visible above ground, though requiring careful interpretation from a knowledge of economic and technical history. Industrial enterprise can thus be placed in a meaningful national and international context. Each manufactory appears

The first iron bridge in the world (1779), spanning the river Severn at Ironbridge, Shropshire. It was constructed of cast iron smelted in Coalbrookdale by Abraham Darby III.

as a cog in a larger commercial machine. Where industrial archaeology requires excavation, the council archaeologist will usually advise on appropriate strategies, perhaps involving a regional history group or university team. At Rothesay on the island of Bute can be seen the site of one of Scotland's earliest cotton spinning mills (1779), where mill machinery depended on a system of lades, ponds and waterwheels. Capital, labour and expertise were inherited from a declining linen industry on site. Slaving and tobacco were threatened as the American War of Independence intensified, but cotton offered excellent profits in India. Rothesay mill was founded by an engineer hopeful to evade legal restrictions imposed by the patent on Arkwright's water-frame in England.

A nexus of social influence, capital and political power underpins industrial success. The most famous Scottish whisky distillery of the eighteenth century was sited at Ferintosh in the county of Ross, arguably not a district in the commercial mainstream. Nonetheless, *Ferintosh* was as much a byword for whisky in its time as *Paisley* was later for printed cotton. The Ferintosh distillery prospered while competitors struggled because of its exemption from excise duties as a reward for the owner, Duncan Forbes of Culloden, whose unflinching loyalty to William III against the Jacobites in 1689 was vital to the new regime's victory. Industrial growth depended on a well chosen site with good natural communications; access to raw materials; a labour force continuing traditional skills with technical expertise; adequate financial resources; returns on capital; and government support. Manufacturers were linked to each other as suppliers, customers, investors or competitors, thus stimulating improvements in products and production methods. When a site, premises, plant, products and packaging are carefully chosen, then goods can be manufactured even in rural agricultural districts. The Stein family in Clackmannanshire were improvement farmers with a surplus of barley. This was used to feed a whisky distillery, whose draff or hogwash was recycled as animal feed on the farm. Communities supported their own tanneries, meal mills, breweries, bakeries, tailoring workshops, wrights' yards, cobblers, chemical works and saw mills. Blacksmiths and engineers manufactured a range of their own products, such as bicycles, and even motor cars, though perhaps never breaking into the national market and ultimately unable to compete with the mass production of Coventry or Oxford. The Bairds of Monklands (Glasgow) were agriculturalists who realised that their land had industrial potential because under their corn lay coal. From 1785 they took mining leases, benefiting from their proximity to turnpike roads, canals and (later) railways. Profit from the pits provided capital for ironworks (1828), which by

The Norwich firm of Boulton & Paul Ltd despatched prefabricated garages by rail anywhere in Britain before the First World War.

To
Keep your Motor Car from Frost

DESIGNERS AND MAKERS
BOULTON & PAUL
LTD. · · NORWICH

Telegrams—Boulton, Norwich   *Telephone Nos. 12 and 911*

1843 required sixteen furnaces. Raw material arrived by rail to be discharged into furnaces fired by Baird coal. Pig iron was loaded into canal boats. Only Dowlais in Wales could rival the Bairds in world iron production.

In 1842 John Summers began his clog-making business. To increase profits he bought out his nail supplier and, in 1851 at the Great Exhibition, invested capital in a nail machine. He then sold nails through the industrial areas of Yorkshire and Staffordshire, expanding his range of iron and going into steel. His works at Shotton on the Cheshire–Flintshire border became a hive of industry in the midst of fields.

A similar mixture of industrial elements underpinned the commercial power in Cheshire of the Marshalls, salt manufacturers. Their salt extraction works are still evident in the landscape, principally as lakes formed by the collapse of shafts. Business archives were preserved in their lawyer's muniment room and indicate that their success depended on the control of collieries to fuel the works, river boats to carry coal and salt, and Liverpool counting houses to fix prices and production for the family's benefit.

Industry affected settlements and the movement of people within regions and across country. Capital was attracted to an area by the presence of a willing workforce. People might be drawn to places where capitalists willingly financed industries and employment. Archives suggest reasons why families were able or obliged to migrate in search of better prospects, for instance agrarian reform or the famines of 1782-3 and 1846. A colony of English nail makers was settled in the Falkirk–Kilsyth area of central Scotland in 1761 in the vicinity of the nascent ironworks of Carron, which itself was initially worked with English labour from Coalbrookdale. The furnaces were sited three miles inland rather than on the coast, to take advantage of coal, charcoal and clay-band iron ore. This immigration is reflected in parish registers, as well as in surnames subsequently found in the area.

The historian investigates the social, racial, political, environmental and financial reasons behind specialisations in certain districts, for instance Hatton Garden for

From medieval times onwards, windmills were an essential power source for the production of meal and flour. At Clayton, Sussex, a clap-boarded post-mill named Jill represents an early type, preserved in working order. Jack (in the background) was a state-of-the-art nineteenth-century tower mill, now occupied as a dwelling.

jewellery, Harley Steet for medicine, Spitalfields for silk weaving, Kirkcaldy for checks and ticks (mattress covers), Macclesfield for silk, Honiton for lace, Perth for silesias (fine linen or cotton), Nottingham for hosiery and Dunfermline for damask. Osnaburghs (brown linens) were manufactured almost exclusively at Dairsie, originally named Osnaburgh, in Fife before the skills and capital were relocated to Dundee to found that town's world supremacy in jute manufacture. Industrial origins are expressed in such place-names as Furnace, Coalville, Leadhills, Ironbridge, Snuffmill Meadow, Brewhouse Croft and Ropewalk. An industrial sponsor is commemorated in Port Talbot and a product in Port Sunlight (soap).

Illicit industries and contraband commerce may come to light during research, perhaps through oral accounts or court cases relating to entrepreneurs detected and prosecuted by the authorities. Business records are unlikely to survive, though the contribution of illegal activity and the black economy to the commercial life of the community may have been considerable; among such activities were smuggling, wrecking, street-corner trading, busking, the selling of political ballads, prostitution and drug-dealing. The activities of a coppersmith, Robert Armour, in Campbeltown, Argyll, during the Napoleonic wars are documented in government archives because, as well as his legitimate business, Armour had a lucrative sideline in the manufacture of whisky stills for sale to illicit distillers. Needless to say, his own records are not informative.

Machinery for edge-tool grinding, textile production, ironworking and corn milling was driven by waterwheels, while windmills were constructed mainly for grinding grain and pumping water from mines. Steam engines from the 1690s – by Savery, Newcomen and Watt – comprised a remote boiler resembling a large kettle, made of riveted iron plates, which was heated by a furnace beneath a tall chimney stack. A stately engine-house sheltered and supported the cylinders and pivoted beam that made up the engine proper. The engine was connected by belts and pulleys or a train of rods to the pumps and equipment it powered. Surviving engines date from 1800 onwards. Sites of dismantled engines maybe inferred from the location of flues, driveshafts, coal bunkers and solid bases. Electricity was applied as a power source from the 1850s, when carbon-arc lighting produced by an engine-driven dynamo was pioneered in lighthouses. Domestic electric light was installed by the armaments tycoon William Armstrong at his home, Cragside in Northumberland, where relics of the original hydro-electric power station and copper cabling can be inspected. Public electricity supplies began from power stations at Godalming and Brighton (1881). Large power stations, such as Ferranti's, at Deptford (1889), and the peat-fired one at Bellacorick in County Mayo, required water for steam turbines and cooling as well as coal or peat for fuel – factors which determined their siting. From such centres of power pylons began their relentless march, eventually being accepted into the rural landscape.

Iron ores occur abundantly throughout Britain, although the early modern iron industry was concentrated in such areas as the Weald, Glamorgan and the Forest of Dean, where timber for charcoal as fuel for smelting coincided with accessible iron ore. When timber supplies became scarce, manufacturers looked further afield and iron smelting was established in ever remoter districts, such as Bonawe in Argyll. Sites are recognisable from ore sheds, crushing mills and charcoal burning stances. Iron ore was smelted in a blast furnace, which basically comprised a hearth superheated by a blast of air supplied by water or steam. Coke-fired smelting was pioneered by Abraham Darby at Coalbrookdale, Shropshire, in 1709. Manufacture then shifted to the coalfields, notably those of south Wales and central Scotland. Iron tapped from the furnace was sold as pig iron for remelting and forging into cast iron for bridges (see illustration on page 194), machine parts, window frames, cooking pots and even, at the height of iron's popularity, for tombstones. Pig iron was also refined in coke-fired hearths, coal-fired reverberatory furnaces and rolling mills into wrought iron, the raw material of blacksmiths, nail makers and chain makers. From 1856 steel was manufactured by means of the Bessemer converter and Siemens open hearth.

Metal trades were conspicuously localised: edge tools and cutlery in the rural hinterland of Sheffield; files around Warrington; pins and needles by colliers' wives at Kingswood, Gloucestershire, and Redditch, Worcestershire. Lead ores in Somerset, Swaledale, Derbyshire, Northumberland, Glamorgan, Montgomeryshire and Galloway were exploited by underground mining or by washing away topsoil with controlled flooding (hushing), scarring the landscape for generations. Ore was crushed in mechanical mills and smelted in furnaces served by zigzag underground flues and remote stone chimney stacks. Lead was rolled into sheets for roofing; shaped into gutterings and water pipes; cast into printers' type; and rounded into gun shot by dropping molten lead into water inside tall shot towers.

Copper was mined in Cornwall, Cumbria, Cheshire and Anglesey. Smelters were sited close to ores and charcoal fuel, for instance in the seventeenth century at Brigham near Keswick, or to coal and water power, for example in the valleys of the Neath (Aberdulais, 1584) and Tawe (Llangyvelach, 1717). Swansea coal attracted brassfounders previously established beside the Avon in Somerset. Business attracted business. At Llanelli the broad manufacturing base of coal, iron, tin, lead, silver, copper and pottery transformed a rural neighbourhood to a major port of 15,281 inhabitants by 1881. In central England brass was machined into scientific instruments, clock mechanisms, interior door furniture, candlesticks, candelabra, gas fittings and water taps.

Deep mines for tin in Devon and Cornwall are signalled by gaunt engine-houses powering drainage pumps. Workings below are seldom accessible for survey without the assistance of expert cavers. Tinplate, a thin layer of tin laminated to sheet iron, was a Swansea speciality at Ynyspenllwch from 1747 and Ystalyfera, 1838, supplied to tinkers and tinsmiths for conversion into a variety of household vessels. Tin was a constituent

A stationary steam engine. Such engines powered the industrial revolution.

At Southwick, Sussex, a single chimney of Portslade (Brighton B) power station – begun 1947, demolished 1987 – is the chief visible monument to Brighton Corporation's enterprise as an electricity generator from 1891 onwards. Shoreham harbour was enlarged to accommodate the corporation's fleet of colliers.

in bronze for cannon, machine bearings and 'copper' coins. Bronze bells are usually inscribed with the foundry name. Tin alloyed with lead and known as pewter was used for tableware, which was often stamped with a pewterer's mark.

Aluminium was first identified in 1828 and first produced in 1848. The metal remained an expensive curiosity – classed as 'precious metal' – used chiefly for trinkets and statuary until the end of the nineteenth century. Large-scale commercial smelting required electric power. The British Aluminium Company (1896) smelter at Foyers on Loch Ness was powered by its own hydro-electric scheme. Alumina extracted from imported bauxite (aluminium ore) at Larne, County Antrim, and Burntisland, Fife, was reduced at Foyers for export to rolling mills in Cheshire.

The mining of anthracite, lignite, cannel and steam coal was a rural industry in Wales, Northumberland, Durham, Lancashire, the West Riding of Yorkshire, Staffordshire, Nottinghamshire and central Scotland. From the eighteenth century technological advances, especially in pumping, allowed the exploitation of deep seams. Shafts of abandoned mines, dangerous to the unwary but susceptible to investigation by experienced cavers, are the means of investigating old workings,

A field sketch of the blast furnace at Bonawe, Argyll, drawn by C. Clerk in June 1987.

On Penwith Downs, Cornwall, the engine-house of the Ding Dong tin mine makes a picturesque ruin, but the engine itself was the centre of a bitter patent battle between Boulton & Watt and Trevithick the younger.

which may be dated according to the techniques employed. Stoops of coal supported galleries before about 1860, but thereafter roofs were propped with timber or, still later, with mechanical jacks. Extraction by pick and shovel and underground transport involved men (and some women) until the 1840s, when ponies and railways were introduced. The researcher will wish to photograph engine-houses, winding gear, storage areas, pithead baths and the conical or scarp-and-dip profiles of slagheaps, overshadowing the standardised tied housing of the pitmen; some of these modest homes may still house those who can remember the heyday of the coal industry. At gasworks across Britain coal was baked into coke, a valuable smokeless fuel. Gases released in the process were collected for heating and power; a range of tars and chemicals was recovered; and, on the grim side, toxic pollutants saturated the ground, to the danger of properties subsequently built there. Gas lamps were installed on London streets from 1812. Gasometers towered over communities throughout Britain, storing coal gas for lighting and subsequently for cooking and heating. Even tiny Ratho, Midlothian, had a gasworks, its annual make of 296,000 cubic feet (8377 cubic metres) supplying just thirty-eight households and thirteen public lamps (1914). The firm of Robert Dempster at Elland, Yorkshire, supplied gasometers throughout the empire, including one towering a monstrous 232 feet (70.7 metres), which served the British Columbia Electric Railway Company at Vancouver.

Water power attracted industry to the gorge of the Dulais near Swansea from 1584. The dressed-stone bastion of a tinplate works of about 1840 fed water to a waterwheel – the wheel pit can be seen in the foreground.

Dartmoor granite was exploited from around 1780. Haytor quarry opened about 1820. A stone-railed tramway smoothed the way for iron-wheeled horse-drawn trucks down to the Stover Canal at Teigngrace 8½ miles (14 km) away. Haytor granite was used for London Bridge in 1825.

Stone was quarried for walling, roofing, road metal, railway ballast, aggregate in concrete, agricultural lime, milling and grinding. By field-walking the historian discovers neighbourhood quarries, sandpits and gravel pits but may have to travel far to find sources of specialised stone. Dinas silica (from the Neath valley) was purchased for the manufacture of firebricks, invented in 1823 for lining industrial furnaces; white Lundy granite supplied the Thames embankment (1864). Slate working reshaped whole mountainsides, notably at Ballachulish (Argyll) and Blaenau Ffestiniog (Merioneth). China clay for potteries was excavated around St Austell, Cornwall, by washing slurries of white clay with high-pressure water jets into settling tanks; this created a landscape scarred with pits and conical white spoil heaps. Field-walking may also reveal masonry remains of the kilns where limestone was roasted into lime for neutralising acid soil or processing into cement. A geologist can be called in to identify the types, properties and uses of stone available in parish quarries, describing where the stones seen in roads, houses, churches and bridges may have originated. Quarry loading platforms, railways, tramways and blondins (aerial ropeways) can be recognised.

Salt was valued as a food preservative and an essential element in the production of chemicals and pharmaceuticals. Brine from sea water trapped in salterns (shallow ponds) was concentrated into salt. At Keyhaven and Lymington in Hampshire nineteenth-century salt houses survive in the vicinity of earth-banked evaporation ponds. Natural underground reservoirs of brine were exploited around Droitwich, Nantwich, Northwich and Middlewich. Brine was boiled in metal pans to form salt crystals. Rock salt, discovered beneath the Marbury estate in Cheshire in 1670, was extracted by conventional mining techniques, notably around Winsford and Marston. Salt workings are evidenced in place-names, abandoned buildings, rusting equipment, boiling pans and flashes (lakes) caused by the subsidence of old workings.

Pottery was a domestic and localised craft for anyone who felt competent to produce mugs or plates for the table. Production on a large scale began in the seventeenth century in districts favoured with the ingredients for success: entrepreneurial expertise, a labour force, investment capital, transport for raw materials such as coal, clay and flint, and a market for competitively priced finished goods. The fieldwork of the industry therefore includes canals, rivers, roads, plate-ways and railways; waterwheels and steam-engine houses for powering machinery; workshops for throwing or slip-casting the clay; and fireproof containers known as saggars for stacking the ware before firing. Flint from southern England or Europe was added to clay to whiten and strengthen the pottery, though first the hard stone was made grindable by calcination (heating) in a top-loaded kiln. Flints were then carried by cast-iron plate-way to the water-powered grinding mill. Pottery was fired in brick cones known as bottle ovens.

Industrial potteries made hygienic earthenware dishes and cups available to all

At North Street, Cromford, Derbyshire, this terrace was built in 1777 to house textile workers who settled following Richard Arkwright's opening of his cotton mill in 1771. Domestic craftsmen operated looms and frames in the garret work rooms, well illuminated by long windows.

social classes, underpinning the sanitary revolution of the nineteenth century which depended upon mass-produced drainage pipes, sinks, basins, chamber pots and water-closet bowls. Pottery was carried by water and road. The wares of provincial potteries supplying the everyday needs of a district may have achieved national distribution if they were particularly attractive or useful as in the case of Belleek, County Fermanagh.

Glass was manufactured from the seventeenth century in London, Bristol, Cork, Waterford, Tyneside and, by Huguenot refugees, at Birr, County Offaly. The ingredients – silica and soda – and furnace fuel were widely available. Manufactories gravitated to Lancashire and central England, where associated pottery and chemical industries were concentrated. Occasionally there survive bottle-shaped brick cones where glassmakers worked around a central hearth. The historian may survey the varieties of glass in windows, for instance crown glass, blown as a flat disc with a central bull's-eye blemish, suitable for cutting into small panes, and sheet glass, blown as a cylinder for larger panes. Plate glass is recorded from the late eighteenth century, its manufacture having been a key element in the development of St Helens. Its production required considerable capital investment in equipment for casting, rolling and grinding. The labour force included numerous female hands for the laborious manual tasks of finishing and polishing. The glass revolution impacted on domestic and commercial life. Houses were designed with convenient bay windows. Shops and shopping were transformed by display windows, perhaps involving the partial demolition and refronting of older properties. Palm houses, conservatories and greenhouses expanded the range of food and plants available. Glass-roofed railway stations and public houses with expanses of etched and silvered glass are symbols of the Victorian age.

The shirts, shifts, sheets and underwear of rich and poor alike were made of wool or linen produced and woven in the district. Fieldworkers may identify linen weaving sheds, bleach-fields, water-powered lint mills where linen flax fibre was scutched (beaten with mechanical hammers), millponds, lades and sluices. Linen was so important that the British Linen Company (1746) became a leading bank. By

Quarry Bank Mill, Styal, Cheshire. A small agricultural community on the banks of the river Bollin was jolted into the industrial age by the capital and vision of Samuel Greg, who founded his cotton mill here in 1784. The chimney stack indicates the later installation of a steam engine.

1780 cotton was booming also. Textile manufacture was mechanised during the eighteenth century, for example with water-powered mills for fulling and carding. Spinning was early mechanised, with the muckle wheel and the treadle-operated spinning wheel, then industrialised with the application of water and later steam power to machines with multiple spindles. Weaving remained a handicraft, practised in both the country cottage and the urban close, for instance tapestries and embroideries at Old Windsor in the nineteenth century. Purpose-built weavers' houses may be identified by the rows of windows lighting upper-storey workrooms. Hand-loom weavers and such craftsmen as framework knitters formed an influential class in early nineteenth-century politics, prospering until the 1830s and thereafter declining to become the backbone of radical movements such as Chartism. Mechanised weaving mills are identified by tall chimney stacks for steam-engine furnaces, by systems of watercourses, ponds and sluices for waterwheels and by the distinctive saw-toothed glass roofs illuminating looms in the weaving sheds.

Before 1750 chemical manufacture depended upon a range of chiefly organic raw materials. Soda for soap makers was refined from wood ash or burned kelp. Soap for

A black powder (gunpowder) manufactory was established on Dartmoor by George Frean of Plymouth in 1844. Three grinding mills were powered by a leat drawing water from Cherry Brook, while plantations of alder provided charcoal. The finished gunpowder was dried by stoves burning Dartmoor peat. Fumes and dangerous sparks were carried by underground flues to be discharged through high chimney stacks standing at a safe distance.

cleaning fleeces combined soda and animal fat in a noisome concoction, its production being concentrated in such textile districts as Bristol. Gunpowder makers refined saltpetre from human excrement collected by urban 'nightsoilmen' or 'petermen'. To minimise explosive risks, the saltpetre was ground in small batches with sulphur and charcoal in water-powered grinding mills remote from towns. Complex systems of lades and ponds supplied water to drive the waterwheels.

Industrial heavy chemicals were required for pottery, paint, bleaching, glass, dyestuffs, fertiliser and explosives. Works were established in the countryside near sources of raw materials and with efficient transport links. Where the industry flourished old plant and premises may be identifiable, perhaps also tell-tale pollutants in the soil – in the shadow of the latest catalytic cracker with its pipework wreathing around its modest parent plant. For the manufacture of sulphuric acid, used to produce soda and bleaches, coke-filled filtration towers loomed over lead-lined chambers. These were mounted on masonry arches above a sulphur furnace and steam boiler. At Billingham on Tees, in a rural landscape producing iron and salt, the Bosch commercial ammonia process was established in 1923 – a seedling enterprise of Imperial Chemical Industries.

Transport

The fieldwork of transport requires walking or cycling along routes perhaps now bypassed and disused. The fieldworker might help future visitors by writing and illustrating a guide with notes on flora, fauna and hostelries along the way. The coast is an interesting place to begin, where sheltered bays and beaches have always attracted traders, fishermen, smugglers and immigrants. To enhance natural anchorages, landowners and town councils financed such improvements as stone breakwaters and moles to enclose lagoons. The construction of artificial harbours was essential for commercial progress and a useful source of income for proprietors. Harbours were equipped with wet docks, preferably unaffected by tides, dry docks for repairs, quays, lighthouses, warehouses, granaries, cranes, customs houses, grain elevators, seamen's missions, fishmarkets, icehouses, salt houses and smoke houses (kipper kilns). Fishing families requiring net lofts, drying grounds and harbour access were rented narrow feus in which houses were set gable-on to the sea. Boats were built and broken up in yards whose slipways and sheds merit surveying. There is also hope of finding out about regional peculiarities of boat design, equipment and fishing methods from the evidence of archives, oral tradition or wrecks. The nineteenth-century craze for salt-water cures and seaside holidays benefited existing towns, such as Tenby in industrial south Wales, and created new

The resort of Newcastle, County Down.

At Maesbury, Shropshire, goods were transhipped between the main road and the Shropshire Union Canal.

(or greatly expanded) resorts, such as Lytham St Anne's, serving the mill workers of Lancashire. Spa waters and country air attracted the middle classes to the assembly rooms, lodgings, bottling plants and medical clinics of Harrogate, Pitlochry, Lisdoonvarna and Tunbridge Wells among others.

Rivers were tamed by private enterprise, generally with the authority of Parliament: water levels were regulated by the dredging of weirs and locks and difficult meanders bypassed or straightened by canalisation. From the 1750s canals lined with brick, stone, timber and puddled clay were built for the carriage of bulky raw materials and manufactures. Boats were dragged along by men and horses on a towpath. Canals of the period 1755-93 that traced contours around hills and marshes were generally narrow with locks up to 7 feet 6 inches (2.3 metres) broad by 72 feet (22 metres) long, reflecting the dimensions of horse-drawn barges. From the 1790s canals were wider and deeper and their routes more direct, requiring tunnels, aqueducts over roads and streams, pumping stations to maintain water levels, bridges, locks for ascending or descending, houses for lock-keepers, wharves, warehouses, bollards and mileposts, many of which survive. Transport interchanges where a canal met a river, road or railway perhaps required inclined planes or mechanical turntables. The canal that linked the potteries and coalfields of Staffordshire with industrial Lancashire and, via Liverpool, with Ireland and America, was opened in 1776. Ports were established for the Trent & Mersey Canal, for example near the medieval township of Barnton, Cheshire, whose salt was sold to the Lancashire chemical industries. A mooring basin was dug for boats to load salt, coal, bricks, pottery, lime, grain and timber and to await entry to the narrow brick tunnel leading north through the hillside. Warehouses, the canal toll office, lodgings for boatmen, dwellings for leggers (who footed vessels through the tunnel), beer shops and a Methodist chapel were constructed in a previously uninhabited corner of the township.

Parish and county authorities maintained roads with rates and statute labour for access to regional markets or moorland. Improvements, such as milestones and guideposts, were sometimes encouraged by legislation. The track was typically unsurfaced and up to two rods (33 feet or 10 metres) broad. When passing through enclosed arable land or plantations the road was bounded with hedges, ditches or walls of stone and earth. Occasionally these survive, as at Spittalwood on the Inverness to Logie Fair track, where the area has remained under moor and old woodland. Roads might be causewayed with soil excavated from side ditches, with a foundation of large stones and a surface of broken stones compacted by hooves and wheels. Repairs were confined to filling potholes with fresh gravel. These early roads are occasionally discovered, sealed under more recent tarmacadam. Drove roads were broad unsurfaced routes by which herds of animals were customarily moved across country to market, bypassing arable fields on high ground. Cattle rested at designated greens, perhaps with hostelries bearing 'drover' names. The typical county bridge is a single-arched humpback of mortared stone. Older histories refer to these as packhorse bridges, supposing incorrectly that the absence of parapets was a design feature specifically to permit the passage of horses with loaded panniers. Heavy horse and cattle traffic was in fact usually diverted to a paved ford alongside the bridge.

Following the Jacobite rising of 1715 military roads were engineered to strategic forts and barracks. Military roads lined with milestones ran determinedly between cleared verges, negotiating steep gradients by uncompromising hairpin bends and crossing streams by arched stone bridges, limewashed or harled (several are still known as Whitebridge) but usually without parapets. Government roads also cut across country to link centres of strategic importance. One network is associated with the work of the 1803 Commission for Highland Roads and Bridges. Even today the road (the A5) from London to Holyhead, the embarkation point for Dublin, follows the alignments and gentle gradients surveyed by Thomas Telford in the early nineteenth century, with technologically advanced bridges at Bettws-y-Coed (iron, 1815) and Menai (suspension, 1819-26) still carrying road traffic. From the seventeenth century trusts were empowered by Parliament to make and repair roads, levying tolls at turnpikes (gates) across the highway at junctions or town boundaries. Tollhouses are identified by a projecting bay with windows for the keeper to watch up and down the road. A board indicated charges. Turnpike roads run straight or in broad curves across the rectilinear fieldscape. Surfaces were of small angular broken stones, packed hard on beds of large stones and slabs. Streams were bridged with single arches of stone.

Railed ways, tramways, dram roads, wagonways and plate-ways were constructed from the sixteenth century onwards, with wagons pulled by men or horses and, later, by cable, powered by a stationary steam engine. Wooden railed ways were in use from 1597 at Lord Middleton's Wollaton Hall colliery in Nottinghamshire. During the seventeenth century railed wagonways carried coal from Durham

The octagonal tollhouse on Telford's Holyhead road at Llanfairpwllgwyngyll, Anglesey, where charges were prominently displayed.

Steam power for locomotion and mining at Middleton, from George Walker's 'The Costumes of Yorkshire', 1814.

and Northumberland collieries to wharves on the Tyne and the Wear. Causey Arch (1727) at Tanfield is probably the oldest surviving wagonway bridge. Plate-ways with L-section iron rails on stone sleeper blocks linked the furnaces, ironstone pits and coal mines of the Coalbrookdale district in the eighteenth century. The first stage of a strategic land route from London to Portsmouth, the Surrey Iron Railway, was authorised as a plate-way in 1801 from Wandsworth along the industrialised Wandle valley to Mitcham and Croydon with branch lines to mills and to Carshalton. The enterprise functioned until 1846 and is traceable in street alignments, perhaps two bridges and the modern Mitcham-Croydon line. The more rural extension to Merstham (1803-5) is easier to follow. Further construction was abandoned following the end of French invasion threats. Plain iron, later steel, rails for wagons with flanged wheels became standard during the nineteenth century. Narrow-gauge horse tramways are still evident from cropmarks or low relief features marking the curve of the railway line or from surviving stone sleepers, stone or brick loading platforms, bridges and culverts under streams. Steam traction by locomotive engines from 1804 required substantial trackbeds, strong rails, gentle gradients and wide-radius curves cutting through fields and suburban settlements. Railway archaeology attracts enthusiasts for main lines as well as narrow gauges, considering tracks, cuttings, tunnels, embankments, bridges, stations, company offices, signal boxes, water towers, engine sheds, locomotives, trucks and carriages. Railway companies built new towns and expanded existing settlements to accommodate their works and workers, at Swindon, Crewe and Darlington. The arrival of the railway ensured prosperity for such communities as Oban, where a terminus of ferries for the Hebrides was established. The railway transformed villages into suburbs as people could travel further to work. With the arrival of the railway the Middlesex village of Ealing, some 6 miles (10 km) west of Hyde Park Corner, became part of the metropolis of London. Ealing Common was ringed with new villas, while the old high street was laid out with less august developments, though retaining a vestige of village green, the parish workhouse and the church. A fashionable broadway at the District Railway terminus was built up with shops, a town hall and a Gothic church.

Agriculture and horticulture

During the 'little ice age' of about 1490-1720 snow and frost might last three months or more even in southern England, affecting winter ploughing and sowing. The freezing of rivers and wells affected water supplies, sanitation and transport, though frost fairs on the Thames from 1607 to 1814 contributed positively to the quality of metropolitan life. Annual rainfall and temperatures fluctuated dramatically, with hot dry summers and cold wet ones blamed equally for crop failures, distress and famine. Wet weather in Scotland ruined grain harvests in 1695-9, 'King William's ill years', when many people died or emigrated. Drought and heat caused sanitary problems in towns. Fires threatened woodland and buildings.

The period 1720-1850 was milder, with plentiful rainfall but, neverthless, recurrent crop failures. Thereafter temperatures rose slightly but consistently into the twentieth century, exacerbating the effects of pollution and urban smogs. Meteorological data can be found in official and family records as well as being recorded in oral traditions.

Agricultural improvers increased production and profits through the enclosure of open arable fields, communal pasture and woodland by agreement with landowners and tenants or by parliamentary authority. New rectangular fields were marked out on the ground with ditches, enclosed with banks of earth or turf, which were in due course supplanted by – or surmounted – with hedges, fences, walls or wire. Trees for timber and enhancement were planted around fields, in shelter belts and as copses where foxes and game birds were bred for sport. Fields were drained with underground clay pipes, replacing ridges and furrows. Land was ploughed in straight lines and seed mechanically sown in straight drills, facilitating the introduction of horse-drawn hoeing implements. The productivity of agricultural land was enhanced through scientific crop rotation, the use of sown grasses, liming, fertilising with manufactured chemicals and imported guano, and the improvement of livestock by selection and cross-breeding. Farms, nurseries and market gardens produced (and distributed to growing urban markets and ports) annual crops of wheat, barley, oats, vegetables and fruit, incidentally encouraging neighbourhood baking, brewing and distilling industries. Fields were accessed by a rectilinear grid of unpaved tracks, some now taken over as roads, others surviving as grassy paths. Estate networks

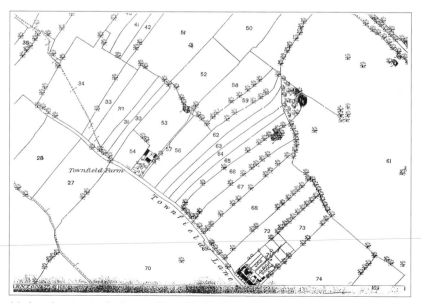

Medieval strips in the former Town Field of Barnton, Cheshire, had still not been amalgamated into the modern rectangular enclosures when the Ordnance Survey visited in the 1870s (OS first edition, XXXIII, 4). The numbers refer to a reference book listing owners, occupiers, acreage and state of cultivation.

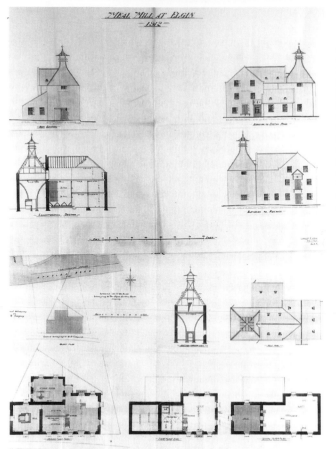

Plans, elevations and sections of a meal mill, powered by an internal combustion engine, with a traditional drying kiln attached, drawn by C. C. Doig, architect, of Elgin.

joined at awkward angles, evident even today to the unwary motorist. The land was divided into compact blocks, each tenanted by an individual farmer paying a rent and occupying a new farmhouse, steading and stack-yard at a strategic site in the holding. From around 1760 crofting landscapes were created by the reallocation of lands on Scottish and Irish estates among peasant tenants. Each arable croft of about 5 acres (2 ha) had a cottage and steading with rights to extensive moorland grazings and peat cuttings. Enclosure and crofting landscapes, rectilinear fields and standard housing convey the impression of a tamed, cultivated landscape. In 1887 Parliament permitted the provision of allotments, where urban workers could grow food for the family table. From 1892 county councils created agricultural smallholdings, each with a house, outbuildings and up to 50 acres (20 ha). These were ranged along key routes and specialised in soft fruit and market gardening.

The gentry created walled parks around their houses – fantasy worlds planned by landscape gardeners. Roads and villages spoiling the view were shifted, though parish churches were often left undisturbed on account of legal and administrative problems, the costs of demolition and rebuilding, or superstitious prejudice against disturbing graves, or because they harmonised with the visual effect of the park. An isolated church is thus an indicator of village removal. A wall-and-ditch barrier known as a ha-ha kept stock away from the house without marring the vista or even betraying its presence. Ornamental lakes, streams and waterfalls were created by damming or diverting streams. Trees were moved in an attempt to improve upon nature. Fanciful temples, statues, grottoes and follies provided visual focus. Formal

(Left) Oast houses were for drying hops or malt, an essential element in the competitive and progressive brewing industry. These buildings at Hawkhurst, Kent, have been converted into dwellings.

(Right) The maltings at Sleaford, Lincolnshire, prospered on a productive agricultural hinterland. The structure, designed by H. A. Couchman, was built in 1892-1905.

(Left) At Bushmills, County Londonderry, whiskey is manufactured from local agricultural and natural products, using know-how developed over centuries of distilling. The pagoda roofs cover malt-drying kilns.

(Right) Profits from Shetland wool and mutton exports increased with the introduction of steamships in 1838. Landowners created sheep ranches and evicted arable farmers, who were given crofts and fishing stances on the coast, as here in Uyea Sound on Scotland's most northerly island of Unst.

beds of exotic and hybridised flowers, as well as mazes of evergreen hedging, delighted house guests, while in walled gardens and greenhouses staple vegetables and exotic fruits were raised for the kitchen. Owners of rural estates, eager to maximise profits, planted commercial woodland, particularly black poplar, sycamore and oak for house builders; oak, beech, walnut and pine (deal) for furniture makers; and ash for the picks and shovels of canal navvies. Timber products were widely sought and included clogs, pit props, railway sleepers, furniture, floorboards, charcoal, barrels, packing cases, cartwheels and fencing. British woodland partly satisfied the demand, with industries sometimes relocating, for instance

The park at Llangedwyn, Denbighshire, from which all tenants were removed by law.

shipbuilding from Kingston upon Hull to the River Spey and a new town named Kingston, exploiting the Scots pines of Rothiemurchus. Imported softwoods from the Baltic and exotic hardwoods from the rainforests of Africa and America filled any gap in supply. New species were introduced to Britain, including mulberry trees planted to feed silk worms for an experimental silk industry promoted during the seventeenth century. Giant Wellingtonia graced landscaped parks. Monkey-puzzle trees from Chile and flowering cherries from Japan enhanced suburban townscapes. Fir and pine for softwood, plywood and paper supplies again covered bogs and hillsides that had been treeless since the Bronze Age. Estates were dedicated to the Victorian passions for romantic scenery and blood sports. Landscapes were rigorously managed. Heather moorland was cultivated for the pernickety grouse, Asian rhododendron was densely planted as game cover; and lochs were artificially stocked with trout and salmon. Remote railway platforms serving comfortable lodges, for example Altnabreac station for Dalnawillan in Caithness, sustained the annual exodus to the wilderness.

Towns and villages

Settlements outgrew their medieval bounds as population and economic activity increased. Villages were transformed by enclosure and clearance, with farmers and servants moving to new farmhouses out in the fields and families migrating to the towns. Houses in the village street were rebuilt or subdivided for landless craftsmen, shopkeepers and labourers. Urban main streets were also transformed. General replanning was unusual, even following major conflagrations – most famously the London fire in 1666 but also other places, for example, Marlborough (1653), Newport, Shropshire (1665) and Tiverton (1598, 1612 and 1731). Houses, gable-on to the street and still confined within narrow medieval feus, were reconstructed in brick or stone with two or more storeys, perhaps also with fore-booths, lean-to shops and stair turrets facing the street. Windows and doors were slapped through blank gable walls to enable the establishment to open for business directly on to the market place. New buildings generally now faced the street. By purchasing two adjoining feus an owner could combine the premises and create a vennel (way through to the rear) of double width with the houses on each side sharing the access. A speculator acquiring three or more adjacent feus might demolish the existing buildings to develop a new street at right angles to the high street, stretching to the back lane or town wall. Such cross streets, lined with houses, sometimes followed the curved line of the original feus and – a useful dating aid – were named after the developer or a contemporary celebrity.

Towns or villages founded or replanned from around 1600 were generally laid out as rectilinear grids of streets and open spaces. Protestant Derry (1609) was a walled grid planned around its central square, the Diamond. Inigo Jones created an Italian-style piazza for the polite society occupying the Earl of Bedford's Covent Garden development (1630). City planners favoured townscapes based upon squares, crescents and circuses lined with terraced buildings of consistent height and architectural style. Rectilinear new towns such as Beauly and Fettercairn (about 1760) also housed peasants evicted in rural Scotland. Speculative builders packed the industrial proletariat into tenements, terraces and back-to-back cottages along dreary grids of streets in such towns as Belfast, Preston, Bolton, Leeds and Halifax. Even the model community of Saltaire, built by the alpaca-fleece tycoon Titus Salt, was, for all its polite architecture, planned as a rigid grid. From the 1860s garden suburbs broke with this trend. At Stoneygate (Leicester) and Bedford Park (Chiswick) villas curved along avenues shaded by trees, while Bournville (1878) offered a similar environment for working men. An ambitious garden city was pioneered on a rural site at Letchworth, Hertfordshire (1903), though ribbon developments along arterial roads were more typical of the period 1920-30.

A survey of buildings indicates the range of urban activity. The historian will note commodity exchanges for trading in wool, cloth, corn or coal; the guildhall or town hall for administration; the assembly rooms for holding concerts and balls; the skittle alley; the ring for cock and dog fighting; the prison, post office and market hall; beer and cook shops; and the chop house and restaurant. The hotel offered food, drink, entertainment and accommodation and had a courtyard entered by

stagecoaches through a vennel from the street. Theatres flourished from the sixteenth century and ranged from the open-air Globe at Southwark to houses of fashionable resort, such as the King's in Drury Lane, London, where Nell Gwynne sold her oranges. Bristol's Royal retains its 1764-6 structure. The lower orders patronised the gin palace and music hall. From 1896 cinematographs or bioscopes were improvised in converted roller-skating rinks (as at the Walpole, Ealing) or shooting ranges (the Savoy, Edinburgh). These 'penny gaffs' were located

The Pratt family from Leicestershire founded the new town of Newport, County Mayo, in the eighteenth century. The town was bitterly contested during the rising of 1798 and was the base of Edward Lyons, hero of the independence struggle in 1916-23. By popular demand, in spite of history, the newsagent with an Anglo-Norman surname stocks the 'English dailys'.

Whiteley Village, Burr Hill, Surrey, was created as the Whiteley Homes for the Aged Poor under the will of William Whiteley (1831-1907), a London department-store tycoon known as the 'universal provider'. The self-contained community of vernacular red-brick houses in garden-suburb style clusters around a village green. The charity provided its own nursing home and a Gothic church.

close to the dwellings of their artisan audiences. Purpose-built cinemas appeared from 1910, culminating in the Art Deco Roxys, Regals and Odeons of the 1930s.

The water supply for Londoners was organised in 1613 through Hugh Middleton's New River from Ware to Clerkenwell reservoir, with a supplementary supply from the Thames, raised by tide-wheels in the arches of London Bridge but later modernised with pumps powered by a Newcomen steam engine. Ambitious works required by industrial towns included the Vyrnwy dam in Montgomeryshire (1880-90) for Liverpool and the Gothic splendour of Green Lanes pumping station and the monstrous Cornish engine and water tower of Kew Bridge for Londoners. Waste disposal was resolved by rivers, such as the Fleet in London and the Irwell in Salford. From 1848, a year of cholera panic, the modern London sewerage system depended on stone and brick-lined tunnels constructed beneath the streets. Abbey Mills pumping station (1865-8) with a Gothic and Byzantine-style hall for its beam engines, was designed for the Metropolitan Board of Works to propel the contents of the northern outfall sewer. Town councils followed London by providing sewage farms, settling beds, engine-houses, treatment plants and underground works.

Deserted settlements are numbered in thousands and were usually the result

Bristol's Palladian corn exchange, designed by John Wood of Bath in 1740-3, has a public clock showing both Bristol and London time (an innovation necessary with the coming of the railways, which ran on metropolitan time). On bronze Renaissance-style balusters or nails in the street, payments were publicly made and bargains sealed, hence 'paying cash on the nail'.

On Achill Island, County Mayo, a medieval village on the slopes of Slievemore was replanned during the eighteenth century. Stone cottages were built along an unpaved main street. Economic isolation, famine and the lure of the New World combined in the end to depopulate the countryside, and Slievemore was deserted.

of decisions by the ruling classes. At West Raynham, Norfolk, the village street was diverted in 1644 because the houses spoiled the landowner's view along a new avenue. At Houghton, Norfolk, Viscount Townshend closed the public highway and moved the village outside the park gates during an estate reorganisation in 1722-39. The villagers of Fochabers, Moray, were relocated in 1776-7 from their homes in front of Gordon Castle to a new village. The market cross of Old Fochabers was retained on its original site as a feature of the landscaped park. In 1851 some 450 peasant families were evicted from Glenveagh, County Donegal, in advance of the construction of J. G. Adair's shooting lodge (1870). Villages were removed during agrarian reorganisation, as at Lilford, Northamptonshire, in 1755, when inhabitants were resettled in the estate village of Wigsthorpe. Old Milton Abbas, comprising around a hundred houses, shops, four inns and a grammar school, was obliterated in 1771-85 and replaced with forty semi-detached dwellings of vernacular charm, though out of Lord Milton's immediate prospect. Thousands of townships in the eastern lowlands of Scotland, from John O'Groats to Berwick-upon-Tweed were cleared following the reaffirmation of the law of removal in 1756. In Knoydart some thirty deserted townships are identifiable. The least obtrusive remains are the grass-grown stone foundations of timber-framed turf-and-wattle dwellings built before 1760. Such creel (wickerwork) cottages, perhaps with cruck trusses, were the usual type of pre-'improvement' Irish and Scottish dwellings. These at Knoydart can be described as 'class I' deserted houses because they were abandoned early, between

The harbour of Bunbeg, County Donegal, was built in the course of inland agricultural clearance.

1771 and 1854. The ruins of class I deserted houses may be recognised from their fire-blackened central hearths, each usually a flat stone to avoid fire risk to the turf gable wall. At Airor the lower courses of clay-bonded rubble walls of improved rural houses (class II) stand to knee height. Built after 1760, they were deserted before 1854. The most substantial Knoydart ruins (class III) are of stone farmhouses and steadings constructed under supervision by the Annexed Estates Commission after 1760 and were deserted perhaps within living memory. Sheriff court cases of just the one year, 1766, document the clearance, replanning and enclosure of the county of Moray. Hundreds of townships were replaced by new farms and farm-houses, often confusingly bearing the old settlement name. Dispossessed peasants were encouraged to migrate to planned new settlements established by the land-owner, where crafts were encouraged or a harbour was constructed to facilitate commercial fishing. The old turf and timber townships are rarely visible, having been ploughed out by 'improving' farmers. The latest of the Scottish clearances, on the Sutherland estates, left a legacy of bitterness and folklore that is intriguing to research.

Houses

By investigating the development of house sites the historian can generate a register of the annual number and situation of inhabited dwellings as a basis for estimating population, allowing from four to six persons per house. A multiplier of this order has been found suitable for a crude, but not too far wide-of-the-mark estimate of population. Of course family size and household size vary through time and according to social class. Researchers who wish to go more deeply into this area of investigation and to develop their statistical technique may make a start in quantitative analysis with guidance from *Historian's Guide to Statistics* (1971) by C. M. Dollar and R. J. Jensen. The living standards of the occupants are affected by and reflected in a house's layout, size, architectural style, situation, ornamentation, building materials, water supply and heating system. Mansions offer a glimpse into the lifestyle of the ruling classes, their modern conveniences having provided models for more modest builders. Sometimes the landed classes were conservative, in Scotland perhaps occupying a draughty towerhouse with open fires long after the homes of ordinary folk had been improved. New trends in housing seem to have travelled from Europe to south and east Britain, from lowlands to highlands, from town to country. Each region is divided into a kaleidoscope of sub-regions with overlapping traditions of structure, style and material. The historian places paro-chial housing within a broad context, discovering where and when a particular style or feature originated and explaining how and why the characteristic travelled across country.

Housing stock reflects epochs of rebuilding financed with the profits of trade or agriculture. The farmers of Glamorgan and Monmouth were rehoused from around 1560. The rebuilding of central England took place in the generations around 1600. English and Welsh highland districts were rebuilt from around 1670; south and east Scotland 1740-1815; Ireland 1780-1845. Urban Britain was built or rebuilt between 1840 and 1939 and from the 1950s onwards. War, fire, flood and enclosure might result in the renewal of housing stock as at Warwick and Blandford Forum, rebuilt after conflagrations of 1694 and 1731 respectively. The renovation of housing in the Hebrides may date from 1886 when the legal position of crofters was redefined. In the Pennines, Shaw Hall is an example of an old house altered piecemeal over the centuries. The hall was the home of the Shaws of Saddleworth. In 1632 the family replaced their timber-framed medieval hall with a two-storeyed gabled stone house with mullioned windows, fashionable decorative features and internal conven-iences. This rebuilding pleased the family for more than a century until, in 1798, the requirements of fashion and social standing demanded comprehensive remodelling. Part of the old Stuart structure was demolished and replaced by a two-storeyed plain

At Dedham, Essex, modern brick houses were built during improvements in the 1730s. Pevsner asserts that, except for the Congregational church, 'there is nothing at Dedham to hurt the eye' and approves the structure shown here as a 'lively, somewhat restless composition'.

classical Georgian residence in deep-coursed local stone. About 1830 the owner, George Shaw (an architect), researched the history from archives and folk memory. His reconstruction drawing of the old hall is preserved with his diaries for 1829-48 at Manchester Central Library (MS 927.2 S15). Shaw demonstrated his antiquarian passion by commissioning vernacular and antique features, including stone transoms, mullions and label moulds for the Georgian sash windows, fancy tracery in the fanlight, floral decoration on the severe classical architrave of the entrance, gables above the cornice, a porch with a spire and a panelled room in Commonwealth style. The owner renamed his house 'St Chad's' to complete its Gothicisation! This analysis comes from the reliable old method of observation on site, assisted by unpublished manuscript sources. Standard textbooks may hardly help: Professor Nikolaus Pevsner summarises Shaw Hall simply as 'St Chad's House (Urban District Offices). C17, apparently altered'.

Typical and exceptional ground plans of houses are surveyed as a means of dating structures and fitting regional styles into a general pattern. Ordinary houses built until about 1720 anywhere in the British Isles usually consisted of just one room for living, sleeping and storage, with walls and roofing constructed of materials acquired near the building site. The compact axial-stack house with a central chimney

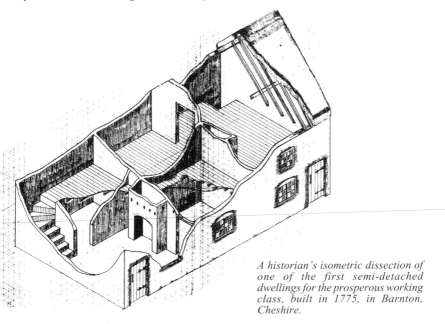

A historian's isometric dissection of one of the first semi-detached dwellings for the prosperous working class, built in 1775, in Barnton, Cheshire.

stack above back-to-back fireplaces originated in the houses of yeomen in Essex and Kent, spreading thence into Oxfordshire around 1585, to northern towns, such as Chester and York, by 1610 and to rural Wales by about 1660. The style was favoured for only two or three generations in each region but came again into fashion for redeveloped estate houses in Scotland about 1815-30. The two-and-a-half roomed house dominated the rural highland zone and post-clearance Scotland from around 1770. The front door opened into a central lobby with a box-bed, a pantry and, if appropriate, a staircase. The kitchen (living room) and the chamber (bedroom) opened to the left and right with fireplaces in the gable walls. Rural two-and-a-half roomed houses were generally single-storeyed with a loft lighted by iron-framed fanlights or dormers, added as an improvement from 1870 onwards. In town the style rose to two or even three storeys and an attic above ground-floor shops and business premises. In the two-plus-one house (1570-1800) an additional room across an entrance passage was added to a basic two-roomed plan. There might be chambers under the thatch above the ground-floor living rooms. The ubiquitous Irish two-plus-one house (1780-1850) added to a basic two-roomed highland house an inner chamber warmed by a small hearth back-to-back with the kitchen fireplace. Double-pile houses (two rooms deep from front to back) appeared at gentry level around 1600, spreading into central England by the end of the century and thereafter into highland regions. A more homely type was created when owners of traditional houses one room deep added a rear extension for a pantry or dairy, covered by a cat-slide extension roof. In smart double-fronted double piles the front door gave access to a hall and stairwell, into which opened all the other ground-floor rooms – parlour, dining room or master bedroom at the front with two service rooms (kitchen, dairy, library, office) at the rear. This centralised plan ushered in a new age of privacy because family members no longer passed through one room to reach another. This, and a fireplace in every room, made the curtained beds of earlier times redundant. Privacy was enhanced and the separation of the classes ensured by the separate circulation of the family and servants using their own stairs. The typical single-fronted house was in effect one half of a double front. The front door opened into a hall and stairwell with rooms ranged one behind the other. This was a style used for the terraced residences of wealthy capitalists in Bloomsbury, Dublin and Glasgow Woodlands, rising four storeys, with servants' attics, basement kitchens and the principal drawing room on the first floor. Lower down the social scale the single-fronted house and its descendant, the surburban semi-detached, consisted of two

At Eochaill, Inis Mhor, Aran, 'An Charraig' is a three-roomed improvement house with whitewashed rubble walls and straw thatch secured with ropes and stones against the Atlantic gales.

principal rooms on each floor. From about 1740 there might be a scullery beneath the stairs or in an extension at the rear, while from 1840 artisans expected a string of backyard extensions, including a kitchen, scullery, washroom, bathroom, ashpit, water or earth closet and coal shed. The single-fronted design was further sub-divided from around 1790 into blocks of back-to-back dwellings with one room on each floor.

Churches

The enlargement and renovation of medieval churches after the Reformation often coincided with periods of parochial prosperity. A chronology of such altera-tions can be compiled from the observation of features and fittings, with help from standard textbooks and archival sources. Religious structures built since 1530 are usually neoclassical in style, characterised by columns, domes, pediments, pilasters and elaborate plasterwork. Severe classicism was favoured by nonconformists in the slated Bethels of Wales and the awesome brick Ebenezer chapels of the industrial north of England. In the parish church a classical renovation often conceals earlier Gothic architecture. During the eighteenth century Gothic Revival architects re-introduced crockets, spires, battlements, gargoyles, vaulted ceilings and pointed-arch windows. Gothic features crept into Telford's spartan Parliamen-tary churches in Scotland (1823-35) and even into prefabricated corrugated iron chapels and halls, popular with nonconformists around 1900. Inside the church the nave was fitted out with a sounding board above the pulpit to amplify the preaching. During long services ordinary parishioners were permitted desks or box pews, while the squire enjoyed cushioned seats and perhaps even a fireplace. The poor and the urban guilds were accommodated in galleries and lofts. Musicians accompanied the singing, though certain sects deplored church music other than unaccompanied psalmody. The Church of England met the Methodist challenge by reviving reli-gious music with a choir and harmonium or pipe organ.

By the sixteenth century fairs and sports were banished from church environs, which became cluttered with memorials and gravestones recording the names, achievements and lifespans of gentlemen, merchants and farmers. Before acid rain and vandalism obliterate them, the wise historian photographs and copies inscrip-tions on graves as a means of gaining information on ordinary parishioners. There are also the lich-gate (literally 'body gate') where corpses were rested, the manse, the almshouses, the sexton's cottage, various encroachments around the perimeter of the churchyard and family mausoleums with stone coffins, iron-caged graves and a watch-house (testifying to the activities of resurrectionists). At Forres, Moray, neglected tombs on the churchyard mound, the result of eight centuries of burials, were cleared during landscaping in 1973-5 without record. A plan dated 1825 in a lawyer's archive and photographs taken in 1906-36 provide some evidence of family burial sites, while masses of bones dislodged in 1996 show how swiftly bodies decay and jumble in that particular soil. Thomas Hardy warns the sentimental historian:

> Here's not a modest maiden elf
> But dreads the final Trumpet,
> Lest half of her should rise herself,
> And half some sturdy strumpet!

Religious idealism inspired such settlements as Gracehill, County Antrim (1746), built for refugee Moravians. Howell Harris's Protestant monastery at Trefecca, Breconshire, was a significant socialistic community established away from the distractions of a town. Under the Chartist land plan, settlements were created at Lowbands (O'Connorville) and Snigs End, both in Gloucestershire, and at Great Dodworth, Worcestershire. Anarchists established their alternative community at Whiteway, Gloucestershire, in 1898. Suburbs of existing towns were developed on sectarian lines as in Belfast, where Catholics settled along the Falls Road, segre-gated from Protestant communities at Springmartin and Shankill.

A funerary monument at Shrewsbury Abbey, Shropshire.

Warfare

Landowning families continued to inhabit castles, though chimneys, fenestration and other building works after about 1550 were for comfort rather than defensibility. Occasionally such government policies as the pacification of Ireland and Scotland demanded reforditfication in earnest. Numerous towerhouses for the gentry were improved or newly built in the highland zone during the sixteenth century, their apparent strength belying the comparative comforts within. In studying castles the historian detects stages in the decline of the military capability of the subject and the parallel rise of state power. Castles were progressively dismantled and their stones used for other purposes until the tourist advantages of ruins were appreciated. The royal castle of Forres, Moray, was demolished as late as 1933, when the foundations of the curtain walls and keep were removed in an unemployment relief scheme to construct a new road to the municipal rubbish dump. The castle motte was reshaped and levelled as a public park.

As a defence against the French in 1539 a chain of squat stone blockhouses was constructed around the English coast; with cloverleaf plans achieving wide fields of fire, engineers maximised the space for mounting heavy artillery. Castles were hastily remilitarised during the Civil War by the creation of gun loops and the repair of walls and gates. New structures consisted of earthen defences, proof against shot and shell, where batteries, assembly points and siege platforms are detectable as low-relief features or cropmarks. At Tilbury (1667) brick-faced earthen ramparts provided gun positions guarding the Thames estuary. In response to the Jacobite threat medieval clan castles were demolished and newer towerhouses refurbished, including Braemar, with battlements for musketeers, and Corgarff, with a star-shaped curtain wall pierced with gun loops. Forts and barracks, such as Ruthven on a medieval motte and Fort George at a ferry point on the Moray Firth, guarded against native Jacobites and their French allies. Copied from the French fort of Cape Mortella, Corsica, in 1794, circular martello towers, each mounting a single heavy gun, looked seaward against the French and American threat from 1804. National security was further buttressed by entrenched camps and the Royal Military Canal linking the Kent front line with the national canal network. Features associated with reforms of the nineteenth century include model hospitals and musketry and gunnery schools. Rifle ranges and halls where territorials drilled were established across Britain, initially to meet the threat of Napoleon III and subsequently to accommodate a permanent territorial force.

The varied landscape of the Second World War presents exciting possibilities for

Drumcoltrum towerhouse, Dumfries-shire, was erected early in the sixteenth century and occupied into the eighteenth; the family had one principal room on each level, accessed by the stair wing.

the recording and analysis of regional strategies. Historians consider such features as the concrete 'dragon's teeth' protecting coastlines against amphibious landings, the public air-raid and private Anderson shelters, airfields with grassy runways and camouflaged bunkers, barrage balloon sites and prisoner-of-war camps. Concrete 'pill boxes' used as minor fortresses for the ordinary soldier or Home Guard have been the subject of a five-year study by the amateur archaeologist and historian Henry Wills of Wilton. Military landscapes of the Cold War attract interest and include a communications centre tunnelled into a hillside at Armagh and one beneath the famous Wentworth golf course. One of Scotland's secret bunkers, near St Andrews, has at last opened as a heritage site. Regional seats of government and observer posts may be identified as evidence of the strategic importance of a particular locality in the nuclear age.

War memorials, honouring sacrifice and celebrating parochial pride, challenge the sensitivity and detachment of the historian in analysing the motives of those who

The principal military distinction of this artillery fort at Pendennis, Cornwall – one of a pair erected around 1543 to protect the Fal estuary against the French – was its five-month defence against landward siege during the Civil War.

Oldcastle, County Meath, remembers a local hero, James Cogan, aged twenty-three, 'killed in action against the English' on 22nd July 1920, and a revolutionary comrade killed in 1921: 'their task remains unfinished'. The Times of 23rd July 1920 reported that Sinn Fein volunteers refused to stop their car for the military and were shot at. 'A cap with a bullet hole through it' was found at the scene.

commissioned the monument, the exploits commemorated, the phrasing of inscriptions and the iconography of images. At Kilrush, County Clare, a monument immortalises, in Irish, French and English, the Manchester martyrs of 1867, 'patriots judicially murdered by a tyrannical government'. The heroes so honoured were terrorists or freedom fighters – depending on your viewpoint – hanged in Manchester for murder and buried in quicklime. Adverse public opinion precluded a memorial in 1867, but nationalism was ascendant, romantic and respectable in 1903, so the community paid for an extravagant monument to the lively spirit of Ireland, carved with a belated tribute to the renowned dead, here translated from the Erse by Brother Gleeson:

> There is not a headstone over the members before they are put in lime, nor stone or cross which would show where they are from or who were their ancestors; people will be thinking in their native town forever on the two quatrain where those famous men lie.

International conflict, clan raid, religious pogrom and dynastic struggle have inflicted untold suffering. Whole families have been wiped out, their records and oral traditions scattered, their homes abandoned to decay. But history teaches that gaps are not unfilled for long, that migrants soon enrich their neighbourhood with skills – and their genes. When new people settle a wasted landscape, community history begins all over again.

Bibliography

The date of the first edition is given unless otherwise stated.

DISCOVERING LOCAL HISTORY

Adams, C. V. Phythian. *Re-thinking English Local History.* Leicester University Press, 1987.
Everitt, A. *Ways and Means in Local History.* National Council of Social Service for the Standing Conference for Local History, 1971.
Dymond, D. P. *Archaeology and History: a Plea for Reconciliation.* Thames & Hudson, 1974.
Dymond, D. P. *Writing Local History: a Practical Guide.* Bedford Square Press/National Council of Voluntary Organisations for British Association for Local History, 1981.
Finberg, H. P. R. *The Local Historian and His Theme.* Leicester University Press, 1952.
Finberg, H. P. R., and Skipp, V. H. T. *Local History: Objective and Pursuit.* David & Charles, 1967.
Friar, S. *The Batsford Companion to Local History.* Batsford, 1991.
Gardiner, J., and Wenborn, N. (editors). *The History Today Companion to British History.* Collins & Brown, 1995.
Hey, D. *Family History and Local History in England.* Longman, 1987.
Hey, D. *The Oxford Companion to Local and Family History.* Oxford University Press, 1996.
Hoskins, W. G. *English Local History; the Past and the Future.* Leicester University Press, 1966.
Hoskins, W. G. *Local History in England.* Longman, 1959.
Kease, J. Campbell. *A Companion to Local History Research.* A. & C. Black, 1989.
Lewis, C. *Particular Places: an Introduction to English Local History.* British Library, 1989.
Macfarlane, A., Harrison, S., and Jardine, C. *Reconstructing Historical Communities.* Cambridge University Press, 1977.
Mitchell, B. R. *British Historical Statistics.* Cambridge University Press, 1988.
Richardson, J. *The Local Historian's Encyclopaedia.* Historical Publications, New Barnet, second edtion 1986.
Riden, P. *Local History: a Handbook for Beginners.* Batsford, 1983.
Rogers, C. D., and Smith, J. H. *Local Family History in England.* Manchester University Press, 1991.
Tiller, K. *English Local History.* Alan Sutton, 1992.
Williams, M. *Researching Local History: the Human Journey.* Longman, 1996.

STEPPING INTO THE PAST

Adams, C. V. Phythian. *Local History and Folklore.* Bedford Square Press for Standing Conference for Local History, 1975.
Aston, M. *Interpreting the Landscape: Landscape Archaeology in Local Studies.* Batsford, 1985.
Aston, M., and Rowley, T. *Landscape Archaeology: an Introduction to Fieldwork Techniques on Post-Roman Landscapes.* David & Charles, 1974.
Bodey, H., and Hallas, M. *Elementary Surveying for Industrial Archaeologists.* Shire, 1977.
Bord, J. and C. *The Secret Country: an Interpretation of the Folklore of Ancient Sites in the British Isles.* Paul Elek, 1976.
Brown, A. *Fieldwork for Archaeologists and Local Historians.* Batsford, 1987.
Cameron, K. *English Place-names.* Batsford, 1961.
Clark, A. J. *Seeing Beneath the Soil.* Batsford, 1990.
Darton, M. *The Dictionary of Scottish Place Names and the Elements that Go to Make Them Up.* Lochar Publishing, 1990.
Falkus, M., and Gillingham, J. *Historical Atlas of Britain.* Kingfisher Books, revised edition 1987.
Farrar, R. *Survey by Prismatic Compass.* Council for British Archaeology, 1987.
Field, J. *Place-names of Great Britain and Ireland.* David & Charles, 1980.
Gelling, M. *Place-names in the Landscape.* Dent, 1984.
Gelling, M. *Signposts to the Past: Place-names and the History of England.* Dent, 1978.
Gelling, M., Nicolaisen, W. F. H., and Richards, M. *The Names of Towns and Cities in Britain.* Batsford, 1970.
Gomme, A. B. *The Traditional Games of England, Scotland and Ireland.* 1894; reprinted Dover, New York, 1964.
Greene, K. *Archaeology, an Introduction.* Batsford, 1983.
Harvey, N. *The Industrial Archaeology of Farming in England and Wales.* Batsford, 1980.
Lamb, H. H. *Climate, History and Modern World.* Methuen, 1982.
Longworth, I., and Cherry, J. *Archaeology in Britain since 1945.* British Museum, 1986.
Luff, R. M. *Animal Remains in Archaeology.* Shire, 1984.
Mackay, J. *Collecting Local History.* Longman, 1984.
Mallory, J. P., and McNeill, T. E. *The Archaeology of Ulster from Colonization to Plantation.* Institute of Irish Studies, Queen's University of Belfast, 1991.
Mitchell, F. *The Shell Guide to Reading the Irish Landscape.* Country House, 1986.
Muir, R. *History from the Air.* Michael Joseph, 1983.
Muir, R. *Shell Guide to Reading the Celtic Landscapes.* Michael Joseph, 1985.
Muir, R. *Shell Guide to Reading the Landscape.* Michael Joseph, 1981.
Nicolaisen, W. F. H. *Scottish Place-names.* Batsford, 1976.
Opie, I. and P. *Children's Games in Street and Playground.* Clarendon Press, 1969.

Parry, M. L. *Climatic Change, Agriculture and Settlement*. Dawson, 1978.
Rackham, O. *Ancient Woodland; Its History, Vegetation and Uses in England*. Edward Arnold, 1980.
Rackham, O. *Trees and Woodland in the British Landscape*. Dent, 1976.
Ravensdale, J. *History on Your Doorstep*. BBC, 1982.
Renfrew, C., and Bahn, P. *Archaeology: Theory, Methods, Practice*. Thames & Hudson, 1991.
Riley, D. N. *Aerial Archaeology in Britain*. Shire, second edition 1996.
Riley, D. N. *Air Photography and Archaeology*. Duckworth, 1989.
Rackham, O. *The History of the Countryside*. Dent, 1986.
Rodell, W. *Church Archaeology*. Batsford/ English Heritage, revised edition 1989.
Rowley, T. *Villages in the Landscape*. Dent, 1978.
Scholes, R. *Understanding the Countryside*. Moorland, 1985.
Smout, T. C., and Wood, S. *Scottish Voices, 1745-1960*. Collins, 1990.
Stewart, J. *Shetland Place-names*. Shetland Library and Museum, Lerwick, 1987.
Stirland, A. *Human Bones in Archaeology*. Shire, second edition 1999.
Taylor, C. *Fields in the English Landscape*. Dent, 1975.
Taylor, C. *Village and Farmstead: a History of Rural Settlement in England*. George Philip, 1983.
Taylor, C., and Muir, R. *Visions of the Past*. Dent, 1983.
Taylor, M. *Wood in Archaeology*. Shire, 1981.
Thomas, K. *Religion and the Decline of Magic*. Weidenfeld & Nicolson, 1971.
Thomas, K. *Man and the Natural World*. Allen Lane, 1983.
Wilson, D. R. *Air Photo Interpretation for Archaeologists*. Batsford, 1982.
Winchester, A. *Discovering Parish Boundaries*. Shire, 1990.
Wood, E. S. *Collins Field Guide to Archaeology in Britain*. Collins, 1963.

LIBRARIES AND ARCHIVES
Barrett, J., and Iredale, D. *Discovering Old Handwriting*. Shire, 1995.
Bevan, A., and Duncan, A. (previous authors Cox, J., and Padfield, T.). *Tracing Your Ancestors in the Public Record Office*. HMSO, fourth edition 1990.
Clanchy, M. T. *From Memory to Written Record: England 1066-1307*. Edward Arnold, 1979.
Colwell, S. *Family Roots: Discovering the Past in the Public Record Office*. Weidenfeld & Nicolson, 1991.
Connor, R. D. *The Weights and Measures of England*. HMSO, 1987.
Currie, C. R. J., and Lewis, C. P. (editors). *English County Histories: a Guide*. Alan Sutton, 1994.
Danbury, E. *Palaeography for Historians*. Phillimore, 1998.
Dawson, G. E., and Skipton, L. Kennedy. *Elizabethan Handwriting, 1500-1650*. Faber, 1968.
Devine, T. M. *The Transformation of Rural Scotland ... 1660-1815*. Edinburgh University Press, 1994.
Emmison, F. G. *Archives and Local History*. Methuen, 1966.
Emmison, F. G. *How to Read Local Archives 1550-1700*. Historical Association, 1967.
Emmison, F. G. *Introduction to Archives*. BBC, 1964.
Grenham, J. *Tracing Your Irish Ancestors - the Complete Guide*. Gill & Macmillan, Dublin, 1992.
Hector, L. C. *The Handwriting of English Documents*. Edward Arnold, 1958.
Hunnisett, R. F. *Editing Records for Publication*. British Records Association, 1977.
Iredale, D. *Enjoying Archives*. Phillimore, second edition 1985.
Kinealy, C. *Tracing Your Irish Roots*. Appletree Press, Belfast, 1991.
McNeill, P. G. B., and MacQueen, H. L. (editors). *Atlas of Scottish History to 1707*. The Scottish Medievalists and Department of Geography, Edinburgh University, 1996.
Morton, A., and Donaldson, G. *British National Archives and the Local Historian*. Historical Association, 1980.
Newton, K. C. *Medieval Local Records: a Reading Aid*. Historical Association, 1971.
Nolan, W. *Tracing the Past: Sources for Local Studies in the Republic of Ireland*. Geography Publications, Dublin, 1982.
O'Neill, T. *The Irish Hand*. Dolmen, 1984.
Ryan, J. G. *Irish Records: Sources for Family and Local History*. Ancestry Publishing, Salt Lake City, 1989.
Simpson, G. G. *Scottish Handwriting 1150-1650*. Aberdeen University Press, 1973.
Sinclair, C. *Tracing Scottish Local History: a Guide to Local History Research in the Scottish Record Office*. HMSO Edinburgh, 1994.
Sinclair, C. *Tracing Your Scottish Ancestors*. HMSO Edinburgh, 1990.
Stephens, W. B. *Sources for English Local History*. Manchester University Press, 1973.
Stuart, D. *Latin for Local and Family Historians*. Phillimore, 1995.
Torrance, D. R. *Weights and Measures for the Scottish Family Historian*. The Scottish Association of Family History Societies, 1996.
Young, N. Denholm. *Handwriting in England and Wales*. University of Wales Press, 1954.

FROM ROMANS TO VIKINGS 410-865
Adams, C. V. Phythian. *Continuity, Fields and Fission: the Making of a Midland Parish*. Leicester University Press, 1978.
Alcock, L. *Arthur's Britain: History and Archaeology AD 367-634*. Penguin, 1971.
Backhouse, J. (and others). *The Golden Age of Anglo Saxon Art*. British Museum Publications, 1984.
Bowen, E. G. *Saints, Seaways and Settlements in the Celtic Lands*. University of Wales Press, 1969.
Brown, M. P. *Anglo-Saxon Manuscripts*. British Library, 1991.
Campbell, J., John, E., and Wormald, P. *The Anglo-Saxons*. Phaidon, 1982.
Chadwick, N. *The Celts*. Penguin, 1970.
Finberg, H. P. R. *Roman and Saxon Withington: a Study in Continuity*. Leicester University Press, 1955.
Hall, R. *Viking Age Archaeology in Britain and Ireland*. Shire, 1990.
Harbison, P. *Pilgrimage in Ireland: the Monuments and the People*. Barrie & Jenkins, 1991.

Harting, H. Mayr. *The Coming of Christianity to Anglo-Saxon England*. Batsford, third edition 1991.
Haslam, J. *Early Medieval Towns in Britain c.700 to 1140*. Shire, 1985.
Higham, N. *The Kingdom of Northumbria AD 350-1100*. Alan Sutton, 1993.
Higham, N. *Rome, Britain and the Anglo-Saxons*. Seaby, 1992.
Hill, D. *An Atlas of Anglo-Saxon England*. Blackwell, 1981.
Hodges, R. *Dark Age Economics: the Origins of Towns and Trade AD 600-1000*. Duckworth, 1982.
Hooke, D. (editor). *Anglo-Saxon Settlements*. Blackwell, 1988.
Jackson, A. *The Symbol Stones of Scotland*. Orkney Press, 1984.
Kennett, D. H. *Anglo-Saxon Pottery*. Shire, second edition 1989.
Kirby, D. P. *The Earliest English Kings*. Unwin Hyman, 1991.
Laing, L. *The Archaeology of Late Celtic Britain and Ireland c.400-1200 AD*. Methuen, 1975.
Laing, L. *Later Celtic Art in Britain and Ireland*. Shire, reprinted 1997.
Laing, L. and J. *A Guide to the Dark Age Remains in Britain*. Constable, 1979.
Laing, L. and J. *The Picts and the Scots*. Alan Sutton, 1993.
Lang, J. *Anglo Saxon Sculpture*. Shire, 1988.
Morris, J. *The Age of Arthur: a History of the British Isles from 350 to 650*. Phillimore, 1977.
Morris, R. *Churches in the Landscape*. Dent, 1989.
Raftery, B. *Pagan Celtic Ireland*. Thames & Hudson, 1994.
Richards, J. D. *English Heritage Book of Viking Age England*. Batsford/English Heritage, 1991.
Ritchie, A. *The Picts*. HMSO Edinburgh, 1989.
Ritchie, A. *Viking Scotland*. Batsford/Historic Scotland, 1993.
Ritchie, G. and A. *Scotland: Archaeology and Early History*. Thames & Hudson, 1981.
Ross, A. *Pagan Celtic Britain*. Routledge & Kegan Paul/Columbia University Press, New York, 1967.
Ross, A. *The Pagan Celts*. Batsford, revised edition 1986.
Seaborne, M. *Celtic Crosses of Britain and Ireland*. Shire, reprinted 1994.
Smyth, A. P. *Warlords and Holy Men*. Edward Arnold, 1981.
Taylor, H. M. and J. *Anglo-Saxon Architecture*. Cambridge University Press, 1965-78.
Thomas, C. *Christianity in Roman Britain to AD 500*. Batsford, 1981.
Wainwright, F. T. (editor). *The Problem of the Picts*. Thomas Nelson, 1955.
Webster, L., and Backhouse, J. *The Making of England: Anglo Saxon Art and Culture AD 600-900*. British Museum Press, 1991.
Welch, M. *Anglo-Saxon England*. Batsford/English Heritage, 1992.
Wilson, D. M. (editor). *The Archaeology of Anglo-Saxon England*. Methuen, 1976.
Witney, K. P. *The Jutish Forest: a Study of the Weald of Kent from 450 to 1380 AD*. Athlone Press, 1976.
Wood, M. *Domesday: a Search for the Roots of England*. BBC, 1986.
Wood, M. *In Search of the Dark Ages*. BBC, 1981.
Yorke, B. *Kings and Kingdoms of Early Anglo-Saxon England*. Seaby, 1990.

THE MIDDLE AGES 865-1529
Aberg, A. (editor). *Medieval Moated Sites*. Council for British Archaeology, 1978.
Adams, C. V. Phythian. *Desolation of a City: Coventry and the Urban Crisis of the Late Middle Ages*. Cambridge University Press, 1979.
Adams, C. V. Phythian. *The Norman Conquest of Leicestershire and Rutland*. Leicestershire Museums, Art Galleries and Records Service, 1986.
Ashby, M. K. *The Changing English Village, a History of Bledington, Gloucestershire, in Its Setting, 1066-1914*. Roundwood, Kineton, 1974.
Aston, M., and Bond, J. *The Landscape of Towns*. Dent, 1976.
Bailey, B. *The English Village Green*. Hale, 1985.
Baker, A. R. H., and Butlin, R. A. (editors). *Studies of Field Systems in the British Isles*. Cambridge University Press, 1973.
Barry, T. B. *The Archaeology of Medieval Ireland*. Methuen, 1987.
Bennet, H. S. *Life on the English Manor*. Cambridge University Press, 1937.
Beresford, M. W. *History on the Ground*. Lutterworth, 1957.
Beresford, M. W. *The Lost Villages of England*. Lutterworth, 1954.
Beresford, M. W. *New Towns of the Middle Ages*. Lutterworth, 1967.
Beresford, M. W., and Hurst, J. G. (editors). *Deserted Medieval Villages*. Lutterworth, 1971.
Beresford, M. W., and Hurst, J. G. *Wharram Percy Deserted Medieval Village*. Batsford/ English Heritage, 1990.
Beresford, M. W., and St Joseph, J. K. *Medieval England: an Aerial Survey*. Cambridge University Press, second edition 1979.
Brown, R. J. *Timber-framed Buildings of England*. Robert Hale, 1986.
Cantor, L. (editor). *The English Medieval Landscape*, Croom Helm, 1982.
Clarke, H. *The Archaeology of Medieval England*. British Museum, 1984.
Coppack, G. *English Heritage Book of Abbeys and Priories*. Batsford, 1990.
Davies, W. *Wales in the Early Middle Ages*. Leicester University Press, 1982.
Dodgshon, R. A. *The Origin of British Field Systems: an Interpretation*. Academic Press, 1980.
Fossier, R. *The Illustrated Cambridge History of the Middle Ages*. Cambridge University Press, 1986.
Foster, R. *Discovering English Churches*. BBC, 1981.
Hall, D. *Medieval Fields*. Shire, reprinted 1987.
Harvey, J. *Mediaeval Craftsmen*. Batsford, 1975.
Hatcher, J. *Plague, Population and the Economy of England, 1334-1530*. Macmillan, 1977.
Hewett, C. A. *English Historic Carpentry*. Phillimore, 1980.
Hindle, B. P. *Medieval Roads and Tracks*. Shire, third edition 1998.
Hindle, B. P. *Medieval Town Plans*. Shire, 1990.

Hoskins, W. G., and Stamp, L. Dudley. *The Common Lands of England and Wales.* Collins, 1963.
Kerr, N. and M. *A Guide to Norman Sites in Britain.* Granada, 1984.
Mercer, R. E. *English Vernacular Houses.* HMSO, 1975.
Morgan, P. *Domesday Book and the Local Historian.* Historical Association, 1994.
Muir, R. *The English Village.* Thames & Hudson, 1980.
Muir, R. *The Lost Villages of Britain.* Michael Joseph, 1985.
Muir, R. and N. *Fields.* Macmillan, 1989.
Muir, R. and N. *Hedgerows: Their History and Wildlife.* Michael Joseph, 1987.
Muir, R. and N. *The National Trust Rivers of Britain.* Webb & Bower, 1986.
Nicholson, G., and Fawcett, J. *The Village in History.* Weidenfeld & Nicolson/ National Trust, 1988.
Platt, C. *The English Mediaeval Town.* Secker & Warburg, 1976.
Platt, C. *Medieval Britain from the Air.* Guild Publishing, 1984.
Platt, C. *The Parish Churches of Medieval England.* Secker & Warburg, 1981.
Roberts, B. K. *Rural Settlement in Britain.* Dawson, 1977.
Roberts, B. K. *Village Plans.* Shire, 1982.
Rowley, T. (editor). *The Origins of Open Field Agriculture.* Croom Helm, 1981.
Rowley, T., and Wood, J. *Deserted Villages.* Shire, second edition 1995.
Sawyer, P. H. (editor). *Medieval Settlement: Continuity and Change.* Edward Arnold, 1976.
Stuart, D. *Manorial Records.* Phillimore, 1992.
Taylor, A. Clifton. *The Pattern of English Building.* Faber, 1972.
Taylor, C. *Fieldwork in Medieval Archaeology.* Batsford, 1974.
Taylor, C. *Roads and Tracks of Britain.* Dent, 1979.
Thirsk, J. (editor). *Land, Church and People: Essays Presented to Professor H. P. R. Finberg.* Museum of English Rural Life, Reading, 1970.
Walker, D. *Medieval Wales.* Cambridge University Press, 1990.
Wilson, D. *Moated Sites.* Shire, 1985.
Wood, M. *The English Mediaeval House.* Phoenix House, 1965.
Yelling, J. A. *Common Field and Enclosure in England 1450-1850.* Macmillan, 1977.
Young, C. R. *The Royal Forests of Medieval England.* Leicester University Press, 1979.

THE MODERN ERA
Adams, I. H. *The Making of Urban Scotland.* Croom Helm, 1978.
Alcock, N. W. *Old Title Deeds: a Guide for Local and Family Historians.* Phillimore, 1986.
Alvey, N. *From Chantry to Oxfam: a Short History of Charities and Charity Legislation.* British Association for Local History, 1996.
Andrews, J. H. *A Paper Landscape, the Ordnance Survey in 19th Century Ireland.* Clarendon Press, 1975.
Appleby, A. B. *Famine in Tudor and Stuart England.* Liverpool University Press, 1978.
Armytage, W. H. G. *Four Hundred Years of English Education.* Cambridge University Press, 1964.
Aylmer, G. E., and Morrill, J. S. *The Civil War and Interregnum – Sources for Local Historians.* Bedford Square Press for Standing Conference for Local History, 1979.
Barley, M. W. *The English Farmhouse and Cottage.* Routledge, 1961.
Barley, M. W. *Houses and History.* Faber, 1986.
Barrett, H., and Phillips, J. *Suburban Style: the British Home, 1840-1960.* Macdonald, 1987.
Beaton, E. *Scotland's Traditional Houses.* Historic Scotland/Stationery Office (Edinburgh), 1997.
Beckett, J. V. *Local Taxation: National Legislation and the Problems of Enforcement.* British Association for Local History, 1982.
Bettey, J. H. *Church and Parish.* Batsford, 1987.
Bettey, J. H. *Rural Life in Wessex, 1500-1900.* Moonraker Press, Bradford-on-Avon, 1977.
Bracegirdle, B. *The Archaeology of the Industrial Revolution.* Heinemann Educational, 1973.
Brunskill, R. W. *Brick Building in Britain.* Gollancz/Peter Crawley, 1990.
Brunskill, R. W. *Illustrated Handbook of Vernacular Architecture.* Faber, 1970.
Brunskill, R. W. *Traditional Buildings of Britain.* Gollancz, 1981.
Buchanan, R. A. *Industrial Archaeology in Britain.* Penguin, 1972.
Burton, A. *The National Trust Guide to Our Industrial Past.* George Philip, 1983.
Calder, J. *The Victorian Home.* Batsford, 1977.
Campbell, M. *The English Yeoman.* Yale University Press, New Haven, 1942.
Carruthers, A. (editor). *The Scottish Home.* National Museums of Scotland, 1996.
Chalklin, C. W. *The Provincial Towns of Georgian England: a Study of the Building Process, 1740-1820.* Edward Arnold, 1974.
Chalklin, C. W., and Haviden, M. A. (editor). *Rural Change and Urban Growth, 1500-1800: Essays in Honour of W. G. Hoskins.* Longman, 1974.
Chapman, S. D. (editor). *The History of Working Class Housing: a Symposium.* David & Charles, 1971.
Clark, P., and Slack, P. *English Towns in Transition, 1500-1700.* Oxford University Press, 1976.
Cossons, N. *The BP Book of Industrial Archaeology.* David & Charles, 1975.
Cressy, D. *Literacy and the Social Order.* Cambridge University Press, 1980.
Crossley, D. *Post-medieval Archaeology in Britain.* Leicester University Press, 1990.
Darley, G. *The National Trust Book of the Farm.* National Trust, 1981.
Devine, T. M. *The Transformation of Rural Scotland ... 1660-1815.* Edinburgh University Press, 1994.
Dunlop, J. *The British Fisheries Society.* John Donald, 1978.
Dyer, A. *The City of Worcester in the Sixteenth Century.* Leicester University Press, 1973.
Dyos, H. J., and Wolff, M. *The Victorian City: Images and Realities.* Routledge & Kegan Paul, 1973.
Edwards, P. *Farming: Sources for Local Historians.* Batsford, 1991.
Everitt, A. *The Community of Kent and the Great Rebellion.* Leicester University Press, 1966.
Everitt, A. *The Pattern of Rural Dissent in the Nineteenth Century.* Leicester University Press, 1972.

Fenton, A., and Walker, B. *The Rural Architecture of Scotland.* John Donald, 1981.

Finnegan, R. (series editor). *Studying Family and Community History: 19th and 20th Centuries.* Four volumes, Cambridge University Press/Open University, 1994.

Foreman, S. *Loaves and Fishes: an Illustrated History of the Ministry of Agriculture, Fisheries and Food 1889-1989.* HMSO, 1989.

Foreman, S. *Shoes and Ships and Sealing-wax: an Illustrated History of the Board of Trade 1786-1986.* HMSO, 1986.

Friar, S. *Heraldry for the Local Historian.* Alan Sutton, 1991.

Gaskell, S. M. *Building Control: National Legislation and the Introduction of Local Byelaws.* National Council for Voluntary Organisations, 1983.

Grace, F. *The Late Victorian Town.* British Association for Local History, 1991.

Harris, R. *Discovering Timber-framed Buildings.* Shire, reprinted 1999.

Harvey, J. H. *Sources for the History of Houses.* British Records Association, 1974.

Hay, G. D., and Stell, G. P. *Monuments of Industry: an Illustrated Historical Record.* Royal Commission on the Ancient and Historical Monuments of Scotland, 1986.

Hey, D. *An English Rural Community: Myddle under the Tudors and Stuarts.* Leicester University Press, 1974.

Higgs, E. *Making Sense of the Census: the Manuscript Returns for England and Wales, 1801-1901.* HMSO, 1989.

Jenkins, D. *The Agricultural Community in South-west Wales at the Turn of the Twentieth Century.* University of Wales Press, 1971.

Lobel, M. D. (editor). *Historic Towns: Maps and Plans of Towns and Cities in the British Isles.* Lovell Johns, Oxford, 1969; Scolar Press for Historic Towns Trust, 1975.

Lucas, B. Keith. *English Local Government in the Nineteenth and Twentieth Centuries.* Historical Association, 1977.

McCutcheon, W. A. *Industrial Archaeology of Northern Ireland.* HMSO Belfast, 1980.

Major, J. K. *Fieldwork in Industrial Archaeology.* Batsford, 1975.

Marcombe, D. *Sounding Boards: Oral Testimony and Local Historian.* University of Nottingham, 1996.

Mingay, G. E. (editor). *The Victorian Countryside.* Routledge & Kegan Paul, 1981.

Moody, D. *Scottish Local History.* Batsford, 1986.

Moore, R. *Pitmen, Preachers and Politics: the Effects of Methodism in a Durham Mining Community.* Cambridge University Press, 1974.

Murray, N. *The Scottish Hand Loom Weavers.* John Donald, 1978.

Muthesius, S. *The English Terraced House.* Yale University Press, 1982.

Naismith, R. J. *Buildings of the Scottish Countryside.* Gollancz, 1985.

Oliver, R. *Ordnance Survey Maps: a Concise Guide for Historians.* Charles Close Society, 1993.

Olney, R. J. *Rural Society and County Government in Nineteenth-century Lincolnshire.* History of Lincolnshire Committee, 1979.

Olsen, D. J. *The Growth of Victorian London.* Batsford, 1976.

Palliser, D. *Tudor York.* Oxford University Press, 1979.

Pannell, J. P. M. *The Techniques of Industrial Archaeology.* David & Charles, second edition 1974.

Patten, J. *English Towns, 1500-1700.* Dawson, Folkestone, 1978.

Peters, J. E. C. *Discovering Traditional Farm Buildings.* Shire, reprinted 1991.

Porter, S. C. *Exploring Urban History.* Batsford, 1990.

Powell, C. *Discovering Cottage Architecture.* Shire, reprinted 1996.

Raistrick, A. *Industrial Archaeology.* Eyre Methuen, 1972.

Ransom, P. J. G. *The Archaeology of the Transport Revolution 1750-1850.* World's Work, Tadworth, 1984.

Reid, A. *The Union Workhouse.* British Association for Local History, 1994.

Reid, R. *The Shell Book of Cottages.* Michael Joseph, 1977.

Rogers, A. *Approaches to Local History.* Longman, second edition 1977.

Sanderson, M. H. B. *Scottish Rural Society in the Sixteenth Century.* John Donald, 1982.

Seaborne, M. *The English School: Its Architecture and Organisation, 1370-1870.* Routledge & Kegan Paul, 1971.

Shaffrey, P. and M. *Buildings of Irish Towns.* O'Brien Press, Dublin, 1983.

Shaffrey, P. and M. *Buildings of the Irish Countryside.* O'Brien Press, Dublin, 1985.

Smith, P. *Houses of the Welsh Countryside.* HMSO, 1975.

Storey, R., and Madden, L. *Primary Sources for Victorian Studies.* Phillimore, 1977.

Tarn, J. *Working Class Housing in Nineteenth-Century Britain.* Lund Humphries, 1971.

Tarver, A. *Church Court Records.* Phillimore, 1994.

Tate, W. E. *The English Village Community and the Enclosure Movements.* Gollancz, 1967.

Tate, W. E. *The Parish Chest.* Cambridge University Press, third edition 1969.

Taylor, C. *The Archaeology of Gardens.* Shire, reprinted 1988.

Trinder, B. *The Making of the Industrial Landscape.* Dent, 1982.

Watts, M. R. *The Chapel and the Nation.* Historical Association, 1996.

West, J. *Town Records.* Phillimore, 1983.

West, J. *Village Records.* Phillimore, 1962.

Whetstone, A. E. *Scottish County Government in the 18th & 19th Centuries.* John Donald, 1981.

Whyte, I. *Agriculture and Society in Seventeenth-Century Scotland.* John Donald, 1979.

Williams, W. M. *The Sociology of an English Village: Gosforth, Cumberland.* Routledge & Kegan Paul, 1956.

Wrigley, E. A. (editor). *An Introduction to English Historical Demography from the Sixteenth to Nineteenth Century.* Weidenfeld & Nicolson, 1966.

Wrigley, E. A., and Schofield, R. S. *The Population History of England, 1541-1871: a Reconstruction.* Edward Arnold, 1981.

Useful addresses

FHSoc denotes Family History Society, Group or other association concerned with genealogy and normally a member of the Federation of Family History Societies.
FHCen (LDS) denotes Family History Centre of the Church of Jesus Christ of Latter-Day Saints (Mormons).

Aberdeen City Archives, Town House, Broad Street, Aberdeen AB10 1AQ
Aberdeen FHCen (LDS), North Anderson Drive, Aberdeen AB2 6DD
Aberdeen University Library, Department of Special Collections and Archives, King's College, Aberdeen AB24 3SW
Aerial Photography for England, Central Registry, Ordnance Survey, Romsey Road, Maybush, Southampton SO9 4DH
Aerofilms Ltd, Gate Studios, Station Road, Boreham Wood, Hertfordshire WD6 1EJ
Air Historical Branch, Ministry of Defence, Lacon House, Theobalds Road, London WC1X 8RY
Air Photographs, Central Register of, Welsh Office, Crown Offices, Cathays Park, Cardiff CF1 3NQ
Air Photographs Unit, Scottish Development Department, New St Andrew's House, St James Centre, Edinburgh EH1 3SZ
Aldershot FHCen (LDS), LDS Chapel, St Georges Road, Aldershot, Hampshire
American Archive, Albert F. Simpson Historical Research Centre, USAAF Maxwell Air Force Base, Alabama 36112
Ancient Monuments Society, St Ann's Vestry Hall, 2 Church Entry, Queen Victoria Street, London EC4V 5HB
Anglesey County Record Office, Shire Hall, Glanhwfa Road, Llangefni LL77 7TW
Angus Archives, Montrose Library, 214 High Street, Montrose, Angus DD10 8HE
Archbishop Marsh's Library, St Patrick's Close, Dublin 8
Argyll and Bute Council Archives, Kilmory, Lochgilphead, Argyll PA31 8RT
Army Records Centre, Bourne Avenue, Hayes, Middlesex UB3 1RF
Arts Council of Great Britain, 105 Piccadilly, London W1V 9FN
Ashton FHCen (LDS), Tweedale Street, Rochdale, Lancashire OL11 3TZ
Australian Institute of Genealogical Studies, PO Box 339, Blackburn, Victoria 3130
Ayrshire Archives, County Buildings, Wellington Square, Ayr KA7 1DR
Barking and Dagenham Public Libraries, Valence House Museum, Becontree Avenue, Dagenham, Essex RM8 3HT
Barnet Archives and Local Studies Department, Hendon Catholic Social Centre, Chapel Walk, Egerton Gardens, Hendon, London NW4 4BE; correspondence to Hendon Library, The Burroughs, London NW4 4BQ
Barnsley Archive and Local Studies Department, Central Library, Shambles Street, Barnsley S70 2JF
Barnsley FHSoc, 58A High Street, Royston, Barnsley S71 4RN
Bath and North East Somerset Record Office, Guildhall, Bath BA1 5AW
Bedfordshire and Luton Archives and Record Service, Record Office, County Hall, Bedford MK42 9AP
Bedfordshire FHSoc, PO Box 214, Bedford MK42 9RX
Belfast Central Library, Royal Avenue, Belfast BT1 1EA
Belfast FHCen (LDS), 401 Holywood Road, Belfast BT4 2GU
Berkshire FHSoc, Corner House, Shaw Road, Reading RG1 6JX
Berkshire Record Office, Shire Hall, Shinfield Park, Reading RG2 9XD
Berwick-upon-Tweed Record Office, Council Offices, Wallace Green, Berwick-upon-Tweed TD15 1ED
Bexley Libraries and Museums Department, Local Studies Centre, Hall Place, Bourne Road, Bexley DA5 1PQ
Billingham FHCen (LDS), The Linkway, Billingham, Cleveland TS23 3HJ
Birmingham and Midland Institute and Priestley Library, Margaret Street, Birmingham B3 3BS
Birmingham and Midlands FHSoc, 111 Kenilworth Court, Coventry CV3 6JD
Birmingham City Archives, Central Library, Chamberlain Square, Birmingham B3 3HQ
Birmingham University Information Services, Special Collections Department, Main Library, Edgbaston, Birmingham B15 2TT
Blackpool FHCen (LDS), LDS Chapel, Warren Drive, Thornton Cleveleys, Blackpool
Bolton Archive and Local Studies Service, Central Library, Civic Centre, Le Mans Crescent, Bolton BL1 1SE
Borthwick Institute of Historical Research, University of York, St Anthony's Hall, Peasholme Green, York YO1 2PW
Bradford District Archives, 15 Canal Road, Bradford BD1 4AT
Bradford FHSoc, 152 Baildon Road, Baildon, Shipley, West Yorkshire BD17 6PU
Brent Community History Library and Archive, Cricklewood Library, 152 Olive Road, Cricklewood, London NW2 6UY
Bristol and Avon FHSoc, 103 The Downs, Portishead, Bristol BS20 8BE
Bristol FHCen (LDS), 721 Wells Road, Whitchurch, Bristol
Bristol Record Office, 'B' Bond Warehouse, Smeaton Road, Bristol BS1 6XN
British Academy, 20-1 Cornwall Terrace, London NW1 4QP
British and Foreign Bible Society, Stonehill Green, Westlea, Swindon, Wiltshire SN5 7DG
British Archaeological Association, 1 Priory Gardens, Bedford Park, London W4 1TT

British Architectural Library, Drawings Collection, 21 Portman Square, London W1H 9HF, *and* Manuscripts and Archives Collection, 66 Portland Square, London W1N 4AD (Royal Institute of British Architects)

British Association for Local History, 24 Lower Street, Harnham, Salisbury, Wiltshire SP2 8EY

British Broadcasting Corporation, Written Archives Centre, Caversham Park, Reading RG4 8TZ

British Coal Archives, 200 Lichfield Lane, Mansfield, Nottinghamshire NG18 4RG

British Library, Department of Manuscripts, 96 Euston Road, St Pancras, London NW1 2DB

British Museum, Great Russell Street, London WC1B 3DG

British Record Society Ltd, College of Arms, Queen Victoria Street, London EC4V 4BT

British Records Association, London Metropolitan Archives, 40 Northampton Road, London EC1R 0HB

British Steel, Records Services, East Midlands Regional Records Centre, By-Pass Road, Irthlingborough, Wellingborough, Northamptonshire NN9 5QH

British Telecom Archives, 3rd Floor, Holborn Telephone Exchange, 268-70 High Holborn, London WC1V 7EE

Bromley Public Libraries, Archives Section, Central Library, High Street, Bromley, Kent BR1 1EX

Buckinghamshire Archaeological Society, County Museum, Church Street, Aylesbury HP20 2QP

Buckinghamshire FHSoc, 10 Merrydown, High Wycombe

Buckinghamshire Record Office, County Hall, Aylesbury HP20 1UU

Burnham and Highbridge FHSoc, 1 Greenwood Close, West Huntspill, Somerset TA1 4TR

Burton-upon-Trent Archives, Public Library, Riverside, High Street, Burton-upon-Trent, Staffordshire DE14 1AH

Bury Archive Service, Derby Hall Annexe, Edwin Street, off Crompton Street, Bury BL9 0AS

Business Archives Council, The Clove Building, 4 Maguire Street, London SE1 2NQ

Business Archives Council of Scotland, Glasgow University Archives, 13 Thurso Street, Glasgow G11 6PE

Business Statistics Office Library, Cardiff Road, Newport, Gwent NP9 1XG

Caernarfonshire *see* Gwynedd

Calderdale District Archives, Central Library, Northgate House, Northgate, Halifax HX1 1UN

Calderdale FHSoc, 61 Gleanings Avenue, Norton's Tower, Halifax HX2 0NU

Cambrian Archaeological Association, The Laurels, Westfield Road, Newport, Gwent NP9 4ND

Cambridge FHCen (LDS), 670 Cherry Hinton Road, Cambridge CB1 4DR

Cambridge Group for the History of Population and Social Structure, 27 Trumpington Street, Cambridge CB2 1QA

Cambridge University Committee for Aerial Photography, Mond Building, Free School Lane, Cambridge CB2 3RF

Cambridge University, Department of Manuscripts *and* University Archives, University Library, West Road, Cambridge CB3 9DR

Cambridgeshire County Record Office, Shire Hall, Castle Hill, Cambridge CB3 0AP *and* Grammar School Walk, Huntingdon PE18 6LF

Cambridgeshire FHSoc, 1 Ascham Lane, Whittlesford CB2 4NT

Camden Local Studies and Archives Centre, Holborn Library, 32-8 Theobalds Road, London WC1X 8PA

Canterbury Cathedral Archives, The Precincts, Canterbury CT1 2EH

Canterbury FHCen (LDS), LDS Chapel, Forty Acres Road, Canterbury CT2 7HJ

Cardiff FHCen (LDS), Heol-y-Deri, Rhiwbina, Cardiff CF4 6UH

Cardiganshire FHSoc, Trebrysg, Tregaron SY25 6LH *see also* Ceredigion

Carlisle FHCen (LDS), Langrigg Road, Morton Park, Carlisle, Cumbria CA2 5HT

Carmarthenshire Record Office, County Hall, Carmarthen SA31 1JP

Catholic Archives Society, Innyngs House, Hatfield Park, Hatfield, Hertfordshire AL9 5PL

Catholic Central Library, 47 Francis Street, London SW1P 1DN

Catholic FHSoc, 2 Winscombe Crescent, Ealing, London W5 1AZ

Catholic Record Society, 12 Melbourne Place, Wolsingham, County Durham DL13 3EH

Centre for Kentish Studies, County Hall, Maidstone ME14 1XQ *see also* East Kent

Centre for Scottish Studies, University of Aberdeen, Taylor Building, King's College, Old Aberdeen AB9 2UB

Ceredigion Archives, Swyddfa'r Sir, Marine Terrace, Aberystwyth SY23 2DE *see also* Cardiganshire

Channel Islands *see* Guernsey *and* Jersey

Charity Commission for England and Wales, St Albans House, 57-60 Haymarket, London SW1V 4QX

Cheltenham FHCen (LDS), Thirlestaine Road, Cheltenham, Gloucestershire GL53 7AS

Cheshire FHSoc, 11 Thornway, High Lane, Stockport SK6 8EL

Cheshire, North FHSoc, Windyridge, Jackson's Lane, Hazel Grove, Stockport SK7 5JW

Cheshire Record Office, Duke Street, Chester CH1 1RL

Cheshire, South FHSoc, 47 Thorn Road, Halton Lodge, Runcorn WA7 5HJ

Chester Archives, Town Hall, Chester CH1 2HJ

Chester FHCen (LDS), 50 Clifton Drive, Blacon, Chester CH1 5LT

Chesterfield and District FHSoc, Park View, Hall Drive, Sutton Scarsdale, Chesterfield S44 5UR

Chetham's Library, Long Millgate, Manchester M3 1SB

Chief Herald of Ireland, Genealogical Office, The Castle, Dublin 2

Chorley FHCen (LDS), 33-41 Water Street, Chorley, Lancashire

Church Commissioners, 1 Millbank, London SW1P 3JZ

Church Monuments Society, Royal Armouries, Tower of London EC3N 4AB

Church of England Record Centre, 15 Galleywall Road, South Bermondsey, London SE16 3PB

Church of Jesus Christ of Latter-day Saints, Branch Library, Hyde Park Chapel, 64 Exhibition Road, London SW7 2PA

Churchill Archives Centre, Churchill College, Cambridge CB3 0DS

Civic Trust, 17 Carlton House Terrace, London SW1Y 5AH

Cleveland FHSoc, 1 Oxgang Close, Redcar TS10 4ND
Clwyd FHSoc, 22 Parc y Llan, Henllan, Denbigh LL16 5AS
College of Arms, Queen Victoria Street, London EC4V 4BT
Commons, Open Spaces and Footpaths Preservation Society (Open Spaces Society), 25A Bell Street, Henley-on-Thames, Oxfordshire RG9 2BA
Cork Archives Institute, Christchurch, Cork
Cork FHCen (LDS), Scarsfield Road, Wilton, Cork
Cornwall FHSoc, 5 Victoria Square, Truro, Cornwall
Cornwall Record Office, County Hall, Truro TR1 3AY
Corporation of London Records Office, PO Box 270, Guildhall, London EC2P 2EJ *see also* Guildhall *and* London
Council for British Archaeology, Bowes Morrell House, 111 Walmgate, York YO1 2UA
Court of the Lord Lyon, HM General Register House, Edinburgh EH1 3YT
Coventry City Archives, Mandela House, Bayley Lane, Coventry CV1 5RG
Coventry FHSoc, 61 Drayton Crescent, Eastern Green, Coventry CV5 7EL
Crawley FHCen (LDS), Old Horsham Road, Crawley, Sussex RH11 8PD
Croydon Archives Service, Central Library, Croydon Clocktower, Katharine Street, Croydon CR9 1ET
Cumberland and Westmorland Antiquarian and Archaeological Society, 2 High Tenterfell, Kendal LA9 4PG
Cumbria FHSoc, 32 Granada Road, Denton, Manchester M34 2IJ
Cumbria Record Office, The Castle, Carlisle CA3 8UR *and* 140 Duke Street, Barrow-in-Furness LA14 1XW *and* County Offices, Kendal LA9 4RQ *and* Scotch Street, Whitehaven CA28 7BJ
Customs and Excise, New King's Beam House, 22 Upper Ground, London SE1 9PJ
Denbighshire Record Office, 46 Clwyd Street, Ruthin LL15 1HP
Derbyshire FHSoc, Bridge Chapel House, St Mary's Bridge, Sowter, Derby DE1 3AT
Derbyshire Record Office, New Street, with correspondence to County Offices, Matlock DE4 3AG
Devon FHSoc, 8 King Henry's Road, Exeter EX2 6AL
Devon Record Office, Castle Street, Exeter EX4 3PU *see also* North Devon
Doctor Williams's Library, 14 Gordon Square, London WC1H 0AG
Doncaster and District FHSoc, 125 The Grove, Wheatley Hills, Doncaster DN2 5SN
Doncaster Archives Department, King Edward Road, Balby, Doncaster DN4 0NA
Dorset FHSoc, 7 Coppercourt Leaze, Poole Road, Wimborne BH21 1QX
Dorset Record Office, Bridport Road, Dorchester DT1 1RP
Douglas FHCen (LDS), Woodside, Woodburn Road, Douglas, Isle of Man
Dublin FHCen (LDS), The Willows, Finglas, Dublin 11
Dublin, University College, Archives, 82 St Stephen's Green, Dublin 2
Dublin, University College, Department of Irish Folklore, Belfield, Dublin 4
Dublin University, Trinity College Library, College Street, Dublin 2
Duchy of Cornwall, 10 Buckingham Gate, London SW1E 6LA
Duchy of Lancaster, Lancaster Place, Strand, London WC2E 7ED
Dudley Archives and Local History Service, Mount Pleasant Street, Coseley, West Midlands WV14 9JR
Dumfries and Galloway Archives, Archive Centre, 33 Burns Street, Dumfries DG1 2PS
Dumfries FHCen (LDS), 36 Edinburgh Road, Albanybank, Dumfries DG1 1JQ
Dun Laoghaire Genealogical Society, 14 Rochestown Park, Dun Laoghaire, County Dublin
Dundee City Archives, 1 Shore Street; with correspondence to 21 City Square, Dundee DD1 3BY
Dundee FHCen (LDS), Bingham Terrace, Dundee DD2 4TJ
Dundee University Library, Department of Archives and Manuscripts, Tower Building, Dundee DD1 4HN
Durham County Record Office, County Hall, Durham DH1 5UL
Durham University Library, Archives and Special Collections, Palace Green, Durham DH1 3RN
Dyfed FHSoc, Delfan, High Street, Llandysul, Ceredigion SA44 4DG
Ealing Local History Library, Central Library, 103 Ealing Broadway Centre, London W5 5JY
East Kent Archive Centre, Enterprise Business Park, Honeywood Road, Whitfield, Dover CT16 3EH *see also* Centre for Kentish Studies
East of London FHSoc, 42 Alwen Grove, South Ockendon, Essex RM15 5DW
East Riding of Yorkshire Archive Office, County Hall, Beverley HU17 9BA
East Yorkshire FHSoc, 12 Carlton Drive, Aldbrough HU11 4SF
East Sussex *see* Sussex
Eastbourne and District FHSoc, 22 Abbey Road, Eastbourne, East Sussex BN20 8TE
Ecclesiastical History Society, Department of Medieval History, University of Glasgow, Glasgow G12 8QQ
Edinburgh City Archives, City Chambers, High Street, Edinburgh EH1 1YJ
Edinburgh FHCen (LDS), 30A Colinton Road, Edinburgh EH10 5DQ
Edinburgh University Library, Special Collections Department, 30 George Square, Edinburgh EH8 9LJ
Elgin FHCen (LDS), Pansport Road, Elgin IV30 1HD
Enfield Local History Unit, Southgate Town Hall, Green Lanes, Palmers Green, London N13 4XD
English Folk Dance and Song Society, Cecil Sharp House, 2 Regent's Park Road, London NW1 7AY
English Heritage *see* Historic Buildings
English Place-Name Survey, Grey College, Durham DH1 3LG
Essex FHSoc, Old Granary, Justice Wood, Polstead, Suffolk CO6 5DH
Essex Record Office, County Hall, Chelmsford CM1 1LX *and* Colchester and North-East Essex Branch, Stanwell House, Stanwell Street, Colchester CO2 7DL *and* Southend Branch, Central Library, Victoria Avenue, Southend-on-Sea SS2 6EX
Essex Society for Archaeology and History, Hollytrees Museum, High Street, Colchester CO1 1UG
Exeter Cathedral Library and Archives, Bishop's Palace, Exeter EX1 1HX

Exeter FHCen (LDS), Wonford Road, off Barrack Road, Exeter
Exeter University Library, Stocker Road, Exeter EX4 4PT
Falkirk Council Archives, History Research Centre, Falkirk Museum, Callendar House, Falkirk FK1 1YR
Family History Library, 35 North West Temple Street, Salt Lake City, Utah 84150
Family History Societies, Federation of, The Benson Room, Birmingham and Midland Institute, Margaret
    Street, Birmingham B3 3BS
Family History Societies of Wales, Association of, Hafod el Wy, 32 Ystad Llewelyn, Denbigh LL16 3NR
Family Records Centre, 1 Myddelton Street, London EC1R 1UW
Felixstowe FHSoc, 16 Western Avenue, Felixstowe, Suffolk IP11 9SB
Field Studies Council, Preston Montford, Montford Bridge, Shrewsbury, Shropshire SY4 1HW
Finsbury Library, 245 St John Street, London EC1V 4NB
Flintshire Record Office, The Old Rectory, Hawarden CH5 3NR
Folkestone and District FHSoc, 41 Reachfields, Hythe, Kent CT21 6LS
Folklore Society, University College London, Gower Street, London WC1E 6BT
Forest of Dean FHCen (LDS), Wynols Hill, Queensway, Coleford, Gloucestershire GL16 5SX
Francis Frith Collection, Charlton Road, Andover, Hampshire SP10 3LE
Furness FHSoc, 15 Kirkstone Crescent, Barrow-in-Furness, Cumbria LA14 4ND
Gateshead Central Library, Prince Consort Road, Gateshead NE8 4LN
Genealogical Society of Utah (UK), 185 Penns Lane, Sutton Coldfield, West Midlands B76 1JU
General Register Office for England and Wales, Smedley Hydro, Trafalgar Road, Birkdale, Southport PR8
    2HH
General Register Office for Ireland, Joyce House, 8/11 Lombard Street East, Dublin 2
General Register Office for Northern Ireland, Oxford House, 49-55 Chichester Street, Belfast BT1 4HL
General Register Office for Scotland, New Register House, Edinburgh EH1 3YT
Georgian Group, 6 Fitzroy Square, London W1P 6DX
Glamorgan FHSoc, The Orchard, Penmark, Barry CF62 9BN
Glamorgan Record Office, Glamorgan Building, King Edward VII Avenue, Cathays Park, Cardiff CF1 3NE
    see also West Glamorgan
Glasgow City Archives, Mitchell Library, 201 North Street, Glasgow G3 7DN
Glasgow FHCen (LDS), 35 Julian Avenue, Glasgow G12 0RB
Glasgow University Archives and Business Record Centre, 13 Thurso Street, Glasgow G11 6PE
Glasgow University Library, Department of Special Collections, Hillhead Street, Glasgow G12 8QE
Gloucestershire FHSoc, Stonehatch, Oakridge Lynch, Stroud GL6 7NR
Gloucestershire Record Office, Clarence Row, off Alvin Street, Gloucester GL1 3DW
Greater Manchester County Record Office, 56 Marshall Street, New Cross, Ancoats, Manchester M4 5FU
Greater Manchester Museum of Science and Industry, Liverpool Road, Castlefield, Manchester M3 4JP
Greenwich Local History Library, Woodlands, 90 Mycenae Road, Blackheath, London SE3 7SE
Grimsby FHCen (LDS), Grimsby Ward Chapel, Linwood Avenue, Waltham Road, Grimsby DN33 2PA
Guernsey: Greffe, Royal Court House, St Peter Port GY1 2PB
Guernsey: Island Archives Service, 29 Victoria Street, St Peter Port GY1 1HU
Guernsey: La Société Guernesiaise, Candie Gardens, St Peter Port GY1 1UG
Guild of One-name Studies, 14 Charterhouse Buildings, Goswell Road, London EC1M 7BA
Guildhall Library, Aldermanbury, London EC2P 2EJ see also Corporation and London
Gwent FHSoc, 1a Melbourne Way, Newport NP9 3RE
Gwent Record Office, County Hall, Cwmbran NP44 2XH
Gwynedd: Caernarfon Area Record Office, Victoria Dock, with correspondence to County Offices, Shirehall
    Street, Caernarfon LL55 1SH and Merioneth Archives, Cae Penarlâg, Dolgellau LL40 2YB
Gwynedd FHSoc, Cwm Arian, Penysarn Fawr, Penysarn, Anglesey LL69 9BX
Hackney Archives Department, 43 De Beauvoir Road, London N1 5SQ
Hammersmith and Fulham Archives and Local History Centre, the Lilla Huset, 191 Talgarth Road, London
    W6 8BJ
Hampshire Genealogical Society, 44 Southway, Bridgemary, Gosport PO13 0XD
Hampshire Record Office, Sussex Street, Winchester SO23 8TH
Harborne FHCen (LDS), 38 Lordswood Road, Harborne, Birmingham B17 9QS
Haringey Archive Service, Bruce Castle Museum, Lordship Lane, London N17 8NU
Harrow Reference Library, PO Box 4, Civic Centre, Station Road, Harrow HA1 2UU
Hastings and Rother FHSoc, 65 Vale Road, St Leonards on Sea, East Sussex TN37 6PT
Helston FHCen (LDS), Clodgey Lane, Helston, Cornwall TR13 8PJ
Heraldry Society, PO Box 32, Maidenhead, Berkshire SL6 3FD
Hereford Record Office, The Old Barracks, Harold Street, Hereford HR1 2QX
Herefordshire FHSoc, Halfar, Coldwells, Holmer, Hereford HR1 1LH
Hertfordshire Archives and Local Studies, County Hall, Hertford SG13 8EJ
Hertfordshire FHSoc, 6 The Crest, Ware SG12 0RR
Highland Council Archive, Inverness Library, Farraline Park, Inverness IV1 1NH see also North Highland
Hillingdon FHSoc, 20 Moreland Drive, Gerrards Cross, Buckinghamshire SL9 8BB
Hillingdon Local Heritage Service, Central Library, 14-15 High Street, Uxbridge UB8 1HD
Historic Buildings and Monuments Commission for England (English Heritage), Fortress House, 23 Savile
    Row, London W1X 1AB
Historic Buildings Council for Scotland, Longmore House, Salisbury Place, Edinburgh EH9 1SH
Historic Buildings Council for Wales, Crown Building, Cathays Park, Cardiff CF1 3NQ
Historic Monuments and Buildings Branch, Department of the Environment for Northern Ireland,
    Commonwealth House, Castle Street, Belfast BT1 1GU
Historic Society of Lancashire and Cheshire, Southport Reference Library, Lord Street, Southport, Lancashire
    PR8 1DJ

Historical Association, 59A Kennington Park Road, London SE11 4JH
Historical Association of Ireland, Department of History, University College, Belfield, Dublin 4
Honourable Society of Cymmrodorion, 30 Eastcastle Street, London W1N 7PD
Honourable the Irish Society, 214 Carey Lane, London EC2V 8AA
Hounslow Local History Collection, Local Studies Department, Hounslow Library, 24 Treaty Centre, Hounslow TW3 1ES
House of Lords Record Office, House of Lords, London SW1A 0PW
Huddersfield and District FHSoc, 31 Kingshead Road, Mirfield, West Yorkshire WF14 9SJ
Huddersfield FHCen (LDS), Dewsbury Chapel, 86 Halifax Road, Dewsbury, West Yorkshire WF13 4JD
Huguenot Library, University College London, Gower Street, London WC1E 6BT
Hull City Archives, 79 Lowgate, Kingston upon Hull HU1 1HN
Hull FHCen (LDS), 725 Holderness Road, Hull HU8 9AN
Hull University, Brynmor Jones Library, Cottingham Road, Hull HU6 7RX
Huntingdonshire FHSoc, Lowood, Somersham, Huntingdon PE17 3DL
Hyde Park FHCen (LDS), 64/8 Exhibition Road, South Kensington, London SW7 2PA
Imperial War Museum, Department of Documents, Lambeth Road, London SE1 6HZ
Industrial Archaeology, Association for, The Wharfage, Ironbridge, Telford, Shropshire TF8 7AW
Institute of Field Archaeologists, University of Manchester, Oxford Road, Manchester M13 9PL
Institute of Heraldic and Genealogical Studies, 79-82 Northgate, Canterbury, Kent CT1 1BA
Institute of Historical Research, School of Advanced Study, University of London, Senate House, Malet Street, London WC1E 7HU
Institute of Irish Studies, Queen's University of Belfast, 8 Fitzwilliam Street, Belfast BT9 6AW
Institution of Civil Engineers, 1-7 Great George Street, London SW1P 3AA
International Society for British Genealogy and Family History, PO Box 3115, Salt Lake City, Utah 84110-3115
Inverness FHCen (LDS), 13 Ness Walk, Inverness IV3 5SQ
Ipswich FHCen (LDS), 42 Sidegate Lane West, Ipswich, Suffolk IP1 3DB
Irish Architectural Archive, 63 Merrion Square, Dublin 2
Irish Family History Foundation, PO Box 36, Naas, County Kildare
Irish Genealogical Association, 164 Kingsway, Dunmurry, Belfast BT17 9AD
Irish Genealogical Research Society, The Irish Club, 82 Eaton Square, London SW1W 9AJ *and* 6 Eaton Brae, Orwell Road, Dublin 14
Irish Manuscripts Commission, 73 Merrion Square, Dublin 2
Ironbridge Gorge Museum, Library and Archives, The Wharfage, Telford, Shropshire TF8 7AW
Isle of Axholme FHSoc, 4 Cheyne Walk, Bawtry, Doncaster DN10 6RS
Isle of Man Civil Registry, Registries Building, Bucks Road, Douglas IM1 3AR
Isle of Man FHSoc, 5 Selborne Drive, Douglas
Isle of Man Public Record Office, Unit 3, Spring Valley Industrial Estate, Braddan, Douglas IM2 2QR
Isle of Man Manx National Heritage Library, Manx Museum and National Trust, Douglas IM1 3LY
Isle of Wight County Record Office, 26 Hillside, Newport PO30 2EB
Isle of Wight: Newport FHCen (LDS), Chestnut Close, Shide Road, Newport PO30 1YE
Isle of Wight FHSoc, Rose Cottage, Burnt House Lane, Newport PO30 2PW
Islington Archives, Central Reference Library, 2 Fieldway Crescent, London N5 1PF
Jersey Archives Service, The Weighbridge, St Helier JE2 3NF
Jersey: Channel Islands FHSoc, PO Box 507, St Helier, Jersey JE4 5TN
Jersey: Judicial Greffe, States Building, 10 Hill Street, Royal Square, St Helier JE1 1DD
Jersey: La Société Jersiaise, 7 Pier Road, St Helier JE2 4XW
Jersey: St Helier FHCen (LDS), Rue de la Vallée, St Mary, Jersey
Jewish Historical Society of England, 33 Seymour Place, London W1H 5AP
John Rylands Library, 150 Deansgate, Manchester M3 3EH
Keighley and District FHSoc, 2 The Hallows, Shann Park, Keighley, West Yorkshire BD20 6HY
Kensington and Chelsea Libraries and Arts Service, Central Library, Phillimore Walk, London W8 7RX
Kent *see* Centre for Kentish Studies *and* East Kent
Kent Archaeological Society, Three Elms, Woodlands Lane, Shorne, Gravesend DA12 3HH
Kent FHSoc, Westgate House, Dickley Wood, Maidstone ME17 1BL
Kent, North West FHSoc, 6 Windermere Road, Barnehurst, Bexleyheath, Kent TN3 0BA
Kilmarnock FHCen (LDS), Whatriggs Road, Kilmarnock, Ayrshire KA1 3QY
Kings Lynn FHCen (LDS), Reffley Lane, King's Lynn, Norfolk PE30 3EQ
Kingston Museum and Heritage Service, North Kingston Centre, Richmond Road, Kingston upon Thames KT2 5PE
Kirkcaldy FHCen (LDS), Winifred Crescent, Forth Park, Kirkcaldy, Fife KY2 5SX
Kirklees District Archives, Central Library, Princess Alexandra Walk, Huddersfield HD2 2SU
Lambeth Archives Department, Minet Library, 52 Knatchbull Road, London SE5 9QY
Lambeth Palace Library, London SE1 7JU
Lancashire FHSoc, 17 Victoria Street, Haslingden, Rossendale BB4 5DL
Lancashire Record Office, Bow Lane, Preston PR1 8ND
Lancaster FHCen (LDS), Lancaster Ward House, Overangle Road, Morecambe
Lancaster FHSoc, 94 Croston Road, Garstang, Preston PR3 1HR
Leeds District Archives, Chapeltown Road, Sheepscar, Leeds LS7 3AP
Leeds FHCen (LDS), Vesper Road, Leeds LS5 3QT
Leeds University, Brotherton Library, Leeds LS2 9JT
Leicester FHCen (LDS), Wakerley Road, Leicester LE5 4WD
Leicester University, Department of English Local History, University Road, Leicester LE1 7RH
Leicestershire and Rutland FHSoc, 11 Faldo Close, Rushy Mead, Leicester LE4 7TS

Leicestershire Record Office, Long Street, Wigston Magna, Leicester LE18 2AH
Lerwick FHCen (LDS), South Road, Lerwick ZE1 0RB
Lewisham Local Studies Centre, Lewisham Library, 199-201 Lewisham High Street, London SE13 6LG
Library Association, 7 Ridgmount Street, London WC1E 7AE
Library of Congress, Washington, DC 20540-4840
Lichfield FHCen (LDS), Purcell Avenue, Lichfield, Staffordshire
Lichfield Record Office, Lichfield Library, The Friary, Lichfield WS13 6QG
Limerick FHCen (LDS), Doraddoyle Road, Limerick
Lincoln FHCen (LDS), Skellingthorpe Road, Lincoln LN6 0PB
Lincolnshire Archives, St Rumbold Street, Lincoln LN2 5AB *see also* North East Lincolnshire
Lincolnshire FHSoc, 135 Baldertongate, Newark, Nottinghamshire NG24 1RY
Linnean Society of London, Burlington House, Piccadilly, London W1V 0LQ
Liverpool and SW Lancashire FHSoc, 8 Paltridge Way, Pensby, Merseyside L61 5YG
Liverpool FHCen (LDS), 4 Mill Bank, Liverpool L13 0BW
Liverpool Record Office and Local History Service, Central Library, William Brown Street, Liverpool L3 8EW
Liverpool University, Department of Special Collections and Archives, PO Box 123, Liverpool L69 3DA
Local Population Studies Society, 78 Harlow Terrace, Harrogate HG2 8AW
London and North Middlesex FHSoc, 7 Mount Pleasant Road, New Malden, Surrey KT3 3JZ
London: Hyde Park FHCen (LDS), 64/8 Exhibition Road, South Kensington, London SW7 2PA
London Library, 14 St James's Square, London SW1Y 4LG
London Metropolitan Archives, 40 Northampton Road, London EC1R 0HB (Corporation of London) *see also* Guildhall *and* Corporation
London: Museum of London, 150 London Wall, London EC2Y 5HN
London, University College London, Manuscripts Room, DMS Watson Library, Gower Street, London WC1E 6BT
London University Library, Palaeography Room, Senate House, Malet Street, London WC1E 7HU
Londonderry FHCen (LDS), Race Course Road, Belmont Estate, Londonderry
Lowestoft FHCen (LDS), 165 Yarmouth Road, Lowestoft, Suffolk NR32 4AF
Lyon *see* Court
Maidstone FHCen (LDS), 76B London Road, Maidstone, Kent ME16 0DR
Manchester and Lancashire FHSoc, Clayton House, 59 Piccadilly, Manchester M1 2AQ
Manchester FHCen (LDS), Altrincham Road, Wythenshawe, Manchester M22 4BJ
Manchester Local Studies Unit, Archives, Central Library, St Peter's Square, Manchester M2 5PD
Manchester University, John Rylands Library, 150 Deansgate, Manchester M3 3EH
Mansfield and District FHSoc, 2 Cranmer Grove, Mansfield, Nottinghamshire NG19 7JR
Mansfield FHCen (LDS), Southridge Drive, Mansfield, Nottinghamshire NG18 4RT
Medieval Settlement Research Group, Planning Department, County Hall, Bedford MK42 9AP
Merseyside Maritime Museum, Albert Dock, Liverpool L3 4AA
Merseyside Record Office, 4th Floor, Cunard Building, Liverpool L3 1EG
Merthyr Tydfil FHCen (LDS), Nantgwenith Street, George Town, Merthyr Tydfil CF48 1DE
Methodist Archives and Research Centre, John Rylands Library, 150 Deansgate, Manchester M3 3EH
Middlesex, West FHSoc, 92 Nelson Road, Whitton, Twickenham TW2 7AY
Midlothian Council Archives, Library Headquarters, 2 Clerk Street, Loanhead, Midlothian EH20 9DR
Mid-Norfolk FHSoc, 35 Colleen Close, Toftwood, Dereham NR19 1NL
Mid-West Regional Development Organisation, 104 Henry Street, Limerick
Military Historical Society, National Army Museum, Royal Hospital Road, Chelsea, London SW3 4HT
Montgomeryshire FHSoc, 1 Moreton Road, South Croydon, Surrey CR2 7DN
Monumental Brass Society, Lowe Hill House, Stratford St Mary, Colchester, Essex CO7 6JX
Morley and District FHSoc, 23 Denshaw Drive, Morley, Leeds LS27 8RS
Museum of London Library, 150 London Wall, London EC2Y 5HN
Museum of Welsh Life, St Fagan's, Cardiff CF5 6XB
Museums Association, 42 Clerkenwell Close, London EC1R 0PA
National Archives and Records Administration, National Archives Building, 8th Street at Pennsylvania Avenue, NW, Washington DC 20408
National Archives, Cartographic and Architectural Branch, 8601 Adelphi Road, College Park, ND 20740-6001
National Archives of Ireland, Bishop Street, Dublin 8
National Army Museum, Department of Archives, Royal Hospital Road, Chelsea, London SW3 4HT
National Art Library, Archive of Art and Design, Blythe House, 23 Blythe Road, London W14 0QF
National Council for Voluntary Organizations, Regent's Wharf, 8 All Saints Street, London N1 9RL
National Film and Television Archive, British Film Institute, 21 Stephen Street, London W1P 2LN
National Library of Ireland, Kildare Street, Dublin 2
National Library of Scotland, Department of Manuscripts, George IV Bridge, Edinburgh EH1 1EW
National Library of Wales, Department of Manuscripts and Records, Aberystwyth SY23 3BU
National Maritime Museum, Manuscripts Section, Greenwich, London SE10 9NF
National Monuments Record *see* Royal Commission
National Museum of Labour History, 103 Princess Street, Manchester M1 6DD
National Museum of Photography, Film and Television, Prince's View, Bradford BD5 0TR
National Museums and Galleries of Wales, Cathays Park, Cardiff CF1 3NP
National Museums and Galleries on Merseyside, Maritime Archives and Library, William Brown Street, Liverpool L3 8EN.
National Museums of Scotland, Chambers Street, Edinburgh EH1 1JF
National Railway Museum Reading Room, Leeman Road, York YO2 4XJ (Science Museum)

National Register of Archives, Quality House, Quality Court, Chancery Lane, London WC2A 1HP *see also* Scottish Record Office
National Sound Archive, 29 Exhibition Road, London SW7 2AS
National Trust, 36 Queen Anne's Gate, London SW1H 9AS
National Trust for Scotland, 5 Charlotte Square, Edinburgh EH2 4DU
Natural History Museum, Cromwell Road, London SW7 5BD
New Zealand FHSoc Inc, PO Box 13301, Armagh, Christchurch
New Zealand, Genealogical Research Institute, PO Box 36-107, Moera, Lower Hutt, Wellington
Newcastle Emlyn FHCen (LDS), Neuadd Emlyn Hall, Newcastle Emlyn, Dyfed
Newcastle-under-Lyme FHCen (LDS), PO Box 457, The Brampton, Newcastle-under-Lyme, Staffordshire ST5 0QW
Newcastle upon Tyne University, Robinson Library, Newcastle upon Tyne NE2 4HQ
Newcomen Society for the Study of the History of Engineering and Technology, Science Museum, Imperial College Road, South Kensington, London SW7 2DD
Newham Local Studies Library, Stratford Library, Water Lane, London E15 4NJ
Newport FHCen (LDS), Chestnut Close, Shide Road, Newport, Isle of Wight PO30 1YE
Norfolk FHSoc, Oak Cottage, Bellaport, Market Drayton, Shropshire TF9 4AZ
Norfolk Record Office, Gildengate House, Anglia Square, Upper Green Lane, Norwich NR3 1AX
North Devon Record Office, Tuly Street, Barnstaple EX31 1EL *see also* Devon
North East Lincolnshire Archives, Town Hall, Town Hall Square, Grimsby DN31 1HX *see also* Lincolnshire
North Highland Archive, Wick Library, Sinclair Terrace, Wick, Caithness KW1 5AB *see also* Highland
North Lanarkshire Archives, 10 Kelvin Road, Lenziemill, Cumbernauld G67 2BA
North Meols FHSoc, 108 High Park Road, Southport, Lancashire PR9 7BY
North of Ireland FHSoc, School of Education, Queen's University of Belfast, 69 University Street, Belfast BT7 7HL
North Yorkshire County Record Office, Malpas Road; with correspondence to County Hall, Northallerton DL7 8AF
Northampton FHCen (LDS), 137 Harlestone Road, Northampton NN5 6AA
Northamptonshire FHSoc, 19 Ridgway Road, Kettering NN15 5AQ
Northamptonshire Record Office, Wootton Hall Park, Northampton NN4 8BQ
Northumberland and Durham FHSoc, 10 Melrose Grove, Jarrow on Tyne NE32 4HP
Northumberland Record Office, Melton Park, North Gosforth, Newcastle upon Tyne NE3 5QX
Norwich FHCen (LDS), 19 Greenways, Eaton, Norwich, Norfolk NR4 6PA
Nottingham FHCen (LDS), Hempshill Lane, Bulwell, Nottingham NG6 8PA
Nottingham University Library, Manuscripts Department, Hallward Library, University Park, Nottingham NG7 2RD
Nottinghamshire Archives, County House, Castle Meadow Road, Nottingham NG2 1AG
Nottinghamshire FHSoc, 10 Lyme Park, West Bridgford, Nottingham NG2 7TR
Oldham Archives Service, Local Studies Library, 84 Union Street, Oldham OL1 1DN
Oral History Society, Sociology Department, Essex University, Colchester CO4 3SQ
Ordnance Survey, Phoenix Park, Dublin 7
Ordnance Survey, Romsey Road, Maybush, Southampton SO9 4DH
Orkney Archives, Orkney Library, Laing Street, Kirkwall KW15 1NW
Ormskirk and District FHSoc, 85 Wigan Road, Westhead, Lathom, Lancashire L40 6HY
Orpington FHCen (LDS), New Village Hall, High Street, Orpington, Kent
Oxford University, Bodleian Library, Department of Western Manuscripts, Broad Street, Oxford OX1 3BG
Oxfordshire Archives, County Hall, New Road, Oxford OX1 1ND
Oxfordshire FHSoc, 19 Mavor Close, Woodstock, Oxford OX20 1YL
Paisley FHCen (LDS), Johnstone Ward, Campbell Street, Johnstone PA5 8LD
Pembrokeshire Record Office, The Castle, Haverfordwest SA61 2EF
Perth and Kinross Council Archive, AK Bell Library, 2-8 York Place, Perth PH2 8EP
Peterborough and District FHSoc, 7 Newby Close, Peterborough PE3 6PU
Peterborough Central Library, Broadway, Peterborough PE1 1RX
Peterborough FHCen (LDS), Cottesmore Close, Off Atherstone Avenue, Netherton Estate, Peterborough
Plymouth and West Devon Area Record Office, Unit 3, Clare Place, Coxside, Plymouth PL4 0JW
Plymouth FHCen (LDS), Hartley Chapel, Mannamead Road, Plymouth, Devon
Pontefract FHCen (LDS), Park Villas Drive, Pontefract WF8 4QF
Poole FHCen (LDS), 8 Mount Road, Parkstone, Poole, Dorset BH14 0QW
Portsmouth City Museums and Records Service, 3 Museum Road, Portsmouth PO1 2LJ
Portsmouth FHCen (LDS), Kingston Crescent, Portsmouth, Hampshire PO2 8QL
Post Office Archives and Record Centre, Freeling House, Mount Pleasant Complex, London EC1A 1BB
Powys County Archives Office, County Hall, Llandrindod Wells LD1 5LG
Powys FHSoc, Cwm Kesty Farmhouse, Newchurch, Kington HR5 3QR
Presbyterian Historical Society of Ireland, Church House, Fisherwick Place, Belfast BT1 6DW
Principal Probate Registry, Duncombe Place, York YO1 2EA
Principal Registry of the Family Division, Somerset House, Strand, London WC2R 1LP
Public Record Office, Ruskin Avenue, Kew, Richmond, Surrey TW9 4DU
Public Record Office of Northern Ireland, 66 Balmoral Avenue, Belfast BT9 6NY
Quaker FHSoc, 5 Rad Valley Gardens, Shrewsbury SY3 8AW
Railway and Canal Historical Society, 17 Clumber Crescent North, The Park, Nottingham NG7 1EY
Rawtenstall FHCen (LDS), Haslingden Road, Rawtenstall, Rossendale, Lancashire
Reading FHCen (LDS), 280 The Meadway, Tilehurst, Reading, Berkshire RG3 4PG
Reading University Library, PO Box 223, Whiteknights, Reading, Berkshire RG6 6AE

Reading University Rural History Centre, PO Box 229, Whiteknights, Reading, Berkshire RG6 6AG
Redbridge Central Library, Local History Room, Clements Road, Ilford, Essex IG1 1EA
Redditch FHCen (LDS), 321 Evesham Road, Crabbs Cross, Redditch, Worcestershire B97 5JA
Religious Society of Friends Library, Friends House, 173-7 Euston Road, London NW1 2BJ
Representative Church Body Library, Braemor Park, Rathgar, Dublin 14
Rhyl FHCen (LDS), Rhuddlan Road, Rhyl, Clwyd
Ripon, Harrogate and District FHSoc, 18 Aspin Drive, Knaresborough, North Yorkshire HG5 8HH
Rochdale Libraries, Local Studies Department, Arts and Heritage Centre, Esplanade, Rochdale OL16 1AQ
Rochester upon Medway Studies Centre, Civic Centre, Strood, Rochester ME2 4AW
Romford FHCen (LDS), 64 Butts Green Road, Hornchurch, Essex RM11 2JJ
Rotherham Metropolitan Borough, Archives and Local Studies Section, Brian O'Malley Central Library, Walker Place, Rotherham S65 1JH
Royal Agricultural Society of England, National Agricultural Centre, Stoneleigh Park, Kenilworth, Warwickshire CV8 2LZ
Royal Air Force Museum, Research and Information Services, Grahame Park Way, Hendon, London NW9 5LL
Royal Archives, Windsor Castle, Berkshire SL4 1NJ
Royal Botanic Gardens, Library and Archives, Kew, Richmond, Surrey TW9 3AB
Royal College of Physicians of London, 11 St Andrew's Place, Regent's Park, London NW1 4LE
Royal College of Surgeons of England, 35-43 Lincoln's Inn Fields, London WC2A 3PN
Royal Commission on Historical Manuscripts *and* National Register of Archives, Quality House, Quality Court, Chancery Lane, London WC2A 1HP
Royal Commission on the Ancient and Historical Monuments of Scotland *and* National Monuments Record, John Sinclair House, 16 Bernard Terrace, Edinburgh EH8 9NX
Royal Commission on the Ancient and Historical Monuments of Wales *and* National Monuments Record, Crown Building, Plas Crug, Aberystwyth SY23 1NJ
Royal Commission on the Historical Monuments of England, National Monuments Record Centre, Kemble Drive, Swindon, Wiltshire SN2 2GZ *and* London Search Room, 55 Blandford Street, London W1H 3AF
Royal Historical Society, University College London, Gower Street, London WC1E 6BT
Royal Institute of British Architects *see* British Architectural Library
Royal Institution of Cornwall, Courtney Library, River Street, Truro TR1 2SJ
Royal Institution of Great Britain, 21 Albemarle Street, London W1X 4BS
Royal Irish Academy, 19 Dawson Street, Dublin 2
Royal Society Library, 6 Carlton House Terrace, London SW1Y 5AG
Royal Society of Antiquaries of Ireland, 63 Merrion Square, Dublin 2
Royston and District FHSoc, 60 Heathfield, Royston, Hertfordshire SG8 5BN
St Albans FHCen (LDS), London Road at Cutenhoe Road, Luton, Bedfordshire
St Andrews University, Archives, North Street, St Andrews, Fife KY16 9TR
St Austell FHCen (LDS), Kingfisher Drive, St Austell, Cornwall PL25 3AZ
St Helens Local History and Archives Library, Central Library, Gamble Institute, Victoria Square, St Helens WA10 1DY
St Helier FHCen (LDS), Rue de la Vallée, St Mary, Jersey, Channel Islands
St Patrick's College Library, Maynooth, County Kildare
Salford Archives Centre, 658-62 Liverpool Road, Irlam, Manchester M44 5AD
Sandwell Community History and Archives Service, Smethwick Library, High Street, Smethwick, Warley, West Midlands B66 1AB
Scarborough FHCen (LDS), Stepney Drive, Whitby Road, Scarborough YO12 5DP
School of Scottish Studies, 27-8 George Square, Edinburgh EH8 9LD
Science Museum Library, Imperial College Road, South Kensington, London SW7 5NH *and* National Railway Museum Reading Room, Leeman Road, York YO2 4XJ
Scots Ancestry Research Society, 29B Albany Street, Edinburgh EH1 3QN
Scottish Association of Family History Societies, 51-3 Morton Hall Road, Edinburgh EH9 2HN
Scottish Borders Archive and Local History Centre, Library Headquarters, St Mary's Mill, Selkirk TD7 5EW
Scottish Catholic Archives, Columba House, 16 Drummond Place, Edinburgh EH3 6PL
Scottish Genealogy Society, Library and Family History Centre, 15 Victoria Terrace, Edinburgh EH1 2JL
Scottish History Society, Department of Scottish History, University of Edinburgh, 17 Buccleuch Place, Edinburgh EH8 9LN
Scottish Record Office *and* National Register of Archives, PO Box 36, HM General Register House, Edinburgh EH1 3YY *and* West Register House, Charlotte Square, Edinburgh EH2 4DF
Scottish Record Society, Department of Scottish History, University of Glasgow G12 8QH
Scottish Records Association, Glasgow City Archives, Mitchell Library, 201 North Street, Glasgow G3 7DN
Selden Society, Faculty of Laws, Queen Mary College, Mile End Road, London E1 4NS
Shakespeare Birthplace Trust Records Office, Shakespeare Centre, Henley Street, Stratford-upon-Avon, Warwickshire CV37 6QW
Sheffield and District FHSoc, 18 Furniss Avenue, Sheffield S17 3OL
Sheffield Archives, 52 Shoreham Street, Sheffield S1 4SP
Sheffield FHCen (LDS), Wheel Lane, Grenoside, Sheffield S30 3RL
Sheffield University Library, Archives, Western Bank, Sheffield S10 2TN
Shetland Archives, 44 King Harold Street, Lerwick ZE1 0EQ
Shropshire FHSoc, Redhillside, Ludlow Road, Church Stretton SY6 6AD
Shropshire Records and Research Centre, Castle Gates, Shrewsbury SY1 2AS
Society for Medieval Archaeology, Archaeology Unit, Winston Churchill Building, Radbrook Centre,

Radbrook Road, Shrewsbury SY3 9BJ

Society for Post-Medieval Archaeology, Department of Medieval and Latin Antiquities, British Museum, London WC1B 3DG

Society for Promoting Christian Knowledge, Holy Trinity Church, Marylebone Road, London NW1 4DU

Society for the Protection of Ancient Buildings, 37 Spital Square, London E1 6DY

Society of Antiquaries of London, Burlington House, Piccadilly, London W1V 0HS

Society of Antiquaries of Scotland, Royal Museums of Scotland, Chambers Street, Edinburgh EH1 1JF

Society of Genealogists, 14 Charterhouse Buildings, Goswell Road, London EC1M 7BA

Soil Survey and Land Research Centre (Soil Survey of England and Wales), Silsoe Campus, Silsoe, Bedford MK45 4DT

Somerset and Dorset FHSoc, 7 Burch's Close, Galmington, Taunton, Somerset TA1 4TR

Somerset Archive and Record Service, Obridge Road, Taunton TA2 7PU

South Lanarkshire Archives and Information Management Service, 30 Hawbank Road, College Milton, East Kilbride G74 5EX

Southampton Archives Service, Civic Centre, Southampton SO14 7LY

Southampton University Library, Highfield, Southampton SO17 1BJ

Southwark Local Studies Library, 211 Borough High Street, London SE1 1JA

Staffordshire Record Office, County Buildings, Eastgate Street, Stafford ST16 2LZ

Staines FHCen (LDS), 41 Kingston Road, Staines, Middlesex TW18 4LH

Stevenage FHCen (LDS), Latter-Day Saints Chapel, Buckthorn Avenue, Stevenage, Hertfordshire SG1 1TU

Stirling Council Archives, Unit 6, Burghmuir Industrial Estate, Stirling FK7 7PY

State Paper Office, Dublin Castle, Dublin 2

Stockport Archive Service, Central Library, Wellington Road South, Stockport SK1 3RS

Suffolk FHSoc, 123 Cedarcroft Road, Ipswich IP1 6BP

Suffolk Record Office, Bury St Edmunds Branch, Raingate Street, Bury St Edmunds IP33 2AR *and* Ipswich Branch, Gatacre Road, Ipswich IP1 2LQ *and* Lowestoft Branch, Central Library, Clapham Road, Lowestoft NR32 1DR

Sunderland FHCen (LDS), Linden Road, Queen Alexandra Road, Sunderland SR2 9AU

Surrey, East FHSoc, 27 Burley Close, London SW16 4QQ

Surrey History Centre, 130 Goldsworth Road, Woking GU21 1ND

Surrey, West FHSoc, Deer Dell, Botany Hill, Sands, Farnham GU10 1LZ

Sussex, East Record Office, The Maltings, Castle Precincts, Lewes BN7 1YT

Sussex FHSoc, 54 Shirley Drive, Hove BN3 6UF

Sussex University Library, Manuscript Collections, Falmer, Brighton, East Sussex BN1 9QL

Sussex, West Record Office, Sherburne House, 3 Orchard Street; with correspondence to County Hall, West Street, Chichester PO19 1RN

Sutton Coldfield FHCen (LDS), 185 Penns Lane, Sutton Coldfield B76 1JU

Sutton Heritage Services, Archive Section, Central Library, St Nicholas Way, Sutton SM1 1EA

Swansea FHCen (LDS), Cockett Road, Swansea

Tameside Archive Service, Local Studies Library, Astley Cheetham Public Library, Trinity Street, Stalybridge SK15 2BN

Teesside Archives, Exchange House, 6 Martin Road, Middlesbrough TS1 1DB

Telford FHCen (LDS), 72 Glebe Street, Wellington, Shropshire TF1 1JY

Thetford FHCen (LDS), Station Road, Thetford, Norfolk IP24 1AH

Tower Hamlets Local History Library amd Archives, Bancroft Library, 277 Bancroft Road, London E1 4DG

Trafford Local Studies Centre, Sale Library, Tatton Road, Sale, Manchester M33 1YH

Trinity College Library, College Street, Dublin 2

Tunbridge Wells FHSoc, The Old Cottage, Langton Road, Tunbridge Wells, Kent TN3 0BA

Tyne and Wear Archives Service, Blandford House, Blandford Square, Newcastle upon Tyne NE1 4JA

Ulster Folk and Transport Museum, Cultra Manor, Holywood, Belfast BT18 0EU *and* Witham Street, Newtownards, Belfast BT4 1HP

Ulster Historical Foundation, Balmoral Buildings, 12 College Square East, Belfast BT1 6DD

Ulster Local Studies, Federation for, Institute for Ulster Local Studies, 8 Fitzwilliam Street, Belfast BT9 6AW

Ulster Museum, Botanic Gardens, Belfast BT9 5AB

University of Wales, Bangor, Department of Manuscripts, Bangor LL57 2DG

Valuation Office, 6 Ely Place, Dublin 2

Vernacular Architecture Group, 16 Falna Crescent, Coton Green, Tamworth, Staffordshire B79 8JS

Victoria and Albert Museum, Cromwell Road, South Kensington, London SW7 2RL

Victoria and Albert Museum, National Art Library, Archive of Art and Design, Blythe House, 23 Blythe Road, London W14 0QF

Victorian Society, 1 Priory Gardens, Bedford Park, London W4 1TT

Wakefield Headquarters, West Yorkshire Archive Service, Registry of Deeds, Newstead Road, Wakefield WF1 2DE

Walsall Archives Service, Local History Centre, Essex Street, Walsall WS2 7AS

Waltham Forest Archives and Local History Library, Vestry House Museum, Vestry Road, Walthamstow, London E17 9NH

Waltham Forest FHSoc, 1 Gelsthorpe Road, Romford, Essex RM5 2NB

Wandsworth FHCen (LDS), 149 Nightingale Lane, Balham, London SW12 8NG

Wandsworth Local History Collection, Battersea Library, 265 Lavender Hill, London SW11 1JB

Warrington Library, Museum Street, Warrington WA1 1JB

Warwick University, Modern Records Centre, University Library, Coventry CV4 7AL

Warwickshire County Record Office, Priory Park, Cape Road, Warwick CV34 4JS
Wednesfield FHCen (LDS), Linthouse Lane, Wednesfield, West Midlands
Wellcome Institute for the History of Medicine, 183 Euston Road, London NW1 2BE
Welsh Folk Museum, St Fagans, Cardiff CF5 6XB
West Glamorgan Archive Service, County Hall, Oystermouth Road, Swansea SA1 3SN *see also* Glamorgan
West Lothian Council Archives, 7 Rutherford Square, Brucefield, Livingston, West Lothian EH54 9BU
West Sussex *see* Sussex
West Yorkshire Archive Service, Wakefield Headquarters, Registry of Deeds, Newstead Road, Wakefield
  WF1 2DE *see also* Bradford, Calderdale, Kirklees, Leeds, Yorkshire
Westminster Abbey Muniment Room and Library, London SW1P 3PA
Westminster and Central Middlesex FHSoc, 46 Churchill Place, Harrow, Middlesex HA1 1XY
Westminster: City of Westminster Archives Centre, 10 St Ann's Street, London SW1P 2XR
Westminster Diocesan Archives, 16a Abingdon Road, London W8 6AF
Weston-super-Mare FHSoc, 15 Stanhope Road, Weston-super-Mare, Somerset BS23 4LP
Wharfedale FHSoc, 206 Moseley Wood Gardens, Cookridge, Leeds LS16 7JE
Wigan Archives Service, Town Hall, Leigh WN7 2DY
Wigan FHSoc, 464 Warrington Road, Goose Green, Wigan, Lancashire WN3 6QF
William Salt Library, Eastgate Street, Stafford ST16 2LZ
Wiltshire and Swindon Record Office, County Hall, Trowbridge BA14 8JG
Wiltshire FHSoc, 18 Sarsen Close, Okus, Swindon SN1 4LA
Wirral Archives Service, Reference Library, Borough Road, Birkenhead L41 2XB
Woolwich and District FHSoc, 54 Parkhill Road, Bexley, Kent DA5 1HY
Wolverhampton Archives and Local Studies, 42-50 Snow Hill, Wolverhampton WV2 4AG
Worcestershire Record Office, Headquarters Branch, County Hall, Spetchley Road, Worcester WR5 2NP
  and St Helen's Branch, Fish Street, Worcester WR1 2HN
Working Class Movement Library, Jubilee House, 51 The Crescent, Salford, Manchester M5 4WX
Worthing FHCen (LDS), Goring Street, Goring-by-Sea, West Sussex
Yate FHCen (LDS), Wellington Road, Yate, Avon
Yeovil FHCen (LDS), Latter-Day Saints Chapel, Forest Hill, Yeovil, Somerset
York, City of, and District FHSoc, 4 Chestnut Avenue, Stockton Lane, York YO3 0BR
York City Archives Department, Art Gallery Building, Exhibition Square, York YO1 2EW
York FHCen (LDS), West Bank, Acomb, York YO2 4ES
York Minster Archives, Minster Library, Dean's Park, York YO1 2JD
York University, Borthwick Institute of Historical Research, St Anthony's Hall, Peasholme Green, York
  YO1 2PW
Yorkshire Archaeological Society, Claremont, 23 Clarendon Road, Leeds LS2 9NZ

Index